HEALTHY PERSONALITY

HEALTHY PERSONALITY

An Approach from the Viewpoint of
Humanistic Psychology

FOURTH EDITION

SIDNEY M. JOURARD
TED LANDSMAN

THE UNIVERSITY OF FLORIDA

Macmillan Publishing Co., Inc.

NEW YORK

Collier Macmillan Publishers

LONDON

COPYRIGHT © 1980, MACMILLAN PUBLISHING CO., INC.

PRINTED IN THE UNITED STATES OF AMERICA

Earlier editions entitled *Personal Adjustment: An Approach Through the Study of Healthy Personality,* © 1958 and 1963 by Macmillan Publishing Co., Inc. Copyright © 1974 by Sidney M. Jourard.

MACMILLAN PUBLISHING CO., INC.
866 Third Avenue, New York, New York 10022

COLLIER MACMILLAN CANADA, LTD.

Library of Congress Cataloging in Publication Data

Jourard, Sidney M
  Healthy personality.

  Includes bibliographies and index.
    1. Personality. 2. Mental health. 3. Humanistic psychology.
I. Landsman, Ted, joint author. II. Title.
BF698.J63 1980   158'.1   79-15144
ISBN 0-02-361390-4

Printing: 2 3 4 5 6 7 8   Year: 3 4 5 6

ISBN   0-02-361390-4

PREFACE TO THE FOURTH EDITION

This new edition of *Healthy Personality* comes to its readers some five years after the tragic, accidental death of its originator and senior author, Sidney Jourard. He enjoyed his students, kept each letter written by his readers, and was deeply loving, loyal, and in never-ending dialogue with his friends, who prized his insults and his outrageousness. All the more reason, you must understand, for the difficulties in revising his book. It would have been easier if he could have fought back over every omission and addition. It does not seem quite fair to change a word without his having the privilege of argument.

This edition includes a continued emphasis on high level functioning found in Chapters 1 and 2 particularly and a new section on the self-concept and its related structures. Sidney's special interest in the body and one of his transcribed speeches on marriage, new to this edition, are left largely intact, if only as a memorial to his best writings. Throughout, an effort has been made to update the available research in all areas.

Sidney was not always right but was always interesting. To retain his personal relationship with his readers, I have generally left untouched his use of the first person singular. Therefore, when the reader encounters an "I" or possessive "my" it is Jourard speaking and representing his own point of view. Should you find a "we" or "our" you have come across one of those rare instances where we both agree on a controversial subject. When you come across the phrase "another opinion is as follows"— you have come upon my counterposition to one of his strong opinions. This latter circumstance is illustrated by our finely differentiated positions concerning the use of chemicals to alter consciousness.

The readers of the revised manuscript were loyal friends and fought to retain many of the omissions: Dr. R. Ward Wilson, Dr. William Peters, Dr. John Lelak, and others who choose to remain anonymous. Each contributed considerable substance to the manuscript, and I am grateful for their meticulous reading. The marks of my teacher, counselor, and friend Arthur W. Combs, Jr., will be found in the many corners of this book. The copyeditor, Mary Pickering, put a sharp pencil to many of my professional obscurities and saw to what Dr. Jourard would certainly wish for—that all sexist language was removed. Where sexist pronouns could not be avoided, we have alternated between masculine and feminine forms. Production Supervisor Susan Greenberg was cheerful with my delays and always encouraging. The editor, Clark Baxter, was merciless, demanding, entirely reasonable, and objective—in short, an excellent editor. I rewarded his talents with a canoe trip around Lake Wauburg. We encountered numerous, large alligators, and I would have cheerfully fed Mr. Baxter to any of them, but none would have him.

Mrs. Olivia Berger, as typist for the manuscript, never missed a deadline. My wife, Mary, who loved Sidney as I did, was a constant, gentle encouragement. Mrs. Antoinette Jourard provided the inspiration and enthusiasm for this supplement to her husband's work.

I think Sidney would have wished to dedicate this edition to those whom he loved—his family and his friends. It is so dedicated.

T. L.

Micanopy, Florida

Preface to the Fourth Edition

PREFACE TO THE THIRD EDITION

SOME ways of behaving in the world are life-giving to the person and not destructive to other people, to animals, or to the environment which supports us all. These are the ways I call healthy personality.

Not only do these ways enhance life and health for the person, they also stimulate, or at least do not impede, the growth and actualization of his more desirable possibilities. Healthy personality fosters personal growth and sustains health and well-being.

In this book, I have presented what we have learned in psychology—through clinical experience and through research in laboratories and natural settings—about healthy personality.

The point of view from which this book is written is that of humanistic psychology.

Humanistic psychology is the study of man based on the assumption that, as a human being, he is free and hence responsible for his actions and their consequences to his well-being and growth. The humanistic orientation in psychology has flourished in the past decade, and I have sought to incorporate some of the vigor of that approach into my efforts to discuss healthy personality.

The two previous editions of this book were entitled *Personal Adjustment: An Approach Through the Study of Healthy Personality*. In this third effort of mine to portray man at his human best, I have made enough changes and have added enough new material to justify changing the title to the one I have now employed.

I have added four new chapters. The first of these, on consciousness, brings to the students' attention the more recent efforts to study human experiencing in its own right. I have tried to provide a point of view from which a student can make sense out of the contributions that phenomenology had made to psychology, and to comprehend the bewildering array of material on "altered states of consciousness."

Work and play are parts of life that I neglected in the previous editions; I have corrected that omission in this volume and have related these themes to man's need for meaning as well as security in his life.

The third new chapter is on religion. I have seen the strength which good religion gives, and I have seen the destruction wrought in people's lives by misguided piety. I have attempted to show the reader ways to distinguish between true, life-enhancing religion and mere church attendance and literal belief in unexamined scripture.

Each of the other chapters has much new material. In the first, I have added the contributions to the concept of healthy personality made by F. Perls, W. Reich, A. Lowen, A. Ellis, A. Assagioli, B. F. Skinner, E. Berne, V. Frankl, and J. Wolpe. I have discussed recent work in the study of body experience and techniques of re-embodiment and psychotherapeutic advances. I have added a chapter which seeks to clarify the humanistic approach to the study and practice of psychology as a profession.

This book was written for undergraduate courses in personality development and as a humanistic introduction to psychology in those colleges where only one course may be available, or where such an approach is of interest, to supplement the more standard introductory course. I believe, however, that what I have written will be useful to students and practitioners of any of the "helping professions" at undergraduate and graduate levels of instruction. Certainly, counselors and psychotherapists, nurses, social workers, and clergymen would find some guidance for their work in these pages.

In 1955 the late Abraham Maslow read the first draft of *Personal Adjustment* and dictated a forty-page, line-by-line critique which helped me immeasurably and which confirmed me as a beginning author. I gained much from the example of his courage and persistence in pursuit of truth about man and his possibilities. I dedicate *Healthy Personality* to his memory.

Preface to the Third Edition

Sidney M. Jourard

CONTENTS

ix

Contents

HEALTHY PERSONALITY

1

WHAT IS HEALTHY PERSONALITY?

INTRODUCTION

Does humankind face a fate of evolutionary destruction of self? Or do humans continually strive for the higher aspects of their own possibilities, to be more compassionate; loving; creative; to create great, beautiful parks and vast, wild, free lands; more exquisite poetry and buildings—to perfect themselves and the world about them? Most humanistic thinkers see evidence for both in the works of humans today. However, they are confident that the struggle, the movement of humankind is toward the development of the self to levels of superb functioning for perhaps a few persons who become models *of human effectiveness and for higher levels of living, joy of living, for much greater numbers. Humans have sought to perfect themselves throughout history. Early Jews sought purification of self in the face of temptation. The Christians sought salvation. The Buddhists and Hindus were seekers of liberation, and the Sufis underwent training for rebirth in love and enlightenment. In all these cases it was recognized that humans are capable of states of being that far surpass present levels in beauty and goodness.*

The term healthy personality *is used here to describe those ways of being that surpass the average in actualization of self and in compassionate relationships with others.*

The human can be studied as a natural phenomenon, with methods appropriate to the study of zoology or ethology. But humans have the capacities for speech and for self-consciousness. People give meaning to their world and are capable of communicating meanings to other persons. If we wish to understand human behavior, we must not view it as we would the behavior of animals struggling to survive in a given environment; we must regard behavior as action, as a kind of speech. Humans "say" something to the world and to their companions by their actions. If we wish to understand humans in their existence as human beings, we must find out what they mean to say, and how they say it in words, action, and even in physiological responses. Of course, we also find out what they mean by asking them to tell us.

The study of healthy personality could be undertaken from a behavioristic standpoint, and some parts of our discussion show a behavioristic influence. However, we shall try to illumine the person in its uniquely human characteristics, basing our discussion on a view of the person as conscious, meaning-pursuing, capable of freedom and responsibility in the conduct of his or her life, and capable of greatness yet unreached.[1]

The Images of the Person: Of Mice and Angels

When some scientists dare to study the human being, they think of the subject as being like a laboratory rat. At least it would seem that way from the large amount of research in psychology based upon that particular animal. And there is no doubt that many things about the white rat are similar to aspects of the human being, including some motivations—sex, hunger, safety, and so on. However, another image of the human being has been expressed in the Psalms (Psalm 8:5), that of being "just a

Healthy Personality

little lower than the angels." [2] This implies many powers and capacities and almost suggests "sainthood" capabilities. However, in this book we are not exploring such, nor is the "normal" person the principal subject. There is a group of persons who are entirely mortal, who have their imperfections, and yet have discovered a way of life that is beyond what most people attempt to create for themselves. One of the characteristics of such people seems to be that they do have a compassion, or caring, for others; but it is a very human kind of love. In this chapter and in later chapters we shall examine some of these and other images of human beings presented by a wide variety of the major thinkers in the early history of adjustment psychology, such as Freud, Adler, and Jung. But we shall also examine some of the more recent views of the human, such as those of Rogers and Maslow.

Why Study the Healthy Personality?

People who care about themselves, respect themselves, and like to present their best self to others also take care of their bodies. They jog or exercise in some other way, watch the intake of their food, and avoid either smoking or being where heavy smokers are taking up the good air. They recognize that having a healthy body is in great part controllable by the individual. Similarly, having a healthy personality is in greatest part under the control of the person who owns it. While there are genetic factors that seem to influence the personality and there are environmental forces that have an effect upon one's style of interacting with people, the humanist also recognizes the tremendous power of the person to affect his or her own personality-destiny. This is perhaps the most important reason for studying the healthy personality. All of us want to be as fully functioning, self-actualizing, and healthy as we can be. Knowledge of what constitutes a healthy personality should help you to develop this type of personality.

What Is Healthy Personality? Secondly, the impact of the environment, especially of the people in your environment, has a great effect upon your personality. This still does not leave you helpless in the face of the influence of your friends, because you can choose your friends and even choose many other aspects of your environment. There are those people, friends, relatives, teachers, companions, who, when you are with them, make you feel that you are growing, becoming. McMillan [3] refers to these kinds of persons as "personality growth facilitators." And there are also those who can destroy you psychologically. We call these "lethal personalities." Thus, the second reason for the study of the healthy personality is so that you may truly distinguish those people who are personality growth facilitators and find ways to be close to them.

What about your effect upon others? How do you influence others so that they will feel they are growing? In particular, almost all of us will have some role in raising children in our lifetimes, either through being parents, teachers, or neighbors. A third reason for studying the healthy personality is to be better able to have a good effect on the people who are close to us, particularly friends and children.

Science claims the privilege of exploring the unknown, if only for the reasons of pure curiosity. Science searches for basic laws and principles that may have no immediate benefit or that might be explored without any specific benefit in mind. Often these discoveries of basic principles and laws do have important applied use. More often, however, the advantages and benefits are not immediately apparent, and legislators impatient for solutions are prone to cut off funds for all but the most applied research. Science for its own sake, for the sake of pushing back ignorance and darkness, even if there is no trunkful of diamonds deep in the darkness of the cave, is a viable reason for studying the healthy personality.

Contemporary Concepts of the Healthy Personality

A. H. MASLOW'S SELF-ACTUALIZING PEOPLE

A. H. Maslow [4] devoted his life to studying the conditions under which human beings develop their capacities to the fullest degree. He believed the key to such development was gratification of basic needs. These needs exist in a hierarchical sequence. Humans must meet the demands of lower needs before those of the higher levels can emerge, according to Maslow. However, there is doubt among some researchers about the primacy of the lower needs.[5] This hierarchy, from lowest to highest, includes physical needs, such as the need for food and water; safety needs, illustrated by the quest for a milieu relatively free from threats to life and fostering a sense of security; belonging and love needs, illustrated by the hunger for affectionate, accepting relationships with other persons; esteem needs, manifested in the desire to be respected by others for one's accomplishments and in the quest for recognition and prestige. Once a person has successfully learned to cope with these needs as they arise, his or her energies will then be more readily freed for self-actualization. Actualization of self cannot be sought as a goal in its own right, however; rather, it is a byproduct of active commitment of one's talents to causes outside the self, such as the quest for beauty, truth, or justice. Without some such mission in life, a person is likely to experience boredom and a sense of stultification. Once this person finds a purpose (or purposes), his or her energies and talents can then be dedicated to its fulfillment. As the individual meets challenges, personal growth or actualization will be fostered as a byproduct of the quest. The task awakens the person's dormant capacities; without the mission, the person would never discover his or her hidden resources. Maslow emphasized the importance of actualizing one's self through productive, meaningful work. He wrote (1970, p. 49), "I have seen a few cases in which it seemed clear to me that the pathology (boredom, loss of zest in life . . .) was produced in intelligent people leading stupid lives in stupid jobs." Other higher needs described by Maslow later included *cognitive* and *conative* needs (need to know and to understand the world). He also strongly suggested that some special people have a basic *aesthetic* need, a craving for beauty—"They get sick from ugliness and are cured by beautiful surroundings" (1970, p. 51).

Maslow developed his ideas through the study of people who met his criteria for being well along in the process of actualizing themselves. Some of the traits that appeared consistently in his self-actualizing (S-A) cases were the following:

What Is Healthy Personality?

1. A more efficient perception of reality and more comfortable relations with reality than occur in average people. His S-A cases seemed to detect the spurious, the fake, and the dishonest in interpersonal relationships and to be attuned to truth and reality in all spheres of life. They rejected the illusory and preferred to cope with unpleasant reality rather than to retreat to pleasant fantasies.

2. A high degree of acceptance of themselves, of others, and of the realities of human nature. They were not ashamed of being what they were, and they were not shocked or dismayed to find shortcomings in themselves or in others.

3. Spontaneity; simplicity; naturalness. The S-A people displayed spontaneity in their thinking, emotions, and behavior to a greater extent than average people. They prefer company that enables them to be free and natural.

4. Problem-centeredness. Maslow's subjects seemed all to be focused on problems outside themselves. They were not overly self-conscious; they were not problems to themselves, and could hence devote their attention to a task, duty, or mission that seemed peculiarly cut out for them.

5. A need for privacy. The S-A people could enjoy solitude; indeed, they would even seek it on occasion, needing it for periods of intense concentration on subjects of interest to them and for meditation.

6. A high degree of autonomy. The S-A people seemed able to remain true to themselves in the face of rejection or unpopularity; they were able to pursue their interests and projects and maintain their integrity even when it hurt to do so.

7. A continued freshness of appreciation. The S-A people showed the capacity to "appreciate again and again, freshly and naively, the basic goods of life . . . a sunset, a flower, a baby, a person." It was as if they avoided merely lumping experiences into categories and then dismissing them. Rather, they could see the unique in many commonplace experiences.

8. Frequent "peak experiences." The S-A people seemed subject to periodic experiences that are often called "mystic" or "oceanic"—feelings that one's boundaries as a person have suddenly evaporated and feeling

*Healthy
Personality*

6

that one has become a part of all humanity or of all nature.

9. Gemeinschaftsgefühl. The German word *gemein-schaftsgefühl* means brotherly feeling, the feeling of belonging to all humanity (related to the mystic experiences); the attitude was found to be characteristic of S-A people. They felt a sense of identification with humanity as a whole, such that they could become concerned not only with the lot of members of their immediate family, but also with the situations of persons from different cultures.

10. Close relationships with a few friends or loved ones. Maslow found that his S-A subjects, although not necessarily very popular, did have the capacity to establish truly close, loving relationships with at least one or two other people.

11. Democratic character structures. The S-A people tended to judge people and be friendly with them not on the basis of race, status, religion, or other group membership traits, but as individual persons.

12. A strong ethical sense; *discrimination between good and evil*. The S-A subjects were found to have a highly developed sense of ethics. Though their notions of right and wrong were not wholly conventional, their behavior was always chosen with reference to its ethical meaning.

13. Unhostile sense of humor. The S-A people had senses of humor that made common human foibles, pretensions, and foolishness the subject of laughter, rather than sadism, smut, or rebellion against authority.

14. Creativeness. The S-A people were creative and inventive in some areas of their existence, not followers of the usual ways of doing or thinking.

15. Resistance to enculturation. The S-A subjects could detach themselves somewhat from complete brainwashing or imprinting by their cultures, permitting them to adopt critical attitudes toward cultural inconsistencies or unfairness within their own society.

Truly, this is a most impressive collection of attributes. One would like to meet or to become such a person.

What Is Healthy Personality? Maslow continuously pondered what humans might become, in the hope of learning how more of us might grow toward those seemingly Utopian levels of being. In a sense, this book is devoted to further exploration of paths to self-actualization.

Maslow's work remains as one of the most helpful sets of principles governing the development of the healthy personality. He suggested the existence of two kinds of motivation: *B*, or being motivation, and *D*, or deficiency motivation. D-motivations are those that grab us when we are deeply deprived or have a loss of some basic need, such as the burglar who may be driven by hunger or the coward who may be driven by fear for personal safety. In contrast, the self-actualizing person is seen as motivated by the *being* needs, to be the fullest possible self, to be able to sing, create, work at highest capacity.

The peak experience concept has met with a great deal of interest. Maslow suggests the existence of these marvelous experiences that overwhelm the person and are great heights of delight and joy or meaningfulness, awesome experiences that may occur to a self-actualizing person but are not exclusively confined to that kind of person.

Here are two contrasting examples of the more moderate peak or positive experiences collected from tenth-grade students:

> Mine happened just last night. I love the summer and hate the winter. So last night when I stepped outside and found how warm it was I just couldn't go back into the house. I walked around the house and then looked all around. You can see all the houses around from our house and just looking around at them and hearing the sounds of the night relaxed me and I felt like I was watching over the whole world. It was a gentle feeling and gave me a little bit of a thrill.

> Yes, in winter I love to walk out in the snow and let it fall lightly on my face. When this happens it seems to make a strange sort of happiness fall on me also.

RICHARD COAN: THE OPTIMAL SELF AND SCIENCE

Healthy Personality   One of the more systematic efforts to illuminate the idea of the healthy personality comes from Coan.[6] He favors the term *the optimal self*, which refers to a person who is functioning at the highest level.

One of the most sophisticated or elegant forms of data analysis is called factor analysis. It involves the use of a great number of scores or measures and an attempt to discover how many of them cluster together, are likely to be related, and therefore are likely to form a *factor* of significance. Coan used a factor analysis for which his psychology students took six hours of testing. About 135 different variables—possible characteristics of the healthy personality or the optimal personality—were involved. Using a factor analysis of these many variables in a way that had not yet been attempted by any researcher, Coan emerged with five main *modes of human fulfillment*, or characteristics of the optimal person. You may wish to compare them with Maslow's list.

COAN	MASLOW
1. Efficiency: functional competence (being able to do things well), effective work autonomy (being able to work independently), and commitment to projects of concern outside of one's self.	1. A more efficient perception of reality. 4. Problem-centeredness: being centered on problems outside themselves. 6. A high degree of autonomy.
2. Creativity: experiences familiar things in fresh ways; openness to the novel, strange, and socially unacceptable; creates new style of life.	14. Creativeness. 7. A continued freshness of appreciation.
3. Inner harmony: likes self; need for some amount of privacy or solitude.	2. High degree of acceptance by self. 5. Need for privacy.
4. Relatedness: compassion, to be genuinely transparent, making self available to receive what others seek to communicate.	10. Close relationships with a few friends or loved ones. 9. Gemeinschaftsgefühl, brotherly love, feeling of belonging to all humanity.
5. Transcendence: mysti-	8. Frequent peak experi-

cal unity with a larger whole, relationship to some all-encompassing totality, to nature or God.

ences, mystic or oceanic feelings.

The emphases of these two major writers have many agreements. Their agreements are even more apparent when further writings of both are compared. For example, Maslow sees his self-actualizers as religious, in the sense that they are ethical and devote themselves to the good of humanity (1970, p. 169). This is close to Coan's first, fourth, and fifth modes. You might wish to keep in mind that one of the reasons for the special significance of these agreements is the fact that these two positions were derived from drastically differing methodologies.

TED LANDSMAN: THE BEAUTIFUL AND NOBLE PERSON

Psychologists have been too timid and guarded in identifying the high-level functioning or healthy personality, argues Ted Landsman.[7] He believes we have disguised the true, human image of this person behind language that is so stiff that the person in the description is lost. The healthy personality is a "beautiful and noble person" (BNP). The beauty described here does not refer to physical beauty, although that may sometimes be found in the healthy personality. It more specifically describes someone whose behavior and work is such that the effect upon self and others is one of producing an essentially aesthetic feeling. The nobility also, of course, does not refer to parentage but to the kinds of behavior and acts performed by such a person.

While some have argued that even psychotic people may sometimes be thought of as healthy, Landsman insists that the BNP must first be normal—perceive reality essentially as it is and be free of bizarre symptoms (such as hallucinations, grimaces, and so on). The first stage in the evolution of the BNP is described as the *passionate self*. Akin to the similar concepts in Maslow and Coan, the passionate self is seen as someone who truly likes, even loves himself or herself, someone who enjoys be-

Healthy Personality

ing alone, and who respects and accepts self. This is not the same as selfishness, but rather is an awareness of self as a worthwhile person. Bragging and possessiveness are avoided.

The second stage involves a concept not dealt with in detail by most other writers: the environment-loving person. A passionate caring for the physical environment is seen in the person at this stage. The human relates to mountains, flowers, music, buildings—the entire physical environment—with appreciation and with joy, preserves it, nurtures it, and delights in it.

The final stage in the evolution of the BNP is described as the *compassionate self*. This is a person who deeply loves others, who cares about people who hurt or are in need, and who takes action, often at great personal risk, to help others. The compassionate person does not only feel for others, but *acts* to alleviate or remedy their pains or injustices.

The peak and positive experience is the springboard for much of the conceptualizations in this system. The following experiences, among others, are identified by Landsman as major positive experiences that lead to the development of the beautiful and noble personality (1971):

1. *Positive experiences* in childhood. Experiences of joy, delight, ecstasy at all levels, not just peak. High levels of intense positive feeling.

2. *Negative experiences* that have been made positive in effect. These are important painful experiences, such as disgrace, failure, death of loved ones, automobile accidents, being fired from a job, which the person has been able to "turn around" and make into significant learning or growth experiences. The following, collected by Smith,[8] is written by a female prisoner:

> Coming to prison. Never thought it would happen to me. Anyone else but not me. It happened. I'm glad I've stopped and reviewed my life up to age 17. Complete destruction for me. I was destroying myself and going at it at top speed. I've met beautiful people here. I've learned a lot about me. This experience I would not change if I could. I needed this. Now maybe I can

be a better person. I can stop and think and reason with myself. . . . Had I not served time I would still be going at top speed I'm sure. Only what would I be into now? [p. 131]

3. *The solitude experience.* Instances in which an individual can escape from the immediate pressures—social, job, interpersonal—and explore the self, one's own feelings, one's relationship to others, to the world. Opportunities to think freely and clearly are usually accomplished in solitude, in intentional isolation, such as a short walk in the woods, or a year's living in the desert alone.

4. *The authentic dialogue.* This, in a sense, is the obverse or "flip side" of the previous experience. You seek the opportunity to converse, deeply, freely, without guile or pretense, with someone you trust totally. Both persons in the dialogue must be committed to authenticity and openness, which differs somewhat from most counseling or psychotherapeutic approaches, where only the client is the communicator about self.

5. *The transcendent experience* is one in which you achieve far beyond what you would normally expect of yourself: writing an unusually beautiful poem, being far more sensitive than one would expect, performing a physical feat such as lifting a beam off of an injured person or winning an athletic contest. These experiences are difficult to predict or create, but when they do occur, they give you the sure confidence that you have possibilities and potential of which you never dreamed.

Like the positions of Maslow and Coan, the approach to beautiful and noble personhood stresses openness, relationship to self and to others. It builds upon Maslow's system of peak experiences to suggest the importance of a whole range of experiences, especially the positive, and also inserts the importance of the relationship, a passionate one, with the physical environment, music, mountains, flowers, lakes, and so on.

THE CONCEPTS OF HEALTHY PERSONALITY: DEFINITION AND OVERVIEW

Healthy Personality   Whenever a conscientious student first looks into abnormal psychology, he or she inevitably finds characteristics of the abnormal that also seem part of the student's self. Can you also see in yourself some of the *healthy* characteristics described by the many thinkers and researchers in this area? Here are some of them:

Openness to new ideas and to people.
Care for self, for others and for the natural world.
Ability to integrate negative experiences into the self.
Creativity.
Ability to do productive work.
Ability to love.

It does no harm to measure yourself in these terms. And if one does come up with some deficiencies, there are ways to learn to improve and develop the self. Some of the traditional ways involve getting into counseling or psychotherapy, finding friends who are constructive and facilitative of one's growth, even reading and practicing what is recommended in authentic self-help books and working with a behavior-modification "manager" who permits you to change aspects of yourself that you chose, rather than making changes dictated by social pressures from friends or authorities.

New institutions of learning and healing have emerged in the past decade, which aim to promote a person's education and training beyond a typical upbringing. There are now *growth centers*, where people can go to learn greater autonomy, creativity, and authenticity. One of the first of these—Esalen Institute—was founded in 1962 at Big Sur in California. Since then more than two hundred have sprung up in the United States and the rest of the world.

What, then, might healthy personality be? How can we recognize it in ourselves and in others? Do the characteristics of healthy personality differ at various age levels? Between the sexes? In different social classes and different cultures? Is healthy personality more than "adjustment" to the norms of one's society? Are there criteria for healthy personality that transcend conformity to the status quo? How can we ascertain whether a family, a work setting, a religious ideology, or an entire society with its culture is good for human beings and other forms of life?

What Is Healthy Personality?

These questions are not merely rhetorical or academic.

We are living in an age when the population is increasing to the point beyond which the earth may not support life. Human beings have destroyed each other by the millions, sometimes praying to the same God, through the same clergy, for guidance for more effective ways to do this. In the name of economic development, people have destroyed entire civilizations; animal species; and the soil, water, and air, making life an uncertainty for the generations that follow, and of dubious quality for those now living. We need now to identify those people who can reverse these processes.

It is difficult, if not impossible, to give a succinct definition of healthy personality. This entire book is given over to the effort to reach such a definition. Nevertheless, for purposes of orientation, we offer this as a preliminary effort: *Healthy personality is a way for a person to act, guided by intelligence and respect for life, so that personal needs are satisfied and so that the person will grow in awareness, competence, and the capacity to love the self, the natural environment, and other people.*

Some Existential Suggestions

A useful exercise at this point is for the reader to ask, "What do I think my best possibilities are? To what extent do I approximate these conceptions of healthy personality? What changes might I make in my life in order to grow more in the direction of my better possibilities? What do I believe is preventing me from further growth? Who are the people who seem to bring out the best in me? What experiences do I long to have that will help me to know my potentialities in work, in my career, in loving and being loved, and in caring for others? How effective is my communication to others? Do I hide my feelings or do I let others know me?"

Descriptions of human beings do not just describe—they *prescribe;* that is, they can function to limit our perceptions of ourselves or to encourage us to transcend or exceed previous limits.[9] I suggest this because it is now apparent that what a person believes to be his or her strengths, weaknesses, and limits are self-fulfilling prophecies. If we are convinced that we have reached our limits,

Healthy Personality

then we will struggle no more. If we believe there is no end to our limits, we may keep struggling.

In "Some Existential Suggestions" at the end of each of the following chapters, a number of questions will be posed to help the reader apply the content of this book in ways that are conducive to growth toward healthier personality.

SUMMARY

Human beings have always striven for personal perfection. Throughout history, this quest has been religious in nature; the goal has been named salvation, purification, redemption, liberation, enlightenment, and rebirth. We only pursue what we believe is a possibility for us.

In contemporary times, psychologists and psychiatrists have offered the authoritative views of humanity at its best as guides to growth, to education, and to psychotherapy. Conceptions of healthy personality are abstracted from the work of Abraham H. Maslow, Richard Coan, and Ted Landsman. These conceptions of humanity at its best all embody different theories of the growth of personality and of the factors responsible for healthy personal development.

Growth centers have been founded where people who are not sick can go to explore further dimensions of their growth.

A preliminary definition portrays healthy personality as a way for a person to act, guided by intelligence and respect for life, so that as his or her needs are satisfied, the person grows in awareness, competence, and the capacity for love of self, others, and the natural environment.

NOTES AND REFERENCES

1. The study of human beings from the standpoint of humanistic psychology has gained momentum since 1962. This volume is written from that perspective. A good introduction to this point of view is provided by J. F. T. BUGENTAL (Ed.), *Challenges of Humanistic Psychology* (New York: McGraw-Hill, 1967).

2. A. COHEN (Ed.), *The Psalms* (London: Soncino, 1960), p. 19.

3. M. R. McMillan, *A Study of Certain High School Seniors Perceived as Growth Facilitating by Their Peers*, unpublished doctoral dissertation, University of Florida, 1965.

4. Maslow was a brilliant and prolific writer. Many consider him to be the father of humanistic psychology. Some of his best works are *Farther Reaches of Human Nature* (New York: Viking Press, 1971); *Motivation and Personality*, Second Edition (New York: Harper & Row, 1970); and *Toward a Psychology of Being* (New York: Van Nostrand, 1962).

5. M. A. Wahba and L. G. Bridwell, "Maslow Reconsidered: A Review of Research on the Need Hierarchy Theory," *Organizational Behavior and Human Performance*, 1976, Vol. 15, pp. 212–240.

6. R. W. Coan, *Hero, Artist, Sage or Saint: A Survey of Views on What Is Variously Called Mental Health, Normality, Maturity, Self-Actualization and Human Fulfillment* (New York: Columbia University Press, 1977); and R. W. Coan, *The Optimal Personality, An Empirical and Theoretical Analysis* (New York: Columbia University Press, 1974).

7. Three related papers are T. Landsman, "The Beautiful Person," *Futurist*, 1969, Vol. 3, pp. 41–42; T. Landsman, *One's Best Self*, in S. M. Jourard (Ed.), *To Be or Not to Be: Existential Psychological Perspectives on the Self*, Social Science Monograph No. 34 (Gainesville: U. of Florida, 1971), pp. 37–49; and T. Landsman, "The Humanizer," *American Journal of Orthopsychiatry*, 1974, Vol. 44, pp. 345–352.

8. S. M. Smith, *Intense Experiences of Black and White Female Prisoners*, unpublished doctoral dissertation, University of Florida, 1973.

9. A psychology of transcendence is presented in S. M. Jourard, *Disclosing Man to Himself* (New York: Van Nostrand Reinhold, 1968), pp. 204–228.

2

HEALTHY PERSONALITY AND UNHEALTHY PERSONALITY

INTRODUCTION

Much of our understanding about healthy personality has actually come from those who had been intimately acquainted with unhealthy personality. These include present-day counseling theorists such as Carl R. Rogers [1] and original psychotherapists such as Sigmund Freud,[2] who dedicated their professional lives to the alleviation of emotional suffering. While it is important to search out the unique characteristics of the healthy personality, the high-level functioning person, there is a wealth of learning that is derived from those clients or patients who have shared their innermost anxieties, fears, and sorrows with counselors.

Even some philosophers have wrestled both with the pain in self and the way to a "higher" state of existence, such as have the Zen Buddhists and the Existentialists. Some of these concepts have appeared to be far-fetched, strange, and even antiscientific to many in the established ranks of human behavior researchers. These concepts must be studied, but studied critically and appreciatively because, like Freud's many of these ideas were greeted with derision and denunciation upon their first presentation and, like Freud's concepts, many of these creative ideas will handily survive the worst of criticism. Some, of course, also like some of Freud's ideas, will only become parts of a significant past. Though for most of their professional lives most of the psychotherapists–theorists dealt with people with adjustment problems of varying degrees of severity, all of them have had something to suggest concerning the nature of the healthy personality. In a sense, the "idealized person," hypothesized at least indirectly by the concept of the healthy personality, represents the goals that the counselor or therapist sets for the client. Therefore, the therapists have had to give considerable thought to the ideal state for their clients.

Experiencing the Here and Now: The Perspective of Gestalt Therapy

Fritz Perls [3] was a German-born psychiatrist who was prescient enough to leave Germany before the Nazi holocaust. He developed Gestalt therapy, which combined diverse traditions, psychoanalysis, and Gestalt psychology (the study of the meaningful patterns in human experience). His view was that the average person comes to fear living and experiencing the *here and now*. Rather, he or she tends to live mainly in the past, through obsessive remembering, and in the future, through anxious expectations of catastrophe. The average person is chronically self-conscious and dreads spontaneous action. Experiencing the self as dependent and helpless, this person turns to others for support and becomes angry when they do not live up to expectations. The healthier personality struggles to emancipate itself from morbidly dependent relationships with others and is capable of direct awareness of perceptions and feelings, rather than engaging chronically in abstract thinking, in recall, or in wishful or anxious imagination. The healthy personality can trust itself to be spontaneous in action. Like Freud and Jung,

Healthy Personality Perls devoted much attention to his patients' dreams. He would ask them to act out all the parts of the dream during the therapy session; the idea was that every aspect of a dream represents some dimensions of a person's experience, much of which the person disowns. By identifying with the different parts of the dream, the person could increase self-awareness, which, in turn, would increase the sense of vitality and foster continuing personal growth.

Perls' emphasis on the importance of self-sufficiency, of standing on one's own two feet rather than relying on others for one's security, is reminiscent of Blatz's views (see p. 22), though these two men did not know each other.

Eric Berne: Transactional Analysis and the Games People Play

The late Eric Berne [4] wrote a book that became a best-seller, called *The Games People Play*. He developed an approach to psychotherapy that he called *transactional analysis*. According to Berne, people suffer in adult life because they will not grow to adulthood, but insist upon struggling, sometimes with ingenious cunning and subterfuge, to get other people to cater to their needs and wishes the way they wanted their parents to serve them during infancy. The sneaky ways in which persons strive to thus exploit others were documented in sometimes hilarious ways in the *Games* book. Thus, an adult might play the game of "wooden leg"—asking for deference from others, and seeking to justify failures, by calling attention to real or imagined handicaps: "I could have been more successful in my career if my stomach hadn't been hurting me all those years."

Berne believed that healthy personality consists of affirming one's personal worth ("I'm OK"), making reasonable demands upon others as befits an adult, and developing simple honesty in one's dealings with others—living a relatively "game-free" existence.

Healthy Personality and Unhealthy Personality

Healthy Personality: An Existential View [5]

The existential philosophers—Kierkegaard and Nietzsche in the nineteenth century and Heidegger, Marcel, Sartre, de Chardin, Tillich, and Buber in the twentieth, to name the more important among them—wrote about the implications of freedom for the human condition.

According to existential writers, humans alone have the capacity to choose their behavior and hence to shape their "essences," that is, their fundamental characteristics, at any time. Healthy adult personalities take responsibility for their actions; make decisions; and seek to transcend the determining, limiting effects on their behavior of handicaps, social pressures to conformity, extreme stress, and biological impulses and feelings. They become aware of the pressures these impersonal forces impose on actions, but they *choose* whether or not they will yield to them or oppose them. Only humans can thus choose, and hence make themselves.

The healthy personality displays *courage to be*. This term implies knowing and disclosing one's feelings and beliefs and taking the consequences that follow from such assertion. It implies freedom to choose between hiding or faking one's real self and letting others know one as one is.

Healthy personality means regarding oneself as a *person*, as free and responsible, not as a passive instrument of impulses or the expectations of other people. In dealing with other people, a healthy personality treats them as persons too, rather than as objects or tools. As Buber puts it, they live in dialogue with their peers in a relationship of "I and thou," rather than between "I and it."

The healthy personality becomes aware of finitude and sees life and what is made of it as *his or her own responsibility*, not the responsibility of others. A person becomes most keenly aware of time-bound existence when he or she squarely faces the fact of death.

From the existential point of view, average people and the mentally ill both suffer some degree of estrangement from their own being, from nature, and from people. They find the responsibility of freedom too frightening, and so they let their lives be lived for them by impulses or by social pressures to conformity. In the process, they lose their selves.

Viktor Frankl,[6] an existentially oriented psychiatrist, shows many of these themes in his writings about *logotherapy*, a term he uses to emphasize the human being's

Healthy Personality

basic need for *meaning* in life. Frankl sees the human as free and responsible for the fulfillment of values and meaning in existence. Life is to be lived, and each person is called upon to fulfill *creative* values, through productive work; *experiential* values, through enjoying the beauties and pleasures that can be sought and found in life; and, finally, when creative and experiential values are not to be found—when a person is lying on the death bed, or has been condemned to live and die in a concentration camp—*attitudinal* values. The person is responsible at these times for giving unique meaning to his or her own suffering and death. Frankl forged his existential psychiatry during more than seven years in Hitler's death camps during World War II, and is himself living testimony to the life-giving importance of a firm sense of meaning in life. He coined the term *noögenic neurosis* to describe neurotic suffering arising from a loss of the sense of meaning in life (akin in meaning to being disheartened or dispirited and to Kierkegaard's concept of despair). Logotherapy is a kind of psychotherapy that aims to help a person find enlivening meanings when older meanings have lost their validity.

Albert Ellis and Rational Thinking

Albert Ellis [7] developed an approach to psychotherapy that he calls *rational–emotive therapy*, to highlight the fact that he is concerned with feelings, but no less concerned with sensible *thinking* about life problems. He regards neurotically disturbed people as individuals who talk nonsense to themselves, who refrain from vital living because they dread catastrophic consequences for ordinary self-assertiveness. They do not think clearly, and they do not check the validity of their thinking. For example, a painfully shy and lonely person may be saying to himself, "I would like to ask that girl for a date, but she might refuse me, and that would be awful." Dr. Ellis might reply to this patient, "Well, suppose she does refuse you; what's so terrible about that? You are 'awfulizing,' and that interferes with life." By virtue of such arguments with a patient's excuses for diminished living, and for not changing self-defeating patterns, Ellis is often

*Healthy
Personality
and Unhealthy
Personality*

able to convince the patient to try ways to live that generate satisfaction and growth. Ellis provides a wholesome reminder that, although excessive thinking can rob a life of feeling and action, wrong thinking can paralyze life itself.

Jurgen Ruesch: Effective Communication

Ruesch,[8] a contemporary psychiatrist, proposed that competence at communication is an indicator of the health of personality. He regards the mentally ill as persons who are deficient in some of the skills essential to full communication with others, for example, ability to transmit "messages" (thoughts and feelings), perceive messages, or decode (understand the meaning of) them. Healthy personality, from this point of view, entails mastery of the many problems involved in communication with others. His work shows how dread of communicating certain aspects of one's experience to others can seriously impair health, whereas frank and free communication makes possible the fulfillment of love and growth.

William Blatz: Independent Security

The late Professor William Blatz[9] founded the Institute of Child Study at the University of Toronto. He developed a theory of security that illumines the study of healthy personality. The theory grew out of his observation of the way children grow and the way adults hinder or help the process. According to Blatz, human beings are born with *appetites*. These include hunger, thirst, elimination, rest, change, and sex. When any of these appetites is deprived, or when a child encounters some problem, he or she is said to be in a state of *insecurity*. Such insecurity is natural for a person; it cannot be avoided. When confronted by insecurity, a person can seek to overcome it in a dependent way, by appealing to others to intervene in one's behalf. *Dependent security* is achieved when a person has been able to assume that the persons upon whom he or she relies to gratify needs and to make decisions are always available and are willing to act in one's service.

Healthy Personality

More desirable, from the standpoint of growth toward maturity, is the quest for *independent security*. This entails learning a new skill in order to gratify the need or to solve the problem by oneself.

Blatz did not make a fetish out of self-reliance, however. He recognized that no human being can face life without help and affection from other people. He emphasized independent security as a goal, to guide the efforts of parents and teachers as they strove to influence a child's growth in wholesome ways. He drew a distinction between *immature* dependent security, which is shown by persons who retain infantile patterns of dependency upon parents, or parent substitutes and authority figures, throughout life. *Mature* dependent security is shown in relationships of mutual love, where each person relies upon the other to provide for those needs that can never be gratified in solitude or without help, such as sexual love and satisfying companionship.

These patterns of independent security, mature and immature dependent security, and the false security based on defense mechanisms are manifested in the major realms of life. These realms include vocational life, one's avocations or leisure pursuits, one's relationships with other people inside and outside the family, and one's philosophy of life. Thus, a person might display independent security in connection with work, mature dependent security in relationships with members of the family, immature dependent security in the use of leisure time, and insecurity with regard to religion or philosophy of life. To Blatz, independent security means

the state of consciousness which accompanies a willingness to accept the consequences of one's own decisions and actions. . . . [It] can be attained in only one way—by the acquisition of skill through learning. Whenever an individual is presented with a situation for which he is inadequately prepared . . . he must make one of two choices—he must either retreat or attack. . . . The individual must, if he is to attack, emerge from the state of dependent security and accept the state of insecurity. This attack will, of course, result in learning. . . . The individual learns that satisfaction results from overcoming the apprehension and anxiety experienced when insecure, and that he may thus reach a state of independent security through learning [1944, pp. 165–168].

Blatz's emphasis on the importance of skills is a valid reminder of an increasing threat to healthy personality—that posed by technology. The more that people rely on machinery, electronic devices, and other apparatus, the more dependent they come to be on that very machinery. In fact, Marshall McLuhan [10] has pointed out that reliance on media, "the extensions of man," robs people of the very powers that are embodied in the gadgets. Periodic excursions to the wilderness, with training in survival skills, are a wholesome corrective to the skill-depleting way of life that is the lot of most people who live in cities. Blatz's ideas are drawn upon in our discussion of work and play and of religion (see Chapters 14 and 15).

Liberation: The Zen Buddhist Version of Healthy Personality

The quest for health and happiness has existed as long as people have been able to reflect upon the human condition. In the East, Hindu, Buddhist, and Taoist monks and philosophers concerned themselves many centuries ago with the problem of how human beings could liberate themselves from cramping habits to attain a happier, freer existence. Some of those who attained "liberation and enlightenment" became teachers, seeking to help others attain the same degree of emancipation from stifling life styles. Alan Watts [11] devoted years to the study of Eastern philosophies and religions; in a series of readable books, he interpreted the major teachings of ancient Eastern philosophers to Western audiences. He saw a parallel between the goal of liberation, which Buddhist monks offer their disciples, and the goal of healthy personality, which psychotherapists offer their disturbed patients. Further, he saw parallels between the various techniques employed by Eastern gurus (spiritual teachers) to elicit "enlightenment" and modern techniques of

Healthy Personality

therapy practiced by present-day psychiatrists and psychologists. Finally, he noticed parallels between the state of enlightenment and the state of healthy personality.

According to Watts, the Zen Buddhists explain neurotic suffering as a result of separating oneself too radically from nature, from other humans, and from one's own organism. Most people equate their very identity with a concept of themselves *instead of with their whole being*. In the process of so separating self, one loses contact with the *flow* or *process* of life, which is essentially spontaneous. People replace spontaneity in their experience, thinking, and behavior with efforts to *make* them happen. Liberation (and, by implication, healthy personality) occurs when a person is able to adopt the attitude of "letting be," or "letting happen." That is, one "lets go" the conscious, controlling ego, or self, and experiences life in somewhat the following fashion: instead of a person's "trying" to swim, "liberated" swimming is experienced as "swimming is permitted to happen" or "swimming is going on." When a person *stops trying* to make things happen, when one stops trying to *make* oneself behave in some desired way, it is argued that the desired events or behavior will spontaneously happen. Learning theorists, surprisingly, offer a similar argument for some skill learning.

In the Zen Buddhist view, healthy personality entails liberation from effortful constraint on, and control over, spontaneous thinking, feeling, and action; it entails attainment of an attitude of "letting oneself be" and letting others and nature "be."

A Behavioristic View of Healthy Personality

Behaviorism has enjoyed a renaissance in the past decade, largely through the influence of B. F. Skinner,[12] the Harvard psychologist, and Joseph Wolpe,[13] a South African psychiatrist now residing in the United States. Skinner developed his views of human beings as organisms subject to laws of *operant conditioning* over a period of nearly forty years. He began his work with studies of rats in "Skinner boxes" and extended it to research in the "shaping" of pigeons' behavior. At present,

25

he and his fellow behaviorists have developed sophisticated techniques for influencing behavior of persons as well as animals.

The behaviorists try to explain human activity without recourse to terms referring to consciousness, such as *reward* or *satisfaction*. Instead, they invoke a circular argument, stating that behavior is "shaped" (into skills, or patterned habits) by *reinforcers*. A reinforcer is any consequence to action which strengthens, that is, increases the probability of the recurrence of, a response. To an observer who is not a behaviorist, the "reinforcing stimulus" may look suspiciously like a reward or a pleasant experience; the behaviorist prefers to avoid such subjectivistic terms.

Skinner and his followers have been consulted by officials concerned with the management of prisoners' behavior in prisons and the behavior of patients in mental hospitals, and by administrators of school systems who wish to make teaching and learning more efficient. There is considerable controversy between humanistic and behavioristic psychologists about the issue of behavior control, and the student should become familiar with the points of debate.

Healthy personality, according to a behavioristic view, calls for competence and self-control—the ability to suppress action that no longer yields positive reinforcers, and to learn action that is successful in attaining the good things. Such rapid adaptability is mediated by the ability to discern the *contingencies*, or rules implicit in nature or in society, according to which needs are gratified and dangers averted.

I have always been uneasy about the behavioristic approach to human nature, because it appeals to the power motive in the behavior scientist. Moreover, research in behaviorism is frequently funded by agencies interested in controlling the behavior and experience of others for the sake of the institution rather than for the person.

Psychosynthesis and Healthy Personality

Healthy Personality   Roberto Assagioli,[14] an Italian psychiatrist, developed a theory of healthy personality and a set of techniques for fostering this goal that he named *psychosynthesis*. He combined contributions from psychosomatic medicine, psychology of religion, study of higher modes of consciousness, parapsychology, Eastern philosophy, personality theory, anthropology, and finally, active techniques for fostering personality growth.

His theory of personality structure states that the human being comprises seven levels, or modes, of functioning:

1. The *lower unconscious*, which includes drives and urges, repressed feelings, and the like (similar in meaning to the id, which harbors primitive sexual and aggressive demands, in Freud's writing).

2. The *middle unconscious*, which comprises the background of our ordinary waking consciousness and is similar to Freud's preconscious, or to the "background" of awareness described by Gestalt psychologists.

3. The *superconscious*, which Assagioli states is the source of "higher" feelings, such as altruistic love, and higher inspirations and intuitions, which give rise to truly creative works.

4. The *field of consciousness*, which designates our ordinary awareness of perceptions, memories, feelings, and urges.

5. The *conscious self*, or "I," designates a "point of pure self-awareness" independent of the content of one's awareness. The self, or "I," he claims, is an enduring center in our consciousness, similar to a light illuminating the objects that are seen.

6. The *higher self*, of which we are generally unconscious, and which transcends the "I," our conscious self. This higher self seems to stand for the possibility of more fully developed experiencing and acting.

7. The *collective unconscious*, a term that Assagioli borrowed from Jung, refers to the beliefs, assumptions, traditions, myths, and symbols that form a source for and background to a person's ordinary consciousness, a source he or she shares with the other members of the society.

Healthy Personality and Unhealthy Personality

Assagioli's conception of personality structure is illustrated by the diagram on page 28.

The task for human beings, says Assagioli, is to free themselves from enslavement by ignorance and unconsciousness, to attain a "harmonious inner integration, true self-realization, and right relationships with others." The goal of such integration—true psychosynthesis—is achieved in four stages:

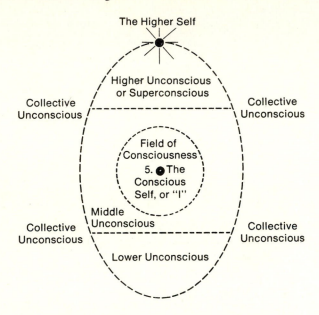

1. Thorough knowledge of one's personality.

2. Control of the various elements of personality. This is achieved by a technique called *disidentification*. Assagioli states, "We are dominated by everything with which our self becomes identified. We can dominate and control everything from which we dis-identify" (p. 22).

3. Realization of one's true self, the discovery or creation of a unifying center. This stage entails the quest for the best, most fully functioning person that one can be through commitment to a worthwhile mission.

4. Psychosynthesis, the formation or reconstruction of the personality around the new center. This phase calls for commitment, study, struggle, and action to actualize the mission and, thereby, the image of the best possible self.

The Freudians [15]

Healthy Personality   Most of the previous writers developed their theories out of an interest in the unhealthy personality. However, almost all of them found it necessary to make some postulations, some suggestions for the concept of the idealized personality. The oldest, most venerable school, that of Freud and psychoanalysis, fixed the pattern of such emphases.

Freud contented himself by stating that health consisted in the ability to love and do productive work. Healthy personality, in psychoanalytic terms, is an outcome of *harmony among id, ego, and superego.*

According to the psychoanalysts, personality is divided into three substructures—the *id*, the *ego*, and the *superego*. *Id* is the term used to refer to instincts. *Ego* refers to the active, controlling, perceiving, learning functions of personality. *Superego* refers to the moral ideals and taboos a person acquires as he or she grows up. It is the task of the ego to scan external reality and inner experience and then choose action that will gratify needs without violating moral taboos—in other words, to mediate between id and superego. A healthier personality would be able to gratify needs and yet remain free of guilt or of social blame. Because one would be less prone to prevent some feelings from coming to the surface (such repression consumes energy), energy would be available for productive work. Because one would not be ashamed of feelings and emotions (because of a reasonable conscience), one could be freer in expressing oneself in loving relationships. Hence, the relationship between ability to love and work, and the concept of harmony among id, ego, and superego, can assume greater meaning.

The psychoanalytic view of healthy personality rests upon a theory of sexuality. According to Freud, children have a rudimentary *pregenital* sex life, involved with fantasies about their parents, and with autoerotic activity. Healthy personality is not possible until a person has overcome childhood fixations and has achieved the *genital* stage of sexual development. At that time, id, ego, and superego are in harmony, and love on an adult basis becomes possible.

Healthy Personality and Unhealthy Personality

Alfred Adler [16] was one of the few psychiatrists in the early 1900s who was deeply drawn ino Freud's ideas. He soon disagreed with Freud, however, about the role of sex in the development of healthy personality and of

neurosis. He saw *gemeinschaftsgefühl* as the most important goal of personal growth and of therapy. The German word *gemeinschaftsgefühl* has been translated as
"social interest" or "social feeling." It refers to a feeling
of oneness, a brotherly feeling toward one's fellow human beings. The concept of social feeling accords with
the highest precepts of ethics and religion and represents
a wholesome corrective to the more pathology-oriented
psychoanalytic writing.

Otto Rank [17] was another of Freud's early followers
who, like Adler and Jung, later went his own way.
Healthy personality, for Rank, implied the courage to
become a separate, distinct person, the courage to express and celebrate one's difference from others, and the
courage to be inventive and creative in various spheres of
existence. I have come to appreciate Rank's view of human being-as-artist more in recent years; I now regard
healthy personality as the ability to respond to the human
situation in inventive, creative ways.

Carl Gustav Jung [18] was at one time a student and colleague of Freud; he too parted with the latter's theories.
Of special interest to us is Jung's view of the structure of
personality. Jung viewed humans as having both a conscious aspect of the psyche and a covert, "shadow" side,
which remains unknown to the individual and invisible
to others. Jung saw personal growth as a gradual unfolding and expression of the unconscious, shadow side and
the integration of these unfolding aspects of personality
into a coherent, meaningful way of life.

Humans experience the world in various ways; Jung
recognized a basic polarity of attention, which he called
extraversion–introversion. The extraverted person is most
attentive to the happenings of the external world. The
introvert is more given to reflection and introspection,
attending to personal experience as it is affected by the
external world. Through upbringing, and perhaps heredi-
tary and congenital influences, persons grow to emphasize one of these fundamental attitudes, while the oppos-
ing attitude remains undeveloped.

Although the attribute of extraversion or introversion
defines direction of interest for the person, that person's
ways of contacting the world are also diverse, as Jung saw

Healthy
Personality

them. He recognized four fundamental ways of experiencing the world, which he designated as *sensing, intuition, feeling,* and *thinking. Sensing* refers to the act of receiving the disclosure of the world by way of one's several sensory systems. *Intuition* refers to a kind of imaginative knowing; it consists of rapid guessing about what lies behind obvious sensory inputs. *Feeling* refers to the emotional quality of experience—its pleasant or unpleasant, frightening, or ugly qualities. *Thinking,* of course, refers to the human capacity for reasoning, conceptualizing, and abstract thought.

The most singular and important characteristic about humans, asserted Jung, was the capacity to *symbolize* experience in dreams, myths, art, and folklore. Jung believed he saw the hints in dreams for the next stages of a person's growth toward fuller self-realization.

Self-realization, becoming an "individuated" person, required that a person become aware of repressed, "shadow" sides in the personality and struggle to express these in his or her way of life. The motive for attempting such self-discovery was to alleviate suffering. Jung treated many people who sought his help because their lives had become stale. They didn't want help in overcoming childhood hangups, which Freud's therapy seemed to focus on. Jung helped them to resume their growth. For Jung, healthy personality entailed the endless struggle to transcend one's initial *socialization* (training to become a *socius,* a citizen) in order to discover and express one's own repressed possibilities of functioning. Integration of the capacities to think, feel, intuit, and sense is fostered by commitment to new purposes for existence. Thus, persons whose growth was adequate to enable them to marry, raise families, and achieve vocational success would arrive at an impasse in their growth and would suffer from it. Their attainment of healthier personality—self-realization—was fostered by relinquishing projects that had animated their youthful years and choosing new aims. The human potential movement in the United States owes a great deal to Jung's writing, whether the debt is acknowledged or not.

Healthy
Personality
and Unhealthy
Personality

An "Unarmored" Body and Healthy Personality

Wilhelm Reich,[19] originally a psychoanalyst, became more and more convinced that healthy personality was impossible as long as a person defended himself or herself from the experience of vitality, sexuality, and other emotions by repression. Such repression produces muscular tension. He gave the name *muscular armor* to those groups of muscles that a person keeps in chronic tension in order not to feel unwanted dimensions of experience. One indication that a person is not living a chronically "armored" life is the capacity to experience a complete sexual climax in lovemaking.

Alexander Lowen[20] adapted some of Reich's ideas and techniques and founded a school of therapy that he calls *bioenergetic analysis*. He observes a person's body, noting peculiarities of chronic tension and posture that are the outcome of the way the person lives. For example, a person with chronically hunched shoulders, who breathes shallowly, may reveal thereby a sense of personal helplessness in a hostile world. Lowen has his patients do certain stretching exercises to identify areas of tension; but he also encourages them to yell, and to beat a pillow or mattress with a tennis racquet, or fists and feet, to release tension. "Unarmoring" a person frees that person from repressions that protect one from pain but also destroy the capacity for pleasure.

Some Existential Suggestions

We have seen that the concept of the healthy personality is nowhere near as old and venerable as the concepts of the unhealthy personality, maladjustment, and neurosis. But we have also seen that ideas about how to make one's self a "better self" or "one's best self" can be found in present-day writings and those from the past. The early Freudians suggest that you can find a way to better functioning by understanding your past, by thinking and interpreting your dreams. Some suggest getting in "better touch" with your body, with specific parts of your body. Full expression of self is indicated by both

Healthy Personality

Freud and Lowen. Of course, such free expression should take place in the proper environment and circumstances—often a psychotherapist's office, but also in one's own home and in the company of understanding, helpful friends.

The newness of the concept of healthy personality gently reminds us that we ought not to put aside any of the many routes to self-actualization or self-realization. These varying methods recognize the necessity, at times, for careful professional help, but they do not deny the value of self-help and help from those who truly love and care about you.

SUMMARY

A series of distinguished thinkers are presented as sources for knowledge about the nature of the healthy personality. These include the following and some of their distinctive contributions.

1. Perls: the significance of the present and of self-sufficiency.

2. Berne: living an adult, game-free existence.

3. Ellis: the impact of wrong thinking.

4. Ruesch: frank and free communication.

5. Blatz: mature, independent security.

6. Assagioli: the attainment of a harmonious inner integration.

7. Freud: acceptance of sexual drives and impact of the past and of the unconscious.

8. Jung: realization of potential.

9. Reich: the significance of the body, of the orgasm.

In addition, the existentialists as a group place more emphasis upon the here and now, the present, in contrast to the deep searches in the past characteristic particularly of the Freudians. The existentialists emphasize being one's self, having the courage to be, regarding one's self as being free and also responsible—not assigning responsibility for one's actions to external sources. Closely related are the ideas of the Zen Buddhists, who invite you to "let be," not to "push the river," to accept the natural forces and flow with them.

Largely in an opposite position are the behaviorists,

who are more atomistic and attend to tiny particles of behavior. They rely heavily upon reward and punishment (aversive stimuli) to control the behavior of the person. Their conception of the healthy personality would include one that avoids behaviors that are not reinforcing. Implicit in their practice is also a conception of the independence of the human being not unlike that of some existentialists, in that the client in the behavior modification program usually chooses the forms of behavior to be extinguished and those to be reinforced. Despite its general rejection by many existentialists, the behavioristic approach must be considered as an additional resource for building the healthy personality.

NOTES AND REFERENCES

1. Recent writings by C. R. ROGERS include *Carl Rogers on Personal Power* (New York: Dell, 1977) and *Carl Rogers on Encounter Groups* (New York: Harper, 1970).

2. Sigmund Freud's view of personality development is summarized in *An Outline of Psychoanalysis* (New York: Norton, 1949). The psychoanalytic conception of the "genital character"—the mature, healthy personality—is well presented in W. REICH, *Character Analysis* (New York: Orgone Institute Press, 1948), pp. 148–199, 254–280.

3. Fritz Perls presents his own ideas in most readable form in *Gestalt Therapy Verbatim* (Lafayette, Calif.: Real People Press, 1969).

4. E. BERNE, *Games People Play* (New York: Grove, 1964). A popular account of the perspective of transactional analysis is given in T. A. HARRIS, *I'm Ok, You're OK* (New York: Harper, 1969).

5. For a review of the impact of existential philosophy on psychology, see R. MAY (Ed.), *Existential Psychology* (New York: Random 1961); see also P. TILLICH, *The Courage to Be* (New Haven: Yale U.P., 1959), and M. BUBER, *Between Man and Man* (Boston: Beacon, 1955), pp. 19–24.

6. V. E. FRANKL, *Man's Search for Meaning*, rev. ed. (Boston: Beacon, 1963).

7. A. ELLIS and R. A. HARPER, *A New Guide to Rational Living* (Hollywood, Calif.: Wilshire Book Co., 1975) and A. ELLIS, *Growth Through Reason: Verbatim*

Healthy Personality

Cases in Rational–Emotive Therapy (Palo Alto, Calif.: Science and Behavior Books, 1971).

8. J. RUESCH, *Semiotic Approaches to Human Relations* (The Hague: Mouton, 1973) and J. RUESCH, *Therapeutic Communication* (New York: Norton, 1961).

9. W. E. BLATZ, *Understanding the Young Child* (New York: Morrow, 1944); see also his posthumous book, *Human Security: Some Reflections* (Toronto: U. of Toronto, 1966).

10. M. McLUHAN, *Understanding Media: The Extensions of Man* (New York: McGraw-Hill, 1965), especially Chapter 4.

11. A. W. WATTS, *Three: (Way of Zen, Nature of Man and Woman, Psychology: East and West)* (New York: Pantheon, 1977).

12. B. F. SKINNER, *Reflection on Behaviorism and Society* (New York: Prentice-Hall, 1978); *Science and Human Behavior* (New York: Macmillan, 1953); *Beyond Freedom and Dignity* (New York: Knopf, 1971); *Walden Two* (New York: Macmillan, 1948). A sensible critique of behaviorism is given in P. LONDON, *Behavior Control* (New York: Harper, 1969). See also the classic debate, C. R. ROGERS and B. F. SKINNER, "Some Issues Concerning the Control of Human Behavior: A Symposium," *Science*, 1956, Vol. 124, pp. 1,037–1,066.

13. J. WOLPE, "Isolation of a Conditioning Procedure as the Crucial Psychotherapeutic Factor: A Case Study" in D. WEDDING and R. J. CORSINI (Eds.), *Great Cases in Psychotherapy* (Itasca, Ill: Peacock, 1979), pp. 121–128. Also see J. WOLPE, *The Practice of Behavior Therapy* (New York: Pergamon, 1966).

14. R. ASSAGIOLI, *The Act of Will* (New York: Viking, 1973).

15. See FREUD, op. cit.

16. Adler's writings are well presented in H. L. ANSBACHER and ROWENA R. ANSBACHER (Eds.), *The Individual Psychology of Alfred Adler* (New York: Basic, 1956).

17. See O. RANK, *Art and the Artist* (New York: Agathon, 1932). A good exposition of Rank's ideas is in FAY B. KARPF, *The Psychology and Psychotherapy of Otto Rank* (New York: Philosophical Library, 1953).

18. Jung was a prodigious writer. A useful introduction to his thought is provided in JOLANDE JACOBI (Ed.), *Psychological Reflections: An Anthology from the Writings of*

C. G. *Jung* (New York: Pantheon, 1953); and Violet de Laszlo (Ed.), *The Basic Writings of C. G. Jung* (New York: Random, 1959). One should read his autobiography, C. G. Jung, *Memories, Dreams, Reflections* (New York: Pantheon, 1961).

19. W. Reich, op. cit., especially Chapter 15.

20. A. Lowen, *The Betrayal of the Body* (New York: Macmillan, 1969), especially Chapter 12.

3

CONSCIOUSNESS AND
HEALTHY PERSONALITY

INTRODUCTION

Consciousness, the capacity to experience the world in its richness, is the evidence for life itself. You may say, "I am experiencing; therefore, I know I am alive!" Certainly a distinguishing characteristic of the healthy personality is openness to new experience. Indicative of the extent of the person's consciousness is the ability to be responsive to new ideas, new thoughts, new perceptions. But does the person have to be selective about the particular experiences that are chosen and even about the ways new experiences are sought? Chemical alterations in consciousness are at best a mixed blessing and need to be engaged in, if at all, with great caution. New experiences that entail genuine effort and accomplishment differ from the chemically induced experience in important ways. Consciousness is a complex and important human characteristic, and the serious student should become familiar with a number of professional points of view concerning the expansion of consciousness in one's own life. This is es-

pecially necessary in a time such as the present, when alteration or expansion of states of consciousness has become a popular and sometimes dangerous recreational activity.[1]

Where Humanistic Psychology and Cognitive Psychology Meet

PSYCHOLOGY REGAINS CONSCIOUSNESS

"After decades of deliberate neglect, consciousness is again coming under scientific scrutiny," writes Natsoulas [2] (1978, p. 906). Most venerable psychologists, while recognizing consciousness as a useful if imaginative construct, did not believe such a state to be a real thing. Watson [3] demanded that psychologists completely dismiss the idea from respectable publications. However, the term never lost meaning to humanistic psychologists, and it is regaining meaning for those involved both in brain psychology and the psychology of thinking.

Natsoulas distinguished seven different kinds of consciousness, as described in the *Oxford English Dictionary*.[4] Some of these are the usual layperson's use of the term, such as "the normal waking state" of the person, definition number 6. Two of these seven, however, are particularly pertinent for the healthy personality. Consciousness definition 3 is *awareness*, "the state of or faculty of being mentally conscious or aware of any thing" (p. 910). Natsoulas agrees that this is the basic concept of consciousness. Within it we may see that one may be conscious not just of people or of their ideas but also of objects, facts, thoughts, and so on. In this chapter, the term *consciousness* is used in conjunction with the terms *awareness* and *experiencing* to mean essentially being aware of anything.

CONSCIOUSNESS IS REFLECTIVE

This important state of being not only refers to the unique capacity to perceive, remember, think about, and imagine the world in its many realities and possibilities. It includes a special human capacity—to *reflect* upon the person's immediate way of being aware. Thus, you can engage in remembering the past; if someone asks, "What

Healthy Personality

38

are you doing right now?" you can reply, "I am trying to remember something." You can tell the difference, through such reflection, between perceiving, remembering, and imaging. Indeed, loss of the capacity for such discriminating reflection, confusion of seeing with imagining, is one of the signs by which students of abnormal personality identify psychosis. The first property of human consciousness to which we call attention, then, is that it can be reflected on. Humans are capable of being self-conscious, as well as conscious of the world beyond themselves. This strange ability of the human to "clamber outside of self" and look back at self is a valuable tool of consciousness expansion. It enables the person to see self as others see the person. It gives one an added foothold on reality.

Consciousness Is Organized into Figure and Background

The work of the Gestalt psychologists, Wertheimer, Lewin, Köhler, and others taught us that perception is organized into the focus of interest, which they designated as *figure*, and the *ground*—a term that describes the rest of the field of awareness and that affords a context or background for the figure. Although figure and ground are most clearly relevant to visual perception, the terms apply metaphorically to the other sensory fields of experience too. Thus, the meaningful words you hear someone utter are *figure* in the auditory field, whereas the sound of passing cars and shuffling feet are present as the *ground*.

THE AFFECTIVE QUALITY OF EXPERIENCING

Our experiencing is always of some meaningful content, such as a person's face, or the sound of a voice, or the recollection of someone's acts. This content stands forth as figure in one's field of awareness. Another basic characteristic of experiencing is that it always has some emotional quality. Thus, my memory of my father is accompanied by feelings of warmth, nostalgia, and sometimes laughter as I recall some of his conversations. My perception of a lovely woman is accompanied by aesthetic

Consciousness and Healthy Personality

and sensual feelings. "Unemotional" experiencing is an outcome of the repression of affect and represents an effort on the part of the unemotional person to imitate a camera or tape recorder. (In Chapter 6, emotional experience is discussed in relation to emotional behavior.)

THE ATTRIBUTION OF REALITY TO OUR EXPERIENCING

One of the most fundamental distinctions we make about the content of our experiencing has to do with whether it is *really there*, whether we are perceiving something or only imagining it. Each person, and for that matter each society, is committed to a set of assumptions about what is real (what can be perceived) and what is unreal. Reality is what a person or group of persons takes to be real.[5] In the last analysis, reality is an attribution, that is, an act or judgment performed by a person, imbuing some experience with the quality of a reality that must be reckoned with. By the same token, we can withdraw our attribution of reality from some experience and view it as not real. Thus, a person may awaken from deep sleep with the conviction that someone is trying to harm him. Upon awakening, he reflects upon this experience and says, with relief, "It is not real—no one is trying to harm me; I was only dreaming." On the other hand, he may experience himself as trapped by a dominating parent and believe that the parent has more power to control his destiny than he has strength to oppose. He lives his life, then, according to this parent's wishes, or what he believes those wishes would be. To an outsider, his estimate of his own strength in relation to the strength of the parent seems unrealistic. But he lives according to what he takes to be the case, what he experiences as real. He attributes reality to his estimates of his strength in comparison with his experience of his parent's power.

People in some societies attribute reality to experiences of ghosts and spirits, and they experience plants, animals, and all of nature as having souls and personalities. The "real world," the world that is real for them, differs from that experienced by the modern Westerner. She regards that world view as mere animism—the ghosts, spirits, and souls with which the "primitive" person lives in her daily life are figments of imagination to the sophisticated person of the modern world. For her, only what can be recorded upon instruments, such as cameras and sound recorders, is taken to be real.

CONSCIOUSNESS IS PERSPECTIVAL

No two persons occupy the same space, and so each has a different place from which to view the world. It follows that, if there are three billion human beings in the world, there are three billion ways for this world to be experienced, none more real or valid than another. If each person embodies a unique perspective, then it is a momentous thing indeed to invalidate or destroy it. This is one cruel feature of colonial exploitation, which destroyed the perspectives of black Africans, Australian aborigines, and American Indians. Women and blacks around the world have complained, legitimately, that their perspectives are often ignored or invalidated by the dominant white male populations. With the advent of the various liberation movements, the neglected perspectives are revealed to the world, and an enriched existence accrues to all concerned. The growing interest of young people in the religion and the life styles of traditional peoples such as the American Indians and Africans, and in Hinduism and Zen Buddhism, is a quest for perspectives upon self and world that are experienced as more life giving than the perspective of white, male, middle-class America.

Ronald Laing, whose writings will be noted in many places throughout this book, has a gift for felicitous expression. About perspectives, he says,[6]

> The human race is a myriad of refractive surfaces staining the white radiance of eternity. Each surface refracts the refractions of refractions of refractions. Each self refracts the refractions of others' refractions of self's refractions of others' refractions. . . . Here is glory and wonder and mystery, yet too often we wish to ignore or destroy those points of view that refract the light differently from our own [p. 3].

Consciousness and Healthy Personality

THE POLITICS OF EXPERIENCING

Laing published a provocative volume called *The Politics of Experience*,[7] the content of which is germane to the theme of this book. The politics of experience implies a contest to see whose perspectives will be recognized and confirmed as right, sane, and true, and whose will be invalidated. Laing points out how members of the psychotherapeutic professions can function as representatives of prevailing views of truth and reality; they are not agents for enlightenment and growth, but agents of social control, dismissing dissenting perspectives as "insane."

There is a sense in which even a conversation is a contest between the participants over the question of whose perspective will prevail. Views of what is real, what is important, and what is possible can be infectious. A person's perspective is vulnerable to being so altered, through contact with others, that the person's action no longer serves his or her own needs, but those of the other person. When this happens, the person is said to be *mystified*.

DIVIDED AND UNIFIED EXPERIENCE:
SELF-CONSCIOUSNESS AND SPONTANEITY

Eastern philosophers are fond of pointing out how Westerners live with a "divided" consciousness, experiencing a gulf between mind and body, between self and nature.

Divided consciousness is a chronic *self*-consciousness, such that the person is aware of self at all times. Whether the person is watching a sunset, making love, or playing a game of tennis, he or she is always aware of self as the "subject," whereas that which the person is noticing is experienced as the "object," as "out there," distant from the self. Even our language, with its grammatical structure, encourages us to enter a chronic state of self-consciousness, of reflection upon our experiencing. A child, before taking on language, apparently has the capacity to perceive in selfless fashion. Eventually, the child learns to learns to monitor experience and action, after having learned that he or she will be called on to give an account of thoughts and actions. The child is to become a spy or witness of his or her own action, and is to give a report to parents upon request.

Healthy Personality   As the child grows older, such self-vigilance becomes habitual, and the rift in consciousness that hinders spontaneity has been permanently inserted. When a happening fully absorbs someone's attention, the person may re-experience the long-lost mode of unreflective, unselfconscious perception.

This is a terrible way to live—always to be watching one's self. The capacity to be self-conscious is unique to human beings, because of the relative size of the human cerebral cortex. Doubtless, the ability to observe the flow of one's experiencing has some adaptive and adjustive value, as noted earlier in this chapter. However, chronic self-consciousness is agonizing, and it destroys enjoyment of living; in extreme instances, self-consciousness can so handicap a person that he or she becomes unable to act at all until having first checked and rechecked the proposed action or communication. When self-consciousness is carried to this extreme, the individual may become nearly paralyzed by doubt and indecision, as in a pattern of neurosis called *doubting compulsion*. When used to "mirror" self and know how you are perceived by others, the gift of reflecting consciousness is helpful.

Zen and Yoga were developed as means of healing the breach in consciousness. The purposes of Zen "sitting," of the disciplines of Hatha Yoga and transcendental meditation, are to help a person "transcend" the ego and experience a unification of self with all that exists. When such enlightenment and unification occur, the person becomes more capable of effortless action, grace of movement, and power of reason, because the person is not doing two things at once, that is, doing something and reflecting upon what is being done. As the Zen aphorism puts it, "Sit when you sit; stand when you stand; don't wobble."

Thus, there is a similarity between the experiences of *samadhi* among followers of Yoga, *satori* among Zen disciples, "rebirth" among followers of the Sufi way, and the "peak experiences" of which Maslow has written so extensively.[8] The experience of overcoming chronic fixation upon a self-conscious, reflective state of awareness, so that one begins to smell and taste, and remember and imagine with greater vividness, can easily be described as "an enlargement of the world," a rebirth, or a self-unification. Yet reflection, or self-witnessing, helps a person to learn skills.

Self-consciousness may rob action of its spontaneity

Consciousness and Healthy Personality

and of its joy. The aim of healthy personality is to be able to reflect upon experience when it is appropriate to do so, and to engage unself-consciously like a child in action, and in personal relationships, when there is no need to reflect.

Action is one way to obtain temporary respite from self-consciousness. Warm-up exercises, followed by intense involvement in a game of tennis or basketball, or in dance, enable a person to be engaged without reflection. Other means for temporarily suppressing the act of reflection include listening to music, engaging in hobbies, and absorption in a book or a drama. Dialogue with another person that fully engages one's attention is also a means of overcoming self-consciousness. When such dialogue is going on, each person is responding to the other without premeditated efforts to produce a particular impression in the experience of the other.

Two Other Views of Divided Consciousness

In addition to the issue of self-consciousness versus spontaneity, there are two other views of the concept of divided self that are of great consequences: the multiple self and the two sides of the brain.

AWARENESS OF MULTIPLE SELVES

One of the strangest forms of adjustment to emerge in our times centers about the person who has not merely divided into two selves but into a number of selves. The most dramatic accounts of this phenomenon are found in the books *Three Faces of Eve* and *Sybil*,[9] both of which are true histories of individuals with multiple personalities. One may have sympathy with a multiple-selved person in the light of the classic work of Kelly [10] identifying the need for self-consistency as being the fundamental drive. Neither of the two, Eve or Sybil, was able to function constructively as long as the "person" kept switching identities or consciousnesses of self. The phrases that speak of this phenomenon have now become standard in our language, "putting it all together," "getting my act together," "getting my head together." While Eve had three selves, Sybil had sixteen, each a distinct personality.

Healthy Personality

Other psychiatrists have since reported similar conditions in rare instances, and one might predict that this phenomenon of divided consciousness will become more frequent, since many of the psychoses seem to have cultural or temporal connections—that is, they are products of the social situation. Something in our divided society seems to favor the emergence of this behavior syndrome.

THE TWO SIDES OF THE BRAIN

In sharp contrast to the previous logical, philosophical, or psychological views of divided consciousness is the position of Ornstein [11] that each side of the brain controls widely differing functions.

> Both the structure and the function of the two "half brains" in some part underlie the two modes of consciousness which simultaneously coexist within each one of us. Although each hemisphere shares the potential for many functions, and both sides participate in most activities, in the normal person the two hemispheres tend to specialize. The left hemisphere (connected to the right side of the body) is predominantly involved with analytic, logical thinking, especially in verbal and mathematical functions. Its mode of operation is primarily linear. This hemisphere seems to process information sequentially. This mode of operation of necessity must underlie logical thought, since logic depends on sequence and order. Language and mathematics, both left-hemisphere activities, also depend predominantly on linear time.
> . . . The right hemisphere (again, remember, connected to the left side of the body) seems specialized for holistic mentation. Its language ability is quite limited. This hemisphere is primarily responsible for our orientation in space, artistic endeavor, crafts, body image, recognition of faces . . . the right hemisphere is more holistic and relational . . . [pp. 51–53].

Consciousness and Healthy Personality

Ornstein and others have suggested that the existence of the two functions implies the need for developing both sides and for seeing these as complimentary functions rather than as polarities in the human being. The high-level-functioning person will effectively utilize both functions in work and life style.

There are many other views that should be considered. A third viewpoint needs to be mentioned, even though its full exposition is well beyond the scope of this book. The relationship between self or self-consciousness and the brain, considered as a physiological entity, has been fully explored in a rare dialogue between two distinguished thinkers, one, Karl R. Popper, a philosopher, and the other, Sir John Eccles, a brain researcher.[12] Both are dualists and espouse the separate existence of mind and brain. Eccles describes their view:

> According to the dualist–interactionist philosophy presented . . . , the brain is a machine of almost infamous complexity and subtlety, and in special regions, under appropriate conditions, it is open to interaction with . . . the world of conscious experience [p. 226].

Modes of Experiencing

We experience the world in a variety of ways, or modes, all of which are essential for the fullest personal functioning.[13] The most fundamental mode of experiencing is *perception*.

PERCEIVING THE WORLD

Our sense organs, like the radio with many stations, permit us to receive a many-faceted disclosure of the world. With our eyes, we receive the impressions of things that are transmitted by light refraction. Our ears receive the sound of things, brought about by vibration. With our olfactory and taste receptors, we receive the scents and flavors emitted by things, and our touch receptors receive impressions produced by direct physical contact—texture, pressure, and pain. The state of our muscles and joints and the location of our arms, hands, legs, and feet are communicated to our reflective awareness by means of kinesthetic sense organs. Our position in relation to vertical posture is mediated by receptors located in the semicircular canal of our ears (equilibratory senses). Finally, the condition of our body—its

Healthy Personality

comfort and discomfort, our fullness and emptiness, the need to eliminate—is detected and received by visceral receptors located in our stomach, intestines, and other hollow organs of the body.

A most unique and important development in the history of the reflective consciousness of the human is seen in the biofeedback movement.[14] The enthusiastic advocates of this approach have been able to successfully demonstrate that the person can control many more internal functions once he or she is helped to "hear" or "perceive" them with a range of instruments. Thus, persons have the ability to speed up or slow down their respiration rate, their heartbeat, and even their blood pressure. We consider this to be a significant step in the development of the human being's independence through knowledge of self—in this case, knowledge of the internal physical aspects of self. "Know thyself," originally found on the temples of Isis and Osiris in North Africa, has become a commandment of the humanistic movement. Its history and its current usage in biofeedback suggest further ways in which a person can control and maximize the self.

What we perceive, and the sensory modalities by means of which we receive disclosure, depend on what is there, what we have been told is there, and also on our needs and projects of the moment. Generally speaking, the salient figure in our field of perception is always related to our immediate needs and goals. Everything else is blurred into the background of experiencing.

When we perceive, that is, receive the disclosure of, something, we always give it *meaning*. We name the objects and persons in the world and make inferences about what the world is "promising" or "threatening" to do to us. We experience the world "inviting" us to do some things and not others and to be in some way. Perception, whether visual, tactual, auditory, or visceral, is a kind of hearing. All our sense organs function in a way analogous to the hearing of speech. In a profound sense, we do not merely see the world; we read the world as we read a sign or a letter. Just as writing is a form of speech, so seeing something and calling it a car is analogous to the car saying, "I am a car; drive me." If all our sense organs are variable ways of hearing, then there is a sense in which our entire body functions as a voice, speaking our replies to the "voices" of the things and beings heard in the world. Our acts, seen by ourselves or by others, have meanings equivalent to speech. To kiss someone can be another way of saying "I am fond of you," and it can mean "hello" or "good-bye."

The act of giving meaning to the perceived beings in our world is called *construing*.[15] As indicated earlier, construing is a kind of listening. We give the meanings to things in the world that our parents and teachers have given them. If mice are frightening to our mothers, then we will hear mice say "Beware," metaphorically speaking, every time we see them. There is a sense, more than metaphorical, in which the world speaks with a voice, with warnings and invitations.

Some whole systems of humanistic psychology have been based upon perception, notably that created by Snygg and Combs, and by Combs, Richards, and Richards.[16] They have suggested that all behavior of humans can best be understood in terms of the subject's perceptions of self and of the outside world. Thus, a teacher who knows that a child in kindergarten has seen running water only in a health clinic understands why the child would run away at the first sight of the tiled bathroom. The child is perceiving it as a place to be hurt. Knowing that your roommate perceives something you say as an insult enables you to understand his or her refusal to talk to you. Our behavior and that of others can be best understood in the light of the perception of the event or activity. Dramatic differences in the way two persons behave in the midst of the same event are explainable in terms of their differing perceptions. Your father may perceive your current boyfriend as someone who is taking his daughter away from him; you will perceive the boyfriend as a white knight. The differences in perception will demand differences in behavior between your father and yourself in relationship to the boyfriend.

CONCEPTUALIZING: CONCEPTS, METAPHORS, AND ANALOGY

Healthy Personality   To conceptualize something is to fit it into a class. Such abstracting and classifying is essential in human existence, because it frees a person to act in service of needs once the person has classified what has just been perceived. If I classify that person over there as a woman, and a married woman at that, I act differently toward her than if I classify her as an unmarried woman. When we conceptualize, however, we "close down" our perception, and we no longer notice the continuing disclosure of the being in question. Once I identify someone as "Mother," I assume I know her, know what to expect of mothers in general and of mine in particular. In fact, concepts of persons and things inevitably go out of date, because every person and every thing is more than we presently believe to be the case; and everything changes in time. My mother today is not identical with my mother yesterday.

Poets and writers make use of metaphors, analogies, and symbols to express truths of experience that cannot be expressed in more prosaic terms.[17] For example, how else can one describe the experience of being in the company of a very dependent person except to say, "He is a leech who sucks my blood every time he comes near." To say, "He is a leech," is not to classify him as a zoologist would, but it does point to a characteristic of his that is real. The ability to see such similarities between things, people, or actions and other phenomena that seem remote aids a person to develop an enriched understanding of the world. Metaphor and analogy are ways to foster insight in a person who is having difficulties in living; psychotherapists frequently interpret a patient's dilemmas in metaphoric and analogical ways, in the hope that the patient will be aided, thereby, to see the situation more clearly or in a new perspective. Thus, a patient might complain that he cannot give up his girlfriend, even though she no longer wishes to see him; he suffers the tortures of the damned when he is not in her company, yet he only fights with her when they are together. The therapist might say, "You are addicted to her company the way an addict is to heroin. You have withdrawal symptoms." The patient might then discover that he can "kick" the habit of seeing his girl, and get on with a livable life.[18]

Metaphor is a way to make sense out of something new that appears within one's horizon. Novel phenomena may be frightening. To use metaphors, analogies, or symbols to describe them is to "tame" them, to note the similarity between something novel and something old and familiar. Metaphoric thinking is also a way to bring about "break-throughs" in scientific fields of inquiry.[19] For example, the behaviorists say that the human being is an organism, like a dog or a beetle. They then proceed to study human beings with methods proven useful in the study and control of dogs. Actually, such description is a case of subtle use of metaphor, or more precisely, *analogy*. To say that human beings are animals conceals the fact that they are like animals, but not entirely like them; they have some capacities that differ from those found in animals. To say that human beings are machines is likewise to conceal the analogy that has been seen by the discerning inquirer. Human beings are not machines, but they function in ways that resemble machines, so that to understand a machine is to understand something about human beings. Scientists who have the capacity to employ new metaphors, similes, and analogies are frequently more creative in their fields of research and theory than those confined to only one model or metaphor.

REMEMBERING

Remembering past perceptions of the world is another way to experience it. As with conceptualizing, we close down the "gates of perception" when we experience the world recollectively. The capacity for vivid and relevant recall of the past is essential for effective action. Anything that hinders our ability to recall jeopardizes our access to healthy personality. We tend to recall schematically in the rush of a busy existence, searching the storehouse of our memory for ways to solve problems of living and to discern the meanings of things; but memory also serves a function of enriching the experience of life itself. When the immediate world of perception is grim and joyless, and there is nothing to be done to ameliorate it, vivid recollection of a happier past may enable a person to endure the present until circumstances change. Such eidetic recalling can, of course, also serve an escape function. Reminiscences of the past can prevent a person from addressing problems of the present with passion and energy.

Healthy Personality

The act of disciplined thinking about one's world, in order to make sense of what has been going on and to solve problems, is another way of experiencing the world with the doors of perception temporarily shut. In fact, when people want to reason and argue with themselves in order to arrive at some conclusion, they seek quiet surroundings. Thinking in a disciplined way, according to rules of logic, is a skill that contributes to effective action. But we can think wishfully, and fearfully, too, when our needs and passions are aroused. Such *autistic* thinking may lead us to conclusions that conform to our feelings but misinform us about the way the world really is. Autistic thinking calls for reality testing—a way to review the argument the thinking embodies and to check the conclusions by means of fresh perception (see Chapter 4).

Compulsive thinking interferes with living; it blocks perception and inhibits effective action. Indeed, one of the functions of meditation is to still one's chattering mind. Such stilling is akin to learning how to discipline the act of speaking. Compulsive thinking is like compulsive talking; it does the person no good.

Disciplined thinking to solve a problem is illustrated as follows: the person carries on an inner dialogue, saying, "If I act in this way, it is likely to produce these consequences, whereas if I don't, the problem will persist." Whether or not this type of thinking will lead to effective action can then be tested. Autistic thinking is a kind of reverie where the person's inner dialogue is deliberately allowed to proceed unchecked by the discipline of reason, and merges into imagination; for example, "I wish I had ten people in love with me at once, wouldn't that be grand?" and so on. Alienated thinking, or chatter, is akin to being in the company of a boring chatterbox who will not allow you to see, hear, or think as you wish because of the constant din of talk.

IMAGINING

When we imagine, we are envisioning possible ways for the world to be. Imagination is play with the possibilities of transforming the world from the way it is now perceived to be to some new form. Of course, it takes action to transform an image of a possible self in a pos-

*Consciousness
and Healthy
Personality*

sible world into an actuality that can be perceived by others and by oneself. Imagination is a way of "traveling," of overcoming one's present situation, in order to envision possibilities that might make life more livable, more fulfilling. The free play of imagination, then, is the way in which we experience new possibilities for the world. It is one of our most precious gifts of evolution, because it is only through such vision that we can save ourselves when our situation has become unlivable.

Anything that diminishes or makes banal our imagination chains us more tightly to a here and now that may not be viable. Every compelling goal and project, whether projected for five minutes or five years into the future, rests upon our capacity to imagine another way for the world to be, with us in it. Such a vision of a transitional utopia may function as an irresistible temptation or invitation that the person may accept, showing this acceptance through action.

Just as imagination can enliven us, ordering and directing our life, so it can demoralize us, even kill us. If one imagines oneself to be weak or helpless, it is but a short step from imagination to belief that such is the case. Healthy personality calls for the ability to discriminate among modes of experiencing. Under conditions of intense need or emotion, a person may confuse imagination with perception and with confirmed truth. There is another aspect of imagining, or literally "image-ing," that when misunderstood can affect a person's body and action in deleterious ways but that, appreciated, can serve the person's well-being and growth. When a person engages in imagining, it is done not just with the mind, but with the entire body. Indeed, the art of acting on the stage is a deliberate, imaginative imitation of some other person. One "becomes" the imagined person, acting and experiencing the world as the role requires. Being hypnotized is another kind of embodied imagination. Hypnotists tell subjects that they *are* tired, or strong, or that they can remember the past so well that they will become three years old again, and the compliant subjects "yield." They fulfill the hypnotists' suggestions by being as they imagine a tired or strong person is, and they act as they imagine or remember what it was like to be three years old.[20] One's body image is the way in which one chronically imagines the body to be, whether weak or strong, energetic or exhausted, vulnerable to disease or resistant. Fisher and Cleveland [21] were able to show that an image of one's own body as only weakly "bounded" was related to increased susceptibility to diseases and malfunction of the internal organs, such as stomach ulcers; an image of one's body as rigidly armored against the world—excessively so—was related to diseases of the skin, bones, and muscles, for example, arthritis.

I have been so impressed by the influence of imagination upon one's body and one's capacities to act that I say to my patients, "Be careful how you imagine yourself to be, because you might become that way." So-called psychocybernetics and positive thinking work in this way, as a kind of self-hypnosis or intense argument with oneself, by saying, "I can do this, I can survive, I can succeed," and believing the statement. This self-persuasion can affect a person in beneficial ways, just as imagining oneself as dead, or as a failure, can bring the image of doom to reality.

DREAMS AND FANTASY

Freud called dreams "the royal road to the unconscious." Recent research has shown that everyone dreams several times during each night. When people say they never dream, the probability is that they do not *recall* their dreams. We tend to recall dreams only when they have been especially intense or dramatic and when we have some special interest in recalling them.[22] Busy, extraverted people seldom pay attention to their dreams and would find it a waste of time to write them down. Yet, increasingly, it is being found that recording one's dreams and thinking about them, seeking hints of new possibilities for personal growth, is an enterprise rewarded by new insight.

Dreaming is a way of being aware of the world, although, paradoxically enough, it is a kind of consciousness that "happens" when we are asleep, when our waking consciousness is suppressed. Laing believes that the dreaming consciousness is active, as a kind of underground

Consciousness and Healthy Personality

53

or background to our waking consciousness.[23] He calls this underground mode of experiencing *fantasy*. Fantasy is a form of perception, a way to perceive the world by noting the effect one's situation is having upon one's body. Our vocabulary for describing bodily states is scant, and so we employ metaphors, symbols, and analogies to describe the way our situation and the people in it are affecting us. Thus, when a person says, "I have just been stabbed in the back," she is speaking metaphorically, but she is also talking about a real experience. If one says of another, "You turn me on," he may be speaking of an enlivening effect that the other person is inducing. These somatic metaphors are efforts to describe one's real condition as a human being. They are attempts to assess whether a relationship or a situation is enlivening, or whether they are devitalizing and debilitating. Fantasy and dreaming are, in a sense, guardians of one's existence, because the content of dreams and of somatic experiencing is always found to be related to one's survival, wellbeing, and growth. Gestalt therapists and followers of Jung and Freud have been able to help persons overcome impasses in their lives through serious consideration of dreams.

Careful attention to the way one's body feels as one lives life can also be useful for growth and wellbeing. One's body can function as did the canaries that miners used to take into the depths of a mine, where oxygen depletion was a grave danger to life. If the canary stopped singing, the miners would know that the air was becoming unfit for humans, and they would improve ventilation or get out. Vague feelings of being "shafted," "sucked dry," "turned on," "ripped apart," tell a person something about his or her situation that should be explored by more direct perception. Fantasy, that waking dream that lurks behind our ordinary consciousness as vague feelings metaphorically described, is a way of knowing. So is dreaming.

Characteristic Ways of Experiencing the World

Healthy Personality   Now that we have explored some of the ways in which the world *can* be experienced by everyone, we turn to the problem of how persons actually *do* experience their world, as a function of their culture and individual upbringing. Both Rorschach and Jung called attention to *erlebnistypus* (literally, "experience type"). Rorschach made inferences about the ways people habitually experience the world from their responses to his famous ink-blot test, whereas Jung inferred "type" on the basis of his psychotherapeutic interviews. The widely used Myers-Briggs Personality Type Indicator uses Jung's analysis of consciousness to describe such types. Persons who emphasize thinking and judging, in their usual waking consciousness, as opposed to persons who are more emotional and intuitive in their approach to the world, are examples of types.

People become specialists at some kinds of experiencing. For example, creative writers are specialists at imagining and at remembering. Many college professors become specialists at thinking, with diminished or repressed ability to pay perceptual attention to what is going on around them. Eliade [24] points out that shamans, in primitive tribes, are specialists at the self-induction of ecstatic states of consciousness, during which time they are capable of "seeing" the future, healing illnesses, walking on coals, and other such feats. It may be that such capacities lie within everyone's capabilities, but upbringing and the need to adjust to the specialized environments within which we live prevent us from discovering and cultivating such ecstatic states.

IS EXTRASENSORY PERCEPTION POSSIBLE?

There continues to be much dispute over the human ability to transmit messages to others by thinking about the message with great intensity of concentration, and to receive such messages transmitted by others. Disciplined scientific research into ESP is being done under J. B. Rhine, at Duke University Parapsychology Laboratory; by workers at the Menninger Clinic, in Kansas; at Maimonides Dream Laboratory in Brooklyn; and in several European countries.[25] I have not been in any of these laboratories, or seen any demonstrations, but I cannot neglect the reports of findings that I take to be true, written by reputable and competent scientists. I regard it as a

Consciousness and Healthy Personality

reasonable hypothesis that some such capacity for extra-sensory communication is an innate human capacity that is but rarely developed because few people believe that it is possible, and perhaps, too, because it is not valued. Indeed, if persons were capable of "tuning in" on everyone's thoughts, or of intruding into the thoughts of others, everyday life would be impossible because of the constant inundation of messages. From the perspective of this hypothesis, the known adepts at sending and receiving messages must have been persons who were not trained for it, but who retained the ability in spite of their socialization. In short, they could conduct extrasensory communication because nobody in their culture told them that it was impossible.

POSITIVE EXPERIENCE

Maslow proposed the term *peak experiences* to describe occasions of great joy, moments of intense happiness and satisfaction that may be occasioned by knowing one is loved, by a fulfilling sexual climax, by the completion of a long and difficult project, or even by eating simple fare after a period of long privation. An intensely contested game of golf, tennis, or handball can be a "high." Maslow argued that the world is seen in its essence, as it really is, during and after such occasions of peaking. He further asserted that such moments are times when a person "has it together," is more integrated, less self-conscious; indeed, is more fully functioning and less armored against the world.[26]

Although Maslow chose the term *peak experiences* (current slang uses the terms *highs*, or *ups* as opposed to *downs*), I would like to extend its meaning and use Ted Landsman's term *positive experiencing*.[27] Positive experience refers to all occasions of pleasure, fun, satisfaction, completion of projects, fulfillment of hopes—the good moments of life. Of course, positive experience can also include pain and suffering, when these are undergone in order to bring about some meaningful and hoped-for outcome.

Positive experience, then, is what life is *lived for*. This statement is not a return to a hedonistic theory of human life, because meaningful positive experience goes beyond, though it includes, sensuous pleasure. Positive experience

Healthy Personality

includes the experience of the fulfillment of meaning.[28]

When a person lives a life that does not yield its due measure of positive experiencing, that person begins to lose morale. He or she becomes increasingly dispirited and hopeless, and under these circumstances may even attempt suicide. Certainly, sudden reductions in customary positive experience, and long intervals without positive experiences, and with no apparent hope of amelioration, are likely factors in reduced resistance to infectious ills. Positive experiencing is good for physical, psychological, and spiritual health.[29] Indeed, one definition of love for another is concern that positive experiencing will come his or her way more often. Healthy personality entails the ability to act in ways that produce positive experiencing for the self and for others.

Two particular kinds of experiences seem to contribute to the development of the healthy personality or to becoming a "beautiful and noble person," as described by Landsman [30]—first, the positive experience, significant experiences of joy, happiness, warmth, and so on; and secondly, those particular negative or unhappy experiences that result in a strengthening of the self or in learning about the self.

The positive experience of being loved, for example, is clearly a growth-facilitating happening. Healthy children and adults need a consistent flow of these experiences to, at the very least, be sure that life is a joyous experience or that life holds the potential for joy, delight, ecstasy, compassion, warmth, and so on. Rizzo and Vinacke [31] asked a sample of people of wide age ranges about their critical experiences and found that those who described these experiences as being happy (or positive or mixed) also made high scores on the Personality Orientation Inventory, indicating high self-actualization.

Some seven kinds of experiences especially stand out as significant in studies by Landsman and others:

1. Completion—the last stroke as you complete the painting of a fence, the final sentence in your term paper, attaching the last shelf of a bookcase you have built.

2. Beauty—discovering a beautiful flower, being in a magnificent home, seeing a beautiful child, hearing lovely melodies.

3. Conquest of a skill—the feeling of rolling away as

you discover you can ride a bicycle, being able to completely play a piece of music on your violin, discovering you can paint a portrait.

4. Excitement—a wide variety of feelings of high intensity, such as one's first dance, participating in a hard-fought race, walking out into space.

5. Earned success—being awarded your Eagle Scout badge, being elected to head your sorority after working for a year toward it, reaching the top of a mountain climb.

6. The human relationship experience—falling in love, feeling close to another person, helping someone in difficulty, being helped by someone through a confusing class assignment.

7. The mystic or supernatural experience—feeling the presence of a spirit, being moved by spiritual conversion, sensing the impact of a deity in one's own life.

Some significant, helpful information has emerged from this research:

1. The most frequent sources of our positive experiences are relationships with other human beings.

2. The second most frequent source for all age groups is the earned success experience.

3. Beauty experiences are less frequent, which suggests that this potential resource for healthy personality growth has been undeveloped.

4. For the "strong" or macho type person, it is important to know that positive experiences come from letting one's self be helped as well as in helping others.

Studies by Fuerst [32] and McKenzie [33] also suggest that some negative experiences have positive effects upon the personality. The death of a parent may result in one child's becoming stronger and more self-reliant. A failure in a class may motivate the student to be more systematic in his or her method of study. A disgrace to the family may spur growing children to more "pro-social" behavior. In particular, McKenzie's study suggested that when negative experiences are turned around to become positive, the probability of there having been a helping person involved, such as an uncle, aunt, or friend, is high, *Healthy* especially for women.
Personality

Altered States of Consciousness

We have mentioned the experiences of ecstasy [34] and of unification; these states are in contrast with the usual ways in which we experience ourselves and our world in the usual conduct of daily life. When we go about the regular business of living in our usual roles with others without having our basic needs satisfied (see Chapter 10), we experience the world, most often, under the influence of *deficiency motivation*. Many people never have the opportunity to experience the world in other than this everyday way, or even have a conception of the possibility of such experience.

Deficiency motivation (or D-motivation) is one of two ways identified by Maslow [35] to perceive the world. The other approach is through *being motivation* (B-motivation). Persons functioning under D-motivation are governed and determined in their perceptions or consciousness by their deprivations, and they can only see the world in terms of what satisfaction for basic needs (such as safety) it can give. People and the world are seen only in terms of their use or exploitations of them. On the other hand, persons who are basically need-satiated can see the world in a broader, cosmic fashion, as it is and as it might be. They can react to the world with their inner being, their irreducible nature.[36] Being-motivation perception is akin to many of the "letting be" philosophies of the Zen Buddhists and other Eastern thinkers.

> Perception must then be gentle, delicate, unintruding, undemanding, able to fit itself passively to the nature of things as water gently soaks into crevices. It must not be the need-motivated kind of perception which shapes things in a blustering, over-riding, exploiting, purposeful fashion . . . [Maslow, 1968, p. 38].

Thus, consciousness that has as its base the person who has largely satiated his other deprivation needs can move on to become B-motivated and manifest the "gentle perception" indicated by Maslow.

Consciousness and Healthy Personality

Suspension of Striving and Altered States of Consciousness

The two authors of this book were at odds for years on some aspects of altered states of consciousness.

After considerable experimentation with ways to alter his usual ways of being conscious of his world, Jourard arrived at a hypothesis that made such alterations intelligible to him. He believed that anything that ends a searching, striving attitude toward the world triggers off an alteration in all modes of experiencing, even when the objective state of the world has not changed. Thus, the psychedelic drugs, such as marijuana and LSD,[37] seem to work by rapidly disengaging a person from commitment to the usual projects and roles. Once this disengagement happens, there is no reason for the person to repress hitherto distracting modes of being conscious; so the person will then smell, taste, touch, and hear more than usual; recall will be more concrete and eidetic; and imagination will be more playful. Landsman, however, sees these "expanded" states of consciousness as largely false, unreal perceptions, sought after specifically as an escape from a dimly perceived, threatening, or boring reality. Both authors agree on the value of periodic, healthy disengagement, as in meditation.

The revelatory power of prayer perhaps stems from a similar cause; a person may pray for divine guidance when personal struggles have come to naught. If the person authentically "surrenders" and begins to pray, this disengagement from the struggle may bring to light solutions that always were there, although the person could not see them. Meditative disciplines alter and enlarge a person's perceptual and other experiential modes by way of disengagement. One cannot truly "get into" the various Hatha Yoga postures until one disengages from one's customary modes of experiencing and striving.

Hypnosis appears to work in similar fashion. When one is being persuaded by the hypnotist's suggestions, one is actually being seduced into suspending usual ways of being conscious of the world. If one yields, one's consciousness is indeed altered.

Healthy Personality

The "outsiders"—a theme Colin Wilson[38] addressed

with such insight—were people "who saw too much" for their time and place. They were not wholly in the clutch of the norms, goals, and standards of their place, and so their consciousness of the world within which they were living was radically "altered," different from that of the typical person. Thus, such characters as Meurseault, in Camus' *The Stranger*, and such real persons as William Blake, Nijinsky (the great ballet dancer), and Lawrence of Arabia were all outsiders, and as Wilson pointed out, their "vision" wrecked them because they did not understand why their vision was different or how to protect themselves.

R. D. Laing has said that what has hitherto been regarded as the madness of schizophrenics is likewise an authentic but different way of experiencing the world that happens when a person gives up an identity that is no longer viable. The act of surrender triggers off such alterations of consciousness as hallucinations, visions, and the like.[39] Of course, any deviations from ordinary consciousness give rise to action that appears strange to the average person. This is why "altered consciousness" can be troublesome unless a person learns how to use the richer experience as a guide to more effective action.

SOLITUDE, ABSTINENCE, AND "HIGHER" CONSCIOUSNESS

Shamans and persons in search of their God have for millennia pursued a path of disengagement, and not only from the worldly pursuit of wealth, power and fame; they have also renounced sex, food, drink, drugs, and the company of other persons. Jourard experimented with many of these routes to altered and enlarged awareness, short of total commitment to the way of a holy man. He was persuaded that his hypothesis about the relation between disengagement from one's situation and the enlargement of consciousness retains high explanatory power. Food, sex, alcohol, and narcotic drugs appear to shrink consciousness. The sensuous pleasure and anesthetic effects "fix" a person into only one of many possible ways to experience the world: pleasant, but confining. Perhaps this was why Odysseus had his men tie him to the mast as their ship passed the island of the Sirens,

Consciousness and Healthy Personality

whose seductive songs might have diverted him from his mission.

The reason for solitude is apparent. We all are readily influenced by others' perspectives, which they transmit as they talk to us. Disengagement from others enables us to reflect in silence, to discern what our own perspective might be. It should not be forgotten, however, that another basic way to alter and enlarge consciousness is through listening to a person speak who is more aware of the world's possibilities than oneself.

EXPERIENCING THE UNEXPECTED

Kurt Goldstein described a condition among brain-damaged patients that he called the "catastrophic reaction." Treating German soldiers during World War I who suffered gunshot and shrapnel wounds in the brain, he noted that such patients, after some time for recovery, were able to function reasonably well if their world was kept tidy and unchanging, and if their time was ordered in rigidly scheduled ways. For example, they needed to know where their clothes were located and when to expect meals. If some sudden alteration was introduced in the way their time and space was arranged, they would not welcome it as a respite from boredom; rather, it was experienced more as a disaster, a catastrophe with which they could not cope. They would become furious, panicky, and might even faint.[40]

This reaction to the unexpected is but an exaggeration of a similar reaction that occurs in average people. We are all socialized so that we acquire a set of assumptions about the world that enables us to live our customary lives. If something new, different, and unexpected enters our world, we may react with panic or with violence. It is as if the unexpected reality that has just been experienced calls upon inadequate capacities to respond. Accordingly, we may try to deny that anything new has appeared, saying, "Why, it's nothing but something old, in new clothes"; or we may try to destroy that which is new or different. Many young men who were among the first to appear with long hair in America experienced varying degrees of violence from people who felt that men were supposed to have short hair. If a man experi-

Healthy Personality

ences tender, or even sexual, feelings for another man, he may undergo panic, even though he does not express the feeling.

For healthy personalities, the experience of the unexpected serves as an occasion for new learning and growth. To be surprised, or to encounter something that challenges one's assumptions about oneself and the world functions for healthy personalities as a motive for reality testing (see Chapter 4), as well as an opportunity for the enlargement of one's awareness of the world.

On Recognizing a Consciousness Larger than One's Own: A Hypothesis

A person's experience of the world is invisible to others. All that anyone can perceive directly of another person is action, body, and speech. The gulf between one consciousness and another cannot be crossed, except through acts of intuition, empathy, and imagination and through communication with shared understandings. If the other person experiences the world in more dimensions, in greater depth, and with more breadth of vision than oneself, one cannot even imagine what that experience might be, because one can imagine only within limits set by one's own experience. How, then, can a person recognize when he or she is in the presence of a teacher?

One answer lies in surprise and unpredictability. If the other person presents ideas that come as a surprise to the listener; if the other person's actions are of surprising skill and grace; or if he or she achieves truly lofty, noble objectives that seem unthinkable to the average person; the possibility arises that the other person is an enlarged consciousness. Boris Spassky, the Russian chess master, may have had a moment of suspicion that Bobby Fischer was a larger awareness, when finally he yielded the championship to him. A second key lies in *authenticity*. There must be some clear evidence of this attribute; one indicator, as discussed earlier, is that the teacher always permits the follower to be psychologically and physically free to leave immediately. Instances of mind control by various colorful, seductive cult leaders require the immediate freedom test.

A person with a larger awareness faces a problem in communicating with those of lesser awareness. In all the traditions of enlightenment, different paths are recommended by the teacher, to bring the seeker to the desired "light." Socrates followed the path of dialogue, questioning his student until the latter suddenly achieved an understanding. The Zen master assigns *koans*, impossible problems to solve, such as, "What is the sound of one hand clapping?" The seeker would be obliged to ponder this paradox until, after enough struggle, the enlightenment would occur. Moses enjoined the Hebrews to live in a very particular way that he could see would lead to an enriched life. If they would follow in the disciplined way, they would live more fruitfully and experience more. The yogis guide their followers toward a larger awareness of the world by assigning them the disciplines of Hatha Yoga, meditation, good works, and simple living. The Sufi masters assigned discipline and employed wine, stories, and ecstatic dancing to lead their pupils to a larger awareness of their possibilities.

It is an interesting hypothesis, then, that great religious teachers, such as Buddha, Jesus, Moses, and Patanjali, were men of very high awareness, whose teachings constituted instruction to followers on how they might arrive at comparable levels of awareness.

Indeed, we cannot help but realize that all training schemes, even those devised by "behavior modification" experts, are ways to alter and enlarge consciousness. The art instructor does not teach the skill of drawing so much as he or she invites a student to persist in making marks on paper, while really looking and really seeing what the student looks at. Artists teach a way of being aware as much as they teach a manual skill.

Enlarged consciousness is infectious. Thus, dictators of authoritarian nations and cult leaders seek to censor writers and artists, to avoid having their awareness of tyranny and control transmitted to the masses, who then would be less manipulable.

Awareness is *power*, the power to affect others for their betterment or to their detriment. Perhaps this is why, in all the mystical and religious traditions, the "mysteries and secrets" are never revealed to novices un-

Healthy Personality

64

til they have proven to their elders that they will employ the knowledge that is revealed to them for the good of humanity, not to exploit this knowledge.

Carlos Castañeda was subjected to many tests by Don Juan, his teacher of the "Yaqui way of knowledge," before true knowledge and seeing became possible for him.[41] And in the traditions of primitive peoples, young people must undergo tests of their maturity and virtue before they are initiated into the knowledge and responsibilities of adulthood.[42]

Enlarged Consciousness and Healthy Personality

Whether or not the enlargement of consciousness is conducive to healthier personality depends upon several factors, including the projects to which a person is committed and the person's ability to acquire skills commensurate with the enlarged awareness. Healthy personality rests upon *competence*, the ability to act effectively in pursuit of the gratifications and meanings that make life possible and worth living. If a person has become excessively aware of self and of the world, as sometimes happens with unwise users of psychedelic drugs, that person cannot deal effectively with everything of which he or she has become aware. Maslow[43] was aware of this when he cautioned of the "dangers of Being-cognition." The hyperconscious individual may arrive at a sense that all things are of equal importance and value. Such a stance is equivalent to valuelessness, and it results in paralysis of action. Old people prepared to die may have such enlightenment, but it is not of much use to younger persons with a life yet to be lived. There is some optimum harmony among the magnitude of a person's awareness of the world, the goals and projects to which that person commits his or her life, and the skills and capacities for effective action. If enlarged and altered consciousness enriches one's sense of meaning and is accompanied by increased effectiveness at living a life-engendering existence, then such alteration is conducive to healthy personality; otherwise, it might be pernicious.

Consciousness and Healthy Personality

Another point of view that should be considered is that many forms of changed consciousness, particularly those that come from the use of chemical substances such as LSD and alcohol, are not really enlarged, expanded, or higher, but rather are simply changed, and changed in such a fashion to disguise reality and prevent the person from dealing with the problems of real life, of responsibility for others, and even of maintaining personal health and sanity. The nature of experience itself is such that it cannot be checked and validated by scientific methods; Castañeda's experience cannot be validated by Don Juan. This is particularly true of reported experiences of "higher" consciousness and greater awareness of self. Substantiated evidence for this is difficult to develop. For some, these enlarged consciousnesses are the stuff of which dreams are made.

Some Existential Suggestions

It is good to be able to reflect upon one's own experiencing, but excessive reflection makes action difficult, if not impossible. Nevertheless, there is value in examining the structure of one's field of consciousness, especially in the light of a quest for further self-development.

A different kind of warning is sounded by Schur [44] with regard to the current consciousness fascination. He has raised the question about whether or not the emphasis upon individual consciousness will lead young, committed persons to concern themselves entirely with themselves and turn away from the hard work involved in righting social wrongs. Schur points out that all of our societies are riddled with problems that cannot be correctly seen as originating even in collective consciousness. Social problems require social answers. Particularly in the sphere of chemical alterations of consciousness, including alcohol and the mind-altering drugs such as LSD, is the phenomenon of escape from social responsibility apparent.

What modes are predominant in your consciousness? Is there some one sensory modality that is not functioning? When was the last time you really looked at something, smelled it, tasted it, fondled and touched it? There *Healthy* are "sensory awakening" exercises that are fun to do and *Personality* that enrich the quality of experience. Bernard Gunther's books [45] are good as guides to this. Burl I. Payne [46] has a useful collection of consciousness-expanding exercises in *Getting There Without Drugs: Techniques and Theories for The Expansion of Consciousness.*

Dreams offer us glimpses of other ways to live, as well as flashes of truth about ourselves and our situation. Ann Faraday's book *Dream Power* [47] offers a useful guide to recording and making existential sense out of one's dreams.

"Openness" is becoming one of the few characteristics of the healthy personality that is agreed upon by all writers. Maslow, Coan, Landsman, and others cite it in one form or another in their classification systems. Objective evidence is provided by Schaeffer, Diggins, and Millman,[48] who found, in their study of self-actualized individuals, that creativity, among men particularly, was highly correlated with openness to theoretical and aesthetic experiences. This suggests the "natural" consciousness expansion as being characteristic of the high-level-functioning person. Can you maintain your openness to new ideas in the face of threats?

One of the most popular forms of consciousness expanding all over the world, which has claimed the allegiance of large numbers of students, is transcendental meditation. This practice often involves two periods of serious meditation daily. Impressive support for this position has come from a large body of research published by the Maharishi International University. The research does not at this moment establish the superiority of TM over other forms of meditation. However, it strongly suggests that such activities that "quiet down the outer and inner voices" and enable one to listen to self are worthwhile for personal growth. In the harried and hassled world of learning and of the marketplace, it is a rare person who can systematically, daily put aside the external world for short periods of time. However, there is much to say for such an effort. Ferguson and Gowan [49] studied three groups of volunteer male and female students—short-term meditators, long-term meditators, and nonmeditators. The results strongly indicate that the TM program reduces anxiety, depression, and neuroticism and increases self-actualization.

Consciousness and Healthy Personality

The readers might examine their ways of meditating or of reaching "higher" levels of awareness. Are they dependent upon mind-expanding drugs, or can they detach from their usual consciousness through meditation, fasting, or other "natural" means?

The significance of the positive experience in developing the high-level-functioning person is shown in a study of "critical experiences" by Rizzo and Vinacke.[50] They tested persons ranging from undergraduate students to octogenarians and found that those persons who reported their critical experiences as being essentially happy were more self-actualized. They also suggest that their study indicates, as did Lynch's and Horn's,[51] that the high-level-functioning person is able to derive positive results even from painful experiences. Do you bemoan misfortunes or make the most of them? Is your consciousness governed by D-motivation? Can you recognize teachers and companions who are consciousness-expanding influences? Equally important, can you distinguish between those who do open your consciousness and those who are simply looking for others to share their short-term escapes from reality? Which "side" of your brain needs developing, the analytical or the emotional?

SUMMARY

Consciousness is the human being's unique and supreme gift. It is difficult to define and talk about, because one can only do so in terms of consciousness itself. Some basic properties of consciousness are that it is reflective; it is always intentional, that is, of some meaningful content; it is organized into figure and ground; it always has some affective, or emotional, quality; the quality of reality or unreality is attributed by a person to his or her experiencing; each perspective upon the world is unique; there is a "politics" of experiencing, that is, competition between people to see whose definition of the common situation is held to be authoritative; it may be divided and unified; and finally, it always occurs in some mode.

Healthy Personality

The modes of consciousness include perception, conceptualizing, remembering, thinking, imagining, and dreaming and fantasy. Each person develops a charac-

teristic way of experiencing the world (in German, an erlebnistypus), *where some sensory modality, such as vision or touching, is highly developed and some experiential mode is predominant, for example, imagination or thinking.*

The brain, in a sense the tool of consciousness, may be thought of as mediating two kinds of consciousness: analytical and emotional.

Consciousness of self may also be split or fractionated, but the healthy personality owns a unitary, organized self.

Extrasensory perception, positive experience, and altered states of consciousness, as well as the effect of experiencing the unexpected, were discussed. The problems of recognizing a consciousness more developed than one's own and the relationship between enlargement of consciousness and healthy personality were explored.

NOTES AND REFERENCES

1. The content of this chapter is based upon the philosophical position known as *existential phenomenology. Phenomenology* refers to the science of "phenomena"—the way the world appears to human beings. *Existentialism* is a philosophical position that concerns itself with the study of what it means to be in the world as a human being. Edmund Husserl is viewed as the founder of phenomenology as a modern philosophical school; existentialism is associated with Kierkegaard, Nietzsche, Heidegger, Jaspers, Sartre, Berdyaev, and Buber. One of the better discussions of this point of view in the professional literature is provided by H. MISIAK and V. S. SEXTON, *Phenomenological, Existential and Humanistic Psychologies: A Historical Survey* (New York: Grune, 1973). An introduction to existential phenomenology is provided in W. LUIJPEN, *Existential Phenomenology*, 2nd ed. (Pittsburgh: Duquesne, 1971). Humanistic psychology draws heavily upon this discipline in its concern with the study of people as human, rather than as animal or mechanical, beings. Two recent books by psychologists that illustrate this approach are E. KEEN, *Psychology and the New Consciousness* (Monterey, Calif.: Brooks-Cole, 1972), and A. GIORGI, *Psychology as a Human Science: A Phenomenologically Based Approach* (New York: Harper, 1970).

Consciousness and Healthy Personality

2. T. Natsoulas, "Consciousness," *American Psychologist*, 1978, Vol. 33, pp. 906–914; and T. Natsoulas, "Consciousness: Consideration of an Inferential Hypothesis," *Journal for the Theory of Social Behavior*, 1977, Vol. 1, pp. 29–40.

3. J. B. Watson, "A Schematic Outline of Emotions," *Psychological Review*, 1919, Vol. 26, pp. 165–196.

4. *Oxford English Dictionary* (New York: Oxford U.P., 1933), pp. 847–848.

5. The phenomenon of attribution has been studied most thoroughly by Fritz Heider in his book *The Psychology of Interpersonal Relations* (New York: Wiley, 1958). Laing applied Heider's concepts to the study of disturbed human relationships. See R. D. Laing, *Self and Others* (New York: Pantheon, 1970), especially Chapter 11; and *The Politics of Experience* (New York: Pantheon, 1967), Chapter 1.

6. R. D. Laing, H. Phillipson, and A. R. Lee, *Interpersonal Perception, A Theory and a Method of Research* (New York: Springer, 1966).

7. Laing, *The Politics of Experience*, op. cit.

8. A fine introduction to the ideas presented in this section, or a source for further study, is C. Naranjo and R. E. Ornstein, *On the Psychology of Meditation* (New York: Viking, 1971). A further source is D. Goleman, "The Buddah on Meditation and States of Consciousness"; Part I: "The Teachings"; Part II: "A Typology of Meditation Techniques," *Journal of Transpersonal Psychology*, 1972, Vol. 4, pp. 1–44; 151–210.

9. F. B. Schreiber, *Sybil* (New York: Warner, 1974); and H. Thigpen Corbett and H. M. Cleckley, *Three Faces of Eve* (New York: Popular Library, 1957).

10. E. C. Kelly, *Education for What Is Real* (New York: Harper, 1947).

11. R. E. Ornstein, *Psychology of Consciousness*, 2nd ed. (New York: Harcourt, 1977).

12. Karl R. Popper and Sir John C. Eccles, *The Self and Its Brain* (Berlin: Springer International, 1977).

13. This analysis of consciousness is adapted from Laing. See R. D. Laing, *The Divided Self* (New York: Pantheon, 1969); also the references cited in notes 6 and 7. See also S. M. Jourard, *Disclosing Man to Himself* (New York: Van Nostrand Reinhold, 1968), especially Chapters 13 and 14.

14. B. B. Brown, *New Mind, New Body: Biofeed-*

back: New Directions for the Mind (New York: Harper, 1974).

15. See G. KELLY, *The Psychology of Personal Constructs*, Vol. 1 (New York: Norton, 1955) for a thorough analysis of the act of construing and a development of the point of view Kelly called "constructive alternativism."

16. See A. W. COMBS and D. SNYGG, *Individual Behavior*, 2nd ed. (New York: Harper, 1959); and A. W. COMBS, A. RICHARDS, and F. RICHARDS, *Perceptual Psychology* (New York: Harper, 1978).

17. See W. A. Shibles, *Metaphor: An Annotated Bibliography and History* (Whitewater, Wis.: The Language Press, 1971). See also C. M. TURBAYNE, *The Myth of Metaphor*, 2nd ed. (Columbia, S.C.: South Carolina U.P., 1970).

18. H. R. POLLIO, "*The Whys and Hows of Metaphor and Their Measurement*," paper presented at Southeastern Psychological Association, 1972. J. R. BARLOW, "Metaphor and Insight," paper presented at Southeastern Psychological Association, 1972.

19. T. S. KUHN, *The Structure of Scientific Revolutions*, 2nd ed. (Chicago: U. of Chicago, 1970).

20. For a review of theories of hypnosis, see T. X. BARBER, *Hypnosis: A Scientific Approach* (New York: Van Nostrand Reinhold, 1969); and E. HILGARD, *The Experience of Hypnosis* (New York: Harcourt, 1968).

21. S. FISHER and S. CLEVELAND, *Body Image and Personality* (New York: Dover, 1968); see also S. FISHER, *Body Consciousness: You Are What You Feel* (Englewood Cliffs, N.J.: Prentice-Hall, 1973), especially Chapter 2.

22. A splendid, most readable review of scientific studies of sleeping and theories of dreaming is ANN FARADAY, *Dream Power* (New York: Coward, 1972). She presents the approaches of Freud, Jung, Perls, and Calvin Hall to the interpretation of dreams and then shows the reader how to make sense of his or her dreams. But everyone should read primary sources: S. FREUD, *The Interpretation of Dreams* (New York: Basic, 1955); C. G. JUNG, *Memories, Dreams, Reflections* (New York: Pantheon, 1963); F. PERLS, *Gestalt Therapy Verbatim* (Lafayette, Calif.: Real People Press, 1969); C. HALL, *The Meaning of Dreams* (New York: McGraw-Hill, 1966). I have always liked E. FROMM, *The Forgotten Language: An Introduction to the Understanding of Dreams, Fairytales and Myths* (New York: Holt, 1970).

Consciousness and Healthy Personality

23. Laing, *Self and Others*, op. cit., Chapters 1 and 2; *The Politics of Experience*, op. cit., pp. 30–32.

24. M. Eliade, *Rites and Symbols of Initiation* (New York: Harper, 1958), pp. 94–96.

25. Articles on ESP appear frequently in the *Journal of Transpersonal Psychology;* there is also a journal devoted exclusively to parapsychological phenomena. A useful book with which to begin study in this area is Sheila Ostrander and Lynn Schroeder, *Psychic Discoveries Behind the Iron Curtain* (New York: Bantam, 1970).

26. A. H. Maslow, *Toward a Psychology of Being*, 2nd ed. (New York: Van Nostrand Reinhold, 1968), Chapters 6 and 7.

27. T. Landsman, unpublished manuscript, University of Florida, 1973.

28. V. E. Frankl, *Man's Search for Meaning*, rev. ed. (Boston: Beacon, 1963).

29. S. M. Jourard, *The Transparent Self*, 2nd ed. (New York: Van Nostrand Reinhold, 1971), Chapters 9 and 10.

30. This material is discussed in greater detail in a paper by Ted Landsman, "Positive Experience and the Beautiful Person," presidential address: Southeastern Psychological Association meetings, 1968. A brief recapitulation is found in "The Humanizer," *American Journal of Orthopsychiatry*, 1974, Vol. 44, pp. 345–352.

31. R. Rizzo and E. Vinacke, "Self-Actualization and the Meaning of Critical Experience," *Journal of Humanistic Psychology*, 1975, Vol. 15, pp. 19–30.

32. R. E. Fuerst, *Turning Point Experiences*, unpublished doctoral dissertation, University of Florida, 1965.

33. D. H. McKenzie, *Two Kinds of Extreme Negative Experiences*, unpublished doctoral dissertation, University of Florida, 1965.

34. Besides Eliade (note 24), Marghanita Laski has investigated the experience of ecstasy. See Marghanita Laski, *Ecstasy: A Study of Some Secular and Religious Experiences* (London: Cresset, 1961).

35. Maslow, op. cit.

36. A. H. Maslow, *Farther Reaches of Human Nature* (New York: Viking, 1971).

37. D. Solomon (Ed.), *LSD: The Consciousness Expanding Drug* (New York: Putnam, 1964); see also A. Hoffer and H. Osmond, *The Hallucinogens* (New York: Academic, 1967).

38. C. WILSON, *The Outsider* (Boston: Houghton, 1960).

39. LAING, *The Politics of Experience,* op. cit., Chapters 5 and 6. See also the account by Mary Barnes of her experience of surrender to a wish to regress to infancy in order to re-enter the world in a more authentic and life-giving way: MARY BARNES and J. BERKE, *Mary Barnes: Two Accounts of a Journey Through Madness* (New York: Harcourt, 1971).

40. K. GOLDSTEIN, *Human Nature from the Point of View of Psychopathology* (Cambridge, Mass.: Harvard U.P., 1940); K. GOLDSTEIN and M. SCHEERER, "Abstract and Concrete Behavior," *Psychological Monographs,* 1941, Vol. 53, pp. 1–151.

41. C. CASTAÑEDA, *Teachings of Don Juan: A Yaqui Way of Knowledge* (New York: Ballantine, 1968); *A Separate Reality: Further Conversations with Don Juan* (New York: Simon & Schuster, 1971); *Journey to Ixtlan* (New York: Simon & Schuster, 1972).

42. ELIADE, op. cit.; A. VAN GENNEP, *The Rites of Passage* (Chicago: U. of Chicago, 1960).

43. MASLOW, op. cit., Chapter 8.

44. E. SCHUR, *The Awareness Trap: Self-Absorption Instead of Social Change* (New York: McGraw-Hill, 1976).

45. B. GUNTHER, *Sense Awakening* (New York: Macmillan, 1968); *What to Do Till the Messiah Comes* (New York: Macmillan, 1971).

46. B. PAYNE, *Getting There Without Drugs: Techniques and Theories for the Expansion of Consciousness* (New York: Ballantine, 1973).

47. FARADAY, op cit.

48. D. E. SCHAEFFER, D. R. DIGGINS, and H. L. MILLMAN, Intercorrelations Among Measures of Creativity, Openness to Experience and Sensation Seeking in a College Sample," *College Student Journal,* 1976, Vol. 10, pp. 332–339.

49. P. FERGUSON and J. GOWAN, "TM: Some Preliminary Findings," *Journal of Humanistic Psychology,* 1976, Vol. 16, pp. 51–60.

50. R. RIZZO and E. VINACKE, op. cit.

51. Two highly interesting studies of the effects of positive and negative experiences are S. LYNCH, *Intense Human Experience: Its Relationship to Openness and Self-Concept,* unpublished doctoral dissertation, University of Florida, 1968, which showed that positive experiences gen-

erally open the person to further experiencing; and M. L. HORN, *The Integration of Negative Experience by High and Low Functioning Women*, unpublished doctoral dissertation, University of Florida, 1975, which showed that high-level-functioning women could integrate negative experiences and remain open to the world.

4

REALITY, PERCEPTION, AND HEALTHY PERSONALITY

INTRODUCTION

If one knows how to function effectively, one has a sound basis for the development of a healthy personality. The ability to perceive reality as it "really is" is, therefore, fundamental to effective functioning. It is considered one of two preconditions to the development of the beautiful and noble person. Our need systems heavily affect our ability to perceive reality—we often perceive what we want to see rather than what is really there.

Our behavior is always undertaken with reference to the world as we believe it to be. We can hardly make sense out of anybody's behavior unless we somehow learn from individuals how the world appears to them— what they are paying attention to, how they interpret the things they see and hear, and what their expectations are regarding the world about them, according to Combs [1] and others. We will be puzzled if we see someone run in terror from an automobile engine as it starts up, because to us the automobile is simply something to get us from place to place. However, if the person is a primitive who has never seen an automobile, that person may perceive it as a punishing instrument of the gods that is about to engulf someone. If we know how the person perceives the situation, we can understand the situation better and offer help.

A person's perceptions and beliefs will be inaccurate or distorted unless the person takes steps to verify them. Reality contact is not a given; it is an achievement! Efficient contact with reality must be worked for, because there are powerful forces at work at all times, tending to distort perception, thinking, and recall.

Some Influences on Perception of the World

In the first place, the content of our field of perception is necessarily selective; it cannot include all inner and outer reality that exists at a given moment. Only part of the ongoing flow of feelings, thoughts, and external events is detected by our sense organs and represented in our field of awareness. Our sense organs resemble TV or radio receivers, in that they are differentially sensitive to stimuli of different intensities and qualities. But even within the receptive range of our senses, we still notice only a fraction of all the sensory information reaching our brain. Some of the important determiners of *figure*, that is, of our focus of attention, are unfulfilled needs.

Our feelings and our needs direct our perception, thinking, remembering, and fantasy, so that the figure will be that perception, thought, or memory most relevant to our needs of the moment. Our cognitive processes are thus servants of our needs. When we are hungry, we think and dream about food, we search for it, and we tend to ignore everything in the world that is inedible or that will not help us to get food. If we are sexually deprived, we tend to have fantasies with erotic themes, we find it difficult to think about other things, and we look at the world from the standpoint of the sexual gratification and frustrations it is likely to afford. If we are anxious because of some threat to our security, we are unlikely to notice the beauties of nature; we are too busy seeking the source of danger so that we might escape

Healthy Personality

76

from it. There have been many experiments conducted to demonstrate how needs determine our attention and the content of our consciousness, and so we need not dwell further upon this point. More germane to our discussion is the manner in which emotions and unfulfilled needs operate to distort our perceptions and beliefs.

INFLUENCE OF IMMEDIATE NEEDS UPON PERCEPTION

Perception is perhaps one of the most important processes in psychology and is essential in understanding human behavior. According to Combs and Snygg,[2] *all behavior* is related to perception. A student attends a university because she perceives it as being helpful to her career or because a parent perceives it to be helpful to her offspring's development. A thief robs a bank because he perceives it as the source of money, according to Willie Sutton, one of the most famous of bank robbers. A child cries when seeing a clown because he sees it as a monster rather than as a funny creature.

The most important influence upon perception and misperception is the perceiver's own needs. At about noontime, if you are driving through a strange city, should you see painted on a store window the name of the owner, *Sandwharf*, you are likely to perceive it as *Sandwich*. If you are embarrassed by sex-laden words and are asked to read a list quickly, you are likely to misread *breast* as *beast*. In a passionate political or personal argument, one's need is so great to win that we may avoid perceiving the other person's position at all.

The presumption, of course, is that since we are all human, others would perceive things the same way we would. A healthy personality is by no means exempt from this law. These persons too may momentarily see only themselves as "right" in their perceptions of complex political situations, for example, but they are able to look back upon themselves, their arguments, and their behavior and recognize when their needs are causing them to misperceive reality—or at least to miss other possible realities. This capacity for reflection back upon self is a uniquely human characteristic and is exceedingly valuable in keeping a certain openness to new ideas, new friends,

Reality, Perception, and Healthy Personality

and new joys. If someone perceives all new sports or new challenges as producing probable failure, that person will avoid tackling new, exciting experiences.

The perception principle is useful also in understanding the behavior of others, particularly of those whose cultural backgrounds may be different. The Russians see our election system as inefficient because it enables popular rather than competent persons to be elected to office on the basis of the amount they spend for advertisements. We see their system of nominating only one candidate as a farce. Some of the most cherished beliefs may rest upon doubtful perceptions of reality. The need to be right is so strong that we will defend our perceptions most vigorously and violently when we are least sure of them. A child who perceives a kitten as something warm, soft, and playful will run to play with it on a visit to a friend's home. Another child who sees a kitten as something that will bite and scratch you will run in terror from the animal. Any effort on the part of an adult to force contact with the kitten can only increase the terror unless the child's perception is gradually helped to change. A young (or old) man who has great need to prove his uncertain manliness will perceive every date as a challenge to conquest rather than to relationship and may be expected to display himself, posture, and go to all lengths to seduce or conquer rather than to relate.

This viewpoint is often termed a *phenomenological* or *perceptual point of view*. It suggests that we would better understand our associates and children through knowing how they and we perceive reality.

Our needs and emotions not only make us believe things that are untrue; they also blind us to truth. If a perception gives rise to devastating depression or hopelessness, there is a tendency for people simply to ignore the disquieting truth. Anyone who has suffered the death of a loved one will know how difficult it is to realize that the deceased will not be seen any more. People tend to forget, or more accurately, to repress the memory of painful or humiliating events.

Many needs can be gratified only through relationships with other people. This means that strong emotions are mobilized in our interpersonal relationships. Reliable information about another person is difficult to obtain, because much of that person's behavior goes on at times when we cannot see it. Furthermore, the person's consciousness of the world is not accessible to our direct vision. We can only learn the subjective side of another person if he or she confides in us, and the person may not be willing to entrust us with personal information.[3] Often we are obliged to form our concept of another person on the basis of overt behavior alone. We infer, as accurately as possible, what an individual's perception might have been, so that we can predict his or her behavior in similar situations in the future.

OTHER PEOPLE'S INFLUENCE ON OUR SENSE OF REALITY

Reality is what we take to be real. This, in turn, is powerfully influenced by what significant other people have told us is true, real, and important in the world. We are continuously told by newspapers, comics, friends and family members, movies and television programs about the way things are. Sometimes this influence is subtle; someone merely describes some aspect of the world to us, and we find that this description impels us to see the world as we were told it is. One teacher played a classroom game; she asked the children to pretend that blonde, blue-eyed children were evil. In time, the black-haired children came to loathe the blondes, who in turn felt inferior.[4]

Other people, then, can so influence one's ways of perceiving, and of attaching meaning and value, that one loses one's own autonomous perspective. If other people are strong, with high status, they may invalidate one's own perspective on reality; the weaker person accepts the perspective of the stronger.

For example, when high school seniors in the minority are confronted by perceptions or judgments from a majority identified as college students, the high schoolers conform to the perceptions of the higher status college student.[5]

Reality, Perception, and Healthy Personality

A person may need to disengage from other people and go into solitude, in order to separate other people's perspectives on reality from one that is more truly individual.[6]

Ontic projection is Thomas Hanna's [7] term to describe what a person takes to be real—attributions of reality. Each language provides words that sensitize a person to those aspects of the world that are most important for survival in that place. Thus, we have only one word for snow, whereas Eskimos have many, corresponding with different qualities of snow, which indicate whether hunting or igloo building are possible.[8] We do not see the world; rather, we "read" the meanings of what we see, just as we read the words in a book. These meanings are provided for us as we grow up by the person who teaches us to speak our "mother tongue." It is our mothers who give the first meanings to our world, who give the world the "voices" with which it tells us of dangers and gratifications. In developing countries like Indonesia or India, each child learns three languages, each of which highlights some aspects of the world more than others, and which gives different meanings and emotional qualities to the perceived world. Thus, a child will learn the language of the village from his or her mother; in India or Indonesia, it will be one of the several hundred local languages, which differ so much that people fifty miles apart cannot understand one another's mother tongues. At school an Indonesian child will learn Malay, and an Indian child will learn Hindi—both languages are the national tongue, which facilitates communication throughout the country. Finally, both Indonesians and Indians may learn English, which makes communication beyond national boundaries possible.

In each case, the language that is spoken affects perception. In order really to perceive what is there in the world, a person will have to suspend language and really look and listen, to discern the reality *beyond* language (pp. 67–69).

Reality Testing

Healthy Personality   Our chances of behaving effectively are increased if we perceive the world accurately and form valid beliefs about it. But we know that unfulfilled needs and strong emotions can so shape our experience that we misinterpret facts, arrive at erroneous conclusions, and, indeed, frequently fail to see and hear what is there. How does a person go about increasing the efficiency of perception and thinking? How does a person carry out reality testing? Indeed, why would a person seek the truth when unreality is often more pleasant in the short run?

Reality testing means applying the rules of logic and scientific inquiry to everyday life. When we engage in reality testing, we are systematically doubting our own initial perceptions and beliefs until we have scrutinized them more carefully and checked them against further evidence. We do this when we have learned that truth, ultimately, is the best servant of our needs and is a value in itself.

AN EXAMPLE OF REALITY TESTING

A nineteen-year-old woman once consulted me, seeking help with a problem that was bothering her. She believed her roommate was stealing her money, jewelry, and even stationery. She noticed various items missing from her dresser from time to time, and she concluded her roommate was guilty. However, she dared not confront the roommate with her suspicion. Instead, she felt distrust and resentment and struggled to conceal these feelings from her. Their relationship gradually deteriorated to one of formality, forced politeness, and false expressions of friendship.

I asked the young woman why she didn't bring the whole issue out into the open. She stated that if she did this, her roommate would hate her, and she couldn't stand this. I asked if there were any other possible way of interpreting the loss of her money and jewelry. She replied that she hadn't thought of any. Rather, she had concluded that if her things were missing, they must have been stolen by the person closest to her. When I suggested that her roommate might be saddened at the way their friendship had deteriorated and that she might welcome some frank talk to settle things, the young woman admitted that this might be possible, but she was afraid to talk about the problem. However, she agreed to broach the subject.

Reality, Perception, and Healthy Personality

The next time I saw her, she was happy to report that she had discussed the whole affair. She learned that her roommate was puzzled by the way their relationship had changed. Moreover, she was glad to discuss the loss of the articles with her and she was able to clear herself of any blame. In fact, the roommate too had been missing some money, and investigation by the dormitory counselor brought forth the fact that other women had been robbed and that the guilty party was a cleaning woman, who was promptly discharged.

The example illustrates how some initial, untested beliefs that one person forms about some aspect of the world—in this case, about another person—can lead to misunderstanding in interpersonal relationships and to considerable unhappiness.[9] At first, the woman was afraid to carry out any efforts at reality testing to see if her assumption of the guilt of her roommate was warranted. This illustrates another aspect of reality testing; frequently, people may be reluctant to go after the information that is crucial to the formation of accurate beliefs. Yet if a person gives in to the fear of getting at the truth, that person is almost sure to become increasingly out of touch with reality.

RULES FOR REALITY TESTING

The search for the "real" reality in contrast to the perceived reality is a difficult one even for the scientist. Here are some rules that may help you become far more effective in reality testing:

1. State the belief clearly.

2. Ask, "What evidence is there to support this belief?"

3. Ask, "Is there any other way of interpreting this evidence?"

4. Try to determine how consistent the belief is with other beliefs that are known to be valid.

Living in the "Raw World":
The Return to Experience

Healthy
Personality

It is probably the lot of human beings that once they have learned speech, then perceptions of reality are always filtered through, and guided by, their *concepts* of reality. For example, if you learn the concept *gun* and then look at a gun, you probably see something entirely different from what a primitive savage might: guns have no place, nor even a word to describe them, in his or her culture.[10]

Words limit what a person will actually experience in a concrete situation. Once a concept has been learned, a person will look at a given object long enough to place it in its proper category or to assign an appropriate name to it. The person may then ignore much of what is actually there. We are all familiar with the bigoted person who, once he or she has determined that a person is a Jew or a black, never looks further at the person. The bigot "knows" the properties of all members who fall into those classes. In reality, the bigot fails to observe the enormous amount of variation among members of any class.[11]

The ability to break down categories and discern uniqueness is as essential for healthy personality as the ability to classify. But the ability to see what is there, to transcend labels and classes and apprehend the thing before one's view, is a means of enriching one's knowledge of the world and of deepening one's contact with reality. Fritz Perls [12] would have his patients in Gestalt therapy go through exercises of simply looking at something or somebody, in order to discern the reality beyond the concept. To be able to sense the "raw world" involves the ability to abandon presently held concepts and categories. This ability is possessed by the productive scientist who deliberately ignores the orthodoxies, and looks ever afresh at the raw data that prompted the formation of present-day concepts and categories. The artist probably possesses to a marked degree the ability to apprehend the unique, the individual object.

The ability to set conventional categories and concepts aside and to look fully at the world with minimal preconceptions seems to be a trait that facilitates scientific discovery, art, human relations, and, more generally, an enrichment of the sensory experiences of living.

Reality, Perception, and Healthy Personality

The capacity to let oneself see or perceive what is there seems to entail the *temporary cessation of an active, searching, or critical attitude.*[13] Need-directed perception is a highly focused searchlight darting here and there, seeking the objects that will satisfy needs, ignoring everything irrelevant to the need. Being-cognition, as Maslow has called it, refers to a more passive mode of perceiving. It involves letting oneself be reached, touched, or affected by what is there so that the perception is richer. In Maslow's own words,[14]

> The most efficient way to perceive the intrinsic nature of the world is to be more passive than active, determined as much as possible by the intrinsic organization of that which is perceived and as little as possible by the nature of the perceiver. This kind of detached, Taoist, passive, non-interfering awareness of all the simultaneously existing aspects of the concrete, has much in common with some descriptions of the aesthetic experience and of the mystic experience. The stress is the same. Do we see the real, concrete world, or do we see our own system of rubrics, motives, expectations and abstractions which we have projected onto the real world? Or, to put it very bluntly, do we see or are we blind? [p. 38]

This mode of cognition, however, seems to be possible only at those times when we have adequately fulfilled the basic needs. When we are anxious, sexually deprived, or hungry, it is as if our organs of perceiving and of knowing have been "commandeered" to find the means of gratification. Our consciousness seems most free to play, to be most receptive to new impressions, when the urgency of needs is diminished. The implication is clear— if we want to know hitherto unnoticed features of the world that confronts us, our chances of so doing are increased when our basic needs are satisfied.

The direction of our cognition by needs has adaptive value, because it increases our chances of finding the things that will satisfy our needs and it permits us to avoid dangers in our environment. However, if persons are *always* perceiving the world under the direction of their needs, they will simply not perceive much that exists. The aesthetic, appreciative contemplation of reality, with no purpose other than the delight of looking at

Healthy
Personality

it, or experiencing it, lends a dimension of richness to an existence that is ordinarily characterized by the search for satisfaction. Competence at gratifying one's needs frees one from time to time of the necessity to be forever struggling and permits one the luxury of aesthetic sensing.

Some Existential Suggestions

The next time a friend does something that puzzles you, try thinking about how he or she has perceived the situation and see if you can understand the behavior better. To really exercise this principle, try inferring the perception of someone who is quite distant from you ethnically and make a real effort to understand the person.

The experience of being in a minority is an extremely healthy one, provided you can stalwartly resist efforts of those of higher status or authority to make you change your mind. Be sure, of course, that you are taking the position because of your genuine perception of what is the right thing to do, rather than merely to be inflexible. This is the kind of experience that makes for true intellectual integrity—an important component of the high-level functioner.

One of the exercises Gestalt therapists ask their patients to engage in is really looking at someone familiar to them. This is a way to break up one's concepts so that one really sees what is there, not what is *said* to be there.

Try bracketing off previous knowledge about yourself and really look at yourself naively.

Be careful what you believe to be true, because as long as you believe it, then for you it is true. But your beliefs about reality, your *attributions of reality* or your *ontic projections*, profoundly influence your life. Of especial importance for healthy personality are those beliefs about limits, about your weaknesses and lack of aptitude. If you believe you cannot learn to play a musical instrument because you lack talent, get a musical instrument and learn to play it. If you believe you cannot do without food for three days, go on a five-day fast. Challenge your own beliefs, especially about yourself and others, because what you believe to be true about self and others functions more as persuasion than as description.

Reality, Perception, and Healthy Personality

85

Healthy personality depends upon accurate perception of and knowledge about the world. One of the best ways to help understand another person's behavior is to know how that person has perceived the situation. Our perception and our thinking is subject to influence by needs and emotions, and we are vulnerable to confusion of perception with imagination. Consequently, our perception may be very selective and distorted, and our beliefs unfounded. Reality testing is the technique of verifying our perceptions and beliefs by seeking further information and by engaging in rational thinking about the implications of our perceptions. Other people can influence our perspective, even to the point of replacing it with their own. Reality testing entails disengaging oneself from action and querying one's views of a situation to discern whether they are compatible with fresh perceptions and with reason.

The "return to experience" involves viewing the world afresh, uninfluenced by language and ongoing needs and projects. This basic perception is what Maslow described as B-cognition and appears to be the aim of the enlightening disciplines, such as Zen, Taoism, Sufism, and as the Yaqui sorcerer Don Juan called it, "stopping the [speech of] the world," so that one can really see it.

NOTES AND REFERENCES

1. The phenomenological or perceptual approach to understanding behavior was developed by Arthur W. Combs and Don Snygg. A recent revision of their text is A. W. COMBS, F. RICHARDS, and A. RICHARDS, *Perceptual Psychology* (New York: Harper, 1978).

2. A. W. COMBS and D. SNYGG, *Individual Behavior*, 2nd ed. (New York: Harper, 1959).

3. S. M. JOURARD, *Self-Disclosure: An Experimental Analysis of the Transparent Self* (New York: Wiley-Interscience, 1971) provides a review of Jourard's research into factors in self-disclosure.

4. This experiment was carried out by Ms. Jane Elliott and is reported in the documentary film, *Eye of the Storm*.

5. D. L. WIESENTHAL, N. S. ENDLER, T. R. COWARD, J. EDWARDS, "Reversibility of Relative Competence

Healthy Personality

86

as a Determinant of Conformity Across Different Perceptual Tasks," paper presented at the meeting of the Eastern Psychological Association, Chicago, May 1973.

6. See R. D. Laing and A. Esterson, *Sanity, Madness and the Family* (London: Tavistock, 1964) for dramatic illustrations of the way the perspective of one member of a family is invalidated by others.

7. T. Hanna, *The Other "Is,"* unpublished manuscript, University of Florida, 1973.

8. B. L. Whorf, *Language, Thought and Reality*, J. B. Carroll (Ed.) (Cambridge, Mass.: M.I.T., 1956). Also see S. Hayakawa, *Language in Action* (New York: Harcourt, 1941). See also H. Werner, *Comparative Psychology of Mental Development* (Chicago: Follett, 1948), Chapters 9 and 12; R. Brown, *Words and Things* (New York: Free Press, 1958).

9. G. Ichheiser, *Appearances and Realities: Misunderstandings in Human Relations* (San Francisco: Jossey-Bass, 1970), pp. 1–120.

10. See note 8.

11. G. W. Allport, *The Nature of Prejudice* (Reading, Mass.: Addison-Wesley, 1954), especially Chapter 2.

12. See F. Perls, P. Goodman, and R. Hefferline, *Gestalt Therapy: Excitement and Growth in the Human Personality* (New York: Dell, 1951), Chapters 2–4, for examples of these exercises.

13. This difficult art is central to classical phenomenological philosophy and is known as the Epoche; it requires bracketing off one's previous knowledge of the object or phenomena perceived. Developed by E. Husserl, *Ideas: General Introduction to Pure Phenomenology* (London: Allen & Unwin, 1931).

14. Maslow, op. cit., pp. 67–96. See also E. Schachtel, *Metamorphosis: On the Development of Affect, Perception, Attention and Memory* (New York: Basic, 1959), pp. 220 ff.

5

BASIC NEEDS, HIGHER NEEDS, AND HEALTHY PERSONALITY

INTRODUCTION

In Kurt Weill's Threepenny Opera *a major melody is sung around the theme "First feed the face and then talk right and wrong." The human has needs for survival, food, shelter, and so on that are shared in common with other animals. He or she also has needs for self-development, for the appreciation of beauty, that are very characteristic of a high-level or human existence. Healthy personality calls for competence at gratifying basic needs. One is then free to pursue goals beyond personal security. It is difficult to be concerned with truth, justice, or beauty when one is starving or frightened for one's life. First things come first.*

In similar fashion, those interested in helping others must first demonstrate that they can take care of themselves. The person who can meet his or her needs through individual skill is independently secure. The child relies on grownups to devote their time and skill to its needs; to the extent that the parents can do this, the child is de-

pendently secure. As the child grows and becomes an adult, he or she gradually takes over more and more of the security needs—providing sustenance, buying a car, earning a living. A young adult who remains dependent upon others to meet his or her basic needs (except for love and companionship) may pay dearly for their intervention; this person may be obliged to conform to restrictive demands, which call for unhealthy suppression of action and repression of experience. Immature dependent security is costly.

To be deprived of basic need gratification is painful. There is no denying the agony of starvation, fiery thirst, or terror from someone who is threatening your life. Other needs of a different order, such as love, companionship, freedom from political tyranny, and unfettered artistic and thought expression are to be considered in understanding the healthy personality. The development of the healthy personality extends beyond the basic needs alone. The healthy person is one who partakes generously of all the joys that life provides—including the artistic or aesthetic satisfactions.

Some people try to deal with the pain of deprivation of basic needs by denying that it exists or by anesthetizing themselves to their suffering with drugs, alcohol, or immature religion, but these responses only postpone the inevitable recognition that problems and pain do not go away until one has acted.

Definition of Basic Needs

The term *basic needs* usually refers to those needs that have to be satisfied first, before other, usually higher, needs can be dealt with. While there are many systems of basic need classification, most agree that the body needs—safety, survival, food, shelter, and so on—are the basic needs. While personal freedom or political freedom and artistic creativity are often thought of as higher order needs, there are many examples of individuals who would give up their safety, their bodily needs, to satisfy the need for political or personal freedom. There are also many instances of starving artists who prefer to paint rather than take jobs that would permit them to eat more

Basic Needs, Higher Needs, and Healthy Personality

regularly. But these cases are rather rare, and the concept of the basic needs, the bodily needs, including sexual expression, is of reasonable validity for most of us.

It is often difficult to distinguish between a need and a want. Wants are infinite in number, and they change moment by moment. I want a yacht, but I don't need one to survive. I may, however, need a yacht to achieve the status that is essential to me. Wants are a person's interpretation of what he or she needs in order to achieve happiness or wellbeing. Needs are what scientists agree a person requires to sustain life and to foster growth of desirable human potentialities.

Incentives, rewards, and reinforcers are what other people believe will move you. A man needs food. His wife knows he really likes rare roast beef. She may reward (or reinforce) his attention to her wishes by cooking it for him. Whoever possesses the means of gratifying needs and wants has power to influence action. This makes a person vulnerable to being controlled by others in ways that can undermine personal freedom and dignity. A person is vulnerable in this way, however, only when others know what he or she needs or wants—what it takes to "buy" that person.[1] Competence at gratifying one's basic needs can protect one from being controlled by others. There are situations in which self-concealment may be required in order to elude control.

On the other hand, if persons wish the love of others, they must "open" themselves and disclose their needs and wants to the beloved ones, who can then act in their behalf. It takes trust to accept the love of another. The other must earn this trust by being trustworthy.

What do persons need for a healthy personality? What does one need for oneself in order to be free to give to the world as well as take from it?

Maslow presents an authoritative analysis of needs. He stated a need can be adjudged basic if

1. Its deprivation breeds illness (mental or physical).
2. Gratification of the need prevents illness.
3. Identification and gratification of the need restores health in a person who is presently ill.

Healthy Personality

4. The deprived person prefers gratification of this need over any other, under conditions of free choice.

5. The need is not in a state of tension or privation in healthy persons.

6. A subjective feeling of yearning, lack, or desire prevails when the need is not fulfilled.

7. Gratification of the need feels good; gratification produces a subjective sense of healthy wellbeing.[2]

There is further implied the idea that when the need is met, the person does not think about it until the next time it arises; he or she is free for other pursuits.

While there are many systems of needs, Maslow's hierarchy is perhaps the best known. Without specifying which of the needs are explicitly basic, the system does imply that the lower needs are *prepotent*, that is, that they must be satisfied before the other, higher needs can be taken care of. Maslow's list from basic to higher order is as follows:

1. Physiological needs.
2. Safety needs.
3. Belongingness and love.
4. Self-esteem.
5. Self-actualization.
6. Cognitive and conative.
7. Aesthetic needs. (pp. 35–51)

Keeping in mind the entire range of needs, one may get a perspective on the importance of the basic needs. The concept of the basic need is easier to demonstrate with animals than it is with humans. In animals the maternal drive is usually considered to be the most fundamental. Even Maslow's system for humans has been challenged by some recent research [3] suggesting that the hierarchy of needs is not unassailable as theory. Nevertheless, the system is useful in providing a perspective over the whole need system of the human.

Opinions among biologists and psychologists vary about the precise number of basic needs in humans. Agreement can be reached on what is required for sheer physical survival, but not on what humans need to fulfill their unfathomed potentialities. The following section offers a hypothesis about such needs, the test of the hypothesis being a judgment of the quality of life with and without the gratification of these needs.

Basic Needs,
Higher Needs,
and Healthy
Personality

Some Basic Needs in Humans

TO VALUE LIFE ITSELF

Most basic of all human needs is the affirmation of life, the desire to continue living. When life is under threat, a person will do almost anything, break laws, kill others, and sacrifice wealth, to eliminate the threat and preserve existence. Such occasions are rare. It will suffice merely to remind the reader that the wish to live is the most powerful determiner of action that we can know. A person may, however, decide to sacrifice his or her life for love of another or for country.

Paradoxically enough, a person can be persuaded that further existence is neither meaningful nor possible. A long period of suffering or joylessness may so dispirit someone that he or she resigns from life. This person may commit suicide or yield to a sickness that would not be lethal had he or she retained the desire to live. Loss of zest for life and the choice for sickness or death can be induced in a person by misfortune and tragedy such as prolonged illness, failure, or an intense sense of lack of worth. One's choice of friends and companions takes on added significance when you consider that good choices of friends can help one through these otherwise lethal crises.

PHYSICAL NEEDS

Physical needs refer to food, drink, relief from pain and discomfort, and adequate shelter. Modern society does a better job of satisfying these needs than was true in earlier times, and so the quests for food, shelter, and comfort are less powerful determiners of everyday action than they used to be. However, when we experience a threat to our supplies, or to our access to supplies, of food and shelter, we may take desperate measures to secure these vital things.

LOVE

It is not only the poets who think of love as having fundamental significance in one's fate. Two fundamental kinds of love may be identified: natural or unconditional love, and earned or conditional love.[4] The former is seen

Healthy
Personality

92

in the parent's love for the child, which is unconditional, in that the love exists regardless of how "bad" the child is. It is not "earned," in that the child ordinarily receives it without reciprocation. In ordinary development this love proceeds to become reciprocal, with the maturing person recognizing that he or she must do things for the other person, parent, peer, or even later, lover. This is the earned, conditional love of most of contemporary human relationships—despite the myth of unconditional love among adults.

The first phase of learning to love—receiving parental or adult love—is fundamental; a child needs it to survive, to grow, and to know how to carry on that most joyous of human activities: loving, giving and receiving love from peers. If the person has been deprived of parental love, his or her ability to participate in the adult conditional love may be seriously impaired. The early Freudian psychologists felt that such love was irreplaceable and that withholding such love by the parent led to serious personality problems in the child. Many contemporary psychologists, however, while they also feel such love to be critical, desirable, and nurturant, also feel that one can learn to love on an adult level, while an adult, even if one is originally deprived. It is nevertheless clear that parental love, unconditional and spontaneous, as seen in the dignity-devoid father or mother playing with and cooing to an infant, is crucially important for a happy adult life and for the healthy personality.

STATUS, SUCCESS, SELF-ESTEEM, AND COMPETENCE

Human beings need to feel recognized and approved by other members of the groups within which they live. Without such recognition they tend to feel inferior. The quest for power and prestige is universal, though the means of attaining status differ from society to society. A man or woman may work to the point of exhaustion, neglecting personal health and the needs of his or her family, in order to purchase a Rolls Royce. The status symbolized by the Rolls seems worth the cost. The person may not enjoy the work, may not enjoy seeing his or her family suffer from neglect, the limousine may not transport the family any better than a less costly vehicle, but so urgent is the quest for status that the person is willing to pay the price.

Let us not underrate the strength of the status drive in modern humans. The puzzling thing is, how does it become so powerful? One hypothesis is that the fanatic quest for status is in compensation for lack of love or for physical deprivations associated with poverty. It is as if the "success-starved" person is trying to make up in adult years for childhood privations and can never get enough. Related is human beings' need for a feeling and experience of competence, a confidence that they can control their environment.[5]

FREEDOM AND SPACE

Humans need varying degrees of freedom to conduct their lives according to their own wishes and plans. Many wars have been fought in the name of freedom. We can distinguish between *objective* freedom, which refers to the relative absence of real restrictions on one's behavior, and the *feeling* of freedom. The latter refers to persons' estimates of how free they are to express themselves. Healthy personalities find an environment within which there is the greatest possible amount of objective freedom. Unhealthy personalities may dread both objective freedom and the feeling of freedom. They find it anxiety-producing. They can only carry on as long as they feel that they are under authoritarian rule or in surrender to charismatic leadership.[6]

Human beings not only need room to move and to express their unique ways; they need personal space for solitude and to facilitate uninterrupted intimacy with others. In the absence of such assured space, people tend to become irritable and chronically defensive. As we enter an age of vastly increased population and the concentration of this population in crowded cities, the need for more space becomes increasingly urgent.[7]

SOLITUDE

Parallel to the need to love and care for others is the *Healthy* need to be alone for predictable periods of time. The *Personality* crowding of cities, the constant interaction with other

94

humans, require periods of time for an individual to contemplate the self, to consider personal growth, and to place self in perspective with the rest of the world. It is for this reason that monks and other ascetics seek long periods of solitude. The popularity of transcendental meditation [8] is partly ascribable to the deprivation from the solitude experience. This solitude is not the same as loneliness, which is a result of deprivation from the company of others. A solitude experience is created by a healthy person out of a positive need to be alone for contemplation or intense meditation. Solitude is harder to create for oneself than is the companionship of a good friend and requires careful planning in our heavily socialized culture. Moustakas [9] has suggested that such experience is essential to the development of the healthy personality.

INTIMACY

To be close to another person physically and emotionally, to be held tightly, to share one's deepest self-secrets—all of these represent a basic need largely ignored by most behavioral scientists. This tender need seems to be uniquely human in its manifestation.[10] Obviously related to the sexual needs, intimacy yet has a meaning of its own that includes the physical union, but that can be expressed and can be experienced in the psychological realm alone. Its opposite is true loneliness—just being in the presence of others is insufficient. The need is for a real closeness that affirms the existence of the person. One's existence as an individual is not only highlighted, like a back-lit photograph, in separation from others, but is also manifested in the phenomenon of intimate closeness.

CHALLENGE

Deprivation of challenge is experienced as boredom, or as emptiness in existence.[11] The need for challenge manifests itself most keenly when a person has made a "successful adjustment" to life, when he or she has been able to fulfill the material needs, and cannot then find anything to do. Without challenging goals, people eat or drink to excess or pass the time getting high on marijuana.

Basic Needs, Higher Needs, and Healthy Personality

Just as human beings need intense involvement to foster full functioning and growth, they also need disengagement. They need to get away from their customary consciousness of themselves and their world. The "getting away" can be literal, as in travel; but it can also take the form of what are now called *altered states of consciousness*.[12] There are two ways to alter one's consciousness of one's situation. One of these is literally to change situations. The other is to suspend the customary way of experiencing a situation, to allow new modes of consciousness to appear. One's situation functions hypnotically, influencing a person to perceive, recall, think and even imagine in stereotyped ways. One way to break the quasihypnotic spell is to engage in meditation. Za-zen, or sitting-Zen meditation, is one such method. It entails sitting cross-legged, or in any comfortable position, letting one's stream of consciousness simply "happen." Another technique is that of transcendental meditation, which also calls for the attainment of a state of quiescence, where one's "chattering" mind is stilled. Hatha Yoga, together with deep, slow breathing, is yet another method through which a person can disengage from the usual situation. The significant aspect of these meditative disciplines is not the state itself, but rather the effect they have on persons' awareness of their situation when they return to it. New aspects of the situation are perceived, and they can imagine, think, and remember in more flexible ways.

Psychedelic drugs, such as lysergic acid diethylamide (LSD), cannabis derivatives (marijuana and hashish), mescaline, psylocybin, and peyote, are all pharmacological means by which persons can leave their situations (in a metaphorical sense). Indeed, in current jargon persons who ingest LSD or mescaline are said to be "tripping." Although these drugs often produce an absorbing and sometimes pleasant change in experience, they can have deleterious effects upon the capacity to cope effectively with problems.

COGNITIVE CLARITY

Healthy Personality   Human beings cannot endure ambiguity or contradiction in their knowledge. In the face of uncertainty, they seem impelled to construct answers, because they can act only when they have made a satisfactory interpretation of the situation. Their interpretation may not be valid, but it seems true that humans prefer a false interpretation to none. Thus, a person may hear unidentifiable noises in the sky. The experience of not knowing may fill the person with anxiety. He or she may be virtually paralyzed until the noise is explained.

In addition to the need for some interpretation of situations, human beings need consistency among their presently held beliefs. When new cognitions—perceptions and knowledge—are not compatible with those already held, the state of *cognitive dissonance* is said to exist. Cognitive dissonance influences behavior like any other basic need.[13] When there is a conflict between present knowledge and new information, people may deny and distort truth to eliminate dissonance. Healthier personalities can tolerate ambiguity better than unhealthy personalities; they resolve cognitive dissonance in ways that do the most justice to logic and evidence (see Chapter 4).

MEANING AND PURPOSE

To ask about the purpose of human life is to raise an existential question, rather than one answerable through experiment or logic. Existential questions are answered by the way one lives. Every person's life, and the daily actions and decisions that comprise it, represent that person's answer to the question, "How, then, shall I live?"

These answers are almost by definition the embodiment of a person's religion. The chief function of religion is to provide ultimate answers to the questions that existence poses (see Chapter 15). In the absence of credible and lifegiving answers to the questions, "How shall I live, and why?" a person enters the state Frankl calls noögenic neurosis—a kind of despair or cynicism.[14] Much depression and neurotic suffering stem from a failure to find meaning in life or to find new meaning when old goals have been consummated or have lost their inspiriting power.

Basic Needs, Higher Needs, and Healthy Personality

Fromm regards "a frame of orientation and devotion" to be as essential to healthy personality as food. The process of self-actualizing, of which Maslow wrote, and the achievement of selfhood (in Jung's sense) appear to be impossible without such a religious orientation. Of course, it does not matter whether the religion is theistic, and it is possible to judge whether or not a person's objects and ways of worshiping are life-giving. But life for human beings is impossible without something to live *for*.

VARIED EXPERIENCE

The human needs varied stimulation, not just to avoid boredom but actually to preserve the ability to perceive and to act adequately. When a person is radically deprived of the customary variety of sights, sounds, smells, conversation, and so on—as happens in solitary confinement—he or she begins to feel strange and may show signs of deteriorating as a person. "Sensory deprivation" experiments show that when volunteer subjects are placed in a special room that is soundless, with their vision closed off by special goggles, and immersed in warm water kept at body temperature (to reduce the experience of tactile stimulation), some begin to hallucinate and go through other psychoticlike experiences. I have been in such an isolation chamber, and I found it tranquil and conducive to meditation. Variety in "stimulus input," then, may be regarded as a basic need, even though deprivation as extreme as that produced in the laboratory seldom occurs in everyday life.[15]

The "evil twin" of varied experience is boredom—a form of dispiriting in style of life. Travel, risk-taking, excitement, and simply trying something new in the way of clothes, reading, vacations, or challenges are the antitheses of boredom—varying one's experience of life. Even moonrises and sunsets can get monotonous for the jaded taste of the daily skywatcher. The healthy personality is also nurtured by meaningful variety.

Excitement has often been thought of as a need for the young only. We now recognize that it is part of the fullest of lives in all generations. The excitement experience is one of the most difficult to create. Not all excitements involve risk-taking, and excitements are quite individually determined. One person may be thrilled by the first parachute jump—another is equally excited about the first sighting of the sandhill crane.

Healthy Personality

A substantial proportion of the world's population lives in cities where trees and grass are seldom seen, where the sounds of birds and babbling streams are not heard. The air they breathe is either filtered through air-conditioning units or heavily polluted with smog. Such persons adapt to the milieu within which they live, but it is an unnatural environment. Contact with the physical world, with the seaside, forests, and parks, with fields and animals, gives persons a sense of rhythm that contrasts with the rhythms of industrialized urban life. These experiences remind the person that he or she does not simply have a body, but that the person *is* a body, an embodied being who is in and of nature. Chronic physical and muscular tension, accelerated rhythms of speech and movement, are common to people who live apart from their own nature and the nature around us all.

Just as a person may suffer from estrangement from the rest of nature, the person may also suffer a kind of alienation and distance from the body (see Chapter 7). From infancy, the human needs physical contact with other human beings and with the world. Infants and grownups alike need caressing, sensuous massage, enjoyable exercise, and dance in order to feel the vitality of their bodies. As Reich, Lowen, and Rolf have pointed out, growing up leaves a person with many muscular systems chronically tensed, as part of an overall defense against danger and pain. This "muscular armor" interferes with fullest respiration, with proper posture, with sleep and rest; it often requires specialized massage and manipulation before the muscular system is restored to the pliability most compatible with a health-giving life. Reich especially pointed out that a chronically defensive attitude reduces a person's capacity for the fullest sexual climaxes. Of course, orgasm is also an exquisite experience.[16]

Our culture, with its puritan heritage, has encouraged people to repress sensuality, perhaps because it interferes with compulsive work. Recent counterculture developments have introduced a variety of approaches to a re-engagement with nature and with one's own body that seem compatible with healthier personality.

*Basic Needs,
Higher Needs,
and Healthy
Personality*

99

The concept of needs implies a drive toward the satisfaction of these needs. They operate at different levels of demand upon the person and at differing times, and blocks or barriers to the satisfaction of any one of these needs results in *frustration*. The word is most often paired with sex, and for some, frustration implies sexual frustration. However, as frustrating as the classic eros is, it is not alone in capability of producing severe blocking—any one of the needs can be frustrated and can result in one of two classic patterns: *aggression* and *regression*. The latter refers to reversion to earlier childhood patterns of handling unhappy events. The adult executive who gets angry, shouts, and pounds a table when her staff does not do her bidding fast enough for her is reverting to a childhood temper tantrum pattern of handling frustration. Similarly, the husband who drinks himself into oblivion in a bad marriage mimics his own infancy when sucking upon the nipple brought relief from pain.

The aggression reaction is a commonly observed pattern among children and adults. The child who cannot wait for his turn to use the nursery school tricycle may knock the present pilot off the driver's seat and peddle away to the tune of the classmate's wails. The adult who for the third time finds that her quarter does not bring her the canned soft drink will violently kick the anal retentive machine.

The adult who is rude or insulting to a companion after the soft-drink machine frustration is *displacing* anger from the true source to a convenient, innocent substitute. Displacement is a favorite form of reaction to frustration for many.

SOME FACTORS INFLUENCING
FRUSTRATION THRESHOLDS

There is a level of tension below which the person can think rationally and act effectively. When tension increases above this point, efficiency breaks down, and irrational thinking and expressive behavior take the place of rational thinking and effective action. This point on the tension continuum is called the *frustration threshold*. It varies from person to person, and within the same person at different times.

Healthy
Personality

A mother wants her house to be clean and orderly. In the forenoon, her three-year-old daughter might spill a glass of milk, leave her toys in disarray, and scatter magazines all over the newly cleaned living room. The mother's reaction at the time is one of mild anger, followed by efficient attempts to set things straight. At five-thirty in the afternoon, the child repeats her efforts at messing up the house. This time the mother "explodes"—she spanks the child, hurls some chinaware herself, and is unable to prepare supper until she has vented her tension.

Health. Optimum physical health produces a high frustration threshold. A sick or exhausted person has less energy to cope with tension and is more easily frustrated than one who is fit.

A Strong Sense of Meaning and Purpose in Life. People who managed to survive the extremely stressing conditions of wartime concentration camps in Germany—so-called death camps—have pointed out that a strong commitment to life and a sense of a mission to fulfill were definite factors in survival. Individuals with such a sense of mission were less readily frustrated by the deprivations, stresses, and pressure of extremely hostile environments.

Opportunities for Release. When Zorba the Greek was unable to express his grief following the death of his beloved son, he danced a Cretan dance until he dropped from exhaustion. On another occasion, when he felt he had at last found the solution to a problem of bringing logs down a mountainside, again he danced. Finally, when the plan to bring logs down the mountain failed, and his boss's investment was dismally lost, the boss asked Zorba to show him how to dance, and the two men danced and laughed like madmen.

When someone has access to such means of self-expression, as in dance, violent exercise, painting, or song, that person can release the inevitable frustration of life without recourse to mindless, destructive outlets of tension. As Reich pointed out,[17] sexual orgasm also provides a natural means for the dissipation of tension. In fact, prolonged sexual privation is a common cause of frustration. It is however, a mistake to think that other frustrations, such as marital misunderstandings, are all relieved by sexual activity.

It is common for a person to experience conflict between wishes. He or she may want to study and also to go to the movies. Someone may want to marry one person and at the same time be in love with another. A person may want to have fun but also to be "good."

The healthy thing to do with conflict is to acknowledge its existence within the self, study all the alternatives as rationally as one can in the light of one's value system, make a decision, act on it, and accept all the consequences. Among the consequences to be accepted are regrets over what one has lost in connection with the abandoned alternatives. No decision can ever be made without some fear that it is the wrong decision. There is nothing inconsistent with healthy personality in the idea that a decision, once made, will still leave the person uncertain that it is the best or "rightest" one.

Existential conflicts frequently arise where each choice has positive values and negative implications associated with it. Any alternative, if chosen, will affect one's life profoundly. To make decisions, such as whether to marry or not, to take this job or that, calls for courage. The ability to decide such conflicts is an attribute of healthy personality. Such courage seems to grow out of past experiences at decision-making, experience that fosters independent security.

DECISIONS AND THE SELF

The existentialists also have pointed out that the self is made through decisions. You become what you decide. If, in the choice between running away or facing an unpleasant task, you choose to face up to the issue, you have become a better person. If you choose the weaker and more cowardly alternative, you become, at that moment, on the basis of your own choice, a weaker, lesser person. The behaviorists have, on the other hand, suggested that you have no "choice" but that your choices are determined by factors that control you, such as your parents' wishes, your genes, and social demands upon you. Again the existentialists reply that one can also choose to let others make decisions for oneself but that the responsible direction is to recognize that, in almost all difficult decisions, the choice is still yours.

Healthy
Personality

Need Privation and Sickness

People may sicken in consequence of excessive life stress or from infection ensuing from lowered resistance. An inability to gratify needs by effective action contributes to physical sickness in direct ways. If a person is obliged to persist in ways of acting that are required by familial, occupational, or age roles, when these ways fail to produce basic need gratification, the person will gradually become *dispirited*. Dispiritation refers to a state of lowered morale, diminished zest in living, and a sense of hopelessness that lowers one's resistance to infection by germs, bacteria, and viruses. A student may develop the flu after being rejected by his girlfriend. A woman may be deprived of fulfilling sexual love, affection, and appreciation and yet persist in living the joyless life because she can envision no other; her chances of contracting various illnesses are increased. Any prolonged need deprivation dispirits a person and reduces that person's commitment to life. This reduced commitment to living appears to be responsible (in ways not fully understood) for alterations in the efficiency of the immunity mechanisms of the body.

Everyday life itself is stressing, and persons rest in order to regain strength to cope with the challenges of existence. If a person is living a joyless existence, and cannot alter it, it is necessary for that person to force himself or herself to fight the impulse to flee the scene. This unremitting struggle to *remain* in a thwarting situation imposes even more stress and can contribute to cardiovascular diseases and respiratory and eliminative disorders.[18] But perhaps more importantly, the dispirited person finds less and less joy or fun in work, family, or life itself. Thus, in the same fashion that one needs to see a physician or change some part of one's life in the face of continuous physical illness, one also needs to attend to the self in the condition of dispiration. How does one defeat dispiritedness? First, recognition of the state and of the need for change is helpful. On some occasions it may be wise to seek the help of a professional counselor, psychologist, social worker, or psychiatrist. On most college campuses such help is provided by a counseling center or student mental health service. One should not look upon this as an embarrassment but rather as in-

*Basic Needs,
Higher Needs,
and Healthy
Personality*

dicative of your knowing yourself and knowing when it is time to seek help. There are also other roads to escape from being dispirited—changing one's job; changing one's life objectives; getting out and seeking new, successful, yet exciting alternatives. Robert Manry, who for years was a copy editor on the *Cleveland Plain Dealer*, abruptly left his job for a period of time, outfitted a small 16-foot boat, and sailed alone to England. He tells the tale in a charming book named after his craft, *Tinkerbelle*.[19] Seeking good friends who will not try to talk you into their solutions, but who will, rather, help you to talk out your own ideas and seek your own solutions— this is also a successful approach to coping with the very normal occurrence of being dispirited. Normal though it might be, it demands attention in order for one to maintain a healthy personality.

The Unconscious

To be aware of a need means to experience and identify some lack. Thus, a person may be sexually deprived, admit it, and set about the task of obtaining sexual gratification. But suppose the person regards sexual wishes as forbidden? Under these conditions, acknowledgment of real feelings might give rise to powerful guilt or anxiety. The guilt or anxiety will then motivate the person to rid his or her mind of the offending thoughts. This effort is called *repression*. Repression of wishes and feelings does not annihilate them; it renders them unconscious. A healthier direction would be for the person to keep the feelings in the conscious realm, learn to understand them, and choose to either have sexual experience or not, depending upon his or her personal value system and the ethical–religious beliefs that are a part of the person's conscious life. One of Freud's greatest contributions to human understanding was his effort to decipher unconscious motivation through the study of dreams, slips of the tongue, and accidents.[20]

THE INFERENCE OF MOTIVES—
CONSCIOUS AND UNCONSCIOUS

Healthy Personality   We continuously try to "read" our own and others' motives. The most common bases employed for inferring the intentions, feelings, and needs of the other person are (1) observation of facial expression, tone of voice, and gestures, which generally disclose what the person is feeling; and (2) observation of the person's action and its consequences, from which we try to infer what he or she is up to. Ordinarily, we can check our inferences about the other person's motives by asking a direct question.

When are we justified in assuming that our own or another person's motives are unconscious? We can never be absolutely certain, but we can entertain the hypothesis of unconscious motivation (1) when the person acts in ways that produce consequences he or she denies intending to produce; (2) when the person shows many signs of emotion without admitting he or she is experiencing strong feeling; and (3) when there are obvious inconsistencies in action at different times, for example, kindness and brutality, intelligent and stupid behavior.

In addition to these general signs of unconscious motivation, there are other more subtle indicators that a person is not conscious of real influences upon his or her behavior. These include:

1. Dream content that seems bizarre and incomprehensible to the dreamer.

2. Daydreams that surprise the daydreamer.

3. Errors and "slips" in speech and writing.

4. Body postures and evidence of bodily tensions.

5. The forgetting of intentions, and of the names of people and places.

6. Accidents of all kinds.

7. Performance on certain projective tests of personality.

ILLUSTRATIONS OF LIKELY INSTANCES
OF UNCONSCIOUS MOTIVATION

During my training I was influenced by Freud's monumental books *The Psychopathology of Everyday Life* and *The Interpretation of Dreams*, which are full of examples of unconscious motives. Here are some examples collected out of my experience as a psychologist:

An Example from Dreams. A nine-year-old child was judged by all who knew him to be very "good." He was "respectful" to his parents and affirmed his love for his father in almost every conversation. He related this dream

Basic Needs, Higher Needs, and Healthy Personality

to me: "I dreamed that I was a soldier, and we had a very mean captain. One day, when nobody was around, he was beating up a very nice lady. I took my machine gun and shot him a million times. He fell into a lot of little pieces when I was finished."

One does not have to be a professional interpreter of dreams to suspect that the officer was a symbolic version of his father, toward whom the boy had a strong but repressed hostility, and the "nice lady" his mother, to whom he was very attached.

An Example from Daydreaming. A student preparing for the ministry related to me with much embarrassment and guilt that he was afraid to be alone or without some busywork to perform. As soon as he was idle, his mind filled with the most "sinful and voluptuous images of sex." He couldn't understand why this should be, as he was ordinarily an upright, "clean-thinking" young man.

Slips of the Tongue and Pen. The following item came from a local newspaper: A minister had spent some time in Hollywood and was interviewed by a local reporter with respect to his impressions. The article related how the minister deplored the moral turpitude of many movie stars. The article ended with this sentence (the italics are mine): "It is a shame the way our nation's best entertainers, in their lives offstage, are forever making *pubic* spectacles of themselves."

Examples from Body Posturing and Tensions. Variations in the muscle tonus of parts of a person's body may reflect repressed emotions and need tensions.[21] A flaccid handshake may disclose a lack of sincerity. A soft, suckling mouth may reveal unconscious wishes to be passive and dependent.[22] A female student complained that men were forever "making passes" at her, yet she denied any erotic interest in males. Observation revealed her bodily movements were very provocative. She wiggled her hips when walking and pushed her chest high. When talking with a man, she glued her eyes, alternately opened and narrowed, to his. Repressed hostility may be manifested by excessive muscular tension in the forehead, neck, or shoulders, often resulting in headaches, a "pain in the neck," and back pain.[23]

Forgetting of Intentions, Names. I once forgot to

write a letter of recommendation for a graduate student whom I disliked for personal reasons that had nothing to do with his ability. Fortunately, the student received the position without the benefit of my letter.

Accidents. Accidents may result in disadvantage either to the person having the accident or to others, depending upon the unconscious motivation—guilt in the former case, hostility in the latter. A colleague's wife spilled ink on a manuscript her husband was working on (neglecting her as he did the work) as she cleaned his study. A student broke his hand shortly before he had to take an examination for which he felt unqualified.

Examples from Projective Tests (those in which the person projects hidden aspects of self into pictured situations). A twenty-two-year-old undergraduate student once consulted me for help with vague guilt feelings, inability to study, and fierce headaches that occurred whenever he went home or was obliged to spend any time with the dean, one of his professors, or his boss at a part-time job. He appeared to be extremely polite. (He used the word *sir* in almost every sentence when talking to me.) In the test, many of his stories included some expression of violence and hatred toward authority figures. The student told this story about a pictured situation that shows an old man stretching his hand toward the reclining figure of a younger man:

> This boy is having a nap. The old man, his father, is coming in to get him out of bed so he'll get back to his studies. His father has been nagging him for ages about how lazy he is. The boy has been putting up with this for a long time. This is the last straw. When he wakes up, he'll be so mad he'll start beating up on his father. He'll grab a chair and start mashing in his head. When he finishes, his old man will be a bloody pulp. The boy will get the electric chair, but he won't care, it was worth it.

Basic Needs, Higher Needs, and Healthy Personality

It is not too farfetched to infer at least some unconscious hostility toward authority figures in this young man.

There is no discovered way, as yet, to prove that an

inference of unconscious motivation is warranted. Nevertheless, it can be shown that the motives a person will consider as possible influences upon his or her action will change under special circumstances. A patient entering psychotherapy may act in ways that humiliate his wife; yet at the outset he may vigorously deny having hostile feelings toward her. Finally he can admit having hostile feelings, without guilt or anxiety. In addition, his hostility, if rational and warranted, may come to be expressed much more openly than it was before. It often happens that recognition and understanding of irrational hostility will reduce or eliminate it.

Repression, obviously, is not an effective way to deal with problems of existence. People sometimes repress experience because they have a strict conscience; it is often healthier to attempt to change the conscience or to accept the fact that one is not as "good" as one would like to believe. Repression is a way to ward off anxiety, but there are more effective and healthier ways. Repression may ward off painful frustration, but there are healthier ways to avoid frustration, such as learning skills. Only where repression is temporary and permits important action to be completed, or where it forestalls psychosis, can it be regarded as good for healthy personality.

HEALTHY FEATURES OF THE UNCONSCIOUS

Creativity. Healthier personalities have been more successful than average people in gratifying their needs. Consequently, their unconscious is not a dreaded source of evil, but a fount of innovation, self-integration, and creativity. Creative individuals show less fear of the free play of fantasy, and so they can "unrepress" to a greater degree than the average. In freeing their unconscious from its customary bonds, they experience the welcome admission to consciousness of new ideas, solutions to problems, insights into themselves, and other valued creations.

Health-Giving Morality. Sexuality or unacceptable drives such as aggression are not the only aspects of personality that are typically repressed. Mowrer has shown that individuals repress their consciences, and hence are unconscious of the guilt that would arise if the conscience were not repressed. If someone has acquired a conscience

Healthy Personality

that could guide that person in the direction of fullest growth and personal integration, then its repression could thwart his or her healthiest potentials. The individual said to have a "hardened heart," like Scrooge in Dickens' classic *Christmas Carol,* is one who has likely repressed his or her conscience and the guilt to which it might give rise. The unrepression of conscience in such individuals will produce acute guilt. The guilt, if acknowledged, could motivate the person to change his or her usual ways of behavior from self-centered pursuit of satisfaction to more loving concern for others.[24] Thus guilt, often thought of by many theoreticians as unhealthy, can be useful as an indicator to the person that he or she must take action to correct something that is the person's own responsibility. It is a signal that some behavior of yours has wronged someone. Some have seen psychotherapy as assuaging guilt for one's harm to others. Mowrer [25] and others have insisted that this is a misuse of psychological help and is doomed to failure. They strongly suggest an old remedy—righting the wrong that has been done.

SUBLIMATION AND SUBSTITUTION

One of the ways of dealing with wishes and feelings that provoke anxiety or guilt is to substitute another activity, particularly one that is socially desirable. This is called *sublimation* and is an ancient and honorable approach for the individual with specific religious or cultural taboos that he or she chooses to honor. Thus, someone with a great deal of sexual energy but strong feelings of moral commitment to abstinence might throw himself or herself into community leadership, into programs of social justice, or into creative arts such as painting or sculpture. Particularly as a result of greater freedom in sexual activity, many have rejected the concept of sublimation as indicative of the person's avoidance of the problem. However, there is as much evidence for the position that it is a healthy adjustment mechanism as for any other.

Basic Needs, Higher Needs, and Healthy Personality

Glimpses of Growing Possibilities. While Freud showed how people repressed undesirable dimensions of their experience, Jung called attention to the fact that we remain unconscious of our "higher," more fully humanized possibilities.[26] The unconscious is not only a repository of our psychological "sewage"; it is also the source of our most sublime possibilities.

Just as dreams reveal morally repugnant wishes for tabooed sexuality or murder, so they can reveal, albeit in metaphoric language, possible ways for a person to rise above barriers to growth. In dreams, many persons discover the solutions to vexing personal problems.

Our usual waking consciousness is limited by our chronic preoccupation with daily needs and projects. Other possible ways to experience ourselves and the world remain unconscious, or potentially conscious, and may be revealed to us in our dreams.

Goals Beyond Basic Need Fulfillment: Self-Actualization

If a person is successfully satisfying basic needs, his or her energy and thoughts are freed for other interests. The exact nature of these interests will differ from person to person, but the diversity and intensity of involvement in matters outside the self is a good indicator of healthy personality.

Maslow [27] has suggested that having successfully dealt with these basic needs, the person can move on to B-motivation (being motivation), which involves giving joyous vent to the highest aspirations and needs; fullest self-actualization and attending to aesthetic needs; and appreciation of beauty, art, and the higher realms of thought or cognition. When we cease to be a problem to ourselves, because we have fulfilled our needs for security, love, and status, we will begin to see the world in a manner that differs from the way "deficiency-motivated" persons see it. We can forget ourselves and become involved in play, or in another person's problems, and perhaps with the wellbeing of humanity as a whole. It is difficult to become concerned about the hunger or enslavement of another person when one is in the midst of such privation oneself. When we have experienced and transcended these conditions, we can empathize with (i.e., imagine with vividness) the experience of others and devote ourselves to serving them.

Healthy Personality

Many interests and values grow out of a person's earlier quest for the means of gratifying basic needs. Thus, someone may become a physician as a means of assuring economic security. However, once the person is earning the money he or she was seeking, that person may (indeed *should*) find intrinsic fascination in the challenges posed by illness. The motivation for the practice of medicine changes then from a quest for money to a quest for knowledge of new ways to relieve suffering. Whenever an interest in some activity comes into being as a means of satisfying basic needs, and then changes into a spontaneous fascination, the motive is said to be *functionally autonomous* [28] of its more basic origins. We do not fully understand the mechanisms by which functional autonomy of motives occurs; it appears to be a matter of commitment.

THE PROBLEM OF COMMITMENT

Human beings need meaningful activity to give direction and value to their existence. We have little difficulty understanding much human action, because it clearly serves the most basic needs. But when a person has assured access to the basic requirements, the question arises, What shall I do now with the time and energy that have become available? What is worth doing? One can consume only so much food, one can only be loved a certain amount, one can only be safe to some degree. What will I do next with my time and resources?

We are dealing fundamentally with the question of persuasion. Some challenges, tasks, hobbies, and vocations that have little to do with one's basic needs are "invested" with value and worth by our observation of someone else. We see someone doing something with his or her time that seems to give that person much satisfaction. Either by invitation or by self-initiative, persons explore ways to spend their time, and commit themselves to such activity. The billions of interests that absorb persons attest to the fact that we can give value to anything from collecting seedpods to scaling mountains at great risk to life and limb, because they are there. The capacity to commit oneself to activities and projects beyond basic need fulfillment is a further defining characteristic of healthier personality.[29]

*Basic Needs,
Higher Needs,
and Healthy
Personality*

While almost all writers in the field see attention to the self as the primary, basic preoccupation of the normally healthy person, all also see commitment outside of self as being characteristic of the healthy personality. This includes commitment to activities such as political change, social welfare, problems of the aged, commitment to an abstract ideal such as freedom or beauty, preservation of the environment, or commitment to another person—a beloved friend, wife, lover, or trustworthy leader.

It is important also to note that in the search for a direction of commitment, one can choose an unworthy and even dangerous commitment, especially when it is presented under the cloak of religion, politics, or even of psychology or some other abstract ideal. Thus, the many people who accompanied the Reverend Jim Jones to Guyana and to their deaths in 1978 were committing themselves to a leader, charismatic and hypnotic, who destroyed them. There are many effective, meaningful religious and political commitments that a person can make that will better self and society. Some of the false commitments will offer false, cheap surcease for one's personal pain. A wise young person will select commitments with care and with attention both to the maintenance of the freedom of the mind and to the assurance that one can change one's mind and one's commitment without fear of coercion, whether psychological or physical. No commitment or choice should ever be made to renounce your freedom to think for yourself.

Some Existential Suggestions

What has been lacking in your life at times when you have found yourself bored, miserable, or even sick? What can you do about these lacks? Upon whom do you depend to gratify these needs? What does your dependency "cost" you in the way of submission to the wishes of the person upon whom you are dependent? What do you believe you cannot do without? Viktor Frankl showed that it is possible not only to survive, but moreover to transcend lethal circumstances; he wrote most of a book while he struggled to survive for eight years in a Nazi death camp.

Healthy
Personality

Can you identify what you need to enhance your life,

and learn the skills that will enable you to gratify these needs? This is what Blatz has described as overcoming insecurity through action—the way of independent security.

Whenever you become sick—with a cold, flu, mononucleosis, or other illness—reflect upon your life and see if you can identify an episode of dispiritedness brought on by loss of someone's love, an abrupt change in way of life (such as moving to another residence), or some failure. Or consider whether your style of life or family role is preventing you from gratifying certain basic needs; prolonged deprivation may have stressed or dispirited you. Sickness is a splendid opportunity to reflect upon your way of living, so that when you have recovered, you can make changes that will reduce the likelihood of becoming sick again. Sickness is often an indication that one's habitual way of life has not yielded those basic need gratifications that sustain health and keep a person growing in vital ways.

When all is not well in your life, it is good to record dreams for hints as to possible changes you could make to revitalize yourself. Getting back to nature—a walk in the woods or by the sea, away from machinery and work—can provide an opportunity to meditate and gain perspective upon an unsatisfying life style. Sometimes dispiritedness will hit one without the symptoms of physical illness, but rather in signs of disinterest in life, loss of ability to enjoy life, and feelings of worthlessness. The healthy person can recognize these as indicators of time to seek professional help, time to make changes, or time to seek out good, listening friends. In choosing commitments, one needs to examine deeply the possibility of being able to change one's mind, to keep the mind free and to leave psychologically, spiritually, or physically when one chooses. Avoidance of false, unworthy commitments is an indicator of the healthy personality. Especially during periods of dispiritedness are you vulnerable to persons who offer easy ways out.

Basic Needs,
Higher Needs,
and Healthy
Personality

S U M M A R Y

Nobody knows, ultimately, what human beings need in order not merely to survive, but to prevail and to develop

113

their full possibilities. Our most basic needs include the need to affirm life itself; physical gratifications; love, status, and self-esteem; freedom and space; challenge; meditation; cognitive clarity; meaning; variety and change; intimacy in solitude; and contact with nature. There may be more basic needs, and some of those mentioned, such as excitement, may not be essential to life itself, but they certainly make for a richer existence if they have been met.

Prolonged deprivation may bring about a state of frustration, when a person loses contact with reality and may engage in destructive tension-reducing action. Aggression and regression are characteristic responses to frustration.

Frustration thresholds are heightened by good health, recognition of meaning in life, and opportunities for release. Prolonged deprivation of basic needs can sicken a person through diminished resistance to infection, which is brought about by stress or dispiritedness. The healthy personality acknowledges dispiritedness in self when it occurs and seeks help.

Needs and emotions that threaten a person's self-esteem and sense of security may be repressed; they operate as unconscious influences upon action and experience. Such unconscious motives may appear in the content of dreams, in accidents and errors, in body postures, in the forgetting of intentions and promises, and in certain projective tests of personality. The unconscious harbors one's possibilities for achievement and growth as well as for action that is personally or socially reprehensible. Guilt can be a healthy indicator of something being wrong in one's behavior.

Once a person has gratified the basic needs, his or her energies and experience are liberated so that the person can turn to projects beyond basic need satisfaction, such as the pursuit of freedom, justice, beauty, or truth; in other words, B, or being motivation, including self-actualization. The problem is to find goals and projects that are challenging, fascinating, and that keep your mind free. Any choice of a meaningful commitment outside of self must include one's free choice to change one's mind.

Healthy Personality

114

1. This analysis of needs and wants comes from Blatz's thirty-six-year-old book dealing with children. Blatz was one of my first teachers at the University of Toronto, and this book is still valid. See W. E. BLATZ, *Understanding the Young Child* (New York: Morrow, 1944), pp. 80–82, and also Chapter 9, on security. The human vulnerability to control by other people—not only by the physical environment, which "selects" the "right" behavior—is shown in B. F. SKINNER, *Beyond Freedom and Dignity* (New York: Knopf, 1971).

2. A. H. MASLOW, *Motivation and Personality*, 2nd ed. (New York: Harper, 1970).

3. A review of the research on the basic need hierarchy reports only partial support for the hierarchy concept. See M. A. WAHBA and L. G. BRIDWELL, "Maslow Reconsidered: A Review of Research on the Need Hierarchy Theory," *Organizational Behavior and Human Performance*, 1976, Vol. 15, pp. 212–240.

4. This radical view of love was espoused by T. LANDSMAN in "Love: The Serpent's Tooth and the White Knight," paper presented at the conference on new frontiers in counseling, University of Florida, February 11, 1977.

5. D. C. McCLELLAND, *The Achieving Society* (New York: Free Press, 1967). Also see V. PACKARD, *The Status Seekers* (New York: McKay, 1959). For the competence concept, see R. W. WHITE, "The Concept of Healthy Personality: What Do We Really Mean?" *Counseling Psychologist*, 1973, Vol. 4, pp. 3–12.

6. See the article by Frank Barron, which analyzes freedom as a feeling, like affection or anxiety: F. BARRON, "Freedom as Feeling," *Journal of Humanistic Psychology*, 1961, Vol. 1, pp. 91–100; also ERICH FROMM's classic *Escape from Freedom* (New York: Holt, 1941) should be read in this context. In the British edition, this book is entitled *Fear of Freedom* (London: K. Paul, Trench, Trubner, 1941).

7. D. MORRIS, *The Human Zoo* (New York: McGraw-Hill, 1969); R. ARDREY, *The Territorial Imperative* (New York: Atheneum, 1966); A. WESTIN, *Privacy and Freedom* (New York: Atheneum, 1967); R. SOMMER, *Personal Space: The Behavioral Basis of Design* (Englewood Cliffs, N.J.: Prentice-Hall, 1969); S. M. JOURARD, *The Transparent Self*, 2nd ed. (New York: Van Nostrand Reinhold, 1971), Chapter 8, "The Need for Privacy."

8. Many of the benefits of transcendental meditation

Basic Needs, Higher Needs, and Healthy Personality

have been supported by research. An example of such a study is by P. FERGUSON and J. GOWAN, "TM: Some Preliminary Findings," *Journal of Humanistic Psychology,* 1976, Vol. 16, pp. 51–60.

9. Some of the most sensitive writing in humanistic psychology is by this writer. Two short books of great value are C. E. MOUSTAKAS, *Loneliness* (Englewood Cliffs, N.J.: Prentice-Hall, 1961); and *Creative Life* (New York: Van Nostrand, 1977).

10. A. S. SKOLNICK and J. H. SKOLNICK, *Intimacy, Family and Society* (Boston: Little, Brown, 1974); and J. W. RAMEY, *Intimate Friendships* (Englewood Cliffs, N.J.: Prentice-Hall, 1976).

11. Shaw wrote effectively on the need for challenge. See F. J. SHAW, *Reconciliation: A Theory of Man Transcending* (New York: Van Nostrand Reinhold, 1966), posthumously edited by S. M. Jourard and D. Overlade.

12. C. TART (Ed.), *Altered States of Consciousness* (New York: Wiley, 1969).

13. See ELSE FRENKEL-BRUNSWIK, "Intolerance of Ambiguity as an Emotional and Perceptual Personality Variable," *Journal of Personality,* 1949, Vol. 18, pp. 108–143; L. FESTINGER, *A Theory of Cognitive Dissonance* (New York: Harper, 1957); G. A. KELLY, *The Psychology of Personal Constructs, I: A Theory of Personality* (New York: Norton, 1955), Chapter 2; M. ROKEACH, *The Open and Closed Mind* (New York: Basic, 1960).

14. V. E. FRANKL, *Man's Search for Meaning,* rev. ed. (Boston: Beacon, 1963); E. FROMM, *The Sane Society* (New York: Holt, 1955).

15. M. M. SCHWARTZ and L. S. GAINES, "Self-Actualization and the Human Tendency for Varied Experience," *Journal of Personality Assessment,* 1974, Vol. 38, pp. 423–427. D. W. FISKE and S. R. MADDI, *Functions of Varied Experience* (Homewood, Ill.: Dorsey, 1961), Chapter 5; J. P. ZUBEK (Ed.), *Sensory Deprivation: Fifteen Years of Research* (New York: Appleton, 1969); J. C. LILLY, *The Center of the Cyclone* (Garden City, N.Y.: Doubleday, 1971).

16. W. REICH, *The Discovery of the Orgone: The Function of the Orgasm* (New York: Noonday, 1961), Chapters 2 and 8. See also A. MONTAGU, *Touching: The Human Significance of the Skin* (New York: Harper, 1972), for a fine review of evidence on the need for physical contact.

17. W. REICH, *Character Analysis* (New York: Orgone, 1949), Chapter 12.

18. H. SELYE, *The Physiology and Pathology of Exposure to Stress* (Montreal: Acta, 1950), or his less technical book, *The Stress of Life* (New York: McGraw-Hill, 1956). See also JOURARD, *The Transparent Self*, op. cit., pp. 75–102; D. BAKAN, *The Duality of Human Existence* (Chicago: Rand McNally, 1966); and D. BAKAN, *Pain, Disease, and Sacrifice: Toward a Psychology of Suffering* (Chicago: U. of Chicago, 1968).

19. R. MANRY, *Tinkerbelle* (New York: Harper, 1966).

20. S. FREUD, *The Interpretation of Dreams* (New York: Basic, 1955); *The Psychopathology of Everyday Life* (New York: Norton, 1971). These are classics that every student should read as part of a liberal education.

21. REICH, *Character Analysis*, op. cit.

22. E. FROMM, *Man for Himself* (New York: Holt, 1947).

23. See J. C. MOLONEY, *The Magic Cloak: A Contribution to the Psychology of Authoritarianism* (Wakefield, Mass.: Montrose, 1949), pp. 99–101 and also Chapter 13, for a discussion of diverse psychosomatic symptoms that Moloney found to be associated with repressed hostility among people who work in authoritarian settings. Hemorrhoids, back pain, and high blood pressure are not uncommon in persons who daily are provoked to anger but dare not express their feelings. For experimental demonstrations of muscular tension, see R. B. MALMO, C. SHAGASS, and J. P. DAVIS, "Electromyographic Studies of Muscular Tension in Psychiatric Patients Under Stress," *Journal of Clinical and Experimental Psychopathology*, 1951, Vol. 12, pp. 45–66.

24. O. H. MOWRER, *The Crisis in Psychiatry and Religion* (New York: Van Nostrand Reinhold, 1961).

25. Ibid., *The New Group Therapy* (New York: Van Nostrand Rheinhold, 1964).

26. C. G. JUNG, *Two Essays on Analytic Psychology* (New York: Meridian, 1956), pp. 182–197.

27. A. H. MASLOW, *Toward a Psychology of Being*, 2nd ed. (New York: Van Nostrand Reinhold, 1968), Chapter 3.

28. G. W. ALLPORT, *Pattern and Growth in Personality* (New York: Holt, 1961), pp. 226–229.

29. Commitment is a case of attribution of importance to

some possible future. See S. M. JOURARD, "Some Notes on the Experience of Commitment," *Humanitas, Journal of the Institute of Man*, 1972, Vol. 88, pp. 5–8. The entire issue of the journal was devoted to papers on commitment.

Healthy
Personality

6

EMOTION AND HEALTHY PERSONALITY

INTRODUCTION

Emotionality represents a heightened state of being, but use of "cold logic" with an absence of emotion may also be thought of as a heightened state. In the midst of an emotional experience, a person will show definite physiological symptoms: flushing, tremors, and increased heart rate, according to Isaacson and Hutt.[1] However, the physiological symptoms are not necessarily different for each different emotion.

Emotion may be defined as a group of organized feelings, all heightened or strengthened, either in reaction to a threat to the person (such as in anger or indignation) or in reaction to a perceived enhancement of the person, as in joy or ecstasy.

Whereas the use of cool objectivity also has survival value for the person, the inhibition of emotion or the overcontrol of emotional experience is often associated with adjustment problems. The free expression of one's feelings or emotions—as long as it is within control of the person—is considered to be a characteristic of the healthy person. A high-level state of humanness includes the opportunity for the person to express self emotionally, as freely and spontaneously as a hearty laugh, for example, and with a reasonable level of control, as in the case of an angry parent who refrains from physical punishment of a child, and who rather chooses to explain and reason with the child concerning the misbehavior.

Emotion aids life's intensity and meaning. We are amused and we laugh; someone insults us and we become angry. A young woman has just received a proposal of marriage from the man she loves; her excitement and joy are dramatically evident.

Emotion is a quality of experience and an expressive quality of action. We can speak thus of emotional experience and emotional expression. The former is emotion viewed from a phenomenological perspective, that is, from the standpoint of the person, whereas emotional expression is the way emotional experience appears to an observer.

The Varieties of Emotional Experience

There is no authoritative catalogue of emotional experience. Furthermore, there is no precise differentiation of the physiological expression of emotion. Physiological psychologists have difficulty naming the emotional experience that a person is undergoing when their only data are markings on a polygraph that depict alterations in autonomic nervous system activity.

In psychology's earliest days, emotion was an awkward concept for behavioral scientists to define and accept. The effort tended toward minimizing the subject, considering it a part of the motivation process, and most of all, boiling down emotions to as few as possible. In 1919 Watson,[2] the grand old man of behaviorism, suggested the existence of only three emotions in the infant—fear, joy, and lust. In the years following, the direction of the profession may be seen in that Bridges[3] (1932) proposed just one response: undifferentiated excitement, a concept *Healthy* that matches the lack of differentiation in physiological *Personality* symptomology characteristic of almost all emotions.

Clinicians, counselors, and others who have dealt intimately with emotions and whose task it often is to help people understand their own emotional responses very accurately and specifically, do differentiate a far richer spectrum of emotions in the human. The complexity of emotions as seen by the humanists, as contrasted to the parsimonious efforts of the behaviorists, may be seen in the table, an attempt to construct a catalogue, which, as

An Incomplete Catalogue of the Emotions

POSITIVE

joy	hope	safe
ecstasy	desire	radiant
spontaneity	cheerful	vivacious
exhilaration	merry	jubilant
pride	congenial	jaunty
innocence	gleeful	carefree
clean	mirthful	chipper
feeling good	playful	perky
delight	reverent	happy-go-lucky
attraction	frivolous	enamored
tenderness	contented	wanting to take
excited	rapturous	care of
interest	enraptured	enamored
being moved	relieved	solicitous
jovial	blithe	amiable
pleased	enchanted	warm-hearted
elation	transported	affectionate
trusting	blissful	sentimental
thrilled	delirious	amatory
anticipation	rhapsodic	benign
liking	rapture	benevolent
loving	gratified	cordial
erotic	peaceful	generous
pleasure	charmed	ardent
surprise	comfortable	exultant

NEGATIVE

miserable	feeling low	disliking
depressed	sad	ignoring
oppressed	uninterested	fear
lethargic	harshness	anger
shame	bored	perturbed
guilt	annoyed	lustful
dirty	suspicious	anxiety

Emotion and Healthy Personality

dread	intimidated	exasperated
disgust	discouraged	in a huff
rage	repelled	galled
gloom	browbeaten	piqued
jealousy	defeated	enraged
pained	discouraged	infuriated
distress	threatened	ill-tempered
embarrassment	worried	displeasure
dejected	appalled	acrimonious
frightened	daunted	animosity
frenzied, frantic	badgered	indignant
panic	petrified	resentful
terror	startled	irate
horror	disquieted	irascible
dismay	unnerved	displeased
cowed	melancholy	chagrined
shocked	wrathful	impatient
harried	hatred	provoked
make my hair stand	resentful	take umbrage
on end	vengeful	petulant
make my flesh	vexed	in high dudgeon
creep	antagonistic	fretful
put one's heart in	rankled	embittered
one's mouth	peeved	

a helpful feature, attempts to divide the list of emotions into positive and negative. From time to time, humanists have pointed out that most psychology textbooks, when they do give any space to emotions, concentrate largely on the negative emotions, such as hate and depression. The list in the table on pages 121–122 continues that unfortunate tradition and suggests that our colleagues were only reflecting actual usage in our English-speaking society.

One may wish to add to the list a small group of terms that may be either positive or negative, such as:

Being beside oneself (with anger or with joy).

Passionate (fury or love).

Aroused (in anger or erotically).

Yearning (for relief or for love).

Wistful (sad or charming).

Astounded (disappointed or pleased).

Healthy
Personality

Surprised (pleasantly or rudely).

It may be argued that some entries on the list are better

described as *feelings* rather than as full-fledged emotions. Yet in practice, there is little differentiation between the part and the whole, an indifferent synechdoche (whole-part relationship). They comprise, in any event, a stark contrast to the attempt to force this richness of experience into the format of one, two, or three emotions. Freed of the physiological definition, the psychology of emotion assumes a significant role in the description of the healthy personality.

You may want to consider other definitions of emotion. Plutchik,[4] one of the foremost researchers on emotion, suggests that feelings are too unreliable to be used in a definition of emotion. He suggests the following as a definition:

> An emotion is a patterned bodily reaction of either protection, destruction, reproduction, deprivation, incorporation, rejection, exploration or orientation, or some combination of these, which is brought about by a stimulus [p. 12].

Or a supremely general definition offered by Arnold [5]:

> the emotion . . . becomes felt tendency toward anything appraised as good, and away from anything appraised as bad [p. 76].

Izard,[6] who authored a prize-winning publication on emotions, sees emotions, emotional expression and experience, and indeed, even the way we express emotions facially, as crucially related to high-level functioning, which he refers to as optimum or optimal personality functioning. Each society and subculture has stereotyped ways in which persons express, and hence communicate, their feelings to one another. The behavioral, gestural, and facial expressions can be faked—someone can pretend to experience feelings he or she does not actually have. Perhaps the only one who knows with certainty what feelings someone is experiencing is the actual person, and even that person may be unaware that he or she is in an emotional state; it is a human possibility to repress the affective quality of experience.

Emotion and Healthy Personality

In spite of these qualifications, we can identify some common feelings and emotions and recognize them in ourselves and others. From the standpoint of healthy personality, it is desirable to be free to express the fullest gamut of emotion, because of the enrichment it affords to the quality of life. Not to know emotion is to be like a robot or zombie. Further, it is vital that a person's feelings be authentic rather than pretended. Pretended emotion falsifies relationships with other people; such inauthenticity undermines health and distorts personal growth.

THE INTELLIGIBILITY OF EMOTION

Emotional expression is an aspect of communication. If we share a common upbringing and cultural heritage, we will not have difficulty in understanding the subtleties and nuances of emotion that are conveyed by the flare of a nostril, the narrowing of eyelids, or the ripple of muscle along the jawline as a person suppresses rage. When we enter another culture, however, such as happens when an American from New York visits a Southern state or another English-speaking country, we frequently do not recognize when our speech and actions are angering or amusing the local people. Indeed, it may take years to learn the perspective, expectations, and evaluative norms of the natives, and until that happens, a visitor may feel lonely and out of touch. Many students have had the experience of joy and relief at encountering someone from their home when they were abroad.

Understanding one another's feelings is usually immediate between people who know one another. There are occasions, however, when the emotional disclosure of someone well known becomes unintelligible; we cannot comprehend why a friend is terrified, angry, or sexually aroused. This is the case with so-called schizophrenic [7] and neurotic people; their emotionality does not appear to make sense, even to members of their families. Yet, because they are human, it must be assumed that the emotional experience of such sufferers makes sense to them, in the light of their perspective upon the world. If someone is terrified, it is because the person experiences imminent danger; if someone is enraged, it is because someone else has violated that person's space and integrity.

Healthy Personality

All emotion makes sense when we have imaginatively grasped the perspective of the person who is feeling it. It is such empathy, and the willingness to encounter and enter into dialogue with someone with a different perspective, which is so important for therapists, teachers of children, parents, and those who seek to live and work in another country.

Some Particularly Important Forms of Emotional Experience

PLEASURE

It feels good to eat when one is hungry, to drink when one is thirsty, to urinate and to empty one's bowels when the time to do so has come. Physical massage and the sheer sensuality of being caressed yield pleasure not overshadowed by sexual orgasm, which is viewed by most humans as the acme of human pleasures. Although pleasure as such cannot serve as the chief purpose of life— the reality principle discussed by Freud tells us that the quest for pleasure can endanger life itself—a life without pleasure is hardly worth living. Gratification of basic needs is pleasurable in and for itself, and the capacity to feel such pleasure is one of the rewards of healthy personality. Although it may seem surprising, many persons actually dread the experience of pleasure and repress it. Such repression is most likely in persons reared under puritanical regimes in which "self-indulgence" is regarded as a sin.[8]

Pleasure comes not only from the act of satisfying basic needs, however. There is joy to be found in contemplation of beauty in music, art, and nature; in the sound of birds; the sight of a child taking its first steps; the smell of new-mown hay. Another source of pleasure is to be found in the zest accompanying action. Zest is engendered when people engage in activities that will challenge, but not overwhelm them. Thus, a game of tennis or handball, surfing along the perfect wave, skiing down a fast slope, yield pleasure no less than that afforded by a sensuous, passive massage. Similar zest arises in those who love their work, whether it be that of an artist in the studio, a scientist in the laboratory, or a businessperson planning a sales campaign. People who experience pleasure in living do not develop the uptight, armored bodies and grim facial expressions of those whose lives have been hard and joyless or whose religious orientation proscribes pleasure as a sin. And those who find zest in their work and play appear "childlike" or ageless—they do not grow old.

Pleasure engulfs the experience of persons who have just had their hopes fulfilled, or who have just completed a valued project. The delights of winning a prize or receiving an unexpected gift are among the "highs" in life, as are the joys of finishing a difficult mountain climb or writing a book.

Pleasure—whether occasioned by sensuality, physical activity, or the consummation of projects—is a goal and reward of healthy personality.

DEPRESSION

Persons typically become depressed when their lives have lost delight and any sense of meaning or hope. Occasions for depression include the death of a loved person, prolonged failure of one's projects, the loss of beauty or one's health and vitality. When persons are depressed, they experience life as hellish—time slows down; nothing is happening; they may feel worthless, guilty, and beneath contempt. Clearly, when persons are depressed, their lives are not yielding what is needed for vital, enlivening existence. Depressed people frequently make suicidal attempts, and they sometimes succeed—which is a shame, because persons can disengage from hopeless ways of being, and, with a little imaginative help from friends or a psychotherapist, reinvent themselves and their situations in ways that engender more positive experience. Although depression is hellish, it can and perhaps should serve as a motive to the sufferers to change their situations to more life-giving ones. In the same fashion that joy is likely to be a part of every person's experience during a lifetime, depression may also be a factor in everyone's life at some time—including the lives of healthy personalities. Bugental [9] has suggested this radical change in the conception of the role of depression. He implies that depression ought to be "utilized," under-

Healthy Personality

stood, and taken by the person as a normal occurrence to be dealt with and integrated into the personality, to become part of the person's total experience in the same way any other negative experience may be a source of new learning about the self.

ANXIETY AND DREAD

Anxiety or dread is experienced when persons believe their way of life is in jeopardy and there is no possibility of further existence. Anxiety differs from fear in that with the latter, one can see the source of the danger, and can, perhaps, cope with it by combat or flight. Anxiety is more likely to arise when one has violated a personal or a religious taboo and experiences the imminence of annihilation, while feeling helpless to do anything about it. It is also triggered by signals that do not appear to make sense, such as a horror of high places, panic over insects, or a dread of dirt. A simple onslaught of such anxiety or dread is enough to traumatize someone for a lifetime, if the person survives it. Indeed, some of the most rigid character traits and so-called defense mechanisms are developed as desperate means of ensuring that the horror will never again be experienced. Many compulsive habits, like primitive religious taboos and injunctions, persist throughout persons' lives, interfering with their personal relations and with the spontaneous enjoyment of life, in order to prevent the dreaded anxiety. When persons cannot avert the experience of anxiety by regulating their lives or their environment, they may develop any of the life styles that are described by psychiatrists as neurotic or psychotic. These ways of being are themselves devoid of joy, because they are so hemmed in by inhibitions; but the diminished life is preferred by the patients to facing, unaided and alone, that annihilation of their world and their identity that is called anxiety.

It is impossible, however, to live without some encounter with anxiety. The posture most compatible with healthy personality in an encounter with dread is the posture of courage, the "courage to be" of which Paul Tillich wrote so beautifully. The person with courage to face the unknown with resolve and fortitude discovers

Emotion and Healthy Personality

unplumbed capacities to grow and to cope with life. As paradoxical as it may sound, the experience of anxiety is essential for growth.

Spielberger [10] suggests two basic forms of anxiety: state anxiety, which strikes occasionally and for short periods of time, and trait anxiety, which describes the general state of the person and is with that person more or less constantly as a personality characteristic. It may be anticipated that even the psychologically healthy person would be in a state of anxiety on limited occasions, although the adaptive or useful function of the state is by no means entirely clear. It may serve to signal to the person or to peers that a matter of great importance is being considered and the individual needs to mobilize all resources for a successful response to the event—a significant decision, a serious threat to selfhood, or a major turning point in one's life.

Perhaps the most distinguished humanist writing on the subject of anxiety, Rollo May,[11] insists that raw physical courage (in addition to the courage to be noted earlier) is often a triumph over anxiety. He cites the work of William Lloyd Garrison in seeking emancipation for the slaves, who wrote of his knees shaking in anticipation as he faced a large audience. Courage in itself seems to be one of the major dynamics of the high-level-functioning person. Courage is most likely to appear, however, in those persons fortunate enough to have an "encourager" in their lives, whether it be a friend, family member, counselor, or their deity.[12]

ANGER, HOSTILITY, RAGE

The capacity to experience anger, like the ability to become afraid, is a biological endowment; presumably, it served the interests of the human survival as a species. The problem, however, is how to regulate anger, for it can lead to violence between people. Open violence makes family and community life impossible. Chronically suppressed anger is a factor in the development of many psychosomatic illnesses, including peptic ulcers, high blood pressure, asthma, colitis, and so on. Anger typically arises when someone or something enters one's "territory" unbidden, and it arises when people get in the way

Healthy Personality

of one's projects. Finally, it arises, in the form of moral indignation, when one sees people acting in ways that one profoundly feels are evil. Anger energizes a person for attack, just as fear energizes for flight. When persons are at war, their rage will serve them well, enabling them to fight without reserve. In everyday life, however, the recurrent provocation to anger or irritation, without the possibility of full expression of anger or escape from the provokers, undermines health and wellbeing.

A person needs to find respite from nagging irritation and to find socially and personally acceptable ways to express accumulated anger. Violent exercise, such as in handball or tennis, is frequently helpful as a harmless way to express anger that cannot be expressed in other ways. Of course, the attainment of a more positive attitude toward life may reduce the frequency with which a person becomes angered. Very conservative people often become enraged at the appearance and actions of persons with a radically different life style, even to the point of wishing them to be imprisoned or killed; a broader perspective upon what is regarded as acceptable ways to be human certainly diminishes the anger of such persons.

The problem with anger is to learn how to accept it as natural in oneself and to express it in nondestructive ways. One author, Israel Charny,[13] regards marriage and family life, not as a haven of peace and happiness, though it can be that; rather he sees the relationship between husband and wife, and between parent and child, as a place to learn ways to reconcile differences and to deal with anger without destroying the persons with whom one is angry. George Bach has actually provided instructions to married people on ways to fight fairly and nondestructively with one another.[14] Perhaps the most constructive way of dealing with anger or rage is to "work through" the emotion, to understand why you feel that way and through your understanding to reduce the intensity of rage and even, under some circumstances, to have the rage washed away by the flood of understanding. This can be done with a skilled counselor and always involves the person's readiness to express fully his or her anger to the understanding helper.

We are not capable of experiencing guilt until we have formed a conscience. Young children, prior to the internalization of their parents' moral expectations, may experience fear of punishment for misdeeds, but this is not guilt.

Guilt is the experience of self-loathing that arises when persons transgress their own moral principles. It can be so powerful an emotion that guilt-ridden persons may kill themselves rather than endure the onslaught of self-hatred. Common occasions for guilt include hurting another person, stealing, violating one's own sexual morality, or cheating in examinations.

A distinction can be drawn between guilt that arises from the violation of moral taboos that one truly has outgrown and existential or humanistic guilt, which arises when persons have diminished the quality and possibility of life for themselves and others. Maslow calls the former *silly guilt,* as in instances when an adult engages in masturbation and feels a catastrophic loss of self-esteem for what is properly viewed as a harmless solitary sport. Existential guilt is illustrated by the failure to respond to a call for help or the failure to fulfill one's own possibilities through lack of nerve.

Existential guilt, a phenomenon of the psychological realm, is also sometimes seen as a constructive analogue of pain in the physical realm. Guilt helps you to determine when something is wrong with your behavior and, like physical pain, provides an early warning system of something that must be corrected in the self. The capacity for existential guilt is an achievement; of course, the most life-giving response to such guilt is to make restitution and to seek then to live in conformity with one's ideals.[15]

WEEPING

In our society at least, only women and young children can weep without self-consciousness and embarrassment. Grown men are generally regarded as weak if they cry when sad or hurt. Perhaps the only exceptions are instances where a man has lost someone close to him through death. Then tears are grudgingly accepted in a man, or at least regarded as understandable.

Healthy Personality

The ability to cry—in men as well as in women and children—is desirable for healthy personality. It is deemed desirable when it does not preclude more active ways of coping with problems and when it is effective in releasing feelings of despair, joy, anger, or a sense of loss. Such emotional *catharsis*, or release of feelings, frees the person to resume life once more on an active basis. Psychotherapists find that when their patients are finally able to weep during therapy sessions, the course of therapy proceeds more satisfactorily. This is especially true of male patients who find weeping a drastic threat to their self-esteem and their masculine identities. Therapy calls for the fullest disclosure of experience on the part of patients, and if they will not permit themselves to cry when they want to, it indicates a lack of trust in the therapist.

The inhibition of weeping that characterizes the average male in our society seems to be but part of a more generalized suppression of many other kinds of feelings, including tenderness and sentimentality. Such suppression, if carried to extremes, can have unhealthy consequences for the body and can also render men's relationships with others empty and lifeless.

HUMOR AND LAUGHTER

The capacity to see humor in situations and to respond with laughter is an indication of being well. Loss of the ability to laugh at oneself and at comic situations is one of the early symptoms of more serious personality disorders. When a person can laugh even in potentially grim situations, it implies some degree of freedom from the press of fate and circumstances. Prisoners in Nazi concentration camps during World War II could find something to laugh at, though they lived but a hairbreadth from torture and death.

One psychologist, Franklin J. Shaw,[16] regarded laughter as one of the purest examples of characteristically human behavior. Laughter is a response that can be made only by persons who have transcended their animal heritage as well as the conformity-producing pressures of society. Laughter is defiance of brute necessity, a proclamation of freedom, and the ability to transcend the limits of otherwise grim circumstances.

Emotion and Healthy Personality

Of course, there are rough norms defining the appropriateness or inappropriateness of laughter. Schizophrenics will often laugh in situations where a more intact person might weep or become angry. But a good sense of humor, the ability to find something ludicrous in situations, is not only a social asset; it is an indication that a person is able to do more than just struggle to exist. One of the major factors found in high-level-functioning persons is a childlike sense of humor, according to Puttick.[17] In a recent Israeli study by Ziv,[18] children reported that teachers who use humor in the classroom reduce the psychological distance between teacher and child, create a more agreeable atmosphere in the classroom, and make it easier to concentrate.

Frivolity as a Defense. Some persons will joke about things that probably should be taken seriously. People who are afraid to admit their righteous and justified anger, or who are afraid to be taken seriously, may cloak matters of genuine concern in laughter. When they do this chronically, they permit situations to be perpetuated that could be changed for the better if they dropped the humorous façade.

Jokes. A clever and even off-color story can add zest to a gathering, but it takes a certain savoir-faire to be able to distinguish between those times when a joke will contribute enjoyable laughter to a situation and when it will bring agonizing embarrassment to the listeners.

Healthier personalities are able to find humor in situations, they are able to laugh at themselves as well as at others who might strut or huff and puff in phony pretense, but they will not be addicted to jokes that inflict harm or express malice. It should not be forgotten, however, that there are some situations, as in dictatorships, where overt hostility against the leaders of a regime might bring death or imprisonment to the rebels, as occurred to Solzhenitsyn.[19] Under conditions of this sort, satire, jokes, and cartoons that cleverly deride the ruling regime may be the only available outlet for feelings. Furthermore, such humor may serve a valuable function in sustaining morale.[20]

*Healthy
Personality*

In an important theoretical paper, Frank Barron proposed that freedom be defined not only as the repertoire of adaptive responses available to a person in a given situation, but also as a *feeling*. The implication of this view of freedom—seeing it as a feeling in the sense that anger, sex, or guilt are feelings—is that one can study how persons cope with it. Thus, the feeling of freedom can be repressed, projected, and have reaction formations constructed against it, and it can be responsibly acknowledged.

"In what situations, with what other persons, does a given individual feel free?" This question can be used as a guide for students to survey their own life situations. The opposite of the feeling of freedom is the feeling of compulsion, or the feeling of being driven. Maximization of the feeling of freedom is a desirable quality for healthy personality. However, little direct study has yet been made of the conditions upon which the feeling of freedom is dependent. Tentatively, we may propose that persons feel most free when they perceive their environment as safe; when they perceive other people as accepting, trustworthy, and loving; and when they perceive themselves as competent and fundamentally good. This latter point is made because it seems likely that persons who regard themselves as good do not have to watch their own behavior carefully in order to make certain that no evil or dangerous behavior will emerge. Instead, they can permit themselves to be spontaneous. Spontaneity in expression and behavior is one of the forms in which the feeling of freedom manifests itself.[21]

BOREDOM

Boredom arises from doing repetitive, unchallenging work. It arises as a consequence of relationships with persons who lack spontaneity and who do not relate to us in ways that meet our needs for affection, understanding, or intellectual stimulation. Boredom arises when people do not actively choose what they will do, but instead permit their lives to be lived for them by social pressures to conform with rigid roles and concepts of respectability. Boredom is inevitable in human life, but there are

*Emotion and
Healthy
Personality*

healthy and unhealthy methods of coping with it. The unhealthy patterns include (1) permitting it to continue for indefinite periods of time without making an effort to understand its causes, and (2) impulsively seeking excitement or diversion without striving to understand the causes of boredom. For example, some people may drive automobiles at breakneck speeds simply to interrupt monotony. Others flee ennui by attending many movies, drinking too much liquor, staying "stoned" on marijuana or other drugs, watching television for long hours, or reading escape literature. Most of these are harmless as temporary palliatives, but they endanger one's health when they are the sole reaction to boredom. The healthier approach to boredom is to reflect upon one's life, to ascertain what one truly wants and the ways in which existence is failing to provide legitimate satisfaction. If persons are unable to diagnose their own needs, they are serving the interests of healthy personality by discussing their situation and personality with a friend or by seeking counseling.

AFFECTION AND TENDERNESS

Well-loved children feel and express affection for parents, siblings, friends, and animals. As they grow and become socialized to their sex roles, and ultimately their occupational and community roles, they can lose the capacity to feel affection and tender concern for others. Men of our culture especially appear to be subject to a "tenderness taboo." [22]

Their relationships with other men frequently are limited to reserved expressions of friendship or competition in work or in games. The male role, as socially defined, impels many men to regard affection and tender solicitude between men as evidence of homosexuality or effeminacy. Women are encouraged, by contrast, to be more open in experiencing and expressing their affection. There is evidence that such rigid differentiation between the sexes is breaking down in America and other Western countries, so that men can be softer, less aggressive, and more affectionate in their relationships with others, regardless of age or sex. From the perspective of healthy personality, such liberation from rigid sex roles is good for men, women, and children alike, and may even add

Healthy Personality

years to the typical male life expectancy. Affection is life-giving, both for the object of the affection and the one who is feeling and bestowing it.

IDENTIFICATION AND EMOTIONAL RESPONSES

Anyone can observe similarities in emotional habits within a family or between two close friends or spouses. A father and his sons may all display similar emotional responses to politicians, salespeople, women, and animals. A woman, before she became married, may have responded emotionally after the fashion of her mother and siblings; after several years of marriage, her parents and siblings notice she no longer feels about things the way she used to—she has changed. She has come to share some of the emotional habits of her husband, and he in turn has acquired many of hers, so that his former bachelor friends notice striking differences in him. He is no longer amused by the same things, angered or afraid of the same things, as when he was "one of the boys."

The mechanism responsible for the acquisition of emotional responses that resemble those of someone else is *identification*. Identification is a learning process by means of which one person models himself, herself after another. It may be a deliberate attempt to imitate the other person, or it may be an unconsciously purposeful emulation. It is not known whether emotional habits are acquired through direct identification or whether the similarity in emotional habits between two persons derives from identification with each other's values, expectancies, and attitudes. Nevertheless, it can be asserted that, either directly or indirectly, persons acquire certain of their emotional habits by means of identification.[23]

SOCIALIZATION AND EMOTIONAL RESPONSES

A sociologist or anthropologist observes that most members of a given social class or society share many emotional habits. These emotional responses differ, however, from typical emotional responses of people in other classes or societies. For example, the exposure of women's breasts arouses no erotic interest in an African tribesman, whereas it may excite a middle-class American man.

Part of the total socialization process—the efforts of

Emotion and Healthy Personality

parents, teachers, and others to mold and shape the typical personality for that society—is devoted to insuring that the growing children acquire the appropriate emotional habits. It is desired by the society that most members of a group perceive and interpret aspects of the world in a uniform way, and react with similar emotional responses. This uniformity is achieved in part through formal education—children know that pain and fear are associated with danger, and so their elders and instructors teach them to interpret many things as dangerous. It may also be achieved less formally through experiences within the family that have the effect of training most members of the society to react in a uniform way to certain classes of stimuli.

Expression and Control of Emotion

What do persons do when they have been provoked to emotional arousal? The alternative reactions of a person to emotional arousal are (1) immediate uncontrolled expression and release, (2) suppression of emotional behavior, and (3) repression of the emotional quality of experience.

IMMEDIATE EXPRESSION OF EMOTION

Immediate expression is the characteristic pattern among young children when they experience emotional tension. They laugh, cry, strike out, jump up and down, throw tantrums—in short, they appear to be almost out of control. It is as if their cerebral cortex has been dethroned from rational control over behavior and their entire organism is directed by "explosions" of subcortical brain structures, such as the hypothalamus.

On the positive side, immediate expression of emotional tension in this uncontrolled manner is effective in getting rid of the tension. Once it is given expression, the person is able to proceed in a more controlled and less tense way. On the negative side, immediate expression is undesirable, especially in an adult, because:

1. Society condemns uncontrolled expression of emotion in adults on a purely normative and moral basis. Adults who throw tantrums or who cannot control their

Healthy
Personality

emotions are viewed as immature, as persons who cannot be trusted with important responsibilities.

2. While expressing uncontrolled emotion, the person is out of touch with external reality. Persons out of touch with reality do not perceive the world with accuracy—indeed, they are not interested in the external world during the tantrum. Further, they do not protect other important values while in the throes of an "affective storm." They may break things that they value; they may say or do things that cost them their job, marriage, reputation.

SUPPRESSION OF EMOTIONAL BEHAVIOR

Emotional control is made possible through the gradually acquired ability of a person to choose responses to a situation (emotion-provoking or otherwise) that are compatible with the largest number of important values. This choosing in turn is predicated on the ability to postpone immediate responsiveness, to delay responding in order to allow time to reason, plan, or think. Young children cannot do this because they have not yet learned how, and because their nervous systems have not yet matured to the point where it is physically possible for them to tolerate tension and inhibit motor expression.

When the nervous system has matured to the point where delay and purposeful planning are possible, then suppression of emotional behavior becomes possible. There are no precise norms available for the age at which such control becomes possible or for the quantity of tension a person can be expected to tolerate without exploding into expressive behavior; however, it can be expected that the ability increases from infancy to maturity and then probably declines with approaching senescence.

Let us now examine some of the implications of emotion suppression for personality and physical health.

Physical Consequences of Emotion Suppression. When a person is provoked to emotional tension, widespread changes occur throughout the body in consequence of heightened autonomic nervous system activity. If expression is possible in the form of muscular activity, weeping, laughing, sexual behavior, then the physiological processes will shortly be restored to normal.

If no release is possible, if the person suppresses emo-

Emotion and Healthy Personality

tion for a long period of time, then the physical events that constitute part of the emotional response will be prolonged. If the prolongation is marked, it is possible that the functions and even the structure of inner organs may be permanently impaired. The field of psychosomatic medicine is devoted to study of the effects of emotionality on health.[24]

Psychological Consequences of Emotion Suppression. Suppressed emotional excitement interferes with rational activity. Reich coined the term *emotional plague* to describe the far-reaching impairments of logical reasoning and accurate perception produced by prolonged suppression of sexual and emotional tension. A paranoid dread of communists or a chronic belief that one is going to be sexually assaulted illustrate forms of emotional plague.

In addition to the effects on rational thinking, emotion suppression appears to interfere with the efficiency of skilled behavior. One cannot play the piano, repair machinery, or knit with efficient speed and dispatch when one is full of unexpressed fear, hostility, grief, or laughter.

Finally, it may happen that the cumulative effects of suppression may eventuate in such powerful tension that control becomes impossible; the person then explodes with more violent expression than would have been the case had that person reacted much earlier. Many persons have committed acts of destruction when they could no longer suppress conscious hostility.

Healthy Emotion Suppression. The capacity to suppress emotional expression and to delay immediate responsiveness is valued by moralists and also by personality hygienists. But the personality hygienist may differ from the moralist in that the hygienist affirms the value of the capacity to express emotional tensions just as much as the capacity to suppress them. The healthy personality displays neither immediate expression nor chronic suppression of emotion exclusively. Rather, the healthy personality displays a capacity to *choose* between the alternatives of suppression and expression. When it will not jeopardize important values, these people will express their feelings freely, laughing with gusto, crying without restraint, or expressing anger with vigor. If other values would be endangered by such emotionality, they are ca-

Healthy Personality

138

pable of suppressing their feelings and carrying on with whatever behavior was in process at the time of emotional arousal. In the long run, however, this regime of selective suppression and release insures that the persons' bodies and their ability to perform will not suffer the effects of prolonged emotion suppression and that they will not needlessly endanger their job, reputation, self-respect, and other important values by heedless emotional explosions. They can suppress when they choose, and they can let go when they choose—and it is they who do the choosing.

Unhealthy Emotion Suppression. Emotion suppression becomes unhealthy when it is prolonged for any reason. When persons chronically suppress their emotions, they generally do so because they fear the consequences of emotional expression. Fear of emotional expression is often irrational, based on overgeneralization from unpleasant occurrences in the past. Perhaps someone was severely punished, or lost a job, because of an emotional outburst. From this one event, the person may have generalized that all emotional expression is dangerous or bad. Thus the person comes to suppress feelings— though he or she is fully aware of them—without discrimination.

The longer-range consequences of chronic suppression may be psychosomatic illnesses (provided other necessary and sufficient causes are present), such as elevated blood pressure, mucous colitis, asthma, peptic ulcers, chronic fatigue (it consumes energy to suppress hostility and other strong feelings), muscular aches and pains, migrainelike headaches, impaired work and study efficiency, inability to concentrate, impaired reality contact, and impaired relationships with people who want their friends and loved ones to be able to express feeling. The chronic suppressor is often derogated as a "stick," "stone-face," or "iceberg"—someone who is "less than human."

REPRESSION OF EMOTIONAL TENSIONS

Persons are said to repress their emotions when they take active steps to avoid experiencing certain affects, and when, confronted by stimuli adequate to induce an emotional response, they deny (and believe their own denial) that they are experiencing emotion. Repression in the first instance is achieved by regulating one's life so that one will never encounter the objects known to induce feelings, and also by refusing to think about objects or events that might induce unwanted feelings. Repression in the second instance appears to be achieved by means of some form of self-deception or denial—as if the persons say to themselves, and believe, "I am not angry [afraid, sexy, amused]." In order to rid their awareness of the unwanted emotional tensions, they may think about things and perform tasks that induce feelings incompatible with the unwanted emotional tension. Thus, a small child, confronted by a fear-inspiring dog, might say, "Nice puppy"—puppies evoke tender feelings, not fear in the child. The nervous and timid speaker at a banquet, who is afraid he or she will be ridiculed, may address the audience as "My friends." If the speaker believes that they are friends, the fear will evaporate.

Repression occurs automatically and unconsciously, because the emotional tensions trigger off strong anxiety over the anticipated consequences of expressing them; too, the emotional tensions conflict strongly with persons' conscience and self-ideals—if they admitted they had these feelings, they might have to change their concepts of themselves, with accompanying losses in self-esteem.

In most, if not all, instances, professionals condemn repression of emotional tensions as unhealthy. The main reason for this condemnation lies in the fact that in spite of repression, the feelings exist—or at least the capacity to experience these feelings remains present and unchanged. When feelings have been provoked but are not recognized by the person, they produce both physical and psychological effects. In Chapter 4 we discussed some of the ways in which unconscious feelings (and needs) manifest themselves in thinking and behavior. In addition to the psychological consequences, repressed affects produce the same effects on the body as do consciously suppressed feelings, except that the person is not aware that he or she has these feelings.

Healthy Personality   When feelings have been repressed more or less successfully, it is not only the individual who is unaware of their presence. Other persons as well will not know how the person really feels. Thus, a husband may irritate his wife for years by certain of his habits. She, however, may have repressed her annoyance and hostility. Then, at some future date, she leaves him or becomes overwhelmed with uncontrollable rage at some trivial annoyance. Naturally, the husband is surprised and shocked. If she had openly vented her feelings, he might have altered his behavior easily and without complaint.

One of the most important tasks in psychotherapy and in the treatment of so-called psychosomatic illnesses is aiding patients to recognize their own feelings—to "un-repress" them, to experience and express them fully. This uncovering process generally is met with strong resistance on the part of the patient, however, for the experience of these feelings is threatening to security and to self-esteem.

FACTORS THAT PROMOTE CHRONIC SUPPRESSION AND REPRESSION OF EMOTION

In view of the fact that chronic suppression and repression of affect produce such unhealthy consequences, we shall inquire into some of the factors responsible for the adoption of these unhealthy patterns.

Dependency upon Others. When persons must depend upon others for the solution of their problems and the satisfaction of their needs, they are thrust into situations that can promote unhealthy suppression and repression. So long as they are in the dependent role and need the other person's good will, they must express nothing which will incur the displeasure of the other person. Thus, a child, an employee, or an inadequate person may have to withhold honest expression of feelings and express (or pretend to feel) only those that will improve his or her status in the eyes of the dominant one. Most of us have had the fantasy at one time or another of telling someone with whom we have been closely associated in a dependent role just how we really feel toward them. Some people, on achieving autonomy, wealth, or courage, come right out and express long-withheld feelings. Sometimes the dissolution of a dependency relationship will remove only the motives for suppression, so that persons vent feelings they have long been aware of. Sometimes, however, with the breakup of the dependency relationship, long-standing repressions will be undone, and persons will themselves be shocked and surprised at the feelings that well up for expression.

Excessively Strict Conscience and Self-ideal. Persons may chronically suppress or repress certain emotions not only for external reasons, such as avoiding rejection or criticism, but also to conform with demands of conscience. Persons may have acquired values that make their self-esteem contingent on the exclusion of certain feelings and emotions not only from behavior, but even from consciousness. They can accept themselves only as kind, pure, and strong, and so they must repress all those feelings that would produce guilt if they were recognized.

Rigid Role Definitions. Everyone learns a variety of social roles in order to live acceptably in society. Examples of roles include those associated with age, sex, occupation, and one's family position. Each role has strong social norms governing the experience and expression of emotion. For example, a physician is expected to appear calm in situations of illness and crisis, whereas a layperson or a patient can experience and express panic without social blame. Similarly, men in our culture are expected to appear stronger, more competent, and more in control of their emotions than are women (although these roles are changing through the influence of women's liberation advocates). Thus, men commonly feel ashamed if they experience tenderness, weakness and dependency, or the impulse to weep. The necessity to appear before others in conformity with conventional role definitions thus fosters suppression and repression of emotion. If a person cannot find opportunities to be "out" of these roles, in order to experience and express the feelings engendered by life happenings, then that person's roles are endangering his or her health.[25]

DEALING WITH EMOTIONAL EXPRESSION,
OR LACK OF IT, IN OTHERS

Healthy Personality Sometimes persons who themselves are uncomfortable with genuine emotional expression, especially of pain, embarrassment, or sorrow, find it necessary to avoid dealing with such expressions in friends, relatives, children, or others. This makes for non-genuine interactions, since both are pretending to be or feel some way that is not authentic. Someone with a poker face in the midst of an expression of deep emotional feeling on the part of another leaves that person with a feeling of being drastically misunderstood.

Rogers [26] has pointed out that concern for another's feelings is characteristic of a "person-centered" society. He has contributed a simple but effective way of assuring accuracy of communication of feeling through the "reflection of feeling." This is a useful technique in psychotherapy, as it is in all human relationships. One reflects back to the other the sensitive awareness of the other's feelings: "I know you are upset with me" or "You feel very angry, extremely angry." This technique of course requires that the "understander" be fully able to accept the feeling without shock or other negative, basic feelings. Because of the demonstrated difficulty in determining the nature of an emotion from the facial communication only, according to Izard, it seems even more important to make use of the reflection as a check on one's understanding of another person.

The temper tantrum is perhaps the most manipulative of all emotions, and although it is often thought of as characteristic of the "spoiled" child, it can also be found in the spoiled adult. Someone who learns to get his or her way through exaggeration of emotion becomes an emotional tyrant who does damage to his or her own emotional life as well as to that of others.

Healthy Personality and Emotion: An Overview

The dimensions of healthy personality are interrelated. The capacity to experience a broad range of emotion, and to control its expression, is most likely to be found in persons who have been competent at satisfying their basic needs, who have retained a firm grasp on reality, who have achieved a healthy "self-structure" (see Chapter 8), and whose relationships with other people are secure and authentic (Chapter 11). This suggests that if persons re-

Emotion and Healthy Personality

press their emotions or experience troubling emotional responses (such as irrational fears and manias), they should endeavor to improve their competence, their relationships with others, or their view of themselves. On the other hand, the work of behavior therapists has shown that people who complain of excessive anxiety or a specific phobia can be aided to live more fully by a direct attack upon the symptom itself. The techniques of "extinguishing" unwanted emotional responses do work, and they can make life more livable for a person who has been thwarted by hitherto uncontrollable fear or rage. We have helped patients of ours to overcome a fear of the opposite sex, of public speaking, of authority figures, by methods of classical conditioning and behavior modification, as well as through interviews aimed at encouraging patients to learn new skills, alter their self-concepts or self-ideals, and change their relationships with others in the direction of greater authenticity. Patients who have been helped in these ways attest that there is great joy and enlivenment in overcoming the repression of feelings, so that one is free to feel and to express such feelings; and there is comparable joy in being free of a hitherto uncontrolled emotional response that rendered life unendurable.

Some Existential Suggestions

Hardly anyone experiences the fullest range of emotion of which humans are capable. Not only does one's culture impose limits upon the experience and expression of emotion; one's own family will also influence which emotions are aroused and which will be expressed.

Because the expression of emotion is so important to both the quality of life and to health, it is important to reflect upon your own emotional habits. What situations provoke you to anger, for example? And to fear or anxiety? Both fear and anger can enrich life and foster growth, but irrational fears and rage can destroy the quality of existence.

Healthy Personality   If you are chronically in a fury about everything—if everyone's behavior seems imperfect, if their appearance angers you, if the slightest deviation from your view of perfection puts you into an ill-concealed rage—then your life might be enhanced if you could alter your expectations in reasonable ways. You should seek help to achieve better use of your emotional life.

If you are "running scared," it is possible that you view yourself as weaker and more helpless than is warranted; you might be able to challenge yourself to face those situations you dread and discover that you can cope.

Can you express your emotions without guilt or anxiety, and without being destructive to self and others? One of the most wholesome guarantors of health and *joie de vivre* is the freedom to express your feelings. If you are chronically suppressed and emotionally inhibited, it may be worthwhile to "let go" a little, to test whether it is really so dangerous to laugh, cry, become angry, or tender and affectionate. Encounter groups, if available and properly led, can provide persons with the opportunity to explore their possibilities for experiencing and expressing their genuine feelings.

Falsifying emotion can be a pernicious influence upon your life. Let the other people in your life know your authentic feelings toward them, especially those with whom you have a personal relationship (as opposed to a more formal role relationship; see Chapters 10 and 11 for the distinction). To be emotionally dishonest is to set the stage for estrangement from others and for self-alienation.

Furthermore, your sensitivity to others' emotions and your receptivity to their feelings, no matter how different from your own, can help your friends and those about you to grow and "become." Can you show understanding and acceptance of emotions that are strong and even sudden in their expression, or do such expressions frighten you and in turn discourage your friends from expressing themselves authentically?

In dealing with temporary, short-term explosions of feeling, such as in temper tantrums, can you wait them out sympathetically, showing understanding of the person's degree of upset—and yet not reward the child (or adult for that matter) by giving into what he or she wants just to gain quiet? One of the characteristics of good friendships and of good parenting is the freedom of the persons concerned to fully trust each other to express emotionality honestly and openly, especially when the emotional expression is not a particularly pretty one. At the same time, sharing another's joys and delights also facilitates depth in friendships and in parent–child relationships.

SUMMARY

Emotion is a quality of experience and an expressive quality of action. It is composed of strengthened feelings, positive or negative. When persons are stimulated to express emotion, their awareness, their behavior, and their physiological functioning all change.

There is no complete catalogue of emotional experience, but emotional expression is a kind of communication, and some "states" of emotion are identifiable by individuals and by those who associate with them: pleasure, depression, anxiety and dread, anger, weeping, humor, the experience of freedom, boredom, and affection and tenderness. The capacity to experience a broad range of emotion is an indication of healthy personality.

Our emotional habits are acquired through conditioning, through the learning of expectancies, and through identification with significant others in our lives.

Immediate uncontrolled expression of emotion and chronic suppression and repression are incompatible with healthy personality. The ability to suppress and express emotion selectively and to work through and understand one's own emotionality are the patterns of emotional control most compatible with healthy personality.

Growth-producing human relationships are facilitated by being authentically receptive and understanding of the other's emotional expression.

NOTES AND REFERENCES

1. I am limiting my discussion of emotion to those aspects relevant to understanding healthy personality. Students may benefit more from the discussion in this chapter if they review the chapter on feelings and emotions in any recent textbook on introductory psychology. See, for example,

Healthy Personality

R. Isaacson and M. Hutt, *Psychology: The Science of Behavior*, rev. ed. (New York: Harper, 1971), or M. E. Meyer (Ed.) *Foundations of Contemporary Psychology* (New York: Oxford, 1979).

2. J. B. Watson, "A Schematic Outline of Emotions," *Psychological Review*, 1919, Vol. 26, pp. 165–196.

3. K. M. B. Bridges, "Emotional Development in Early Infancy," *Child Development*, 1932, Vol. 3, pp. 324–341.

4. R. Plutchik, "Emotions, Evolution and Adaptive Processes," in M. B. Arnold (Ed.), *Feelings and Emotions* (New York: Appleton, 1970), pp. 3–22.

5. M. B. Arnold (Ed.), *Feelings and Emotions: The Loyola Symposium* (New York: Academic, 1970).

6. C. E. Izard, *The Face of Emotion* (New York: Appleton, 1971).

7. R. D. Laing and A. Esterson, *Sanity, Madness and the Family* (London: Tavistock, 1964).

8. A. Lowen, *Pleasure* (New York: Lancer, 1970); T. Szasz, *Pain and Pleasure: A Study of Bodily Feelings* (New York: Basic, 1957); A. Montagu, *Touching: The Human Significance of the Skin* (New York: Harper, 1972); W. Reich, *The Discovery of the Orgone: The Function of the Orgasm* (New York: Noonday, 1961), pp. 184–220; W. Schutz, *Joy* (New York: Grove, 1967). A discussion of zest is given in E. Schachtel, *Metamorphosis: On the Development of Affect, Perception, Attention, and Memory* (New York: Basic, 1959), Chapters 2 and 3.

9. J. F. T. Bugental, "The Far Edge of Despair," in D. R. Nevill (Ed.), *Humanistic Psychology: New Frontiers* (New York: Gardner, 1978).

10. C. D. Spielberger (Ed.), *Anxiety: Current Trends in Theory and Research*, Vol. 2 (New York: Academic, 1972).

11. Rollo May, *Power and Innocence: A Search for the Sources of Violence* (New York: Norton, 1972).

12. See S. Freud, *The Problem of Anxiety* (New York: Norton, 1936); R. May, *The Meaning of Anxiety* (New York: Ronald, 1950); P. Tillich, *The Courage to Be* (New Haven, Conn.: Yale U.P., 1952).

13. See J. Dollard, N. E. Miller, L. W. Doob, O. H. Mowrer, and R. R. Sears, *Frustration and Aggression* (New Haven, Conn.: Yale U.P., 1939); H. Cason, "Common Annoyances: A Psychological Study of Everyday Aversions and Irritations," *Psychological Monographs*, 1930, Vol. 40, No. 2 (Whole No. 132); I. Char-

NY, *Marital Love and Hate* (New York: Macmillan, 1972).

14. G. R. BACH and P. WYDEN, *Intimate Enemy: How to Fight Fair in Love and Marriage* (New York: Morrow, 1969).

15. This is the view of guilt held by Mowrer; see O. H. MOWRER, *The Crisis in Psychiatry and Religion* (New York: Van Nostrand Reinhold, 1960), Chapter 8. See also M. BUBER, *The Knowledge of Man* (New York: Harper, 1965), Chapter 6, "Guilt and Guilt Feelings."

16. F. J. SHAW, *Transcendence: A Theory of Man Transcending* (New York: Van Nostrand, 1966), Chapter 3.

17. W. A. PUTTICK, *A Factor Analysis Study of Positive Modes of Experiencing and Behaving in a Teacher College Population*, unpublished doctoral dissertation, University of Florida, 1964.

18. AVNER ZIV, *Humor in Education* (Paris: Education Press, 1979).

19. A. I. SOLZHENITSYN, *The Gulag Archipelago, 1918–1956. An Experiment in Literary Investigation I–II* (New York: Harper, 1973).

20. S. FREUD, "Wit and Its Relation to the Unconscious," in A. BRILL (Ed.), *The Basic Writings of Sigmund Freud* (New York: Modern Library, 1938); G. W. ALLPORT, *Pattern and Growth in Personality* (New York: Holt, 1961), pp. 292–294; J. H. GOLDSTEIN and P. E. McGHEE (Eds.), *The Psychology of Humor* (New York: Academic, 1972).

21. F. BARRON, "Freedom as Feeling," *Journal of Humanistic Psychology*, 1961, Vol. 1, 91–100. E. FROMM, *Escape from Freedom* (New York: Holt, 1941).

22. I. SUTTIE, *The Origins of Love and Hate* (London: Peregrine, 1963), pp. 86–100; J. BOWLBY, *Maternal Care and the Growth of Love* (London: Penguin, 1953); MONTAGU, op. cit.

23. O. H. MOWRER, *Learning Theory and Personality Dynamics* (New York: Ronald, 1950), Chapter 21; I. HENDRICK, "Early Development of the Ego," *Psychoanalytic Quarterly*, 1951, Vol. 20, pp. 44–61.

24. Considerable evidence shows that many illnesses arise following some "dispiriting" or demoralizing experiences, such as loss of a loved one. See S. M. JOURARD, *The Transparent Self* (New York: Van Nostrand Reinhold, 1971), Chapter 10; any medical textbook on psychosomatic

medicine, such as F. ALEXANDER, *Psychosomatic Medicine* (New York: Norton, 1950), that reviews the evidence on the influence of emotion on health.

25. W. REICH, *Character Analysis*, op. cit., Chapter 12; JOURARD, op. cit., Chapter 4, "Some Lethal Aspects of the Male Role."

26. C. R. ROGERS, *Carl Rogers on Personal Power* (New York: Dell, 1977).

7

THE BODY AND HEALTHY PERSONALITY

INTRODUCTION

People of the Western world have thought of the human being in dualistic terms, as a nonmaterial mind dwelling within a fleshly body subject to mechanical and biological laws. This tendency to split one's thinking about humans has led to thinking about them as actually split. Moreover, there has been a tendency in the West to depreciate the experience of body as a distraction from salvation and from compulsive work. Many devout people believe the body is a beast to be subdued and that a person should eliminate feelings, appetites, and emotions from life through assorted disciplines. This peculiar perspective upon our actual embodiment has led to a state of being that R. D. Laing calls unembodiment. *In its extreme form, as in schizophrenic sufferers, unembodiment is experienced as being not "in" one's body.[1] Many people appear insensitive to the way their bodies feel and function. Such somatic repression is a factor in physical as well as psychological illnesses.*

PRETENSE AND REPRESSION OF
SOMATIC PERCEPTION

One way for persons to rid themselves of the body is to pretend to be somebody else. In so doing, they are "in" neither their acts nor their bodies.[2] This pretense is abetted if they can obliterate the experience of the body. Such obliteration is carried out through repression of unwelcome somatic experience.

Persons will repress any dimensions of their experience that terrify them, or that have led to unbearable pain. Thus, when parents observe children masturbating, they may punish them severely. To avoid future pain, the children may repress all pleasurable body experience. It is as if they have divested themselves of their genitalia to avoid rejection by parents who cannot love a child with sexual urges.

Chronic repression of body experience must manifest itself in some way. Subjectively, repression of bodily experience is experienced as no experience, as a "hole" or an absence in the person's experience of being.[3] Thus, one person complained, "I feel numb, like a robot." Objectively, somatic repression manifests itself as character structure, or muscular armor—a peculiar configuration of muscular tonus and flaccidity, which results in a person's characteristic bodily posture, style of movement, and tone of voice. Somatic repression has profound effects upon autonomic functions of the body, such as breathing, elimination, circulation, and rest. Wilhelm Reich was adept at looking at a naked body and "reading" from it what impulses a person was repressing, and what kinds of conflicts the person likely had with parents.[4] There is no magic in this. If persons have been obliged to live dutiful, unpleasurable lives, and dare not experience, much less express, their rage and resentment, then they must hold the rage in. If you will clench your teeth, tighten your neck, pinch your buttocks tightly together, and then look in the mirror, you will improve your ability to empathize with others who are repressed.

A person who has repressed his or her sense of vitality may inhibit the vitality of another person who, before the encounter, felt "full of beans and juices," very much alive. On making contact with the unembodied one, the individual begins to feel diminished in vitality and zest for life.

I once had a colleague who affected me in this way. I would arrive at work in the morning, full of plans and projects, literally dancing with excitement. The colleague would simply appear in my room to discuss his work for the day, and I would notice my zest oozing away. This man affected me the way witches must have affected their victims. In fact, I became so fascinated with this man's effect on me that I began to observe my bodily states whenever I was involved in conversation or shared activity with all kinds of people. I noted that, when I was with my favorite people, I burst with vitality, I laughed, my life and actions had meaning and worth. When I was with certain others, my sense of life would flow out, leaving me drained, flaccid, and empty. I suspect that when this happens, I am in the presence of someone who wishes I were dead, or at least, less alive.

I believe we have enough technology available so that a physiologist could take various measurements of activation, using GSR, EEG, pulse and blood pressure measurements, and so on, and record the enlivening, calming, or deadening effects of one person upon another, below the threshold of immediate awareness.

The discipline known as kinesics enables a person to read bodies through characteristic gestures and postures. Thus, Birdwhistell [5] has been able to demonstrate how people's bodily posture may contradict as well as be congruent with their words. A person may say, "I'm open to your suggestions," while holding his or her body "closed," with arms folded, legs crossed, buttocks pinched—nothing could budge such a person from the pledge to sameness. This person may not be aware that the body is saying something which contradicts the words.

Healthy Personality

152

The way in which persons perceive, think about, and imagine their bodies to be (body image) is another way in which unembodiment, or peculiar ways of being embodied, may be revealed. Seymour Fisher and Sidney Cleveland [6] were able to show that persons who saw many things in the Rorschach ink-blot test that had shells, walls, or definite boundaries (high "barrier" scores) differed from persons who saw objects with blurry or shattered boundaries (high "penetration" scores), in styles of behavior and sickness. Thus, patients with cancer of internal organs had higher "penetration of boundary" scores and lower "barrier" scores than persons with skin cancers. Fischer and Cleveland propose that the responses to the ink-blot test reveal the way in which persons unconsciously imagine their bodies to be. However warranted their hypothesis, it does appear that what persons *believe* to be the case about their bodies becomes a self-fulfilling prophesy. I believe that we have been grossly unimaginative in our ways of thinking and theorizing about the body. The way physicians, anatomists, and physiologists see the body, from the outside, has become the way in which schoolchildren and finally adults experience their bodies. We do not yet have a phenomenological anatomy and physiology that would heighten our consciousness of our body from the living inside.

Another person, such as a parent, can take over the function of detecting one's own bodily states and estimating one's strengths and weaknesses. Children who are told that they are weak, hungry, or sleepy by loving, overprotective parents may lose the ability to construe their bodily states and possibilities. Consequently, they may eat when their parents say they are hungry and not be allowed to stop eating until the parents say "You have eaten enough." Such children may become very fat indeed, if their parents' estimates of their food needs do not coincide with what their bodies actually need for maintenance.

The Body and Healthy Personality

If persons underestimate the capacity of their bodies to endure stress and hardship, they may sicken or die long before it becomes a physiological necessity. "Outward Bound" training, for example, teaches young people that they can endure and survive well beyond limits they had been taught to believe were inflexible.

In short, one's body is very plastic indeed—it does what one expects of it. One should be careful what one expects of one's body, because that, likely, is what one will get. Clearly, the Olympic records of endurance and speed, which change periodically, show that we seldom expect enough of our bodies, but instead overestimate their fragility. Actually, our potential toughness and endurance have yet to be put to the ultimate test.[7]

If persons believe with utter certainty that they are going to die—for example, if they learn they have "terminal and inoperable cancer" or a fatal heart condition—then they are likely to *imagine*, even *wish themselves dead*, thereby hastening the advent of their physical demise. "Spiritual" death or imagined nonexistence become prophesies to which the organs and cells of the body respond. There is no way of estimating how many people die, as it were, through being hypnotized or persuaded by symbols and other people's nonverbal expressions that signify, "Your life is finished." I have even argued that cultural expectations about the "right" age to die function in the same way, as hypnotic suggestions or invitations to die; when persons reach eighty or ninety-five years of age, there is nothing for them to do, and they are expected to view each day as their last, thereby hastening their end.[8] If they remained involved with the pleasures and challenges of life, then death would take them by surprise. Kazantzakis tells of the nonagenarian who would flirt with the women at the village well. When asked, "Grandfather, tell us of life," he replied, "It is a glass of cool water." "Are you still thirsty then?" "Of course," said the old man, "I want to drink to bursting."

A challenge confronting scientists is to explore how "inspirited" states of being—being engaged in meaningful tasks and projects—are reflected in bodily states, such that immunity mechanisms are most efficient, the nuclei of cells do not release cancerous growth, and the mechanisms of wound healing and recovery from fatigue are most rapid and efficient.

Healthy Personality

154

Thus far, I have proposed that conventional upbringing in the Western world produces a partial sense of unembodiment in the majority of persons so socialized. This unembodiment manifests itself in interpersonal duplicity (playacting, pretense, role-playing, pseudo-self-disclosure) and in diminished awareness of one's own bodily being. I presented the hypothesis that unembodiment is the outcome of the repression of the early experience of pleasure and pain that young children undergo in the process of growing up, and that such repression produces a loss of a very important dimension of consciousness I call somatic perception.

Somatic perception refers to persons' awareness of the responses of their bodies to the situations in which they find themselves. They perceive the world somatically by "tuning in" on their bodily states as they go through life situations. Thus, their eyes see a person smiling; their ears hear that person say "I love you"; yet they continue to feel tense and on guard. They do not feel loved. Somatically, they are perceiving that all is not well; more information is called for before a less defensive posture will be taken. Reduction of the capacity for somatic perception appears to be a factor in the development of physical and psychological breakdown. If persons cannot discern how their relationships with others and their physical regimens are affecting them, they will continue to live in a way that generates harmful stress. They will be anesthetized to the pain and dispiritedness that are being generated, and hence will not change what they are doing in some life- and health-saving way. Consequently, unembodied persons *behave* their way into situations of stress and entrapment so overpowering that physical and psychological collapse are their only ways out. Medical care that does not seek to "reembody" persons and to sensitize their somatic perception is, at best, only first aid. Any sedating or tranquilizing medical care that further destroys the capacity for somatic perception is ultimately a menace to health, according to this perspective.

The Body and Healthy Personality

If it is true that conventional socialization results in unembodiment in varying degrees, then the salutary functions of certain embodying disciplines and techniques become understandable. These techniques will be discussed later in this chapter. Next let us look at the body from some technical perspectives.

The Body and Personality

THE BODY AND THE EGO

The *ego* is a term psychoanalysts use to designate the functions of coordinating and controlling the movements of one's body. One of the first signs that the ego has developed is infants' capacity voluntarily to control their movements.[9] Mastery of the outer environment and mastery of one's body appear to be correlated. Before such mastery has been achieved, body movements are global, undifferentiated, and not subject to voluntary control. Once such mastery has been achieved, the infant or child is able to suppress undifferentiated responses to events and respond in a discrete, skillful manner. The ability to coordinate eyes, hands, and mouth is probably among the first signs that the ego is developing.

As physical maturation proceeds, children acquire increasing mastery over the body and are able to perform according to their wishes. By the time persons reach adulthood, if suitably trained, they may be able to achieve such levels of bodily control as are found among athletes and dancers.

The loss of control of body functions and performances is experienced as catastrophic by most persons. Not to be the master of one's body—its movements, needs, and functions—is a loss of the most basic level of control. Adults who cannot control their appetite, or their bowel and bladder sphincters, will feel deep shame and will lose confidence in themselves.

Embodiment and the Self

THE BODY AND SECURITY

The unattractive person generally has a more difficult time winning friends and in being popular with the opposite sex, than the person with a pleasing appearance. One of my students demonstrated that a man judged attractive in appearance from his photographs

Healthy Personality

was overwhelmingly preferred as a prospective date by a group of college women over two men judged less good-looking.[10]

Several studies have demonstrated that a person's appearance may be a source of anxiety for that person. Paul Secord and Sidney Jourard showed that measures of the degree to which people liked their bodies were negatively correlated with measures of anxious body preoccupation and security. In other words, the more persons accept their bodies, the more secure and free from anxiety they feel. Persons with a high measured degree of anxiety tended to be dissatisfied with their bodies.[11]

Anxious overconcern with the body is called *hypochondriasis*. Hypochondriacs are individuals who are continually preoccupied with their health. They make the rounds of doctors' offices and dose themselves regularly with laxatives, vitamin pills, and sedatives. Hypochondriacal anxiety is a substitute for, or a displacement of, anxiety that derives from other sources: repressed hostility, sexual difficulties, or achievement problems. The hypochondriac evidently finds it less threatening to worry about health than to think realistically about other problems.

Persons may become excessively concerned about their appearance. This is most likely to occur among persons who use their appearance to gain acceptance from others, to enhance their social status, or to attract attention. The name *narcissistic overconcern* seems appropriate to describe this pattern. Such a person will become panic-stricken if a wrinkle, gray hair, or change in weight appears.

Hypochondriasis and narcissistic overconcern both may be viewed as unhealthy responses to the appearance and functions of the body. They are unhealthy for a variety of reasons: They fail to solve the problems basically responsible for the anxiety in the first place. Furthermore, while these persons concentrate so much attention on themselves and their bodies they neglect other concerns of importance to healthy personality, for instance, productive work and healthy relationships with other people.

Reasonable concern for one's health and appearance is

compatible with healthy personality, but reasonable concern does not place other values in jeopardy. If individuals with healthy personalities become physically ill, they will take the steps necessary to restore or improve health, but then they will turn their attention to other matters. Furthermore, they will live in accordance with a habitual health regime—adequate diet, rest, and exercise—that maintains their health without requiring too much conscious attention. They will take whatever steps are necessary for them to look their best, and then they will take their appearance for granted. They do not rely totally on their appearance for successful living.

THE BODY AND SELF-ESTEEM

A high degree of self-esteem means that persons accept themselves as worthy. A number of studies have shown that self-esteem is highly correlated with a positive attitude toward one's body. In other words, persons who accept their bodies are more likely to manifest high self-esteem than persons who dislike their bodies.

One reason for this correlation lies in the fact that the self-ideal includes a set of ideals pertaining to the appearance of the body, the so-called *body-ideal*. All persons have a more or less clear concept of how they want to look. If their bodies conform in dimensions and appearance with their concept of an ideal body, they will then like their bodies. If their bodies deviate from their body-ideals, they will tend to reject and dislike their bodies.

In one study of college women, it was found that the ideal body proportions (which all women in the sample shared) were 5 feet, 5 inches tall; weighing about 120 pounds; and 35 inches, 24 inches, and 35 inches for bust, waist, and hips, respectively. The women liked their own dimensions if they coincided with these ideals and disliked them increasingly as their bodies deviated from them. The actual measurements of the women were slightly larger than these ideals, on the average—except for bust size, where the average size was slightly smaller than the ideal.

Healthy Personality A comparable study of college males showed that acceptance of the body was related to *large size*. The

women all wanted to be slightly sma[...]
than they actually were, but the me[...]
larger size; they wanted to be ta[...]
shoulders and chests.[12]

It is evident that the body-ideal[...]
these studies are closely related to [...]
of an *ideal body*.

THE BODY-IDEAL AND THE IDEAL BODY

Each society has its idiosyncratic standards of personal beauty.[13] The Bushman of the Kalahari Desert, for example, esteems enormous hips and buttocks on a woman, whereas in America the desired hip measurements are much slimmer. The American woman wants to have large (but firm) breasts, a small waist, and narrow hips, and she wants to be relatively tall. In days gone by, the American glamor girl was considerably heftier than our present beauties. Old pictures of burlesque queens look to the modern eye like advertisements for a reducing salon.

The cultural concept of an ideal body has consequences for healthy personality, because the cultural ideal influences the personal body-ideal and congruence of the actual body with the body-ideal helps to determine self-esteem. If a person in our society is not able to conform with prevailing ideal body concepts, he or she may face problems growing out of diminished self-esteem. If the ideal body concepts in the society are highly restrictive and difficult for many people to conform with, the implication is that *many* people will suffer loss of self-esteem.

The widespread dread that many people have of aging may be an outgrowth of both the rigid concept of an ideal body and the role of bodily appearance in gaining recognition. Although a rational degree of concern for appearance is compatible with personality health, too much concern indicates that the individual's self-esteem is founded on *too narrow a base*. Under optimum conditions, an individual will predicate his or her self-esteem on a variety of grounds, for example, achievement, social status, ethical behavior. Attractive appearance is thus only one of many determiners of self-esteem. The

The Body and Healthy Personality

healthy personality can face the inevitable changes in appearance associated with aging without a loss of self-esteem. He or she does not feel that when youthful beauty is gone, so goes personal worth. The healthy personality believes, in the words of a twelve-year-old girl at a summer camp, "After all, beauty is only skin. Be a beautiful *person*, and don't worry so much about how you look."

SOME PROBLEMS RELATED TO THE CULTURAL
CONCEPT OF THE IDEAL BODY

The prevailing concept of the ideal body is adopted by most people as their personal body-ideal. This is the source of many somatic concerns.

Obesity. The most common difficulty people have with their appearance in America is obesity. This is also a health problem, for overweight people are more susceptible to disease than thinner people. But the cosmetic aspects of obesity are just as acutely worried about as the physical health aspects. America is one of the few countries in the world where overweight is a public health problem, where food is abundant, but a slender body is a cultural value.

Obesity is primarily the result of eating too much. Overweight people seem unable to maintain their food intake at a level that will enable them to lose weight. When a person wants to stop some behavior pattern but finds that will power is ineffective, it is evidence that unconscious motives of great strength lie behind the behavior. The overweight person is overeating for reasons other than hunger.

Clinical studies of chronically overweight people have shown that they have unhealthy personalities. They may, for example, be unable to derive satisfaction from their work. They may be starved for love. Rather than live with no "highs," they resort to a very primitive type of satisfaction—that provided by a rich meal.

Obese persons are not unlike chronic alcoholics in that they are addicted to a practice that harms them at the same time that it relieves anxiety and provides immediate gratification. Like alcoholics, obese persons might make daily renewed vows to "taper off," but they never seem

Healthy Personality

to achieve this end. In some cities, groups of obese people—Weight Watchers—organize as do the members of Alcoholics Anonymous; they are all dedicated to the aim of reducing, and they lend each other moral support in adhering to reducing diets. Such groups are probably the most effective means for achieving and maintaining a weight loss. However, unless the conditions, medical or psychological, responsible for the excessive appetite are removed, persons will be obliged to remain dependent upon their group membership in order to preserve their weight loss once it has been achieved.[14] This is not an unhealthy dependency.

Skinniness. Just as we deplore fatness in our society, so do we pity the "skinny" person. Chronic underweight resulting from undernourishment is a fairly simple malady to remedy if suitable food is available. But many persons are thin in spite of a sizable caloric intake. There are usually reasons for inability to put on weight, for example, overactive thyroid glands or a finicky appetite; but these may derive from more basic psychological causes. An intensive personality diagnosis may disclose many unhealthy personality traits in the chronically thin person. In such instances, psychotherapy may produce as a side effect a desirable increase in weight. Sometimes simply changing the amount of exercise that the person takes will suffice to stimulate appetite and promote a desirable gain in weight.

Breast Cultivation. Men in our society are highly breast-conscious, and many men equate sexual attractiveness in a woman with a prominent bosom. Because most women want to be attractive to men, they consider a flat bust to be a handicap. The reasons for this cultural emphasis on the breasts are not readily determined. Some anthropologists and psychoanalysts believe it is a derivative of painful weaning experiences undergone by male children in our society. Probably, however, the reasons are more complex.

Nevertheless, many women want to have prominent breasts, and if they have not been naturally endowed with them, they may strive to cultivate them by assorted exercises such as are advertised by health clubs, or they will wear brassiere padding of one kind or another.

The Body and Healthy Personality

There is nothing intrinsically unhealthy in a woman who wears "falsies" in order to appear buxom. Personality health is assessed in terms of a number of different criteria, including what the person does to, with, or for her body. So long as males deem breasts to be an index of attractiveness, then women who wish to attract male attention are justified in doing all that is practicable to gain that end.

Noses. We even have rigid cultural ideals pertaining to noses. The ideal nose is not the majestic protuberance of a Cyrano de Bergerac or the proud, delicately curved sweep of an aquiline "beak." Instead, it must, at least in the woman, be a short, medium-width, uptilted "snub" so that an onlooker can see the nostrils. This, obviously, is a Caucasian ideal that does not grant beauty to many Americans. Many women feel their facial beauty is marred because their nose differs from this stereotype, and so they undergo plastic surgery to achieve the valued snub. Whether or not "nose-bobbing" is a healthy thing to do depends on its consequences for the total personality. Some persons may undergo a healthy personality change following the operation, whereas others may go through life after such an operation feeling they are fakes.

Facial Wrinkles. The appearance of wrinkles in the facial skin and on the neck is an inevitable part of aging. Yet many, women especially, become panic-stricken at the first appearance of a wrinkle. This panic derives from a dread of being old and from the cultural over-emphasis on the importance of appearance as a basis for security and self-esteem.

The person who panics at wrinkles and goes to any length to regain, at age forty, the complexion of a sixteen-year-old, is an unhealthy person. Such an individual might well seek to find more stable sources of self-esteem than facial appearance.

Genitalia. People have all kinds of problems in connection with their sexual organs. Some men feel they are inferior if they have what seem to be small genital organs. There are cases on record where an entire neurotic personality structure began from the belief that the sex organs were smaller than those of other men. There is no connection between "manliness" and the size of the genitalia.

Many people in our society are prudish about, almost ashamed of, the reproductive and eliminative functions of their bodies. They become panic-stricken at the prospect of being seen nude. Some may actually avoid a medical examination if it requires that the genitalia be exposed. Indeed, their concept of their own genitalia and those of the opposite sex may be autistic. These unreal concepts may involve notions that the female organs are dangerous and castrating or that penises are destructive weapons. Some women may acquire attitudes of resentment and shame over their menstrual functions and needlessly isolate themselves through the duration of their periods—as is done in some primitive societies.

Muscle Cultivation. In response to the cultural ideal of a muscular male, many sedentarily occupied men undergo strenuous weight-lifting and body-building courses to become visibly muscular. There is nothing inherently healthy or unhealthy in such efforts. They are healthy if they result in an improvement of appearance, vigor, and health without loss of other values. They are unhealthy if they are expressions of unnecesary compensation or overcompensation for other kinds of deficiencies and inferiorities.

Body Image and Healthy Personality

A HEALTHY BODY-IDEAL

The body image comprises persons' body-ideal and their body concept. Each of these will be discussed in relation to healthy personality.

A person's body-ideal can be assessed with respect to its healthy or unhealthy implications. An unhealthy body-ideal is one that is rigid and unchanging and that includes dimensions impossible for the individual to conform with. Thus, we observe an unhealthy body-ideal in a woman who, at age forty, feels she is ugly and unattractive because she no longer looks the way she did when she was nineteen. If she devotes extreme attention to her appearance to the neglect of other values, her body-ideal is unhealthy. Similarly, a young man with a slender phy-

The Body and Healthy Personality

sique who rejects his body appearance because he is not heavily muscled and proportioned like a football hero may be said to have an unhealthy body-ideal.

A healthy body-ideal is one that is not too discrepant from the cultural concept of an ideal body but that is *revised by the person to make allowances for individual, idiosyncratic dimensions and features.* With increasing age, healthy personalities will modify their body-ideals, so that they can continue to regard themselves as reasonably attractive at each stage of life. They do not aspire after an impossible (for them) degree of beauty. Rather, at each stage of life, they strive to look their best and then let the matter drop, in order to attend to other important concerns.

THE BODY CONCEPT AND
HEALTHY PERSONALITY

A person's body concept includes everything the person believes about the structure, capabilities, and limits of his or her body. As with any other concept—one's concept of other people, of animals—the body concept may be accurate or inaccurate, complete or incomplete. An accurate body concept is important for achieving healthy personality.

Accuracy of the body concept is achieved by all of the means employed to arrive at reality-tested knowledge in general: through observation, through continual verification of conclusions, and through contact with reliable authorities and sources of knowledge. But many persons have been taught erroneous beliefs about diet, health requirements, and the like. Further, a person may become so alienated from the body (as part of the more general process of self-alienation) that the person loses the capacity to "listen" to the body, the capacity for somatic perception.

Thus, some people may fail to recognize that inadequate diet, lack of exercise, insufficient rest, and excessive self-indulgence are gradually weakening their bodies. To the extent that a person has knowledge of the effects of various things on health, then to that extent the person's *Healthy* body's welfare is his or her own responsibility. In soci- *Personality* eties where medical knowledge is not available, people may have erroneous beliefs about the causes of health and of illness. Consequently, one may observe that entire sectors of a population suffer from some chronic ailment that they all accept as "natural," as part of the scheme of living, for instance, rickets or TB. It is only from the standpoint of the contemporary scientific concept of the body that it becomes possible to make judgments about how healthy (or sick) an entire society might be.

Some overprotected people grow up ignorant of the process of reproduction; a nineteen-year-old student of mine believed that menstruation only occurred in virgins; once a woman engaged in sexual relationships, she stopped menstruating. She couldn't discuss sexual questions with her mother, and she was too embarrassed to talk about sex with her better informed girlfriends.

Aging persons with false pride may misjudge their strength and endanger their health through overexercise. But just as persons may overestimate their bodies' capacity, so may they underestimate it. We are all tougher than we have been led to believe.

PERSONALITY, THE BODY, AND HEALTH

Personality refers to the characteristic ways in which an individual experiences and acts in life situations. Action affects not only the external environment, but also the health of the body.

A Physical-Health-Promoting Personality. The meaningful question to ask is "What regimen, what ways of behaving in the world will promote health?" The most obvious answer to this question relates to such matters as diet, rest, and sensible exercise. People who have been adequately educated in general hygiene will follow a diet that maintains health, energy, and weight; they will care for their teeth; they will sleep enough to restore their energy; and they will exercise enough to keep fit.

A more subtle factor in the production and maintenance of physical health is morale, or "spirit." Increasing evidence indicates that when persons find their lives challenging and satisfying, their bodies work better and they resist infectious illness better. Meaningful work, enjoyable leisure, love and friendship are inexpensive health insurance.

The Body and Healthy Personality

An Illness-Yielding Personality. A minority of the population is afflicted with the vast majority of illnesses that come to the attention of physicians. Defective heredity or a weak constitution only partly explains this high incidence of recurrent illness. We must look as well into the ways of life of these people with a talent for sickening.

Studies of the frequently ill show they share many traits. Among other things, it is found that they may simply not take care of themselves; that is, they do not eat, sleep, or exercise sensibly. Another, less obvious, factor in frequent illness is stress. Many people encounter more stress in everyday life than is objectively necessary. They find everyday interpersonal relationships lacking in satisfaction, and, indeed, positively stressing. Demanding roles are a source of such stress. If persons must present themselves to others as something that they are not—if they are obliged to seem friendly when they are unfriendly, or if they are obliged to hide their real feelings and wants from others—then every moment spent in the presence of others is stressing. It is as if they are traveling incognito, with their true identity hidden. They feel that if they are "found out" by others, terrible harm will befall them. Consequently they trust no one and keep their guard up. Other people by their very existence then function as stressors, adding to the stress of daily life.

Another factor in frequent illness is an overdeveloped sense of duty. Persons who feel obliged by their consciences to keep working at unsatisfactory jobs or to stay involved in unrewarding relationships are actively creating the conditions for their own illness. Periods of being sick may thus function as periods of respite from a dispiriting way of life. If they could change their work or their ways of relating even slightly, they would become ill less often. A brief vacation from work or family is usually less expensive than a stay of equal length at a hospital—and the vacation may forestall the illness.

Transcending "Handicap"

Healthy Personality

Persons may become "handicapped" by accident or by disease. They may lose a limb, their sight, or their strength. Whatever the impairment, the persons' capacity to come to terms with their environment has not been eliminated completely. A blind person can still be sensitive to all the properties of the physical environment save those mediated by vision.

HEALTHY REACTIONS TO HANDICAP

When a person suffers some affliction that results in a handicap, there may be, quite naturally, some rather devastating emotional reactions. These include a sense of hopelessness, anxiety about the future, and a loss in self-esteem.

Once the fact of handicap has been accepted by the individual, however, the healthy thing to do is to make an assessment of the residual capacities of the body and the person's goals in life. If the person's goals remain fixed, then he or she must experiment to find new ways of reaching those goals. Thus, a professional dancer, following the amputation of a leg, may wish to continue in the profession. The dancer will be obliged to acquire an artificial leg and practice until he or she once again can move with skill and grace.

It is probably easier for persons to retain their goals and seek new ways of achieving them than to change their goals. It is common for handicapped persons to feel hopeless and sorry for themselves, but with resolve, courage, and encouragement, they can find new ways to engage in active life. The most helpful people in rehabilitation work are those who have themselves been handicapped and have found the strength to overcome passive dependency and self-pity.

UNHEALTHY REACTIONS TO HANDICAP

Once blindness, crippling, or debilitating disease have afflicted a person, it is natural that the person's life will be thrown into chaos. Plans for the future will have been disrupted. It becomes a physical impossibility for the person to exploit former sources of satisfaction. If personal security and self-esteem have been dependent upon certain kinds of activity that are now precluded, then his or her life will seem empty and futile indeed. An athlete may become very depressed when a heart ailment makes it necessary to give up active sports. Someone whose self-esteem is predicated primarily on physical beauty

The Body and Healthy Personality

will see little point in living, following an accident that leaves that person with unsightly scars.

The reactions of depression and self-pity are inevitable when handicap occurs. What we are interested in here is the person's reactions to the emotional responses. The healthy reactions already have been described. The most common unhealthy reaction is resignation. Resignation to handicap means giving up, or "digging in" for a life devoid of satisfaction. When resignation occurs, and lasts for more than some period of time, say six months to a year, the resigner may be deriving some kind of enjoyment from the affliction and the power it affords. The person may make claims on intact people, in accordance with the idea, "Since the world has handed me such a dirty deal, I am entitled to a lot of support and consideration from others." [15] Many physically handicapped persons, however, have provided our culture with superb examples of the healthy personality through the courageous manner in which they have been able to integrate their tough physical problems into a fully functioning philosophy of life.

A man began to have "epileptic" seizures some years ago. They were intense, grand-mal convulsions, such that he frequently broke his hands as he thrashed about during the period of unconsciousness. Over a period of years, the medications to control the seizures elevated his blood pressure and damaged his kidneys. It appeared he was going to die from kidney failure or from circulatory failure.

Two psychologists undertook to train this man, through correspondence, to recognize his "auras" and to engage in actions that might forestall his seizures. The frequency of his losses of consciousness with convulsions was dramatically reduced, as was his need for sedating, anticonvulsant medications. Their hypothesis was that once the man had his first seizure, and showed the characteristic "spikes" on his EEG tracing, he became the subject of a hypnotic, brainwashing onslaught of suggestion, as if his doctors were saying,

Why, you lost consciousnes and had a seizure. You are a sufferer from epilepsy. Never mind, there is no shame connected with this. Julius Caesar was an epileptic, Shakespeare and Jesus probably were, and of course Dostoyevsky was. But you are lucky. Advances in medical science have made it possible for us to control seizures with some powerful drugs. Trust us, and put yourself in our hands. Of course, you may feel sleepy, and your gums may get puffy, but if you are careful to take your medicine regularly, you can live a normal life.

It is difficult to resist such a powerfully seductive invitation to view oneself as helpless, with no power to prevent the loss of consciousnes and the seizure; in short, to become dependent upon drugs, to become passive in order to let outside agencies control bodily happenings. There is reason to suspect that many people deemed "epileptic" are leading drugged lives, rather than being helped to find ways of mobilizing their strength and wits in order to stay conscious and nonconvulsing.

Some Approaches to Re-embodiment

At the beginning of this chapter various manifestations of unembodiment, of the loss of a keen awareness of one's body, were spoken of. Clearly a health-giving way of living in and with one's body calls for such awareness. Next we will discuss ways that have been employed by teachers of body awareness and control to "re-embody" their pupils.

PHYSICAL CONTACT

We have had a puritanical attitude toward physical contact in the United States and northern Europe. Touching, embracing, and holding hands all appear to be restricted to relationships between parents and young children or between lovers and spouses. In Latin countries, such as France or Italy, and in Asiatic and African countries, it is more common to see men holding hands as they walk down a street or embracing upon greeting one another. Physical contact is given more meanings there than as a prelude to sexual arousal or an expression of parental concern, as has been the case in our culture.

We appear to observe strong taboos relating to touching, yet touching and massage are direct ways to awaken a dormant sense of embodiment.

Jourard conducted a study of touching among college students, their parents, and their friends. Several hundred students were asked to show, on a questionnaire, the areas of their bodies on which touches had been exchanged with their mothers, fathers, closest same-sex friend, and closest friend of the opposite sex. The data, shown in Figure 1, indicate that not a great deal of touching went on between these students and their parents and their same-sex friends. With the opposite-sex friend, considerably more touching was exchanged, presumably an expression of affection and erotic caressing. But the data showed that many of the students tested did not have a lover and were virtually "out of touch" with the people in their lives. These findings suggest that many Americans may be starved for sensual physical contact without being aware of what they are missing.

The experience of total body massage (not just a back rub) slowly and sensuously conducted can produce extreme relaxation, and a softening of the tense "muscular armor" from which many people suffer. Esalen Institute, the growth center at Big Sur, California, pioneered in introducing such massage to a larger public. Bernard Gunther's books *Sense Relaxation* and *What to Do Till the Messiah Comes* are readable accounts of ways to relax another person through massage, and to heighten one's capacities to sense the world through touch as well as taste and smell. Physical contact is coming gradually to be incorporated into the helping repertoires of psychotherapists, in both the psychiatric and psychological professions, in recognition of the fact that problems of a psychological nature occur to an embodied person, and hence have somatic concomitants that can be treated directly.[16]

ROLFING

Ida Rolf, an extraordinary physical therapist, developed a technique for altering posture by means of deep manipulation of the entire body musculature, muscle by muscle. The purpose is to soften the fascia, those membranes that sheathe each muscle fiber in the body. The fascia become tightened and constrict muscles into chronic tension as a consequence of blows, emotional stress, and occupation-linked postural defects, such as the forward droop of the head found in many scholars. The configuration of muscle spasm and flaccidity that defines a person's characteristic posture pulls the skeleton out of alignment, so that excessive energy is consumed in standing, sitting, or walking. "Rolfers" believe that the change in posture brought about by this "structural integration" technique will improve sleep, energy level, elimination, sexuality, and overall health.

I received a course of Rolfing treatments and found that the pressure of knuckles and elbows upon muscles (in order to stretch the fascia) is painful, but not unbearable. My posture was improved by the realignment of the musculature of my thighs, back, and abdomen, but since my posture and overall health were good before Rolfing, I cannot notice any dramatic changes; however, in some

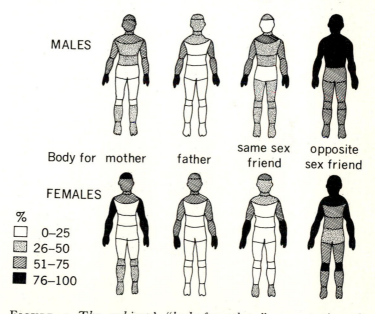

FIGURE 1. The subjects' "body-for-others," as experienced through amount of touching received from others. Percentages are based on N = 168 males and 140 females. The darkest portions signify that from 76–100 per cent of the subjects reported being touched by the target person in question on the body region indicated.

colleagues and friends with bad posture and health, the alterations in appearance have been quite noticeable. They stand taller and are more energetic and more coordinated in their movements.[17]

DIET AND FASTING

People typically eat without consideration of what they need for optimum nourishment or for full consciousness of body and world. Excessive eating is a sedative, insuring that persons will not feel the impact of their life styles upon them. Fasting has played a crucial role in every religious tradition and every discipline that aims at enlightenment. Avoiding food for periods ranging from a day to a month or longer will result not only in some loss of weight, but also in heightened somatic perception and keener senses of touch, taste, and smell. In my own experiences at fasting, I have gone no longer than six days without food; I completed a partial fast of forty days, however, limiting my nourishment to vegetable and fruit juices. The fasting was not unlike a trip to another culture—it gave me a changed perspective upon the situation within which I had been enmeshed.

Many persons in recent years have begun to experiment with vegetarian diets, with organically grown foods, with foods that have not been preserved with chemicals. Such intelligent concern with one's nourishment is quite compatible with healthy personality, and it certainly contributes to the experience of re-embodiment.

HATHA YOGA

In the West, physical bulkiness, with large, prominent musculature, has long been a masculine ideal, and such robustness has been praised in popular magazines and valued by women in their men. Heavy musculature has been cultivated by violent exercise, vigorous calisthenics, and comparable feats of endurance. One function of such heaviness (not obesity, just heavy musculature) is to decrease sensitivity to pain and to enhance endurance. In the East, perhaps because patterns of nourishment have been different, slenderness is more the rule. The disciplines of Hatha yoga have been employed in India for several thousand years as a way to bring the body under more

Healthy Personality

control, so that meditation and contemplation will not be obstructed by an insensitive, or a tense, uncomfortable body.

Hatha yoga is one part of the Hindu religion and is one of the means of achieving the experience of "union of inner and outer," of dissolving the ego and unifying awareness. In the West, Hatha yoga has been undertaken by many, not for religious purposes so much as for exercise to stretch and relax the musculature and produce vigor by releasing energy contained in chronic body postures. Hatha yoga comprises several hundred positions into which one gently folds or stretches the body to the accompaniment of slow, regular breathing. As in all things, a person can only enter fully into one of the yoga postures by "letting go" the muscular commitment to the chronic postures of the body generated by the person's life style. Thus, one position entails bending over, clasping the calves or ankles, to place one's face against one's knees. In the beginning, a person may only be able to clasp the backs of the knees and bend half over. In time, with gentle pressure at the limit of the bend, the person may enter more fully into the position. When an entire repertoire of postures is practiced daily, the person does indeed despecialize the body so that it becomes more limber and better able to sustain diverse forms of effective action.

Body inflexibility and insensitivity are types of over-specialization of one's body in adjustment to a chronic life style. Techniques like Hatha yoga foster a letting go, a metaphoric "erasure" of the muscular and postural configuration that makes up one's character, wiping out the traces of one's way of living, the effects of one's usual roles and projects upon one's body and ways of experiencing the world. Old yogis have surprisingly unlined faces and pliable bodies because of assiduous practice of the postures, with the attendant despecialization of the body.[18] Hatha yoga appears to be a means of producing the effects that Rolfing, does, but the yoga students are despecializing themselves, rather than giving themselves into the hands of the Rolfer.

The Body and Healthy Personality

The martial arts of attack and defense that originated in China, Korea, and Japan call for a rigorous program of discipline and exercise. The beginner must learn to control breathing, remain calm and balanced, and concentrate his or her power in sudden blows, kicks, and slashes with the side of the hand. Although one may wonder why a person would want to learn arts of killing or maiming others through the use of hands and feet, the learner is more fully embodied after the training than before it. In fairness, it must be said that teachers of these arts are always concerned to teach their pupils never to attack, only to defend, to use their power to conserve, not to destroy life.

BIOENERGETIC ANALYSIS

As noted in Chapter 1, Alexander Lowen and his associates have developed a set of exercises designed to identify muscle groups in the body that are chronically tense—the so-called muscular armor that Wilhelm Reich described. Lowen is a practicing psychiatrist, and he developed his physical techniques as adjuncts to the traditional conversational methods of conducting psychotherapy. He had studied with Reich, who, as we now know, was a genius, and adept at seeing how life-depleting ways of existing were revealed in stereotyped ways of acting and in rigid musculature.

Lowen puts the patient into various physical postures that stress the body and asks the patient to hold the position until a tremor comes. Often a patient will spontaneously begin weeping, or become angry, or recall some painful or humiliating event from the past, as he or she enters the diagnostic postures. The purpose of the techniques is to release taut muscles and long-repressed patterns of emotional expression. For example, Lowen may ask a patient to scream, "no, no, no" very loudly, kicking the bed on which the person is lying with great vigor. Or he may ask an inhibited person to strike a mattress with a tennis racquet. These procedures, together with the diagnostic postures, aim at bringing a person's consciousness of the body into a more unified

Healthy
Personality

state, so that the bodyless self and an unconscious body are unified in action and in experience.[19]

Somatic Specialization and Despecialization

The human beings' peculiar genius among living forms, the trait that enabled them to prevail while dinosaurs and other creatures became extinct, is their peculiar lack of specialization. When environments change, inflexible organisms die off. Conventional upbringing and life style encourage a person to become overly adapted to some fixed range of environmental challenges. A person living a sedentary, scholarly life, for example, may become fat, with his or her head jutting forward; someone who works at a machine calling for a strong right arm may develop monstrous biceps in that arm, whereas the left remains the usual size.

Sickness, both physical and psychological, can stem from overadaptation to an environment or culture. Besides so-called occupational diseases, produced by the stresses peculiar to given occupations, there are the symptoms brought about by change in environment. When a person's resources have been committed to coping with one set of demands and challenges, that person may not readily uncommit them to respond to challenges coming from another sector of life. Thus, many persons become sick when they change jobs, neighborhoods, and even family status. The neurotics whom Freud treated were persons overly specialized to survive within the structure of their family of origin. When they were asked to leave home, to start another family, they were unable to despecialize themselves from the role of son and daughter in order to take on new roles of husband or wife.

There is a real sense, then, in which various psychotherapies and the techniques for re-embodiment are despecializing procedures, making it possible for persons to let go their somatic "recall" of the past—to forget their past *somatically*—in order to learn how to act effectively in the present. Memory resides in the muscles, joints, and viscera as much as in the brain cells. Thus, the methods of yoga, Rolfing, fasting, and meditation all are approaches to the erasure of the past, as it is recorded in the musculature and habitual patterns of physiological functioning.

These techniques also function as means to alter one's usual way of being aware of self and the world. We are usually involved in various life projects, such as the pursuit of our profession; and in various interpersonal roles, for example, the role of son to parents, student to teacher, and man to woman. These are commitments of our "embodied" consciousness that influence the way the world appears to us and the way we experience ourselves. Our projects and our roles represent the specialized way in which we appear to ourselves and others in the world. When the somatic aspect of this specialization is "wiped out" so that one truly becomes *no one*, it is possible to re-enter one's old ways with more vigor and with new perspectives, and it is also possible to begin disengaging from chronic roles and projects so that growth of self can occur.

"WARMING UP" AS DESPECIALIZING AND RESPECIALIZING

Athletes and dancers would never think of beginning their contest or performance without a series of "warm-up" exercises. Although they are specialists, dancers and athletes have had to train hard to liberate their musculature so that their bodies become versatile instruments, capable of flexibility unavailable to the average person. But when these people engage in routine daily pursuits, their musculature follows suit. For a performance they must disengage their thinking and their bodies from these mundane involvements. Hence, warming up is a way of disengaging from one way of being in order to re-engage in another. In current slang, "psyching oneself up" to undertake some task or feat is a variety of disengagement and warming up.

The Experience and Somatic Manifestations of Enlivenment

Religion is concerned with life itself, with ways to live that are the most viable. The question is, "What are the experiential and objective signs of being most fully alive?" How can persons tell when their actions, their life

Healthy Personality

styles, their relationships with other people, their diets, are conducive to life itself, and when they diminish life? Sensitive somatic perception clearly is essential to discern when one's way of life is enlivening. To experience one's appetites keenly, to enjoy one's senses, to feel emotion, to breathe deeply, to sleep well, to eliminate adequately—all these vital signs may show a person that his or her life style is good. The experience of zest, vitality, and rich meaning in life are further manifestations of enlivenment.

A useful exercise for students to undertake is to list all the people with whom they have regular dealings, such as parents, friends, and teachers; and all the activities in which they regularly engage, such as studies, sports, and hobbies; and rate themselves in each of these situations for the degree to which they experience themselves as most fully alive. They may find that some relationships, as with a parent or with some one friend, induce in them a sense of being deadened, a loss of enthusiasm for living, and loss of a sense of being themselves. Such a discovery may enable persons to make vitalizing changes in their life situations.

A problem for physiological psychologists is to develop ways to measure how alive a person is at any time. One could envision, for example, taking a series of continuous measurements of blood pressure, pulse, skin conductivity, EEG, and so on. As these readings are obtained, they may be fed into a computer that relates the indices to estimates of reduction of life or propensity for disease. These readings in turn could be transformed into electrical charges and fed into a source of light, such that when a person is most fully alive, the light would shine most brightly. Decrements in enlivenment would cause the light to diminish in brilliance. Just as the simplified electroencephalograph made it possible for persons to train themselves to enter a tranquil, meditative state by observing when the alpha waves appear,[20] so persons might train themselves to heightened sensitivity to their own degree of being alive through such equipment. They could then note when their lives were dispiriting them before they collapsed in illness.

The Body and Healthy Personality

Perhaps one of the most intriguing developments of the 1970s was the biofeedback movement. The discoveries of practitioners and scientists in this area suggest that you can "get in touch" with all parts of your body, from your skin to your brain and internal organs. Barbara Brown,[21] one of the pioneer physiologists in the area, has demonstrated that all of the parts of the body emanate a "language" that, properly interpreted, can signal to the owner of the body significant information about the condition of that part of the body. The excitement and importance of these ideas stem from the well-demonstrated probability that once you know, read, and hear these transmissions from various parts of the body, voluntary control of these organs becomes quite real. Thus, researchers have demonstrated the person's ability, for example, to speed up or slow down the heartbeat; to increase and decrease temperature or flow of sweat in one hand over the other, and to thoroughly relax specific muscles.

In addition to the obvious importance of such control to health and wellbeing, the theoretical significance of not only knowing one's self as a psychological creature but knowing one's body, particularly the internal organs, opens up new vistas in humanistic medicine and intimates more control by the "owner" of the body over his or her own processes and even over the diseases that afflict the body.

Dr. Brown refers to the message electrically transmitted to the person from the skin as "skin talk." In most instances, the person is able to monitor the particular body part through instruments connected to oscilloscopes, which display dots and wavy lines, indicating, for example, variations in heart beat, skin conductance, and so on. Writes Brown,

Each wiggle of the written record of the skin's electrical activity conveys information. As with any communication made by human beings, skin talk gives important clues about the personality, intelligence, psychological state, ability to learn, motivation, memory, awareness, perception, thought processes, sex and age of the communicator. Females and blacks have

Healthy
Personality

better skin electrical conductance than males and Caucasians, but the conductance improves with age in everyone [p. 52].

Use of biofeedback in muscle relaxation is one of the most spectacular techniques to emerge from the movement. Whatmore and Kohli [22] studied the familiar situation where, in anticipation of a problem or decision, your neck muscles, among others, become tense, almost as though you were bracing for a blow. But as the time wears on prior to the decision, you easily forget that your muscles are tense and find yourself with a blistering headache. Whatmore's treatment is to enable the patient to see his or her muscle "talk" on the oscilloscope and to teach the patient to correct these muscle "errors" quite consciously and thus avoid headache and fatigue.

It is in the messages from the brain, perhaps, that the most promise seems to exist for biofeedback. For example, the well-known alpha wave of the brain, found in conditions of rest, appears in measurements of the brains of those persons beginning their meditation exercise. There are many potential uses for biofeedback in psychotherapy and in physical and mental health and well-being. It offers promise for the early identification of disease, for development of special techniques to deal with stress, and for speeding up psychotherapy through rapid identification of some of the special problem areas to be discussed between therapist and client.

Some Existential Suggestions

How many, if any, of the manifestations of unembodiment apply to you? Do you repress much of your somatic experiencing, or is your somatic perception keen and sensitive? You can use your body as a test of others' embodiment; if you feel devitalized in one person's presence, but not in another's, then there is something that is not healthy going on with that other person or with your relationship to that person. As a psychotherapist, I pay keen attention to the way I feel—enlivened or devitalized—when I am with a patient, because this tells me something about the patient's state of being.

What do you believe is beautiful about your body and

The Body and Healthy Personality

what ugly (to you)? Stand in front of a mirror and ask yourself, "What do I feel about my hair, my eyes, nose, teeth?" This exercise will reveal a great deal to you about your own body-ideal, in terms of which you come to either like or to scorn your own appearance.

Especially if you are handicapped, it is good to challenge your own beliefs, including your medical beliefs, about what you are capable of doing. I have suggested to people who run an "Outward Bound" program that they take amputees, blind people, aging people, drug addicts, and grossly overweight people out to the wilderness, to scale mountains and cross deserts and to learn how their concepts of what they can or cannot do are extremely self-limiting.

Learn to give and to receive a massage. An hour of mutual massage each day, between spouses, friends, or strangers, would not solve the problems of the world, but it would certainly improve the quality of daily life.

Experimenting with dieting and fasting is also a good thing to do, to learn how self-limiting and habitual we have become in regard to our eating.

SUMMARY

Partial repression of somatic experience is common among people of the West. "Unembodiment" manifests itself as pretense, as a devitalizing effect upon others, and in autistic body images. Somatic perception sensitizes us to the effect our life styles are having upon our health.

The capacity for control over bodily functions and over the movement of the body is a sign of ego development.

Physical appearance is an important basis for a sense of security and self-esteem. The cultural concept of the ideal body condemns many people who adhere to this ideal to diminished self-esteem, because the ideal is very restrictive. Thus, many people dislike their appearance because they are too fat or thin, or have facial wrinkles or a nose that seems to them to be ugly.

Valid knowledge about the structure, functions, and limits of one's body is essential for healthy personality. Some ways of life associated with culture, occupation, or role are destructive to health.

Healthy Personality

"Handicap" typically leads to depression and helplessness. Healthy reactions to handicap include assessing remaining capacities and readdressing life with vigor.

Some techniques for "re-embodying" oneself, and heightening somatic perception, include massage, Rolfing, biofeedback, special diets and fasting, Hatha yoga, various martial arts, and bioenergetic analysis. These techniques all appear to work by despecializing an overly specialized body. A proposal was made to explore ways to measure degrees of somatic enlivenment.

NOTES AND REFERENCES

1. "Unembodiment" is discussed in R. D. LAING, *The Divided Self* (London: Tavistock, 1960), pp. 67–81.

2. Again Laing has made a fine analysis of the way in which people elude direct experience of themselves in their bodies and acts. See R. LAING, *Self and Others* (New York: Pantheon, 1969), Chapter 3, "Pretense and Elusion," and Chapter 4, "The Counterpoint of Experience."

3. R. D. LAING, *The Politics of Experience* (New York: Pantheon, 1967).

4. W. REICH, *The Discovery of the Orgone: The Function of the Orgasm* (New York: Noonday, 1961), Chapter 8.

5. R. BIRDWHISTELL, *Kinesics and Context* (Philadelphia: U. of P., 1970).

6. S. FISHER and S. E. CLEVELAND, *Body-Image and Personality* (New York: Dover, 1968); also S. FISHER, *Body Experience in Fantasy and Behavior* (New York: Appleton, 1970).

7. E. JOKL and P. JOKL, *Physiological Basis of Athletic Records* (Springfield, Ill.: Thomas, 1968).

8. S. M. JOURARD, *The Transparent Self* (New York: Van Nostrand Reinhold, 1971), Chapter 11, "The Invitation to Die." See also the article on the cultures where it is normal to live past 100 years: ALEXANDER LEAF, "Every Day Is a Gift When You're Over 100," *National Geographic*, 1973, Vol. 143, pp. 93–119.

9. W. HOFFER, "The Development of the Body Ego," *Psychoanalytic Study of the Child, V* (New York: International U.P., 1950), pp. 18–23.

10. Mark Lefkowitz did his master's thesis on this problem. His study is expounded in S. M. JOURARD, *Self-disclosure: An Experimental Analysis of the Transparent Self* (New York: Wiley-Interscience, 1971), Chapter 12.

11. P. Secord and S. M. Jourard, "The Appraisal of Body-Cathexis: Body-Cathexis and the Self," *Journal of Consulting Psychology*, 1953, Vol. 17, pp. 343–347.

12. S. M. Jourard and P. Secord, "Body-Cathexis and the Ideal Female Figure," *Journal of Abnormal and Social Psychology*, 1955, Vol. 50, pp. 243–246; "Body-Size and Body-Cathexis," *Journal of Consulting Psychology*, 1954, Vol. 18, p. 184.

13. Margaret Mead, *Male and Female* (New York: Morrow, 1949), pp. 138–142.

14. See H. Bruch, *The Importance of Overweight* (New York: Norton, 1957).

15. See Horney's discussion of "neurotic claims" in *Neurosis and Human Growth* (New York: Norton, 1950), Chapter 2; also E. Berne, *Games People Play* (New York: Grove, 1964).

16. A. Montagu, *Touching: The Human Significance of the Skin* (New York: Harper & Row, 1972); S. M. Jourard, *Disclosing Man to Himself* (New York: Van Nostrand Reinhold, 1968), Chapter 12; a follow-up study of Jourard's work appears in Jourard, *Self-disclosure: An Experimental Analysis of the Transparent Self*, op. cit., Chapter 11. See also B. Gunther, *Sense Relaxation: Below Your Mind* (New York: Macmillan, 1968) and *What to Do Till the Messiah Comes* (New York: Macmillan, 1971).

17. Ida P. Rolf wrote an excellent summary of her work a few years prior to her death: *What in the World Is Rolfing?* (Santa Monica, Calif.: Dennis Landman, 1975). A brief discussion of several re-embodying techniques, including Rolfing, is found in W. Schutz, *Here Comes Everybody* (New York: Harper, 1972), pp. 202–223.

18. There are hundreds of books available on yoga. I have found R. Mishra, *Fundamentals of Yoga* (New York: Lancer, 1959) reasonable. K. Behanan, *Yoga: A Scientific Evaluation* (New York: Dover, 1937) offers a Western scientific perspective on yoga. See also A. S. Dalal and T. Barber, "Yoga and Hypnotism" in T. X. Barber, *LSD, Marijuana, Yoga, and Hypnosis* (Chicago: Aldine, 1970), Chapter 3. I have just read a book in which the author, a professor at the University of Bombay, shows how the ancient Indian scriptures, called the Upanishads, and the early writings about yoga anticipate current findings in neurophysiology and in the psychology of perception. See T. Kulkarni, *Upanishads and Yoga: An Em-*

pirical Approach to the Understanding (Bombay: Bharatiya Vidya Bhavan, 1972).

19. See A. LOWEN, *Betrayal of the Body* (New York: Macmillan, 1967); also S. KELEMAN, *Sexuality, Self and Survival* (San Francisco: Lodestar, 1971).

20. See J. KAMIYA, "Operant Control of the EEG Alpha Rhythm and Some of Its Reported Effects on Consciousness," in C. T. TART (Ed.), *Altered States of Consciousness* (New York: Wiley, 1969), Chapter 33.

21. An excellent, brief discussion of the biofeedback movement can be found in B. B. BROWN, "New Mind, New Body," *Psychology Today*, August 1974, pp. 48–112.

22. GEORGE B. WHATMORE and D. R. KOHLI, "Dysponesis: A Neurophysiologic Factor in Functional Disorders, *Behavioral Science*, 1968, Vol. 13, pp. 102–124.

CHAPTER

8

THE SELF AND HEALTHY PERSONALITY

INTRODUCTION

Everyone experiences their identities differently, but everyone experiences who they are. We act in the world and interact with other people as the person we believe ourselves to be. Our very names designate our personal, as well as family, identities, and we act in the ways expected of the person so named. I am a Jourard, and of all the Jourards, I am that one named Sidney. People from my home town had little difficulty recognizing me as a Jourard when I was growing up; there was a physical resemblance among us and we all took pride in being hard-working, friendly, and independent. But I am that Jourard named Sidney, and I do not behave in ways identical with my brothers and sisters, nor do I experience the world in the ways they do. My identity is my own. My first name and my surname come to stand for some limits on the ways in which I will act—there are many things I will not do because I am a Jourard, named Sidney, and there are many things that I demand of myself, and that others expect of me, because I am that very person. I am that Jourard named Sidney; but I am called Professor by my students, Doctor Jourard by my psychotherapy clients, Sid by my friends, Daddy by my children, and Dear, at times, by my wife. These are the names for each aspect of my identity and for the social roles (see Chapter 10) that guide my relationships with others. The names prescribe and proscribe what I disclose to and what I conceal from others, and they define what action is appropriate in my relationships with the people who address me in those terms.[1] If a student addressed me thus: "Professor Jourard, darling . . ." I would be confused over which of my possibilities are being summoned.

Identity and the Self-structure

Some psychologists describe a person's sense of his or her identity with the term *self*. This term implies that the individual is somebody in particular (a self), and it also signifies that this individual can experience his or her being in several perspectives, or modes, such as the modes of perception, of conceptualizing, and of imagination.

The structure of the self has a great deal to do with one's success, one's ability to accomplish goals set by self or by others. Here are some of the parts of the self-structure, each of which has a special significance in building the healthy personality:

The *self-concept* is the picture we have of ourselves. In recent years the importance of this concept has become established as a factor in school achievement, social behavior—almost all facets of one's life. It often includes an appraisal or evaluation of self as "good" or "bad," judgments we make about our own intelligence, attractiveness, and abilities.

The *self* is the unique, special identity, the person, the personality. Under its synonym, the personality, the self has a great collection of research behind it, and it is a never-ending cause of concern, wonder, pride, or even sometimes shame for the human being who attempts to discover self.

The *ideal self* is the person or self we think we ought

The Self and Healthy Personality

to be. It includes the voice of our conscience, our hopes and wishes, and, in most but not all instances, our conception of what others think we should be. It is important, in that too big a difference between one's self-concept and one's ideal self indicates a good deal of dissatisfaction with one's self and is often associated with behavior or emotional problems.

The *public self* is the image or picture of ourselves that we give to the general society. It includes the way we want to be seen by others and often involves hiding some aspect of self or showing only certain aspects of self. However, the authentic person discloses his or her whole self comfortably and allows very little distinction between the public self and the real self. Sometimes the public self is also called the *social self*.

The *real self* is a bit of a mystery. It is not as readily defined as other terms about the self. It involves our perception of our own being, being aware of the flow of our own consciousness. We come to know our real self by reflecting upon our experience candidly and through objective observations and evaluation of self. However, in the same manner that philosophers may debate for centuries the nature of reality, so some self-psychologists question the existence of a real self.

Our *best self* is that aspect of the personality that we know as the best of ourselves that we can create, whether in secluded privacy or in blazing public light. It is roughly equivalent to the healthy personality at its best. It is significant as one of many descriptions of the high-level-functioning person.

Healthy personality calls for action that achieves satisfaction of persons' basic needs and that fulfills the projects they undertake to give meaning and direction to their lives. Persons' sense of their identity has a decisive influence upon what action they feel free to engage in and what is taboo for them. Thus, persons can so define themselves that the very action that is essential for their wellbeing and growth is not compatible with their self-concept, their self-ideal, or their public self. Accordingly, they refrain from the activity and live out their identities, even though it may be sickening them. We will be interested in exploring how persons acquire their self-

Healthy Personality

186

structures, how each dimension of these self-structures influences their experience and action, and the conditions under which the self changes in sickening and in health-engendering ways.

The Self-concept

Persons' self-concepts comprise all their beliefs about their own nature. They include their assumptions about their strengths and weaknesses, their possibilities for growth, and their explicit descriptions of their customary patterns of behavior and experiencing. Thus, a person may say, "I am lazy; I always give up when the task becomes difficult. I usually feel happy. I am warm and friendly; however, I need a great deal of help to make it through life." These self-descriptions resemble statistical formulations, in the sense that the individual believes there have been many occasions when he or she acted in those ways.

People describe themselves as if they were describing a fixed essence, or a class of objects of which they are a specimen. When a person says he or she is lazy, or sincere, it is as if the person is saying, "It is my nature to be lazy, or sincere, just as it is the nature of a wolf to be fierce." But human beings do not have fixed natures; neither do wolves. Under most circumstances of life, humans have the freedom to choose how they will be and how they will act. Thus, when persons form self-concepts, thereby defining themselves, they are not so much describing that nature as they are making a pledge that they will continue to be the kinds of people they believe they now are and have been. One's self-concept is not so much descriptive of experience and action as it is *prescriptive*. The self-concept is a commitment. Because our self-concepts are such powerful influences upon our experience and action, it follows that anything or any person who influences what we believe to be true or possible for ourselves will have a powerful influence upon our lives.

If I can convince you that you are strong, when hitherto you believed you were weak, you may then begin to act in ways that befit a strong person. What you believe to be true of yourself *is* your "nature"; what should never be forgotten is that one's beliefs about self are just that—beliefs—and they can be changed. One's self-concept is open to change, just as one's beliefs about God, one's parents, or the world are open to change.

The self-concept exercises almost a tyrannical role in determining behavior. Combs and Snygg [2] suggest that all human behavior is determined by the need for the individual to maintain and enhance the *phenomenal self*—another synonym for the self-concept. The research literature has grown so rapidly in the past 15 years that the new edition of the review of self-concept literature by Ruth Wylie [3] is now in two volumes.

STRUCTURE OF THE SELF-CONCEPT

The self-concept consists of four major entities: the body, other material objects, other people, and a group of abstractions or ideas.

Material objects are an integral part of one's self-concept, regardless of the orientation of one's society to socialism or materialism. Thus, your records, your car, some favorite items of clothing, such as an old pair of work pants or a woolly sweater (or Linus' security blanket), are part of your self. So much are they a part of the self that we hesitate to loan them out, in the same way that we might hesitate to loan our identity to another person. Should your record get damaged, or your car dented, you would be just as upset as if you yourself were wounded. We maintain these objects of self as though they were the self. The list of objects perceived by people as part of the self can be limitless: a camera, pots and pans, home or room, a favorite pen, a violin or saxophone, a guitar, a special book, a special collection of art or of ceramic rhinoceroses, tools, a ring, a watch, a diary, a boat or motorcycle.

The *body*, as discussed in the previous chapter, is not always an integral part of the self-concept, even though for most people there is probably no more certain object in the self-concept. Plato, for example, describes Socrates' pleasure at the impending loss of his body. (He was sentenced to death for corrupting the youth.) Socrates sees himself as freed from the heavy burden of the physical

Healthy Personality

188

self. He sees his "real" self as his soul, which will be freer to function unencumbered by the body. Yet, of course, for most human beings, the body is the central aspect of the self-concept. "How do I look?" we ask our spouse or our roommate or date. We ask asking about our physical appearance. We are worrying over the physical body even more during the present unisex period of our society's development. Whereas indications from early research indicated more attention paid to the concept of the body by women, this seems to be evening out as, for example, men seek hair stylists rather than barbers. In the twentieth century, it would require a great commitment to another, more abstract style of life for a person not to see the body as an important part of the self-concept.

For many, *other persons* also become a perceived part of the self. To parents, their children are often more central to the self-concept than their own bodies. Thus parents might put their children's safety before their own. Mothers and fathers in Nazi concentration camps would save their crumbs of food for their children. Similarly, in close families, spouses, brothers and sisters, parents, even cousins, can be seen as part of the self-concept, some persons being more central than others. Thus, Corrie ten Boom [4] risked her own life many times in a vain effort to help her sister survive the Nazi holocaust in the Netherlands. Love may be defined as wanting fulfillment or happiness for the other person as much as for oneself—there is no doubt that it implies that the loved person is perceived as being part of the lover's self-concept.

Perhaps the most significant composition of the self concept for the healthy personality are the ideas, ideals, or other *abstractions* that are suggested to be particularly characteristic of the high-level-functioning person. These include beliefs and principles. For example, martyrs of all religions have given up their lives and have suffered torture to lesser parts of their self-concept, that is, their bodies, in order to maintain their particular abstract faith. Solzhenitsyn, the Russian dissident author who was expelled from his motherland, was in constant danger of his life, and perhaps still is; yet, he continued to write of the injustices of the Soviet prison system.[5] His belief in "freedom," an abstract concept, was easily as great as his valuation of his own life. Other abstractions that for many people become a part of their self-concept include a particular political system, such as democracy or socialism; a particular philosophy, such as pragmatism or empiricism; even a particular theory in one's profession, such as quantum theory or behaviorism; belief in ghosts, demons, heaven or hell, in science or in witches and magic—all of these are abstractions, or ideas, in many instances held by persons who would willingly give up their bodies to maintain or defend those abstractions.

ORGANIZATION OF THE SELF-CONCEPT

The self-concept itself is an abstraction. Like the "mind," it has no special location and is not comprised of any particular organ. (Children asked to locate their selves usually point either to their chest or their forehead.) The self-concept may be conveniently thought of as being divided into several sub-selves or "roles."

Thus, you may find included in your self-concept your role as a student, as an athlete, as a first child of the family, as a dancer, as a lover, as a spouse, as a parent, as a teacher, or as a merchant. While persons differ widely in their most important sub-self or role, for most people their way of earning a living becomes a major role. Thus, in one of Bugental's [6] earliest self-concept tests, the WAY (Who Are You?), many people replied in terms of their job. In the opening lines to Shakespeare's *Julius Caesar*, Flavius, walking the streets of Rome, is dismayed to find the populace walking about in their best clothes and chides a workman: "What, know you not . . . you ought not walk upon a laboring day without the sign of your profession?" [7]

The Self-appraisal. Another abstraction of great importance in the self-system is one's own evaluation of one's self. Among different researchers this may be called the self-appraisal, self-regard, or self-assessment. It may be expressed in some of the research data, as in the Tennessee Self-Concept Scale, [8] as a single number. A score of 75 would be considered in the normal range for that test. Or it may be expressed in a series of sub-scores, sometimes equivalent to the role concept. One might have a self-appraisal score in relationship to one's primary

Healthy Personality

190

group or family, one's physical self, one's social-self, and so on, or one may appraise oneself as a great lover and a terrible athlete. In many instances, when we speak of the self-concept, many persons mean simply the self-appraisal, the evaluation of self as adequate or not.

The Influence of Other People upon One's Self-concept. Persons' self-concepts are open to influence by views that other people have of them. Beliefs about one-self are not based on conclusions arrived at through in-dependent self-study, but rather are derived by listening to what other people have said about one's nature.[9] Other people define us to ourselves, if we listen to them. Thus, one's mother may say, "You are lazy, like your father." The child didn't know he was lazy until he was told. Once he believes that this is his essential nature, he will act as a lazy person is expected to. When other peo-ple attribute traits to a person, their descriptions function like hypnotic suggestions, inducing or persuading the in-dividual to conform with the others' view. This vulner-ability to others' influence is a liability, if the others de-fine the person as weak or bad; it is also an asset, because one can attribute strength and goodness to a person, who then will discover he or she can be strong and good. Psychotherapists exert a beneficial influence upon their patients by seeing them as potentially strong and self-reliant when all others, including the patients themselves, see them as weak, dependent, and worthless.

People constantly define one another, thereby con-firming one another's self-concepts, for bettter or for worse. Listen to everyday conversations between parents and their children, between close friends, or between spouses: "John, put your coat and hat on; you know you are weak and will catch cold." (John is being led to be-lieve that his body will not tolerate temperature changes without risk of pneumonia.) "Mary, you are such an obliging and generous girl—you could never refuse any-one or say an unkind word." (Mary is being condemned to a life in which she cannot lose her temper or do any-thing to please herself; her nature has just been defined for her.) A husband may define his wife as follows: "Here, dear, let me balance the checkbook; you know you could never add two numbers together." (She is

The Self and Healthy Personality

confirmed in a view of herself as silly, helpless, and impractical).[10]

We Instruct Others on How We Wish Them to See Us. People attribute to the "others" the traits and qualities that they believe define them. Thus, the parents of a student who consulted me told him many times: "You are such a nice, obedient boy. You always do what you are told. Ever since you were a baby, you wanted to please us." Under such a hypnotic and persuasive regime, he came to believe he was nice and obedient, eager to please others. Once he formed his concept of himself, his way of relating to others functioned as an invitation to *them* to view him as he had come to view himself.

It seems strange, but persons' self-concepts represent an answer to the question, "Who am I?" that their parents first answered. If they accept their answer, they transmit it to others who want to know who they are. They tell others who they are, in every relationship that they enter. How odd if you and I are no more than carriers of a view of ourselves that our parents gave us as a kind of legacy. We define ourselves in terms provided by our parents, say, and confirm that definition by our action, which invites and persuades others to believe we are that way.

The student I saw in psychotherapy told me that for years his father had been saying, "You take after your Uncle Billy. He started many things, but always gave up halfway through." His father was defining him as essentially a failure, and he believed that was how he was. He tried to persuade me that he was, essentially, a failure, and there was little anyone could do about it. Of course, I refused to see him that way. Instead, I attributed strength to him and the capacity to overcome self-doubt and the difficulties of study. The student did change his concept of himself under this continuous "invitation" to change it. After having had competence attributed to him, the student not only changed his self-concept, but invited others, including his father, to change their view of him.

This cycle of having one's identity defined by others, believing it, and then persuading others to view oneself in the same way is continuous throughout life. It is the basis for personal growth, and it also can be the basis for

Healthy Personality

endless confirmation of a sense of identity that is self-defeating.

THE SELF-CONCEPT AND THE SENSE OF IDENTITY

People act in ways that confirm their self-concepts. When persons act "out of character," as in the case of persons who think of themselves as kind but then fly into violent rages, they experience threat to their sense of their identity. They may say, "I was not myself when I was so enraged." Such a threat is extremely painful, and people go to great lengths to retain a continuous experience of their preferred identity. Our sense of being who we believe we are can be threatened, not only by action that is out of character, but also by thoughts, feelings, and memories. A person may engage in daydreaming that produces thoughts and feelings of an outrageous nature; for example, a loving mother may find herself entertaining fantasies of abandoning her children.

It is intolerable to lose one's sense of identity, even if it is a "spoiled" identity. For example, obese people and alcoholics may believe they remain addicted to sweets or to alcohol because they "have no will power." This belief may be the basis of their sense of who they are; if they act decisively, they do not recognize themselves. People find it difficult to change their behavior, even when it is destructive to growth and to health, because their self-concepts have not altered.

CONSCIENCE AND THE IDEAL SELF

Conscience is the act of judging one's experience and action, comparing them to the standards of an idealized self. Conscience has been likened to a "still small voice," and it has been described as our imaginative view of how we would like to be and how we believe we ought to be. The standards of conscience, in terms of which persons condemn or approve their conduct, are usually based upon the laws and customs of the society within which they have been reared. Seen from a sociological viewpoint, conscience—our capacity to make moral judgments of our own conduct—is one of the "agencies" for social control. The necessity for controlling behavior

The Self and Healthy Personality

through social pressure, or through threats of imprisonment or violence, is decreased when people have acquired a conscience.

Conscience plays an important role in the development of neurotic and psychotic illness. Moreover, conformity to some moral standards can sometimes force a person to live in ways that are joyless and that endanger the person's physical health.

CONSCIENCE AND HEALTH

Psychological Health. Freud believed that neurosis was partly caused by an overly severe, mainly unconscious, infantile conscience. (He called it the superego.) According to his view, a neurotic sufferer was obliged to avoid sexual behavior, and even sexual fantasies, in order to be free of guilt. One aim of psychoanalytic therapy was to help the patient modify the conscience so that its taboos were less restrictive and more in keeping with adult life.

Mowrer disagreed with the psychoanalytic views. According to Mowrer, a neurotic is a person who persists beyond childhood in the pursuit of irresponsible pleasures, including sexuality, and who represses the conscience to avoid guilt. Neurotic symptoms arise as defenses against guilt, not against infantile sexuality, as the Freudians might maintain. Consequently, Mowrer claims, the aim in therapy is not to render the conscience more lenient, but to make it conscious, so that a person will feel guilt more acutely and seek in future to obey the conscience rather than to repress it.

Clinical experience shows that neither Freud nor Mowrer is wholly correct or wholly incorrect. Some neurotic patients do indeed have a conscience that is too strict; in order to remain guilt-free, they must refrain from all pleasurable activities, including those that society condones. Other patients have the makeup Mowrer has regarded as nuclear to all neurosis—they repress conscience so they can break social taboos without conscious guilt. In still others both patterns of unhealthy conscience may be found.[11]

Conscience and Physical Illness. If a person's conscience is based on a cruel and punitive morality, that person will have an exaggerated sense of duty that makes

Healthy Personality

him or her forego even legitimate pleasures. Thus, a parent may deny himself or herself all fun in life, insisting upon a Spartan existence, in order to provide for the children. The necessity to repress anger, resentment, and temptation to enjoyment can impose excessive stress upon the person and demoralize him or her such that resistance to infectious illnesses is diminished. Conscience can kill a person, if it is inhumanely demanding and restrictive. Such conscience is often found in persons with various forms of stress-induced disease, such as high blood pressure, cancer, and heart disease.

How the Conscience Is Acquired

Conscience is acquired gradually through *identification*. Identification is the process of ascribing to oneself the characteristics of another (usually admired) person. As one identifies with and takes on more traits of the valued model, intrafamilial resemblances in behavior, values, gesture, attitudes, and morals are acquired.

Children come into the world with only the capacity to develop a conscience. They act in accordance with their momentary needs and feelings, and their parents are usually watching them closely, making moral judgments about their behavior. If they act in ways that violate the parents' concepts of what is right, the parents will punish the children for behaving in that way. The parents appear huge, powerful, and admirable from children's standpoint; they want to become like the parents. In order to avoid punishment, to retain the parents' love, and to acquire their wonderful attributes, children strive to become like them in many ways. They identify with their demands and expectations; these gradually become their expectations of themselves. In short, they come to forbid in themselves what their parents forbade. They come to demand of themselves what their parents demanded. They come to expect of themselves what their parents expected. In this manner the conscience commences.[12]

UNHEALTHY CONSCIENCES

Excessively Strict Conscience. This pattern of unhealthy conscience limits behavior more drastically than do law and custom. The unfortunate bearers of such a conscience allow themselves fewer satisfactions than do other members of their social group; they expect more of themselves, more difficult achievements, and have a sterner morality than their peers. Thus, many persons may have been taught that sexy or hostile fantasies and thoughts are equivalent in sinful significance to sexual and hostile action, and so they dare not even think such thoughts.

Authoritarian Conscience. An authoritarian person is one who believes authority figures are omnipotent and must be obeyed without question. Indeed, to disobey or to question authority is synonymous with sin for the authoritarian character; he or she becomes overwhelmed with guilt at even the thought of challenging vested authority. A person may experience his or her conscience in the same way; it is to be obeyed blindly, without question, hesitation, or criticism. Its commands have the feeling of certainty and unquestionable rightness. Fromm has named a conscience with such characteristics an authoritarian conscience.[13]

Repressed and Projected Conscience. To repress is to refuse to think about something or to refrain from engaging in some mental operation, such as thinking, remembering, daydreaming, or evaluating. Conscience functions by means of the comparison of one's own behavior, feelings, or motives with relevant taboos and "shoulds." A person may have learned to refrain from making value judgments about aspects of his or her own behavior in order to avoid the painful experience of guilt. This avoidance of value judgments concerning one's own behavior is what we mean when we speak of the repression of conscience. Laypeople speak, in this connection, of the "hardened heart." Scrooge, in Dickens' classic *A Christmas Carol*, had such a hardened heart until he was overcome with guilt.[14]

Persons can project their conscience as well as repress it. Concretely, this involves repression of self-evaluation and ascribing evaluations of the self to others. Thus persons might engage in some act but deny it is wrong for them to do this. However, they may impute condemnation of themselves to some other person and feel without

Healthy Personality

196

warrant that the other person is criticizing and condemning them. In extreme cases of disturbed personality—for example, paranoid schizophrenia—the patients project all of their self-criticism to others and believe that everyone is criticizing and persecuting them.

Consciences in Conflict. In conflicted conscience, the values, ideals, and taboos contradict one another. Thus, conformity with one value requires violation of another, with consequent guilt. A common source of conflicted conscience is parents who have different standards for judging the behavior of their children—in disagreement with the freer values of the adolescent peer group. The parents may value gentleness, celibacy, and obedience, whereas the peer group affirms aggressiveness, muscular strength, and sexual experimentations. In pleasing their peers, adolescents displease their parents, and vice versa.

Some people attempt to resolve value conflicts by compartmentalizing their lives. They follow one set of values at work, another set in the home, another set when they are among their peers, and so on. More desirable from the viewpoint of personality hygiene is the attempt to reconcile one's values so they constitute a harmonious and hierarchically arranged system.

CHARACTERISTICS OF HEALTHY CONSCIENCE

A person with a healthy conscience will foster healthy personality if he or she strives to pay attention to it. Such attention will have a number of consequences. It will enable the person to obtain enough basic need gratifications to make life worth living, but in a guilt-free manner. The person will enjoy relatively high self-esteem. His or her behavior may be approved by other members of the social group—at least to the extent that the person's conscience is congruent with the group's value system. A healthy conscience will be compatible with continual personality growth; indeed, it may be a strong motivating force toward personal growth. Like pain in the physical realm, a twinge of conscience is a healthy signal that something is wrong. Let us now list some of the more salient attributes of a healthy conscience.

Accessibility to Consciousness. A healthy conscience is one that can be reflected upon. The person is able to formulate its component taboos, ideals, and ethical precepts in words. This accessibility to consciousness is important for resolution of moral conflicts. If a person is faced with a decision, it can be made along moral lines much more readily when the person's ideals can be clearly stated.

When I say that a healthy conscience is conscious, I do not mean the person is always thinking about his or her moral standards. Most of the time, the healthy conscience will be unconscious; the person will conform with the conscience automatically. But when the person does feel guilt, he or she will be able to determine what aspects of the conscience have been violated; and when some conflict has to be resolved, the person will make the relevant moral aspects explicit, so that the decision will be made after due consideration of the moral issues at stake.

Self-affirmation. A healthy conscience is not experienced as an "alien power" within the total personality structure, a power compulsively obeyed out of dread. Rather, it is composed of a set of ideals and taboos, each of which has been examined by the person and affirmed so that it became a true part of the real self. A self-affirmed conscience is one to which the person conforms because he or she wants to, not through fear of disobeying. Another way of saying this is to assert that the person feels he or she owns the conscience. The individual has had a voice in determining the rules by which he or she will live, like the citizen in a democracy who does not mind conforming with rules that the person has helped formulate.

Receptivity to Questioning and Change. A healthy conscience is based upon general values and ideals that remain fixed throughout life or that change only with difficulty. But the specific behavior that these values call for is not rigidly defined. The person can challenge these self-demands when they are no longer relevant to his or her present life circumstances. For example, a student may have been trained to believe that premarital sex relationships are evil and destructive of love. In his college career, he may live with a girl and enjoy sexual intimacies within the context of a loving relationship. He discovers

Healthy Personality

198

that no harm befalls the girl or himself. He may change one of the taboos that is at the root of his conscience. Another student who once believed that premarital sex was permissible may change and accept a taboo against the practice. This openness to change is most possible if the conscience is not authoritarian.

Some Degree of Congruence with the Social Value System. Persons with a healthy conscience are living among other people, and so they will be obliged to share at least some of the other people's ideals and taboos. This is not to say that their conscience must be absolutely congruent with the social mores. It may happen that these persons find their values *more ethical* than the prevailing mores, and so they will follow their conscience rather than the moral expectations of their peers. It may be necessary for persons with a healthy conscience to resist the efforts of others to make them conform to their moral precepts. They may even have to leave home because of moral–ethical differences and seek a group more congenial to their outlook.

It is not implied that a healthy conscience will be highly lenient, permitting any antisocial behavior. Indeed, it may be difficult to conform with the precepts of a healthy conscience. Fromm has stated that the voice of a humanistic conscience may be only dimly heard, because it is readily masked by the authoritarian elements of the conscience. As Fromm puts it, conscience "is the voice of our true 'selves' which summons us back to ourselves, to live productively, to develop fully and harmoniously— that is, to become what we potentially are." He points out further that guilt arising from violation of a healthy conscience may be difficult to identify; we might feel guilt arising from our authoritarian conscience when we ignore its demands in order to pursue the requirements of a healthy conscience.[15]

The Public Self

Persons' self-concepts represent what they believe to be true about their own personalities. Their conscience grows out of an idealized view of how they ought to be. Next, we will explore the identity a person wishes to have in others' experience of him or her—the *public self*. Humans have the capacity to select their actions and their speech, in order to influence the experience others will have of them. Typically, a person wishes to believe that he or she is law-abiding, highly moral, and possesses other traits that evoke a favorable impression.

The layperson's term for the public self is *wanted reputation*. Everyone strives to construct a reputation with respect to their typical behavior; i.e., they choose their behavior before other persons so these others will form the beliefs that they want them to form. Almost everyone draws a distinction between their "public" life and their "private" life. Ordinarily, only those persons an individual trusts are allowed to observe the full range of that individual's behavior repertoire. Outsiders are permitted to observe only the "expurgated" edition of behavior. Goffman speaks in this connection of "on-stage" behavior, as opposed to backstage or off-stage behavior.[16]

The most important reason for constructing public selves of various sorts is *expedience*. It is only when others believe certain things to be true of you that they will like you, marry you, give you jobs, refrain from imprisoning you, appoint you to public office, buy things at your store, or consult you professionally. If for any reason other people believe undesirable things to be true of you, they will ostracize you, jail you, and so on.

A person may construct highly diversified public selves, depending upon his or her goals. The young man seeking a spouse strives to behave in ways that the woman will be likely to value and approve. He does not allow her to see the rest of his behavior, which may vary tremendously from the censored version of the person she does see.

The construction of public selves resembles the art of sculpture. A sculptor manipulates clay, then steps back to see whether the statue being created resembles the image the sculptor has in mind. If it doesn't, he or she continues to work at it, until by successive approximations the sculptor has brought into reality something that hitherto existed only as a preferred idea or image.

Healthy Personality   By the same token, persons may hold images of their own personalities that they want to construct in the mind of another person. Instead of clay, they employ their own carefully selected behavior and conversation. From time to time, the audience will offer feedback, indicating how they have been seen. If the way they are being seen does not yet coincide with the preferred image, the individuals engage in more behavior and talking until they are assured by the other's responses that they are now seen as they wish to be seen.

Persons may "slip" during the process of constructing, or living up to, a given public self. They may want their audience to believe one thing about them, say, that they are morally scrupulous, yet they may forget themselves and use obscene language, and destroy the image they were seeking to create. Such experiences produce embarrassment, to say the least. The reading public has an insatiable curiosity for details that conflict with the public selves of newsworthy people.

SELF-DISCLOSURE AND THE PUBLIC SELF

Self-disclosure refers to the act of communicating one's experience to others through words and actions. If persons wish others to know them the way they know themselves, they will disclose themselves in truth. If they wish to present a false public self, they will lie, pretending to be someone else, as it were. Authentic self-disclosure is not merely a way to make oneself known to others; it is a way to develop relationships with others that are themselves conducive to healthy personality (see Chapter 10).

If a person feels it necessary to mislead others about the kind of person he or she is, that person will engage in false disclosure, like an actor trying to convince the audience of his or her authenticity. But such chronic misrepresentation of self leads to serious consequences. If persons lie chronically to others about their real feelings, wishes, memories, and plans, they will eventually lose touch with their authentic experiencing. They will not know who they really are, so lost are they in their assumed identities. This loss of self, or self-alienation, results from repression of one's real experiencing, as one pretends to be the person projected as the public self. Self-alienation is the source of most psychological illness (neurosis and psychosis), and it also is a factor in the de-

The Self and Healthy Personality

velopment of physical illness. Persons with high degrees of self-alienation are out of touch with reality, especially the reality of their own bodies and needs. Consequently, their actions do not serve their wellbeing and growth; it only protects their public selves.[17]

Self-alienation

Through chronic lying to others and himself, a person may develop a self-structure radically estranged from the reality of spontaneous experiencing. He may believe that he is a devoted husband (self-concept), he may approve of his attitude toward his wife (conscience), and he strives to get his wife to see him as a devoted spouse by the way he speaks to her (public self). Yet his wife may act in ways that infuriate him, and he may be carrying on an affair. If he acknowledged the anger that his wife's actions engendered in him, it might threaten his sense of identity and undermine his self-esteem. If he evaluated the moral significance of his infidelity, it might make him feel guilty. He may avoid the guilt and embarrassment by repressing the unpleasant dimensions of his experience. To the extent that a person represses aspects of his experience, we can assert that he is *alienated from his real self*. He is pretending to be someone other than his real self; he can believe his own pretense only because he continuously represses his experience.

SOME SIGNS OF SELF-ALIENATION

Horney listed a number of indicators of self-alienation that a person can look for in self or in others:

1. The general capacity for conscious experience is impaired. The person is living "as if in a fog. Nothing is clear to them. Not only their own thoughts and feelings but also other people, and the implications of a situation, are hazy."

2. There may be a decrease in awareness or concern for the body, for its needs and feelings, or for material possessions such as a house, car, or clothing.

3. There is a loss of the feeling of being an active, determining force in one's own life.

Healthy Personality The factors that Horney sees as responsible for the process of self-alienation include:

1. The development of compulsive solutions to neurotic conflicts, such as striving for affection, detachment from others, or chronic hostility to others.

2. Active moves away from the real self, such as the drive for glory and striving to live up to an impossible self-ideal.

3. Active moves against the real self, as in self-hate or self-destruction.

The consequence of alienation from the self, Horney says, is that the person's "relation to himself has become *impersonal*." More specifically, in the self-alienated person pride governs feelings—the individual does not react with spontaneous emotion. Instead, the person feels what he or she should feel. Further, the self-alienated person does not feel in possession of his or her own energies; the person's powers are not his or her own. Another consequence of self-alienation that Horney describes is an impairment in the ability to assume responsibility for the self. The self-alienated person is lacking in plain, simple honesty about self and his or her life. The lack of honesty manifests itself, she states, as (1) an inability to recognize oneself as one really is, without minimizing or exaggerating, (2) an unwillingness to accept the consequences of one's actions and decisions, and (3) an unwillingness to realize it is up to oneself to do something about one's difficulties. Self-alienated persons insist that others, fate, or time will solve these difficulties for them.[18]

Self-alienation means, basically, that a person is not choosing action by consulting all components of the real self, such as needs and values; instead, the person serves some *part* of the real self. But if the total self is not the source of direction for the individual's behavior, what is? Let us distinguish among the following partial sources of behavior direction, namely, pride, conscience, authority, peers, impulses, and finally, real-self direction.

Pride and Conscience Direction. Riesman's [19] concept of the "inner-directed character" is an excellent illustration of persons whose behavior expresses the dictates of conscience and self-ideal rather than the real self. When choices for action arise, such persons experience a conflict between what they really want to do and what they believe they ought to do. In this connection, Horney has written of the "tyranny of the should." [20] Implicitly, such persons believe that real selves are unreliable guides to conduct, and so they repress them. The consequence of ignoring the real self in favor of a rigid conscience is that these persons may behave in a moral and exemplary fashion, but their real needs are ignored, and they will be perpetually thwarted.

Authority Direction. The "authoritarian character" is a person who seeks some authority figure to direct his or her conduct. These persons strive to discern what behavior the authority figure expects of them, and they hasten to comply. If there is any conflict between their own wishes and the demands of authority, they habitually suppress their wishes and compulsively comply with the authority's wishes. Indeed, they experience their real selves as evil or weak, not worth considering. Fromm interprets the manner in which authoritarian characters perceive authority as a byproduct of real-self repression, followed by a projection to the authority figure of all of one's own repressed "powers." Hence, authoritarian characters perceive themselves as weak and the leader as all-powerful and possessing unusual strength and wisdom—the "charismatic" leader.[21]

Peer Direction. Riesman's concept, the "other-directed" character, describes an individual who allows the wishes and expectations of social peers to direct personal actions. The other-directed character becomes sensitized to others' wishes and actively seeks to comply with them. The result may be popularity and acceptance, but it is purchased at the cost of knowledge of the real self and of thwarting many basic needs.[22]

Impulse Direction. Impulses and emotions are a part of the real self, just as are will and ideals. Everyone has to struggle to reconcile the conflicting demands of impulses, ideals, and the expectations of other people. An impulse-directed person is one who habitually ignores all demands upon behavior save those imposed by personal impulses and feelings. This person ignores the conscience, the rights of other people, even his or her own long-range welfare and growth. All is subordinated to the immediate gratification of personal needs and impulses and the immediate expression of the feelings. Psychoanalysts refer to such individuals as "instinct-ridden" characters; they

Healthy Personality

idealize and rationalize their drives and emotions because they cannot voluntarily control them. They are like adult children who have evaded growth.

The Real Self and Authentic Being

In all the preceding instances, the person was acting without taking responsibility for *choosing* the action. Instead, it was as if the question "How shall I act?" had been asked once and an answer chosen for all life, no matter what the personal cost. Life was then lived automatically. Thus, the person may evade conflict and the necessity to make decisions by following an inflexible moral code. The authoritarian character never chooses, seeking the leader's wishes and expectations and conforming with them, like a soldier getting orders from a superior officer. The other-directed person likewise does not choose actions, but instead acts as he or she believes peers would wish. In none of these cases do the persons realize that *they are free to choose their actions in every situation they encounter*. They can change their actions at will, though at times it may be difficult. Human beings are free, and hence responsible for their actions and the consequences. But as the existential philosophers point out, awareness of such freedom and its accompanying responsibility may be terrifying: it is certainly common for people to wish to "escape from freedom." Erich Fromm's book of that title is a classic and should be read for the insight into the human situation that it affords. I recommend to my students that they also read some of the writings of Kierkegaard, Sartre, Buber, and Kazantzakis for the same reason. All these authors remind their readers relentlessly that human beings are condemned to freedom, and they must (and do, with or without awareness) choose their responses to life situations, and they are responsible for their choices.

Authentic being, or being one's real self, means that the person explores the opportunities and challenges afforded by each situation and then chooses a response that expresses his other true values, needs, feelings, and commitments. An authentic person is less predictable than an inauthentic, self-alienated person, because each life situa-

The Self and Healthy Personality

tion, each problem, each encounter with a person is experienced as *new*, with different invitations and demands issuing from it. But such authenticity is only possible when the person has not repressed entire dimensions of experiencing, but is, instead, in steady contact with the real self. It takes courage to be real in this sense, because one's own experiencing often gives rise to fright and sometimes disgust. Moreover, such authenticity requires a person to face decisions time and time again, with the awareness that the outcomes of his or her life are the person's own responsibility, not the responsibility of parents, superior officers, or public pressure. Authentic deciding of this nature is most likely to be started by a person after somehow realizing, with intensity, the fact that he or she will die someday. An encounter with death functions as an invitation for many people to live more decisively, more intensively, and more authentically.[23]

Authentic being is a sign of healthy personality, and it is the means of achieving healthy personality growth.

SELF-DISCLOSURE AND AUTHENTIC BEING

When persons are authentic, they not only acknowledge the truth of their feelings, needs, and wishes, but they are capable of revealing their true being to the other people with whom they have personal relationships. We humans can lie to one another, aiming to be seen by others as a person we know we are not. We also have the capacity for entering into true dialogue with our fellows, disclosing what we think, feel, and are planning, without reserve. Obviously, such transparency exposes a person to real danger, because to be that open with others means to be without defenses. The interests of healthy personality are served if persons can disclose themselves honestly and spontaneously to others. People are more likely to be cautious than to be excessively open, with the result that they are relatively safe, but lonely and misunderstood by others.

It may seem paradoxical, but a person comes to know the real self, and becomes able to introspect honestly, as a consequence of spontaneous disclosure of self to another person. The individual who has a trusted friend or relative to whom he or she can express thoughts, feelings,

Healthy Personality

and opinions honestly is in a better position to learn the real self than the one who has never undergone this experience, because by revealing the self to another, *the person is also revealing the self to himself or herself.* The act of stating one's experience to another, making oneself known, permits one to "get outside oneself" and see oneself. This process of self-discovery through making oneself known to another is facilitated if the other person reflects back what he or she has heard you say. This reflection or restatement, like a mirror, then permits you to compare your words with your experience as you feel it directly and immediately. The capacity to be a transparent self in one's personal relationships is a sign of healthy personality.

Some Existential Suggestions

The major suggestion I have to make with regard to the self-concept is to invite you to ask yourself a question: "Just *who* do I think I am?" Once you have answered this question, raise another: "*Why* do I believe those things about myself? Who told me that is who, and how, I am?" Answers to this question may make it possible to ask another: "Who, and how, can I *become?* What new roles would I like to experience?" Can you identify those friends and associates who help you to grow and develop yourself? Can you also identify and avoid those who inhibit your growth? Can you help your friends better become themselves?

As I said in this chapter, I see the self-concept as a self-fulfilling prophecy, as a commitment rather than as a self-description. Thus, if you do not like the way you find yourself just now, it is possible to envision another way to be and then struggle to be that way.

One's self-ideal can be demonic, capable of destroying the quality of life and even life itself. Consequently, it is urgent that a person examine the ideals and taboos that guide conduct. Episodes of guilt should be occasions for examining the ideal that is being faulted rather than the occasion for unthinkingly changing action. It is only good to conform to a humanistic conscience; unreflective obedience to an authoritarian conscience infantilizes a person and blocks the ability to change in ways that enhance life.

Our public selves are among our chief idolatries. The wish to be seen in some special way can so cramp our spontaneity as to make a self-conscious ordeal of social existence. The main suggestion I have to offer in this connection is to experiment with authentic self-disclosure cautiously or boldly, but with tact and a loving heart. Authentic self-disclosure to others keeps one's self-concept from becoming congealed, and others' views of oneself from being traps.

S U M M A R Y

The term self-structure *refers to one's sense of identity of who one is. The self-structure includes the self-concept (the person's beliefs about the self), the self-ideal (one's view of how one ought to be), the public selves (the way in which one wishes to be experienced by others), and one's best self. Persons' self-concepts are powerful influences upon their actions, because all persons act as the person they believe they are and can be. People's views of themselves are strongly influenced by others' definitions of them. Furthermore, we continually instruct others as to how they should perceive us. The self-concept is made up of one's body, special objects identified with the self, other people, and ideas or abstractions about self. The self-appraisal or evaluation indicates one's valuation of self.*

Our self-ideal is the basis for conscience, the act of making moral judgments about ourselves. We acquire our consciences by taking over the moral views of those who raised us. Our conscience, as given, may be too strict, too authoritarian, and incompatible with healthy personality. The interests of healthy personality are served if a person examines and periodically reformulates the self-ideal so that conformity with it is compatible with a health-engendering way of life.

Persons' public selves—how they wish to be seen by others—influence their actions and their self-disclosure before others. Persons act as the persons they wish others to believe they are. If their public selves are radically different from their self-concepts and their real selves, the

Healthy Personality

persons will become increasingly self-alienated. Authentic being and authentic self-disclosure are factors in the attainment of healthy personality.

NOTES AND REFERENCES

1. See R. BROWN and MARGUERITE FORD, "Address in American English," *Journal of Abnormal and Social Psychology*, 1961, Vol. 62, pp. 375–385; also R. BROWN, *Social Psychology* (New York: Free Press, 1965), pp. 51–71.

2. A. W. COMBS and D. SNYGG, *Individual Behavior*, 2nd ed. (New York: Harper, 1959).

3. R. C. WYLIE, *The Self-Concept*, rev. ed., Vols. 1 and 2 (Lincoln: University of Nebraska Press, 1974).

4. C. TEN BOOM, J. SHERILL, and E. SHERILL, *The Hiding Place* (Old Tappan, N.J.: Fleming H. Revell Company, 1971).

5. See TED LANDSMAN, "The Beautiful and Noble Person as Suicidal Rebel," paper presented at the 1974 meeting of the American Psychological Association. The paper centers upon Solzhenitsyn's great risk in exposing the Soviet prison system.

6. J. F. T. BUGENTAL and E. C. GUNNING, "Investigations into Self-concepts: II. Stability of Reported Self-identifications," *Journal of Clinical Psychology*, 1955, Vol. 11, pp. 41–46.

7. W. SHAKESPEARE, *The Complete Works of Shakespeare* (London: Spring Books, undated).

8. W. H. FITTS, *Tennessee Self-Concept Scale: Manual* (Nashville, Tenn.: Counselor Recordings and Tests, Department of Mental Health, 1965).

9. Sullivan was most explicit in stating that the self consisted in "reflections of the appraisals of 'significant others.'" See H. S. SULLIVAN, *Conceptions of Modern Psychiatry* (Washington, D.C.: William Alanson White Psychiatric Foundation, 1947).

10. See R. D. LAING, *Politics of the Family* (New York: Pantheon, 1969), pp. 78–82, for a superb discussion of the way in which a parent's attributions to, and assumptions about, a child function to induce the child to be in that way. Chapter 10, "Attributions and Injunctions," in his *Self and Others* (New York: Pantheon, 1969) is an earlier formulation.

11. The Freudian view of neurosis is presented in O. FENICHEL, *The Psychoanalytic Theory of Neurosis* (New York: Norton, 1945); Mowrer's arguments against it, and his alter-

nate view, are presented in O. H. MOWRER, *The Crisis in Psychiatry* and *Religion* (New York: Van Nostrand Rheinhold, 1961), Chapters 2 and 13.

12. FENICHEL, op. cit., Chapter 6; and O. H. MOWRER, *Learning Theory and Personality Dynamics* (New York: Ronald, 1950) offer accounts of the origins of conscience through identification. J. C. FLUGEL, *Man, Morals and Society* (New York: International U.P., 1945), Chapters 4, 9, 11, and 12, offers an explanation for the strictness of conscience.

13. E. FROMM, *Man for Himself* (New York: Holt, 1947), pp. 143–175.

14. MOWRER, op. cit.

15. FROMM, op. cit., pp. 159 ff.

16. GOFFMAN, op. cit.; also his later volumes *Stigma: Notes on the Management of Spoiled Identity* (Englewood Cliffs, N.J.: Prentice-Hall, 1963).

17. See S. M. JOURARD, *The Transparent Self*, 2nd ed. (New York: Van Nostrand Reinhold, 1971), Chapters 3 and 4.

18. KAREN HORNEY, *Neurosis and Human Growth* (New York: Norton, 1950), Chapter 6.

19. D. RIESMAN, *The Lonely Crowd* (New Haven: Yale U.P., 1950).

20. HORNEY, op. cit., Chapter 3.

21. E. FROMM, *Escape from Freedom* (New York: Holt, 1941); T. W. ADORNO, ELSE FRENKEL-BRUNSWIK, D. J. LEVINSON, and R. N. SANFORD, *The Authoritarian Character* (New York: Harper, 1950); W. REICH, *The Mass-Psychology of Fascism* (New York: Noonday, 1970).

22. RIESMAN, op. cit.

23. M. HEIDEGGER, *Being and Time* (New York: Harper, 1962). Bradley Fisher demonstrated that an encounter with death intensified a person's subsequent experience of his life. See B. FISHER, "Self-Exploration Experience in Death Encounter" (unpublished doctoral dissertation, University of Florida College of Education, 1968); Sharon Graham showed that students who believed in the finality of death were more open and self-disclosing in their personal relations than people who believed in heaven. Her thesis is summarized in JOURARD's book *Self-disclosure: An Experimental Analysis of the Transparent Self* (New York: Wiley-Interscience, 1971). The discussion in this section is influenced by A. W. WATTS, *The Way of Zen* (New York: Pantheon, 1957).

9

DEFENSE VERSUS GROWTH

INTRODUCTION

Persons discover who they are and what they must do to live effectively, and then something changes. Their needs vary moment by moment, sometimes subtly, occasionally in obvious ways. Other people with whom they live change their habits, and their attitude toward them. The machines, the environment, the domestic and foreign policies of the government, even one's own taste in music alter in time. It is our task, no less than it was the task of the dinosaurs, to come to terms with this change. Dinosaurs were endowed with small brains and very specialized bodies. When their world changed too abruptly, they could not change, and so they became extinct. Human beings have vast brains and untapped potential for new ways of experiencing and coping. Our bodies are relatively unspecialized. We can live under fantastically diverse circumstances, ranging from the Australian desert to the concrete of New York. We must specialize in order to survive. The Australian aborigine who wanders the desert carrying nothing but a spear or two is a superb specialist at desert survival, as was the polar Eskimo, who needed nothing more than warm clothes and a harpoon. Aborigines, Eskimos, and city dwellers alike retain the capacity to despecialize when circumstances change, in order to respecialize for living effectively in new circumstances. Anything that blocks our awareness of our capacity to suspend an ineffective way of being (so we can learn another way) is a threat to life itself, or to the quality of life. Our identity can become a glorified image for the sake of which we might sacrifice our vitality and the quality of our existence. We may even choose to die rather than live in ways out of keeping with our identity. It is not easy to be human, because there are so many ways to be, and no guidelines for choosing the identity that is most viable. This is one aspect of the "dreadful freedom" of which the existentialist philosophers speak. We must live with it.

The capacity to experience threat is our margin of safety. Anxiety and guilt are early warning signals. They indicate that unless we change something, our life, our self-esteem, or our very identity may be taken from us. It is good to be able to experience threat.

But threat opens options. It can spur defensive maneuvers that are themselves barriers to life, and it can promote enlarged awareness and greater competence. If every time a person was threatened, he or she put on a heavier suit of armor, then in time that person would be immobile—safe but out of touch. If the person could postpone defensive maneuvers long enough, he or she could act in ways that further growth.

Threats to the Self

Threats to the self originate from external as well as internal sources. We are not concerned here with danger to one's sheer survival, such as war or the destruction of the environment. We are considering threats to the way we feel we *are*, to our sense of our own identity.

EXTERNAL THREAT TO IDENTITY

Healthy Personality

Buber points out that human beings need confirmation from one another: "Man wishes to be confirmed in his being by man. . . . The human person needs confirmation because man as man needs it." [1] Without such confirmation from one's fellow human beings, a person can doubt he or she exists at all. Few people are that "ontologically secure," so firmly grounded in their sense of self that they can withstand a barrage of disconfirmation, or a life in which their perspective is ignored.

Disconfirmation. A person may experience himself being treated like a thing or an animal, for example, by his father. If he says, "You are not treating me right—I feel like a machine or an animal when I'm with you," the father might say, "You're crazy, son. Your mother and I love you, and we are doing what's best for you." The father is disconfirming his son's perspective and threatening his sense of identity. If the son says, "I don't like the Republican party because its policies seem too reactionary," the father may disconfirm him by saying, "You hippies don't know what you are talking about." Such disconfirmation is common, unfortunately, in family life. People who disconfirm one another's perspectives in this way certainly do not contribute to each other's senses of identity, except to help one another feel worthless.

Invalidation. A threat to one's identity related to disconfirmation is invalidation. This is most commonly seen in the behavior of grownups with children, and in members of some dominant group in the presence of those over whom they are dominant. Thus, parents may talk about their child *in her presence*, as if she were a doll or a robot: "She never seems to be happy; she doesn't dress properly, messes up her room, and will not work hard enough at her studies." Physicians may discuss a patient with each other and with students while the patient is present; thus, a psychiatrist may say, "Notice, with this patient, how rigidly he sits, the blank expression in his eyes, and how angry he becomes if I pinch him." The patient's perspective here is not even acknowledged, much less consulted. His sense of being a worthwhile human being is threatened by such experiences. Women are frequently invalidated in similar fashion by insensitive men: "The little woman cooks well, but she doesn't say anything worth listening to about business or politics."

Defense versus Growth Disconfirmation and invalidation do not threaten a person's life, but they certainly undermine the sense of

213

being a person, of existing as that very person. Laing and Esterson showed how an upbringing marked by continuous invalidation and disconfirmation was a factor in the development of schizophrenia. The anger of blacks, women, and colonized peoples, all of whom have felt thus treated, is testimony that no one wishes to be invalidated or disconfirmed.[2]

INTERNAL THREATS TO IDENTITY

Persons' sense of being who they believe they are, and wish to be, is assaulted by some aspects of their own experiencing. Thus, a parent who wishes to be seen as kind and loving toward children will be threatened by the experience of rage toward them. A student who believes she is bright and competent will be terribly threatened by the realization that she does not know enough to pass an exam. A person who believes he is morally pure (whatever that means to him) may be terribly threatened by erotic daydreams involving his brother or sister. Men especially are threatened by the experience of helplessness and dependency. If a man feels unable to cope with some problem, he may accept total failure rather than admit he feels the need for help from others.

What Are Defense Mechanisms?

Defense mechanisms are automatic, reflexlike ways in which a person reacts to threatening perceptions so that the self-structure will remain unchallenged and unchanged. Whenever anything of value is threatened, the person will naturally strive to defend it. But there are realistic and rational ways of defending something of value, and there are shortsighted ways to defend values. If we value our body, and our body is threatened by disease, the rational means of defense is to study the disease, determine its cure, and administer it. The unrealistic means for defense is to ignore the pain, or anesthetize ourselves against the pain, and pretend there is no threat to life and health.

If we value some theory, we can defend it unrealistically by distorting and ignoring conflicting evidence. The earlier discussion of autism (Chapters 3 and 4) illustrates this kind of autistic cognition.

Healthy
Personality

The defense mechanisms are autistic means of defending the self-structure. They make it possible for persons to continue believing they are the kind of persons they want to believe they are when there is much evidence (from the real self) to refute these beliefs.

DEFENSE MECHANISMS ARE INSTANCES OF UNCONSCIOUS ACTION

Defense mechanisms may be viewed as "preconscious" or unconscious. The defensive individual is not always aware he or she is defending the self against threat. As a matter of fact, once a defensive person recognizes he or she is being defensive against some threatening impulse or feeling, the person may achieve voluntary control over the defensive behavior.

HOW DEFENSE MECHANISMS MILITATE AGAINST GROWTH

Growth is change in a valued direction. One of the goals of personal growth is a healthy self-structure, that is, a state where the real self, the self-concept, the self-ideal, and the public selves are all mutually congruent. Whenever such a state of affairs exists, it can be only temporary—an unstable equilibrium. Any change in the real self will disrupt this equilibrium, and such changes are always occurring. The self-structure grows when the necessary adjustments are made following real-self changes. But if the person defends the self-structure, then that person will ignore or distort the messages of the real self, thus preserving the present self-structure despite its increasing alienation from the real self.

The person who defends the self-structure against change is like the aging matron who keeps wearing the clothing of an eighteen-year-old beauty queen, in spite of increasing girth. Her girdle might be so tight that she nearly faints, but she will not admit her clothing does not fit. Such is the case with a defended self-structure; the underlying real self may have become so discrepant from the self-concept, self-ideal, and public selves that the individual is really two distinct persons: the one she believes she is and the one she really is.

Defense versus Growth

The real self inevitably finds its way to expression. A real self that has been excluded by defense mechanisms manifests itself through boredom, frustration, vague anxiety and guilt, depression, unconscious motivation, and the symptoms of alienation from the self—in short, the whole repertoire of clinical psychopathology with which psychiatrists are familiar in their daily practice. Clinical symptoms of neurosis and of psychosis may be regarded as byproducts of the conflict between the real self and the attempt to preserve a self-structure markedly discrepant with it.

Some Common Defense Mechanisms

The mechanisms of defense might just as legitimately be called mechanisms for increasing self-alienation or methods of evading growth, for such are their consequences. They are modes of behavior undertaken by a person with a relatively weak ego when threat to the self-structure arises. If they are effective, they reduce anxiety and guilt, but whenever the defenses are themselves weakened, threat is again experienced, for its causes continue to be operative. A defense is like a drug; it must be kept operative if it is to reduce discomfort. But a defense, like a drug, does not remove the conditions responsible for the pain and discomfort.

What are the major patterns of defensive behavior and how may they be recognized? The individual can seldom recognize his or her own defensiveness, except under special conditions. The observer may be able to infer, from certain signs, the nature of the defense, the consequences of the defense, and the aspects of the real self that are being defended against.

REPRESSION

Repression is the most basic defense.[3] It consists in actively excluding from awareness any thought, feeling, memory, or wish that would threaten the self-structure. Freud introduced the concept of repression to explain some phenomena that he regularly observed in his efforts to treat neurotic patients. He found that his patients displayed resistance to the injunction that they say everything that came to mind. He used the term *resistance* to describe any deviation from unselected, uncensored talk-

Healthy Personality

ing. The term *repression* was invoked to explain the efforts of the person to avoid not merely speaking about embarrassing topics, but even thinking about these topics.

Repression manifests itself by the omission in the person's speech, emotion, and behavior repertoire of responses that might ordinarily be expected under given circumstances. For example, if a person has been deeply insulted by someone and displays no overt signs of hostility, the hypothesis can be entertained that the person has repressed these feelings.

It should not be assumed that because some thought, feeling, or need has been repressed, it simply fades out of existence altogether. Rather, what appears to occur is that the repressed feelings and tensions continue to operate as unconscious determiners of behavior (see Chapter 5), because the causes of these feelings persist in life itself. The represser may betray many signs of the repressed feelings to a keen observer—in dreams, accidents, slips of the tongue, and so on.

Repression also manifests itself as chronic tensing of various muscle groupings. If a person has repressed rage, yet lives continuously among the people who provoke it, that person may chronically display tension in the muscles of the jaw, the neck, and the shoulders. This muscular "armor" is what Wilhelm Reich, Alexander Lowen, and Ida Rolf all addressed directly, through exercises and massage (see Chapter 7). It often happened to patients of these practitioners that, when a set of muscles had relaxed in response to the therapist's manipulations, the patient would express rage, or tears and convulsive sobbing; moreover, the patient might then recall with vividness some childhood events related to the original repression.

An important indicator of repression is a refusal by the person to examine and consider any other motives for a given action than the one he or she presently admits. Thus, a parent may spank his or her children quite severely, may forget their birthdays, never spend time with them at enjoyable activity, and continually scold them. An observer may gather the impression that such behavior expresses hatred and dislike for the children and asks the parent why he or she treats the children so. The parent

Defense versus Growth

says, "Because I love them, and I am trying not to spoil them. I am trying to raise them right." If the observer asks, " Could it be that you don't like your children?" the parent might become quite indignant and refuse to explore the possibility that this might be true. This person is repressing hostility to the children. For the parent to admit disliking the children might threaten his or her self-structure to a profound degree.

Another important indicator of repression is selective recall of the past. In relating aspects of the past, much may be omitted from the account. If the observer knows what has been omitted, he or she may confront the person with these details, only to have the person deny that the events occurred. It is as if this person had a vested interest in forgetting these details, in order to preserve the present concept of self. Many experimental studies have shown how our recall and our forgetting are determined to a high degree by the need to maintain self-esteem and to preserve the present self-concept.[4]

In principle, a person can repress any aspect of the real self, whether it is socially desirable or socially reprehensible. Thus, a person may repress antisocial sexual urges and hostility but may also repress feelings of attraction, his or her own intellect, and strength and resources, if these aspects of the real self imply some threat to the self-structure. The authoritarian character who exaggerates personal weakness and the strength of the hero or boss is repressing his or her own powers and ascribing them (projecting them) to the authority figure in question. Fromm has detailed this point in his discussion of authoritarianism in everyday life and even in religion; he has suggested that the image of an all-powerful God, in contrast with weak, powerless humans, rests on our repression of our own powers and the ascription of these very powers to the deity.[5]

Repression is quite an unstable mechanism, calling as it does for unremitting (but unconscious) effort from the person. Whenever there is any reduction in the energy devoted to repression, there is likely to be a breakthrough of the repressed aspects of the real self. When this occurs, the person may be incredibly threatened by feelings and impulses that he did not know he possessed. It may hap-

Healthy Personality

pen that the feelings are so intense that he explodes into uncontrolled activity—for instance, sexual or hostile violence. Probably many of the sex and homicide crimes which one reads about in the papers ("Nobody would have expected him to do that, he was always so nice, so moral") illustrate the breakthrough of repressed feelings and impulses. When a person is fatigued, or ill, he may be overwhelmed with fantasies, feelings, and impulses that are shocking to him and to those who know him.[6]

Although repression is usually involuntary and unconscious, it can be conscious and deliberate. Every reader will recall occasions when they have had thoughts that were fully conscious, but quite repugnant. On those occations, they may have striven to get rid of the unwanted thoughts by just putting them out of mind or by trying to change the subject of thinking, in order to think of more pleasant things. Such efforts, if successful, may be called voluntary and conscious repression. They are analogous with the conversation between two persons; when an unpleasant subject comes up, the person who finds it is unpleasant will ask that the subject be changed, or else may skillfully guide the conversation so that the dangerous topics are avoided.

RATIONALIZATION

It is striking that whenever persons are asked why they did anything, their motives usually appear exemplary, to them and to the observer. A person will seldom admit intentions of an immoral or antisocial sort. Yet the consequences of many actions are often discrepant with the admitted motive. Thus, a person intends to help a friend and actually interferes drastically with the friend's success. A man loves his wife, yet his behavior toward her may produce grief and discomfort for her.

For any action that a person undertakes, it can be assumed its consequences were desired by the person. If the aim is denied, or if the consequences appear at variance with the aim, then the observer may assume the intent has been repressed. The motive that the person admits may be called a *rationalization*. It is an explanation for an action and its consequences that is compatible with the individual's self-structure. The motive behind ra-

Defense versus Growth

tionalization is not to give a factual account of authentic intent; rather, it is to do justice to the need to explain conduct and at the same time protect the self-structure.

A rationalization, then, is an explanation of one's conduct that has been selected from many possible explanations because it enhances and defends the individual's self-structure.

A theology student had asked a girl for a date. She was known to be quite proud of her sexually "liberated" attitudes. He said he wanted to persuade her to change her ways and denied any sexual interest in her. He was quite possibly rationalizing.

REACTION FORMATION

Persons may defend themselves against unwanted thoughts, feelings, and wishes, first by repressing them and then by compulsively thinking and striving to feel the opposite. It is as if it were not sufficient for them to free themselves of threat by merely eliminating the unwanted thoughts and feelings from the mind. They can only convince themselves (and others?) that they are not that kind of person if, and only if, they display the opposite kinds of behavior in extreme degree. Reaction formation reveals itself through the compulsive and exaggerated nature of the behavior and attitudes that the person manifests; yet the repressed aspects of the real self may still leak out. Thus, a compulsively generous person may betray repressed egocentricity and selfishness by giving gifts that the receiver does not like or cannot use, such as giving expensive cigarette lighters to nonsmokers and bottles of expensive Scotch whiskey to teetotalers. The person who is compulsively kind to animals betrays underlying sadism by the brutality with which invective is leveled against those who experiment with animals. ("I think people who are cruel to dogs should be shot and ground up as hamburger.") The devoted, overprotective parent keeps the child from growing by exaggerated overconcern with his or her health and safety. The guilty, philandering husband showers his wife with lavish gifts and with surprising and unusual tenderness and solicitude. The woman with repressed dependency strivings displays exaggerated self-reliance until she gets sick, when she becomes a virtual baby.

Healthy Personality

The ability to perceive the world accurately is a relatively difficult achievement. The probability is high that persons will perceive the world autistically unless they take active steps to "reality-test" their perceptions. Autistic perception is animistic and "physiognomic." The young child, the regressed psychotic, and, to some extent, primitive people all manifest such "primitive" perception. Primitive perception is characterized by the tendency for the individual to personalize animals, trees, water, and nature—assuming they have motives, feelings, and wishes just as the perceiver has.[7] The defense mechanism of projection is a special case of primitive perception. *Projection* is the name given to the tendency to assume that another person has motives, feelings, wishes, values, or, more generally, traits that the individual has.

Assimilative Projection. If persons assume that someone else is similar to themselves, the term *assimilative projection* is used to describe such an assumption.

Projection as such is not a defense mechanism; rather, it might be called misperception of another person. Or it may be regarded as a sort of logical fallacy—the act of formulating beliefs about another person's motives and feelings without adequate evidence. Thus, I may notice that some man resembles me in age, sex, educational level, and so I assume he is responding to some situation in a manner identical with my own. Both of us look at an attractive woman; I notice I am pleasantly affected by the woman, and I assume that the other person is similarly affected. Further questioning of the other person may prove my assumption is wrong; my assumption itself illustrates assimilative projection.

Disowning Projection. Suppose I have repressed interest in attractive women; to admit such interest would threaten my self-structure. I may assume the other fellow is very interested in the attractive woman, but I would myself vehemently deny any such interest. I would be displaying disowning projection. This unwarranted assumption about the other person's motives would be a defense mechanism. I would be protecting my self-concept by repressing certain feelings in myself and assuming without warrant that other people, not I, are motivated by such unacceptable drives.[8]

Defense versus Growth

The evidence that prompts the observer to suspect disowning projection is to be found in the beliefs that a person holds concerning his or her own motivation and that of others. One suspects disowning projection if (1) the motives imputed to others are derogatory and immoral, (2) such motives are vigorously denied in the self, (3) there is not much evidence to support the belief that the other person has the motives imputed to him or her, and (4) the person himself or herself gives evidence of these imputed motives, but at an unconscious level.

Not only can a person disown and project unsavory aspects of the real self; the person can also repress and project positive potentialities. Where this occurs, the person perceives the self as imperfect, weak, and base, whereas the object of the projection is perceived as perfect, strong, and ideal. Authoritarian characters often appear to do this. Many a romantic lover, too, has seen himself as worthless and evil and has projected his own moral potential onto his beloved, perceiving her as the embodiment of all that is clean, wonderful, and morally perfect. He may become disillusioned in the face of reality.

DENIAL

Repression is really an instance of refusing to see or hear aspects of inner reality, the real self. But one can defend one's self-structure by refusing to see or hear aspects of outer reality if such perception would result in threat to the self-structure. The psychoanalysts coined the term *denial* to describe this tendency to ignore aspects of outer reality that induced anxiety and losses in self-esteem. Experimental psychologists use the term *perceptual defense* to describe the same phenomena. Sullivan spoke of "selective inattention" in this connection.

Humans tend to ignore or reconstruct reality when it is painful. It is such a stubborn tendency that Freud spoke of it as one of the "principles" of mental functioning—the pleasure principle in contrast with the reality principle.[9] When there are two possible meanings that might be assigned to some perception, one pleasant but untrue and the other true but painful, we must actually fight the pleasure principle in order to arrive at accurate cognition. Thus, we do not hear derogatory remarks uttered by someone about us, even though our hearing is quite adequate to notice whispered praise. We do not see the blemishes in our loved ones if our self-esteem rests on the premise that we have made a wise choice of a perfect mate. In extreme forms, among persons with weak egos, we may actually see something quite clearly but then deny we saw it and believe the denial. For some persons the death of a loved one is so catastrophic, calling as it does for much reorganization of behavior and the self-structure, that they will not believe the person is dead.

PSYCHIC CONTACTLESSNESS

The term *psychic contactlessness*, coined by Wilhelm Reich,[10] refers to an inability, or a refusal, to communicate with or get emotionally involved with another person. If one has been deeply hurt in relationships with people, one may protect oneself against further hurt and losses in self-esteem by walling the self off from people. One is *among* people without being really *with* them. Avoidance of close contact and emotional involvement with others serves many defensive functions, not the least of which is the fact that others will never come to know you. Because others are never given the opportunity to observe someone's real self, the contactless person can entertain all manner of grandiose fantasies about the self; these are never known or criticized by others.

DEPERSONALIZING OTHERS

If individuals do not allow themselves to think of others as human beings with feelings and hopes, they protect themselves in many ways. They may be afraid to become personally involved, and so they stubbornly refuse to pay attention to the other person as a feeling, sensitive human being. Instead, other people are seen only as the embodiment of their social role; they are workers, or wives, or doctors, not persons. The act of depersonalizing others may thus protect persons against guilt feelings they might experience if they knew they were hurting others. Or if they suffer from an inability to love, they might protect themselves against such a disquieting

Defense versus Growth

insight through depersonalizing others. Physicians, nurses, and dentists often depersonalize their patients or clients, adopting a "bedside manner" or a "chair-side manner," when dealing with them. The adoption of such contrived patterns of interaction permits them to treat their patient without being disturbed by the latter's suffering. Further, it permits them to hide their true feelings of like or dislike behind a professional mask.[11] Depersonalizing makes it possible for acts of extreme violence to be performed. The Nazis were able to slaughter millions of Jews because they had convinced themselves Jews were not human beings.

SUBLIMATION

A rare defense mechanism in that it calls out positive results is called sublimation. In its narrowest sense, it refers to the substitution of a socially acceptable activity for erotic, sexual strivings that cannot be directly satisfied because of social standards. In a broader sense, it may also be interpreted to mean substitution of a socially acceptable behavior for *any* drive or motivation that is not socially acceptable, including hostility and aggression.

For a person who, for religious or other reasons, can either not marry or chooses not to marry and to live a celibate, sexless life, throwing one's energy into volunteer leadership in the community or into an absorbing job is a good, socially desirable alternative. Sometimes this sublimation may be temporary, as in the case of a teenager who may keep physically active to the point of exhaustion in order to avoid encounters with the opposite sex, or it can also be a permanent lifestyle as in the case of some corporate executives who are "married to their jobs." In any event, sublimation is often seen as an entirely desirable defense pattern.

Evaluating Defense Mechanisms

Although a healthy personality characteristically is free of frequent use of the defense mechanisms, they are *Healthy* in actuality a normal occurrence. Defense mechanisms *Personality* have survived as concepts from earliest days of Freudian psychoanalysis and still are useful as illuminators of some forms of behavior. There seems to be some evidence concerning the relative value of various defense mechanisms. For example, in a study by Barenbaum [12] of people who had lost young sons or husbands in the Yom Kippur war in Israel, denial was one of the most often used defense mechanisms by the bereaved parents or wives. In another study by Jacobowitz,[13] the brighter preadolescent children, facing problems in moral transgressions, would most likely use projection and displacement, whereas the less academically talented peers would use denial. And the value of some of the mechanisms may be seen in a third study by Viney and Manton,[14] who found that university students who used some of the defense mechanisms had reduced anxiety, indicating the therapeutic purpose of the mechanisms.

Defense of the Public Self

Persons' various public selves are important to them. They can feel assured others will like them only when they believe that other people see them as the kind of persons that they can like. And, as Willie Loman pointed out in *Death of a Salesman*, it is important to be well liked. Consequently, it is not enough simply to construct public selves; a person usually feels obliged to defend them.

The most general means of defending the public self is by means of selective suppression of behavior that is inconsistent with the public self, replacing authentic with false self-disclosure. A mother may have heard reports about her son's behavior that conflict with her concept of him. She confronts him with the report, and he denies it flatly. He does not want her to believe that he behaves in such a way. Secrecy is more common than lying as a means of defending our public selves. We can do almost anything without fear (though not necessarily without guilt) if no one discovers what we have done. The secret activities may be incredibly disparate with the public selves of the individual. People at conventions sometimes display behavior markedly different from their usual hometown behavior and are quite disconcerted if

Defense versus Growth

their family and neighbors hear reports of their conduct.[15]

A really intelligent person can construct public selves with ingenuity and finesse—sometimes fantastically diverse and contradictory selves. The more diverse they are, however, the greater the difficulty in maintaining them; persons who hold contrasting concepts of the individual may meet this person simultaneously, and then the individual is at a loss to know how to behave.

Persistence of the Self-ideal

Once a self-ideal has been constructed, the person finds it difficult to change it. Why is this so, especially when the conscience is inhumane and impossibly strict? Consider an individual with incredibly high standards of performance; this person never attains them and believes he or she is a failure. If only the person's self-ideal could be altered, he or she could experience self-esteem, perhaps for the first time. Yet the person, when urged to relax the standards, will refuse, saying, "I wish I could, but I can't."

The reason why persons find it difficult to alter the self-ideal is because it came from sources *they dare not question*—parents, teachers, God, or the Bible. Their values have been acquired in the context of an authoritarian relationship, and they are in dread of horrible consequences should they question the "commands." [16] Freud said, "As the child was once compelled to obey its parents, so the ego submits to the categorical imperative pronounced by its superego." [17]

This fear of obscure consequences if one should change one's conscience presents a powerful conserving force in the personality. A person may anesthetize the conscience with alcohol, lull it with self-deceptive arguments and rationalizations, may even repress it; but one rarely changes it. This refusal has disastrous consequences for one's wellbeing and maturity.

Growth of the Self

Healthy Personality   Thus far, we have discussed the myriad ways in which a person maintains a stable identity in the face of experiencing that threatens it. Such stability is not pathology-producing in its own right; everything depends upon the availability of action that serves the person's needs and fulfills the person's projects. If the different aspects of the self are in reasonable harmony, and the person can cope with the challenges of work, leisure, and personal relationships, a stable self-structure is compatible with healthy personality. But there are times when healthy personality can be achieved only by changes in the self. I shall discuss these occasions now.

THE TIME FOR CHANGE

There are various indicators of the time for change. These include boredom, sickness, chronic anxiety and guilt, failure in work, and failure in personal relationships. In all these instances, the person's self-structure may have gotten out of touch with the real self, and the person is out of touch with external reality. Something has changed, and he or she has not acknowledged or recognized it.

Boredom. The experience of boredom signifies the person's action is not serving his or her true needs and interests. Boredom also arises from prolonged exposure to monotonous surroundings, unchanging relationships, and repetitive work and leisure activity. Boredom is evidence of unperceived change in the self; the person whom one takes oneself to be *used* to be satisfied by those ways of being. Boredom means that one *no longer is that person*, and it is time to discover new dimensions of the self.

Sickness. Illness may signify that the person was not living in health-engendering ways. If a person is recurrently sick, it means, among other things, that the person does not know what he or she needs to do, or to stop doing, to achieve buoyant health; something must be done besides taking medicines. So-called nervous breakdowns—a radical inability to cope with conflict and responsibility in life—likewise indicate that a change in the structure of the self is overdue. Physical and psychological breakdown are the ultimate price one pays for resisting change in the self when life calls for it. If a person "worships" the present self-concept, public image, or self-ideal and is willing to sicken rather than change,

Defense versus Growth

then that person truly is guilty of the sin of idolatry so strongly condemned in the Old Testament. Self-idolatry in this sense is sickening.[18]

Chronic Anxiety and Guilt. An existence plagued by anxiety is hellish. The anxious person feels doom lurking everywhere, that the end of his world is at hand, and that he or she is helpless to avert it. This person may take tranquilizing drugs or engage in compulsive busywork in order never to have "idle thoughts," but the terror is there, appearing in nightmares and obsessional worry about health or imminent failure. Clinical experience with neurotic persons shows that such anxiety arises when life engenders feelings and impulses that the neurotic person dares not acknowledge. The anxiety "replaces" the rage, the sexuality, or the affection that is being provoked in life, but that would devastate the person's sense of identity if it were acknowledged and expressed. Such anxiety is a sign of the time to face personal reality and change the self.

Chronic guilt and diminished self-esteem likewise show that the person is violating the self-ideal and is condemning himself or herself for failing to live up to this vainglorious image. Such guilt indicates that it is time for the person to "straighten up" and live up to ideals—which is a form of growth; or it may rather be a time to change the self-ideal so that it falls more in the realm of human possibility.

Dread of Being "Unmasked." If persons have been disclosing themselves falsely, thereby showing other people a false self, then it is as if they have been living as spies in hostile territory or playing an ungenuine role on the stage of their lives. Under these circumstances they will be obliged to repress all spontaneity in relationships with others and will remain chronically self-conscious. Such cramped and cramping self-scrutiny makes life hardly worth living, yet these persons continue, because they dread the reaction of others, should they ever come to know them as they really are. Such a false public self, with the suffering it produces, likewise indicates that it is time for authenticating change—that is, change for growth.

Healthy Personality

Failure in Work. Success at one's work or one's studies

is essential for self-esteem and for securing one's livelihood. If a person fails dismally at work and does so repeatedly, it may signify that this person is not putting himself or herself wholeheartedly into it. This may happen when the person has not chosen the vocation alone, so that the activities that it calls for fail to arouse and sustain interest. Especially for students, academic failure signifies self-alienation rather than dullness. The failing student is out of touch with his or her real goals and potential strength and ability. Failure is the time for an encounter with one's real self, to make some growth-fostering changes in the self.

Unexpected Failure in Personal Relationships. If a person is rejected by friends or divorced by a spouse without wishing it, it signifies a fundamental incompetence. Interpersonal competence—the ability to be with others in ways that engender their affection and interest—is essential for healthy personality. If one cannot relate lovingly to others, one will indeed suffer a lonely existence. Inability to love others and to be loved by them signifies that one's self-structure is alienated, that one is repressing many possibilities. Such failure points to the time for self-study and change.

The Process of Personal Growth

Growth of the self is not the same as physical growth, although both dimensions of growing are simultaneous in children. Growth of the self is a change in the way of experiencing the world and one's own being.[19] Not all change in experiencing is growth, however. One can speak of growth only when the changes enhance the person's ability to cope with challenges in existence. Some alterations in experience, as occur in psychosis, make effective action impossible; they may be described as regression rather than growth. Yet the experience of growing is almost always confusing, and occasionally frightening. It does not have to be terrifying, however; growing to a larger perspective and a more authentic identity can be exhilarating, perhaps because of the excitement and uncertainty that almost always are involved. Personal growth is often likened to the experi-

Defense versus Growth

ence of a voyage:[20] leaving home (one's present identity, or view of self), traveling to strange places (openness to new dimensions of experience of self and world), and a return, to enlarge home in ways that befit the "larger" person one has become. We outgrow our self-structures just as we outgrow our clothing, cramping family roles, and the way of life accepted in a small town.

"LEAVING HOME"

Growing entails "leaving home," a letting go of one's clutch upon one's present way of being involved with other people and with one's projects. As I pointed out earlier (Chapter 3), our projects and commitments impose structure upon the way we experience the world and our own identities. As soon as a person abandons his or her projects and usual relationships, the world "opens up." To suspend one's usual ways of being involved gives rise to an experience akin to opening a door to a hidden room or to a new world. "Letting go" releases all modes of experiencing from repression. When the person was living the prior identity (which is now in process of enlarging), work and relationships with others required that the person be inattentive to all perceptions, memories, and imaginative productions, save those relevant to that identity. Suspension of this identity opens the person to an enlarged experience of his or her own possibilities and the possibilities of the world.

The means of letting go, of suspending one's present identity, are myriad—as numerous as the means of clinging to one's identity (defense mechanisms) which we have discussed. Earlier (Chapter 2) we discussed some of them. It will be appropriate to review some of them here.

All the meditative disciplines, such as Zen "sitting," transcendental meditation, and various yogas (Hatha yoga, Raja yoga, Tantra yoga, and so on) function as means of disengaging a person from usual ways of experiencing, and they release new dimensions of consciousness. The several "psychedelic" substances, such as marijuana, lysergic acid, mescaline, peyote, and psylocybin mushrooms, also disengage a person from reality and may lead to self-destructive results. Under

Healthy Personality

these circumstances, as in meditation, the person is "leaving home" and opening the self to the free play of perception, thinking, remembering, imagination, and feeling.

Exposure to a perspective larger than one's own can also disengage a person from the commitment to the present view of self and world. Thus, dialogue with a wise person (so that one realizes there are "higher" consciousnesses) can explode a person's view of his or her own possibilities. The same can happen through reading books written by authors who have achieved larger perspectives. Certain authors have always challenged me in this way, for example, Kazantzakis, Henry Miller, Martin Buber, and Sartre.[21] An encounter with death, either through a near escape or the loss of a loved one, can persuade a person to suspend his or her present identity and the way of life that accompanies it, in order to review new possibilities. The realization that one will inevitably die can liberate a person from attachment to unimportant activities, relationships, and confining places.

In other civilizations and times, a variety of techniques for letting go were employed in religious ceremonies and rites; in a sense, they were deemed ways of encountering the gods in the quest for guidance in life. Thus, fasting, chanting, dancing, solitude in the desert or upon a mountain all have been employed to disengage persons from the reminders of who they have been, so that they might become different, more viable selves.

I regard Homer's account of the Odyssey and the story of Moses leading the children of Israel out of the land of bondage (which provided them with security as much as tyranny) as allegories about growth from a limited view of the possibilities in living to a boundless vision.

Literally to leave home, of course, is a way to commence an episode of growing. But it takes vast energy, and courage sometimes, to put one's body into an automobile or an airplane, to go elsewhere. People one is leaving behind may impose astonishing pressure to keep one there, in that place, in that way of being oneself. They may try to make the voyager guilty by suffering

Defense versus Growth

in his or her presence or by reminding the person of duty to "loved ones." Growth, even the initiation of the growth episode, presents the challenge of change to the other people in one's life.[22] They do not always welcome this challenge.

OPENNESS TO EXPERIENCING

The world is always "disclosing" itself to people, but each person "receives"—that is, pays attention to—only a tiny fraction of all there is to be perceived. Each person perceives, remembers, thinks, and imagines only what is relevant for individual needs and projects and what is "appropriate" for a person with that identity to be conscious of. The rest of the world of possible experiencing is closed off. This possible world is the "unconscious" mentioned by Freud, the "shadow" side of existence of which Jung wrote; it is the "ground," as opposed to "figure," which Fritz Perls and the earlier Gestalt psychologists spoke of. The myth of Pandora's box; the knowing that came from eating of the "tree of knowledge"; the Medusa myth; and the myth of Oedipus, who knew too much, all attest the awareness of humans throughout history that there is more possibility for experiencing than we customarily are aware of. All the mystical traditions, such as Sufism, alchemy, kabbala, and shamanism, are recognitions of larger realms of awareness and ways to achieve contact with them. Dreams—the "hidden language," the "royal road to the unconscious"—have always been consulted as paths to a larger awareness of self and world. All point to the "world beyond" our present consciousness and a self that is "beyond" our present awareness.

When a person lets go in any of the ways mentioned, that person does open the self to sights, sounds, smells, feelings, and contact that always were there but to which previously the person was inattentive. Laing believes that the realm of psychotic experience—and of hallucinations, delusions and illusions, cherubs, angels, demons—is a normal, health-giving event that can occur to anyone during the transition from an identity that *Healthy* was destructive to life to another as yet unchosen and *Personality* undiscovered identity more compatible with healthy personality. In other words, schizophrenia is not a disease; rather, it is an intensification of the *experience of transition* from one self-structure that has been outgrown to one that is more authentic and life-giving. Laing believes that such transitional experiences are not diseases to be "treated" by psychotherapy, drugs, and hospitalization; rather, they are experiences of growing that are to be understood, protected, and encouraged by persons who have themselves frequently gone through such growing episodes.

There are many points of view concerning the meaning of openness to experience. The first involves chemical inducers of openness. The second, however, involves the "earned" experience resulting from effort and planning.

A Peyote "Trip." The descriptions of "psychedelic trips" provide one with a more dramatic portrayal of the openness to experiencing that occurs with letting go. On one occasion, I ate a fist-sized peyote button. Its taste was absolutely hideous, and the effort to keep it in my stomach after swallowing each bite was heroic. The content of this cactus is an alkaloid poison, and so as fast as I was eating it, my stomach was reflexly attempting to expel it. Nevertheless, I held it down for about two hours before I finally yielded to the need to regurgitate. I was in Mexico at the time, and a trusted friend was sitting with me on the roof of his house. About an hour after I vomited, I began to shiver from an experience of cold. I huddled in my chair. This ended after a short time, and I felt energized to an extraordinary degree. I began to dance with rhythms that my friend said were African or Indian. I looked at lights from the street, and they had intense blue auras. The heavens appeared to me as they might if one were living inside a volcano, with only the cone open to the skies. I believed I could see the Aztec serpent god Quetzlcoatl flying through the air. During the plant-induced surges of energizing, my perceptions of distance were altered; the street appeared only a footstep away, whereas the actual distance from the roof was more than 25 feet. I recall telling my friend, "Peyote is definitely not for children, or unstable people; I can see

Defense versus Growth

233

how someone would believe he could fly, or step from a building to the ground, and then go ahead and do it, only to die. I at least know that my experience is from the peyote."

During the period of strength and energy I broke a piece of tile about an inch thick with my bare hands, and I pulled a foot-long metal spike out of a brick wall and bent it. (Next morning I could neither break the tile nor bend the spike.) I believed then that I could get into the "rhythm" of bricks and metal and by such contact perform what looked like superhuman feats.

After perhaps two hours of such goings on, I became exhausted and lay on a cot; the period of quiet began a voyage in time to my early childhood, perhaps the years between two and four. I re-experienced some of the vivid visual and auditory memories from that time, which I also had done some five years earlier, when I took lysergic acid (LSD) under the guidance of a physician experienced in those matters. I also could recognize myself again as various animals, for example, a lion, an eagle, a snake, and a dog. After another two hours or so, I slept. On awakening next morning I discussed the experience with my friend and found it enlightening.

I do not believe such drug-induced experiences are growth-enhancing for everyone. If a person is of narrow perspective, immature and incompetent, and not responsibly engaged in work and personal relationships, I believe that powerful disengagement from customary identity can be disturbing, even destructive to the capacity to cope with the world. The other "natural" ways of disengaging are more self-regulating, in that the person can get no further "out" of the identity and customary experience of the world than he or she authentically "earns."

Another Point of View on Openness to Experience

Many see the concept of openness to experience in other ways, and both views should be considered by the person seeking higher levels of consciousness. The second position shares the conviction that openness to experience is a major key to the healthy personality. As a matter of fact, almost all positions concerning high-level functioning, the optimal self, self-actualization, and the beautiful and noble personality include the concept in one form or another (as discussed in Chapter 1). In one sense, the concept of the transparent self implies that the person is open to those who wish to know him or her, to see the person truly—the person's public self is essentially the same as the real self.

However, openness in this position suggests that the person is first of all *passively* open or transparent, in that no blocks are placed before the one who seeks to know the person—more than that, he or she welcomes the other's search, gaze, and discovery of the open self. The person has nothing to hide. In addition, when new experiences present themselves as opportunities, the person readily accepts them, takes them, uses them, experiences them—with no denial, blocking, or suspicion. Thus, as a new flower appears as this person does everyday errands, he or she notices the flower, passively takes in its beauty, its message of a new season. Encountering a new idea while reading, listening to the radio, or watching television, the person can accept the new idea, experience it, as part of the self. The individual's passive openness is seen as he or she meets a new person, largely by chance, standing on a street corner. A conversation is initiated by the other person. The individual responds, accepts the new person, does not close the self off from this new experience.

Furthermore, open, healthy personalities are *active*, enthusiastic seekers of new experiences. They may meticulously plan to learn to play the piano, to ski, to windsurf, to pilot an airplane, to learn a new language, to seek a new culture. They hungrily taste the newness of life; however, they do so *selectively* and with care and preparation. They are ordinarily not satisfied to expand their consciousness through the effortless experience, but rather first plan their openness-realization meticulously, work at it, and joy in their accomplishments when they skim along the water skillfully, play a sonata with distinction, or speak their first phrases to a foreign visitor in the visitor's language. Each of these experiences re-

Defense versus Growth

quires considerable planning and preparation, and usually long days of hard work or study, all of which may be found thoroughly enjoyable by the healthy personality.

Healthy personalities select their experiences in relationship to their possible good and absence of harm. They recognize that some experiences are irreversibly destructive to the self—for example, attempting to cross the Atlantic Ocean in a rubber dinghy without a compass, or ingesting chemicals that might so mask reality that one could not make a good judgment concerning the distance across the road from the corner, or wallowing in an orgiastic group sex experience that might leave some of the group members distressed, diseased, or disgraced. The idea "if you haven't tried it don't knock it" is not "bought" by the healthy personality, which is nevertheless open to experience. These people are open to destructive experience only in the sense that they may consider it, think of it, and discard it. They are open to constructive, joyful, even ecstatic experience. They seek it and even seek variety in experience—but always with an awareness of its negative or positive effect upon the self-concept. The "soul selects its own society," [23] and the high-level personality selects its own experiences.

This does not cheat the high-level personality out of the joy of the spontaneous event, the fun of the belly laugh and the childlike delight of impulsive fun. Yet they participate in all of these with a measure of judgment. Enchanted by a beautiful waterfall while on a hike in the mountains, they may disrobe and walk under the falls—but they do not dive into the pool without first checking the depth of the sharp rocks below. Their joys are often spontaneous, but even then involve a judgment of value.

Finally, the openness to experience involves accepting ideas, thoughts, learnings, new convictions, and choices. It includes the ability to alter one's convictions and beliefs when new evidence or facts are taken in by the person.

This implies, then, that the drug experience—whose impact may be unknown and whose contribution to the self-concept at best is uncertain or unlikely and at worst is deeply destructive—is not only not for children, as indicated by the previous point of view, but may also be of no value and of destructive consequence for adults as well. The rationale behind this is that the drug experience does not bring a feeling of competency or of self-adequacy in coping with or even in enjoying reality—it rather brings a new, distorted view of reality, which brings momentary peace (as in the case of "downers") or momentary excitement (as in the instance of the so-called mind-expanding chemicals). However, it brings no true insights into the self that can be translated into "real" life. It harbors potential for permanent damage.

The research on the effects of drug experiences has been continuing for over 10 years. It seems impossible to come to a reliable conclusion concerning long-term effects, even after these extensive studies have been completed, without the bias of the evaluator predetermining the interpretation. In the face of the possibility of either no harm and momentary joy or great personal destructiveness, the healthy personality utilizes the selectivity principle in choosing experience. In seeking the delights and ecstasies of new experience, this person looks not to chemical ingestion but rather to activity of the whole mind and body in discovering new experience and his or her own undeveloped potentialities.[24]

THE RETURN

Growth, according to the present metaphor, entails a return to the place one had left, in order to make it suitable for living, and moreover, living as a person of enlarged perspective.

A growth cycle is completed when persons affirm their larger experience of self and world and modify their concept of self, their public self, and their self-ideal in the light of the enlarged awareness. They now know they *are* more, and *can be more*, and different, than they hitherto believed possible. This alteration and enlargement of one's sense of self is desirable and conducive to a healthy personality. The process of integrating the larger consciousness of self and world is helped immeasurably by re-engagement in life projects and personal relationships. Indeed, it is the demands, challenges, and

Defense versus Growth

rewards of work, play, and personal relationships that provide the incentive to grow, and the rewards of such growth. Without such ways of being engaged in the world, I believe efforts to let go and to open oneself to new experiencing have destructive and regressive consequences. Chronic users of psychedelic drugs, like fanatics at yoga or meditation, confuse means with ends; they spend their time "in their experience," but out of action.

The return is often difficult, because the people with whom one has been engaged may not have changed; further, they may resent the changes that the growing person has introduced into their world. They may impose considerable pressure upon the individual to revert to the way he or she was prior to the episode of growing. To yield to such pressure is disastrous, for it makes a nonevent out of the person's growth.

OUTCOMES OF GROWTH

Growth is change, but change in the direction of greater awareness, competence, and authenticity. With each episode of growing through which a person passes, that person's knowledge of the world increases and the ability to be more aware of what is going on likewise is enlarged. Growth reveals itself publicly, in the person's action, but the more important dimensions of growing are secret and invisible.

Growth in consciousness makes it possible for a person to see connections between ways of behaving and their consequences for wellbeing.

Typically, a person's growth in awareness and competence occurs imperceptibly, in small increments. Occasionally, however, a person is so well defended against change that it takes an episode of illness or some more dramatic tragedy to dislodge the person from the bastion of immobility. We are often so heavily "reinforced," or rewarded for remaining the same, that it takes powerful pain to make us willing to give up our more familiar ways in order to risk change.

Healthy
Personality
Growing will go on throughout a person's life span, even into the seventies and nineties, if the person has the courage (and the encouragement) to accept threat and

not respond reflexively with mechanisms of defense. Properly understood, the experiences of anxiety and dread will evoke the "courage to be" and they will be harbingers of growth to richer existence. Improperly understood, or encountered in a spirit of timidity, they lead a person to make of the identity an impregnable bastion. The person then leads a safe but often unproductive and joyless life. Courage and encouragers assist one to grow.

The courage to grow can sometimes be generated in psychotherapy and in a properly conducted encounter group. In Chapter 16, psychotherapy as a means for stimulating personal growth is discussed.

AN EXAMPLE OF A GROWING SELF

A woman student, age twenty, consulted me for help with some problems that were so painful that she had been considering suicide. She was attractive, intelligent, and obtained good grades. Our first meeting was dramatic; she had phoned me for a session after spending most of the previous night debating whether to end her life with sleeping pills or with a razor blade applied to her wrists.

The crisis that brought her to this point was the feeling that she did not know who she was. She found herself involved in an affair with another student, yet she did not love him. He wanted her to share an apartment with him, as many of their classmates had been doing. On the one hand, she was tempted to set up housekeeping, because she had never lived with anyone but her own family and her present roommate, who was another woman. On the other hand, she did not like the fellow any more. Yet she could not end the affair, because she was convinced her boyfriend would kill himself. He had convinced her that he found his life possible only if she were his woman. Sometimes subtly, sometimes openly, he controlled her by making her feel guilty over not yielding to his wishes and needs.

To make matters worse, she had been reared by conventional parents who neither smoked nor drank, who went regularly to church, and whom she loved dearly. She lived in the dread they would find out about her

Defense versus Growth

affair. When she reflected upon her situation, it seemed hopeless; she could not displease her lover, nor could she turn to her parents for emotional support. She was convinced that if her mother discovered she had been intimate with a man outside marriage, it would break her heart. Furthermore, like many of her classmates, she smoked marijuana, and this too was opposed to her parents' wishes and their beliefs about her. She was no longer a virgin, obviously, but her parents assumed she was. On her visits home she concealed her birth-control pills.

She described her situation in these terms:

> I feel trapped. I don't know my real feelings. I am such a jellyfish. I please everyone, but I don't know what I want for myself. I feel guilty for my deceptions, and yet I can't be the person my parents thought I was either—I've changed. I really feel terrible. I can't leave John because he'll kill himself, if not right away, then by drinking, and smoking too much dope. He has gone to pieces every time I get selfish. I love my parents, but I can't tell them what I've been up to. They think I'm still their sweet, unspoiled daughter.

We met for therapeutic interviews over a period of a month—about seven sessions in all. During this time, she spoke at length about her background, and the way she had been living, and how she thought about herself. Because I didn't think she was as despicable as she felt she was, she began to feel she belonged within the human race. She examined her conscience and came to the conclusion that she was not living a life that warranted such intensities of self-hate. She had loved, or at least liked, her lover at one time, and their intimacies grew out of what she regarded as mutual love. She stopped condemning herself for entering the affair. But as she talked about herself, she gradually came to see that she had been trying to live out a false self-concept. "It's not like me to act selfishly, to do what *I* want rather than what *others* want. My parents raised me to be unselfish." She recognized the resentment she felt about being controlled by

Healthy Personality

240

both her parents' wishes and her lover's and came to feel that it was all right to experience anger and to express it in appropriate ways.

As she acknowledged more and more of her real feelings, and came to accept herself in the light of this enlarged awareness, she felt that her entrapment was at an end. She ended her affair with John, who did get very drunk when she told him it was over, but he did not kill himself. In fact, he moved in immediately with an older and more motherly student.

She recognized that she had outgrown the perspectives of her parents and could no longer pretend to be a virginal model of propriety. However, she believed that if she confided fully in her mother, as she had when she was a high school student, her mother would be shocked. And so she let her parents know that she was growing and learning a lot at the university, but she kept her private life to herself. She confided in her closest girlfriend, with whom she had a relationship of total honesty.

We ended the sessions when she felt that she had a much larger perspective on her life. She liked herself better, and she felt more honest. In technical terms, she enlarged her self-concept, modified her conscience in humane and mature ways, and presented a public self more in keeping with the realities of her own personality and the demands of the situation. My involvement, as a therapist, was mostly limited to listening to her talk about her situation and confirming her as a worthwhile human being in spite of (or because of) the fact that she had allowed herself ot be trapped in a destructive relationship. She began to live in conformity with her own true feelings and values, rather than others' expectations, and she found this authentic way more life-giving and freeing.

Some Existential Suggestions

The most common sign of excessive defensiveness is frequent experiences of threat. If other people have to be careful about what they say or do in your presence, it can signify that they sense your grasp of your identity is

Defense versus Growth

frail indeed. If you are easily upset by criticism or frightened by your anger or sensuality, it may signify that you are trying to live up to some glorified image.

The time to grow—to begin to let go of one's present self-concept—is evidenced by boredom, failure, and anxiety. These experiences signify that you and your real self have changed but that your self-structure has not. You are *impersonating* an identity that up to yesterday may have been authentic and life-giving. Now, however, it is not. To start a growth episode is frightening, but it need not be terrifying. All it means is that you may have to suspend your usual activities and relationships in order to get a fresh perspective upon your own possibilities and the possibilities of changing some aspects of your life.

If you meditate or retreat to a quiet place from time to time, the chances are that you change aspects of your activity and your self-structure more or less frequently. If, however, you are "locked into" various roles, and a fixed way of being yourself, the experience of threat may be more acute when it happens, and the prospect of change more frightening.

If your present identity is not sustaining a rewarding and health-engendering life and you do not see ways to grow and change, then it might be valuable to find a personal counselor or psychotherapist. Conversations with a professional person can frequently lead to growth-producing changes that are neither drastic nor destructive.

SUMMARY

The self-structure, described in the last chapter, keeps a person from changing. People dread the experience of threat to their sense of themselves. The threat arises from aspects of experience that are not compatible with a person's self-concept, self-ideal, or public selves. One can react to such threat defensively, by resorting to one of a myriad of defense "mechanisms"; and one can acknowledge the threatening experience and alter one's self-structure in the direction of greater authenticity.

Mechanisms for defense of the self-concept include

Healthy
Personality

repression, rationalization, reaction formation, projection, denial, psychic contactlessness, depersonalizing others, fixation, and regression. All these operations that persons perform upon their own experience and behavior enable them to maintain their present belief in their own identity. More to the point, they insure that persons' self-concepts become increasingly estranged from their real self.

Persons maintain their public selves by selective self-disclosure and by inhibition of all action that would adversely affect the way others see them. The self-ideal resists change, usually, because a person has acquired it in an authoritarian fashion and is encouraged to regard challenging the present moral precepts as a sin.

Threat can lead to growth, however. A person can recognize when the self-structure has become estranged from the real self through the experience of boredom, sickness, chronic anxiety and guilt, dread of being unmasked, and failure in work and in personal relationships.

Can you recall painful, tragic, or defeating experiences in your past? Now can you work these in to your self, integrate them into your experiential life so that you can free yourself from defensiveness about them and turn them into positive experiences?

Growth, as a response to threat, is likened to a voyage. It entails leaving home—letting go of one's present sense of identity; opening oneself to all the new dimensions of experiencing that hitherto had been repressed in order to defend the past sense of identity; and then "returning home," reforming one's sense of identity in the light of the enlarged experiencing, and disclosing to others the person one has newly become. Of course, growth as a response to threat is most compatible with the development of healthy personality.

There are many ways to open one's self to new experience. The healthy personality selects carefully those experiences that are constructive and are "earned."

NOTES AND REFERENCES

Defense versus Growth   1. The quote comes from M. Buber, *The Knowledge of Man* (New York: Harper, 1965), p. 71.

2. See R. D. Laing and A. Esterson, *Sanity, Madness and the Family* (London: Tavistock, 1964), for illustrations of disconfirmation and invalidation of experience.

3. See O. Fenichel, *The Psychoanalytic Theory of Neurosis* (New York: Norton, 1945), pp. 148–151.

4. S. Rosenzweig, "An Experimental Study of Repression, with Special Reference to Need-Persistive and Ego-Defensive Reactions to Frustration," *Journal of Experimental Psychology*, 1943, Vol. 32, pp. 64–74; Thelma Alper, "Memory for Completed and Incompleted Tasks as a Function of Personality: An Analysis of Group Data," *Journal of Abnormal and Social Psychology*, 1946, Vol. 41, pp. 403–420; C. W. Ericksen, "Psychological Defenses and Ego Strength in the Recall of Completed and Incompleted Tasks," *Journal of Abnormal and Social Psychology*, 1954, Vol. 49, pp. 51–58.

5. E. Fromm, *Psychoanalysis and Religion* (New Haven, Conn.: Yale U.P., 1950).

6. Bettelheim discusses the difficulty encountered by emotionally disturbed children in establishing "ego controls" upon awakening from sleep. See B. Bettelheim, *Love Is Not Enough* (New York: Free Press, 1950), Chapter 4.

7. H. Werner, *The Comparative Psychology of Mental Development* (Chicago: Follett, 1948).

8. The distinction between assimilative and disowning projection is taken from N. Cameron and Ann Margaret, *Behavior Pathology* (Boston: Houghton, 1951).

9. S. Freud, "Formulations Regarding the Two Principles in Mental Functioning," in S. Freud, *Collected Papers, IV* (London: Hogarth, 1953), Chapter 1.

10. W. Reich, *Character Analysis* (New York: Orgone Institute, 1948).

11. S. M. Jourard, *The Transparent Self* (New York: Van Nostrand Reinhold, 1971), Chapter 20, "The Bedside Manner."

12. L. Barenbaum, "Death of Young Sons and Husbands," *Omega: Journal of Death and Dying*, 1976, Vol. 7, pp. 171–175.

13. M. Jacobowitz, *Personality and Demographic Correlates of Moral Transgression and Psychological Defense Among Preadolescent Children*, unpublished doctoral dissertation, Iowa State University, 1974.

14. L. L. Viney and M. Manton, "Defense Mechanism Preferences and the Expression of Anxiety," *Social Behavior and Personality*, 1974, Vol. 2, pp. 50–55.

15. E. GOFFMAN, *The Presention of Self in Everyday Life* (Garden City, N.Y.: Doubleday, 1954), Chapter 4.

16. FROMM, op. cit.

17. S. FREUD, *The Ego and the Id* (London: Hogarth, 1927), p. 69.

18. E. FROMM, *You Shall Be as Gods: A Radical Interpretation of the Old Testament and Its Tradition* (New York: Holt, 1966).

19. See S. M. JOURARD, *Disclosing Man to Himself* (New York: Van Nostrand Reinhold, 1968), Chapter 13, "Growing Experience and the Experience of Growth," for elaboration of this view. Also F. J. SHAW, *Reconciliation: A Theory of Man Transcending* (New York: Van Nostrand Reinhold, 1966); and his paper "Transitional Experiences and Psychological Growth," *ETC, Review of General Semantics*, 1957, Vol. 15, pp. 39–45; K. DABROWSKI, *Mental Growth Through Positive Disintegration* (London: Gryf Publications, 1960).

20. See the account of a "ten-day voyage" in R. D. LAING, *The Politics of Experience* (New York: Pantheon, 1968), Chapter 7.

21. See JOURARD, *The Transparent Self*, op. cit., Chapter 7, "Self-disclosure, the Writer and His Reader."

22. H. OTTO and J. MANN, *Ways of Growth* (New York: Viking, 1969).

23. EMILY DICKINSON, "The Soul Selects Her Own Society," in OSCAR WILLIAMS (Ed.), *The Centennial Edition of F. T. Palgrave's The Golden Treasury of the Best Songs and Lyrical Poems* (New York: Mentor, 1961), p. 481.

24. For further suggestions of ways to openness in the natural mode, see B. PAYNE, *Getting There Without Drugs: Techniques and Theories and Theories for the Expansion of Consciousness* (New York: Ballantine, 1973); also J. O. STEVENS, *Awareness: Exploring, Experimenting, Experiencing.* (Lafayette, Calif.: Real People Press, 1971). Also a significant experimental study in the area: D. E. SCHAEFFER, D. R. DIGGINS, and H. L. MILLMAN, "Intercorrelations Among Measures of Creativity, Openness to Experience and Sensation Seeking in a College Sample," *College Student Journal*, 1976, Vol. 10, pp. 332–339.

Defense versus Growth

10

SOCIAL ROLES AND HEALTHY PERSONALITY

INTRODUCTION

The self-concept is organized into roles. In this chapter we will discuss the various genuine roles that individuals live out and those that are acted out, how roles are acquired, and, what is perhaps most important, how individuals can be authentic in their roles and avoid the "faking" that characterizes many persons. Some roles are healthy, some are not, and some of those that are not healthy are forced upon the person by usually well-meaning authorities, parents, friends, and even teachers. Healthy personalities need to know how to balance others' expectations of them with their own needs, wishes, and yearnings. The various roles that each individual is called upon to "be" and sometimes to "act" challenge the healthy personality to be consistent rather than to be internally conflicting. Role consistency requires either actual, genuine relationships among the roles played by the person or extreme stress, through the necessity for constant rationalization of the inconsistencies.

Healthy personality is impossible without the ability to enter into a variety of nonintimate social roles and the complementary ability to enter close personal relationships, where mutual self-disclosure and intimate knowing are of the essence.

Roles and the Social System

Social roles make life with others possible, yet they are a hidden source of stress and demoralization that can make people sick. Roles are invisible to us, for they are at the heart of our identities, and we simply *live* them. A sociologist, studying a group like a family, or an entire society, is able to see that people's behavior with others displays recurring patterns. Interpersonal relationships do not occur in random fashion, but instead are seen to follow rules, like a script for a play. Thus, the older male in a family group typically earns the living and protects the woman and the children. The woman nurtures young children, is affectionate and loving to the older man, and is careful to avoid intimacy with other males.

When seen from the perspective of a sociologist, roles are prescribed ways for people to divide the labor of a society and to interact with others. They keep the social system going and prevent it from changing.

Because the stability of a society is so important, people are carefully trained to live within the limits defined by their roles, and strong penalties await those who violate role definitions. The task of training people to their roles is assigned to the agencies and agents of *socialization*, whereas that of keeping people in conformity with their roles is the responsibility of agents and agencies of *social control*. Agencies of socialization include the family, schools, and the mass media, such as television and radio; these are all institutions within society that train people in the "right" ways to act. The *agents* of socialization are the actual persons who shape the behavior of a growing and learning person so that this behavior will fit the definition of the roles the person is to assume. Thus, one's parents, siblings, and peers are all socializing agents, as are the teachers one encounters in school.

Agents of social control are the persons who provide

Social Roles and Healthy Personality

punishment for violation of the rules, laws, and customs. The police are clearly agents of social control. The institutions of the law—the legal system, the courts, prisons, and the police force—are all social control agencies. Parents, peers, and neighbors are social control agents who control our behavior by threatening to withdraw love and friendship, and through criticism and shaming. They also reward and encourage other behavior though approval, gifts, and bestowal of friendship. A more subtle agent of social control is the person's conscience, which functions like an invisible parent or police officer, inflicting guilt and self-hatred at each lapse from the behavior that is deemed right and proper for that person.

All of us define our identities to ourselves and to others in terms of the roles we have had assigned to us and those we have sought to assume because of the status and privilege associated with them. Thus, I define myself as a man (my sex role), father of my children and husband to my wife; son of my parents and brother of my siblings (family roles); and psychotherapist, teacher of my students, researcher, and writer (occupational roles). I had to be trained for some of these roles, whereas I seemed just to "grow" into others. There are norms and rules governing the ways in which I act my age, my sex, my family roles, and my occupational roles. People come to depend upon me to act in stable and predictable ways, and I come to expect such stability of myself.[1]

Each social role that persons embody serves as a kind of badge entitling them to participate in life with others in prescribed ways, and each role sets limits on their freedom and access to material goods. Roles, in short, entitle persons to the privileges associated with high status in a group, or they condemn them to the dregs reserved for those of low status. A white person need only stain his or her skin to discover that the role of a black person has a status lower than that of a white person. Women have become keenly aware that the female role in most societies condemns women to inferior education, lower occupational status, and usually the exclusive responsibility of rearing children, unless they resist this definition. People in their sixties or seventies find themselves treated by younger people as if they were fragile, stupid, and lacking in fundamental human traits such as the needs for companionship, love, and ennobling work. Goffman (1967) has also suggested that persons stigmatized by society (blacks, handicapped, the aged, the gays) are given a role to play by society and are under pressure to play that role. Thus a gay male might be expected to act in certain ways by the rest of the society, and he does so, even though he ordinarily would choose not to do so.[2] Weinberg and Williams found evidence to support this in a large study of homosexual males covering a number of cultures.[3]

Even sickness is governed by social norms. When persons feel unwell, they enter the role of patient, which entitles them to interact with physicians and nurses, or with psychotherapists if they are diagnosed as "mentally ill." [4] Recent research has shown that people are trained to act like a "good patient" in hospitals, and this training has nothing to do with the treatment of illness. Moreover, the hospital itself is a complex web of professions, uniforms, titles, and badges that define status, authority, and responsibility. I worked for several years with a college of nursing; the hospital where the nursing students trained had as employees the graduates of four-year colleges of nursing, who earned a B.A. degree as well as the Registered Nurse (R.N.) diploma; R.N.'s with a degree from a community junior college; licensed practical nurses who had had no college training; and nursing assistants. The bewildering array of backgrounds puzzled the nurses and the physicians as much as it did the patients; the nurses with each type of training felt somehow different from the others and felt entitled to more responsibility, salary, and freedom.

The patients in hospitals are often made to feel like the least important, lowest caste members of the hospital community. They are treated as children about to be disobedient, and they are often kept in the dark about the nature of their illness and the precise nature of the medicines or operations that were prescribed for or conducted upon them.

Social Roles and Healthy Personality

In mental hospitals I visited, even to *be there* as a patient insured that the staff would not treat the patient as a free, responsible human being; rather, the patient was seen and talked about—sometimes in his or her presence—as the embodiment of the mental illness. The patient was required to participate in the therapeutic processes, to take medicine, and so on.

In 1973 a group of psychologists were admitted to mental hospitals as patients, in order to study the career of the mental patient firsthand. They found that they could not convince the attendants and professional staff that they were "sane," though the authentic patients knew they were.[5]

Role Versatility and Healthy Personality

Roles and the badges, titles, and uniforms that identify them enable others to predict how we will act in social situations. The ability to master a variety of roles throughout life is a decided asset for healthy personality, because it facilitates the interactions with others that bring satisfaction of many basic needs. Not to be able to enter roles because of an unhealthy self-structure or irrational fears thus impedes healthy personality development. If a young woman cannot make a career choice because she lacks confidence in her ability to master the training, she may face a life of low economic status. A man with sexual inhibitions may avoid intimate relationships with women and live a life that is safe but devoid of loving relationships.

Although role conformity implies some limitations on one's freedom of expression and action, there is a sense in which the ability to act in ways appropriate to one's family position, age, sex, and profession is *liberating*. Not to adhere to reasonable definitions of appropriate behavior is to invite social censure, which can interfere radically with effective living and the attainment of satisfactions. It sometimes appears hypocritical to students that older people may display politeness and feign delight at being with people they dislike. Actually, the ability to conform to the "niceties" in a variety of situations can be life-giving and liberating, because it clearly separates personal relationships (where spontaneity is expected) from the more formal relationships between strangers. In some cultures, like the English, the French,

Healthy Personality

and the Spanish, much time is spent in ceremonious interaction with others, yet there is room in those cultures for great freedom in the privacy of personal relationships. Europeans often complain that Americans seem friendly in impersonal situations, as in business, but that in private they avoid deepening relationships.

Roles function to aid in the development of the healthy person by structuring the skeleton of behavior, if not all of the substance of behavior. At the party, my role will be that of the great seducer; with my grandparents I shall play the role of the dutiful son; in class, the role of the scholar will help me decide what to do and how to be. The roles provide stability in some cases so that you can know how to behave initially in new situations. They provide a context that enables you, as in the case of a good actor, to also build in your own unique self and characterization of the role. One might expect the healthy personality to utilize the role concept and then proceed onward from there to fashion full selfhood with his other repertoire of roles or through fashioning an entirely new role.

How We Learn Roles

We learn our roles by being trained into them and by imitating, or identifying with, the role models available to us.[6] Thus, as children, our behavior is rewarded by our parents when it conforms to *their* image of the way a little boy or girl should act. At each age level, our behavior is "shaped," by the consequences of approval and of punishment that they provide to our action.

As we get older, we are encouraged to emulate the behavior of people who function as exemplars or role models. This is the way we begin to learn how to be a husband or a father, or a wife or mother, when the time comes, and it is the way we learn our occupational roles. Each person thus serves as a model to be emulated by others.

Social Roles and Healthy Personality

People encounter difficulties in fulfilling their sex roles and family roles when they have grown up without regular contact with role models or when the role models differ from the norms of their group. Some male homosexuals, for example, have grown up without a father in the home or with a father who was so hateful that the boy would not identify with him. When divorce is common, many children grow up without a father because they usually are raised by the mother. Under these conditions, the girls may not learn what adult man–woman or husband–wife behavior can be expected, nor will the little boys. Consequently, they do not learn reasonable family role expectations for self and for others; they may acquire idealized notions of what to expect from their spouses and children when they marry, expectations that their spouses and future children cannot fulfill.

In Harlow's famous and widely publicized study, infant monkeys were raised by artificial mothers, wire or foam rubber mechanical objects that were rigged to provide milk for the infants. Lacking adequate role models, these infants survived infancy handily but were totally unable to carry on adult functions. They were, as Harlow described them: helpless, hopeless, heartless parents.[7]

In professional and vocational training, the learner is both "shaped" by teachers and encouraged by them to copy the teacher's ways of performing skills. I served as consultant to a nursing college and found that the faculty and the staff nurses were not serving as authentic exemplars of the kind of nursing practice they wished the students to learn. They wanted the students to be very open, to be responsive to and empathic with patients, doctors, and colleagues. However, they were *not* functioning in those ways themselves. Many of the nursing faculty had left bedside nursing because they did not like regular contact with the ill. Many floor nurses were afraid of close, communicative relationships with patients, doctors, and each other. My task was to help the faculty and staff *become* the kind of nursing exemplars that the students could emulate. We attempted to do this, first, by encouraging the nursing college faculty to return to regular bedside nursing and, second, by conducting regular faculty meetings where the purpose was to practice open, personal communication with each other. There is some evidence that the strained, formal, and impersonal atmosphere of the college was replaced by one that encouraged greater openness of communication and that the students did become better at relating empathically and warmly with their patients.[8]

Some Common Roles

FAMILY ROLES

The experience of being "in" and "of" a family is essential to a vital sense of identity and fulfills the needs for security and intimacy. It is within the family that most people find their most fulfilling personal relationships, first as sons, daughters, brothers, and sisters; then as spouses, mothers and fathers, uncles and aunts; and later as grandparents. Even when the family breaks down, people seek a "primary group"—a small group of intimate friends with whom life may be lived communally, with or without sexual intimacies. Thus, many young people explore the possibilities of living communally as an alternate life style to traditional family life.

Traditional family roles are socially defined, and each person must learn those ways of being a family member that are acceptable within his or her family. The behavior and experience expected of a person because of his or her family position may be detrimental to healthy personal growth. Laing and Esterson [9] showed how being a daughter in ways deemed acceptable to the parents contributed to the development of schizophrenic behavior in the patients they studied.

The mother role as well has been found to require behavior from the mother that can easily contribute to her personal and physical breakdown. The father's role, in contemporary culture, calls for being a "good provider" and upward social mobility; it frequently imposes a dull or stressful life upon the father. Indeed, the divorce rates attest to the fact that husbands and wives, and mothers and fathers, often find traditional ways of being in these roles unrewarding, and they look to new partners for the satisfactions that were missing in their prior marriage.

David Cooper,[10] a British psychiatrist, wrote a book entitled *Death of the Family*, in which he pointed out the destructive possibilities of family roles as we have known them. He argued in behalf of alternative ways

Social Roles and Healthy Personality

253

for men, women, and children to live together that would avoid such destructiveness. The family, in some form, however, is likely to be with us forever; the challenge and opportunity facing each person is how that person might invent or adapt his or her way of being in various family roles in order to do justice to personal needs for security and for freedom, without stifling the growth and wellbeing of those in the complementary roles. Traditional family roles are "givens," and each person has the freedom and responsibility to do something with what is given—conform to the roles, refuse to enter them, or fulfill them in creative ways.

In perhaps no other institution in society is change in roles so apparent as in the family. While some may disagree, many of the changes appear to be beautifully designed to make the family a more viable, helpful institution in coming generations. Such changes are always controversial, but they also pose special adjustment problems, not just for the old generation but for the new families emerging. Young people establishing families will have role models of limited scope available to them because of rapid change in the family structure. They will have to fashion their roles out of the successful things they have seen their parents accomplish in the past and out of the new knowledge concerning the progressive changes of the present and future.

Some of these changes include:

1. Reduced authoritarianism. Usually the male was thought to be the "boss" of the family. We now recognize the value of democratic decision making in the family, with even children participating at younger ages.

2. Many drastic changes, particularly for the role of the male, in carrying out the child-rearing functions. Your grandfathers probably changed very few diapers and never touched the messiest kind. Now changing diapers, feeding infants, disciplining children, even teaching them sports and helping them making decisions concerning after-school activities and career choices are no longer sex-bound, neither for the child nor the parent. Fathers are entering into these activities and these decisions without apology and with enthusiasm. (However, one may speculate that the reduction in the size of the

Healthy Personality

average American family to 1.9 children may well be a result of fathers now knowing more intimately the inconveniences involved in child rearing.) Even responsibility for birth control can either be a male role, through the use of the condom and vasectomy, or a female role, through the use of the diaphragm, intrauterine devices, or oral medication.

3. Greater flexibility in roles for the female. U.S. government surveys show more than half the American families now contains two "breadwinners." Marriage and family are less likely to interfere with careers and therefore more likely to provide both emotional and physical satisfaction—and also enable the couple to experience that particularly mysterious value—participation in the biological continuity of the human species, that is, experience the pleasures and pains of parenthood.

These changes mean more instability both in family roles and in marriages; they particularly foreshadow greater freedom for the female. Dissolution of marriage has replaced divorce in a number of states. Rather than as a threat to marriage, these new directions can be seen as a great challenge to make the family roles more flexible; more satisfying to children, mother, and father; and even more satisfying to the extended family.

Experiments in newer family roles have always been a part of our civilization, and recent years have brought new life styles into prominence; gay marriages, communal societies, even group marriage. Yet it is safe to say that the major form of the family will remain the monogamous pair bond. However, the high-level-functioning engaged couple would do well to recognize the great challenges to stability and satisfaction involved in ongoing changes and to seek the opportunity to prepare for the new family through the many opportunities now being made available in Parent Effectiveness Training and other such programs.[11]

The task of bringing up children has always been a mixed joy. There can be no doubt but that it provides a special kind of satisfaction, which is most fully obtained when the parents take advantage of the great store of scientific and of experiential wisdom now available to help them. Particularly important in the planning in

coming years will be the clarity of roles in the family
assigned to each parent, and even to each child.

SEX ROLES

Each society differs in its concept of masculine and
feminine behavior. Mead showed that in three New
Guinea tribes, there was considerable difference from
tribe to tribe in the typical male and female roles. In one
group, the Arapesh, men and women alike were passive,
"maternal," cooperative, and nonaggressive. In the
Mundugamor, a tribe geographically close to the Arapesh, men and women alike were fierce, cruel, aggressive,
and self-assertive. A third tribe, the Tchambuli, showed
a different pattern of sex-typing. The men were passive
individuals who spent their time cultivating the arts,
whereas the women were assertive and had to cultivate
the gardens and make a living.

In America, rigid definition of sex roles has broken
down. Thus, many middle-class men take an active role
in child care and housekeeping, and their wives do many
things once deemed to be a male prerogative: they keep
the budget, spend the money, and work at occupations
that formerly were strictly male. In some European
countries, male and female behavior contrasts in certain
ways with the American concept of masculinity and
femininity. Thus, in Latin countries, a man can comfortably kiss another man, and he can cry openly without
shame. But these men might look askance at the American woman who likes to wear trousers. For many of
them, women belong in dresses.

In order to "wear" one's sex role comfortably, a person
has to be trained into it. Yet some men have been reared
in ways that promote the development of traits ordinarily
regarded as effeminate; they may also have acquired, in
the process of growing up, the cultural concepts of the
male role. Therefore, they find it a strain to "be a man."
In acting in manly ways, they are going against their
(acquired) "nature." But if they were to act in the ways
that were most natural for them, they might experience
a considerable threat to their sense of identity as a man
Healthy and expose themselves to much ridicule. The same con-
Personality siderations apply to women. Some individuals are so in-

secure about their sexual identity that they must "over-protest." Instead of being content to be manly, they must be "supermanly." They exaggerate their manly traits as if to convince themselves and others that they are indeed men. If anyone questions the masculinity of such a person, he may become dangerously aggressive. His life involves a continual quest for reassurances of his own masculinity.

Because sex roles are relatively fixed by society, each person, man and woman, must find ways of fitting himself or herself to his or her sex role, of coming to terms with it. Some men and women find their sex roles too constraining, and they adopt many of the patterns of the opposite sex, both sexually and behaviorally.

Healthy personalities are able to redefine their own personal sex roles in ways that dovetail better with their needs. Consequently, they have greater freedom to express and act out their real selves and are much less easily threatened. Thus, a healthy man can do many things that might have once been seen as effeminate, yet he will not experience any threat to his masculinity. He may wash dishes, change babies, and perform jobs such as hairdressing or ballet, yet still feel manly.

To the extent that women have assented to traditional, male-dominated views of what their "true" roles and function might be, to that extent they have realized only a fraction of their potentialities as fully functioning human beings. Healthy personality for the individual and a life-giving culture for a society are no longer possible as long as half the world's population, women, continues to reflect ancient male perspectives, rather than to develop a more truly educated and enlightened womanhood about the world. There seems little doubt that if all women received an enlightening education, then the more enlightened population resulting from such a program would contribute to the solution of problems of untrammeled population increase, destruction of the environment that supports life, and war. Women are too important an influence upon healthy personality growth

Social Roles and Healthy Personality to remain less well educated than men and to limit their involvement in society to maternal roles and subordinate professional and occupational roles.

It is disconcerting to realize that the first influence upon a child's education is the mother—a person who, for millennia, has been denied access to higher education and professional opportunity. I am a champion of women's liberation because I see in that movement a force that contributes to healthier personality for all human beings.[12]

Recent studies support a very close relationship between self-actualization (or healthy personality) and profeminist attitudes. A study by Follingstad, Kilmann, and Robinson showed that in a group of male students led by females, those men who had high self-actualization scores were in agreement with profeminist attitudes, in contrast to a control group, which shifted toward more traditional attitudes. Similar results were found in another study by Doyle. Hjelle and Butterfield also found correlations between profeminist attitudes and self-actualization among women.[13]

AGE ROLES

Each society expects a progression of behavior in its members, a progression that will keep pace with the person's chronological age. If persons are keeping pace with their age roles, they are said to be mature. If they are behind other people their age, they are said to be immature or fixated. If they revert to behavior characteristics of a younger age, they are said to display regression, and if they show a premature development of traits expected from older persons, they are said to display precocity. As with sex roles, age roles may conflict sharply with persons' needs. They may not be ready to progress to the next age role when the time for it comes. Or they may enforce conformity with the age role on themselves, at considerable cost in satisfactions.

By the time individuals have become adults, as this is defined in their culture, they acquire a vested interest in regarding themselves as mature. Yet need gratification may be possible only if they behave in ways deemed immature in their social group.

Healthy
Personality

Healthy personalities can regress when they want to or when they feel like it, without threat to self-esteem or to their sense of identity. Persons who are insecure about their maturity may strive to convince themselves and others that they are mature and avoid regressive behavior like the plague. Thus, some men may not allow themselves to be taken care of even when they are gravely sick because it would imply that they had regressed. Some women may refuse tenderness and solicitude from a man because of the implication that they are not independent adults. Some adults cannot play because being frolicsomeness feels childish to them and threatens their self-esteem.

As with family and sex roles, age roles are part of the "facticity"—the "givens"—with which each person must come to terms. The behavior expected of each person by others (because of chronological age) can be irrelevant to the person's authentic needs and capacities. Older people are often virtually invited by those who are younger to be feeble and helpless, when they have great reserves of vitality latent within them. The fact is that as long as a person has vitalizing, challenging work and projects, and confirming personal relationships, he or she can be fit and active into the eighties and nineties or older. Bodies respond to life style and to people's expectations. I have suspected that people die of "old age" not because their bodies had no more strength, but because they were bored or lonely, with no incentives to stay alive.

Another point of vew is represented by Christiansen,[14] who stresses dignity in old age and in death as an inner characteristic rather than as a role. He also suggests that one may in a fashion foresee the close of one's life and illustrates the point with a moving description of his grandfather's dignified foresight.

There are old people who maintain dignity in later years not so much by power, defiance, interdependence, or isolation as by choosing for themselves some task to carry on with love and skill. . . . my maternal grandfather had cultivated a vegetable garden. It was one of the famous sites of the neighborhood and despite the pain of cancer and radiation therapy, he kept the garden until he died at 80. That last fateful spring, he cultivated, planted, weeded and did everything leaning over a cane.

Social Roles and Healthy Personality

One July evening that year my father sighted Grandpa coming from the garden. . . . He walked only a few steps at a time before stopping and propping himself against the house. . . . My father overheard him bidding farewell to his garden. "Good-bye Andy's backyard. Good-bye. I won't be back." He died two weeks later [p. 48].

Authenticity and Inauthenticity in Roles

It is a human peculiarity that people can *be* in roles, and they can *act* in roles. To be a student, for example, is to commit oneself to the aims of being a student—to pursue learning with seriousness. When one is *being* a student, in unself-conscious pursuit of knowledge, one is not aware of being in a role. But a student can impersonate a serious learner when the person himself or herself is not remotely interested in learning. When someone pretends to be in some role but is committed to objectives other than those appropriate to that role, that person is said to be in bad faith, or to be inauthentic. Thus, salespeople who pretend to be interested in your welfare are being inauthentic, and in bad faith to you, because they may be trying to impersonate someone in the role of friend. In fact, they may be authentic in their commitment to making a sale and inauthentic in their relationship to you. The human capacity for semblance, for acting and impersonating, is at once the means whereby we learn and grow to take on new roles, and also the basis for beginning the process of self-alienation. We begin to learn how to become doctors and lawyers, husbands and wives, by first mimicking those parts at play or in school. But if a woman continues to play-act the part of wife and mother after marriage, without serious commitment to the tasks of a wife and mother, then she has commenced a career of inauthenticity that will lead to painful consequences.

In order to be inauthentic in a role, a person is obliged to imitate authentic action and to repress his or her authentic experience. A son who is unhappy in the *Healthy* career his father chose for him may try to persuade him-*Personality* self and his father that he is contented with the courses he is taking for the career. If the choice is inauthentic, and he is in fact miserable, then each day becomes an ordeal, of forcing himself to seem happy and consuming energy to suppress his spontaneous urges to get away from the scene of his discontent. The student may then find himself becoming very tired, disinterested in his studies, even frequently sick, because of the stress and demoralization engendered by remaining in the inauthentic role. To be authentic in a role, you must be honest with yourself and with others about what you truly are up to, and how you feel about the roles you are committed to. Chronic inauthenticity in one's roles is a factor in physical and personality breakdown. Authenticity, by contrast, although it may lead to personal and interpersonal conflict, is a factor in personal growth to healthier personality.

Authenticity in roles calls for honest self-disclosure to the others with whom one is involved. Faking and dissembling are commonly chosen by many people who dread the reactions of others and the problems they would encounter if they revealed the truth of their feelings about the roles they are living.

Roles and Sickness

The person who is living with others within the limits of his or her roles goes through changes. The way of being son or daughter, parent, student, or teacher that up to yesterday was rewarding becomes boring or meaningless today. To continue being in those roles in the same way gradually becomes stifling and depressing. The person dreads each day, because it means being the same person, enacting the same roles, eliciting the same reactions from others, with no hope of respite from the increased irritation and boredom. A theory of illness has been developed that traces the connection between prolonged involvement in unrewarding roles and physical diseases of all kinds. A person acts in order to meet his or her needs. If this action does not meet the needs but only maintains the stability of a family or work arrangement, then the person is truly neglecting his or her own wellbeing. A prolonged regime of action that neglects

Social Roles and Healthy Personality

one's own needs for love, esteem, full emotional expression, or excitement will generate stress and dispiritation—both factors in physical illness.[15] If a person feels truly trapped in unrewarding roles, he or she may develop psychiatric illnesses, exchanging, thereby, an unrewarding existence as a wife and mother, for example, for a career as a patient in a mental hospital.

Everyone begins to feel locked into their assorted roles at various times in their lives. Other people's expectations provide a powerful force restraining a person from changing roles or from changing the ways of being in those roles. It is astonishing to see how surprised, even outraged, other people become when a person decides to drop out of a role or change role behavior even in trifling ways. For example, a simple change in appearance, such as growing a mustache or shaving one off, will evoke a barrage of commentary, some critical, some complimentary, from the others with whom one is involved. For a woman hitherto docile and dependent upon men to become involved in women's liberation activities may infuriate the men in her life. The obedient son or daughter, after a year at school, begins to act in ways that outrage the parents, who feel that their child is "out of his mind." In all these cases persons find that to remain as they were has become intolerable, yet sometimes immense courage and energy are called for to stop being in roles in the customary ways, in order to act in more life-giving ways.

A strong sense of duty, stemming from an authoritarian conscience, will often keep a person in sickening roles. A woman may feel that her husband will collapse and her children will be neglected if she devotes less time to their needs and more to herself. Accordingly, she may neglect her health, her appearance, and the cultivation of her intellect in order to meet her family's needs. The consequence may be that she suffers and that her spouse and children all feel vaguely guilty. Mrs. Portnoy, the mother in *Portnoy's Complaint*, was expert at inducing guilt in her son and husband by excessive care at the expense of her own pleasures.

Healthy Personality   Opportunities for solitude and meditation help one to disengage from roles in order to discover or invent more life-giving ways of re-entering them. Personal growth calls for creative use of imagination, to ponder ways of reconciling commitments to others with one's personal needs. Such creativity is encouraged by periods of quiet, uninterrupted solitude.

Once a person has discovered a more self-expressive and enlivening way to be himself or herself in relation to others, that person faces a problem: will the other people in his or her life confirm the changes now being inserted into *their* world? Or will they resist the change, refusing to accept or recognize the person unless he reverts to the ways in which they knew him? It is a poignant choice that a growing person often has to face: if she remains as is, as the person locked in roles that were recognized by others, she becomes increasingly angry and dispirited. When she changes in the ways that are most vitalizing, her parents, friends, and associates no longer like her. Growth frequently calls for the sad necessity of "leaving home," in search of people who will accept and confirm a person as the one she has just become.

Some Existential Suggestions

I have been exploring the hypothesis that rigid roles and conformity to them are the main source of physical as well as psychological breakdown in our culture, at least for middle-class people. If the hypothesis is sound, then it means persons can do much to foster their own health by examining the ways in which they are living out their various social roles. One piece of existential research anyone can carry out is to itemize the various roles that he or she is committed to and then do a self-rating as to the degree of *enlivenment* felt in each role (in relation to the others with whom the person regularly deals while in that role—for example, son to mother, son to father, employee to boss, colleague to colleague, husband to wife, and so on). Thus, I could list the following roles for myself: husband; father to each of three *Social Roles* sons; son of my mother; brother to each of five siblings; *and Healthy* friend to each of several people that I see regularly; and *Personality* so on. I could compare how alive I feel in each of these relationships; how authentic I can be in each; how free I feel to disclose myself in each relationship. Moreover, I could try to alter my ways in each role that I found oppressive. Ask yourself, "Can I be flexible and create new roles or adapt to new roles when necessary?"

I have found that when I am serving as someone's psychotherapist, I spend a great deal of time exploring the patient's ways of being in roles, in the quest for more authentic and vitalizing ways. Certainly a person can, with a bit of imagination, begin to experiment with more life-giving ways of being in age, sex, and assorted family and occupational roles, without waiting to get sick. It is not easy, but it is necessary and possible to redefine one's roles. If the other person will not confirm one's changed ways of being in the role, it may be necessary, for one's wellbeing, to withdraw from that relationship altogether. However, many, perhaps most, good friends are able to accept health-giving role changes in others—but be prepared for an understandable period of readjustment on their part to the new "you," the changed role.

SUMMARY

Social roles lie at the heart of our identities. We are trained early to live according to social definitions of behavior that are appropriate to our age, sex, family status, and occupation. Agents of socialization train us to our roles, and agents of social control keep us in them, even when they become stressful and dispiriting. The ability to fulfill the requirements of a variety of roles is essential for healthy personality.

Family and sex roles can so limit a person's degree of freedom that health and growth are undermined. Women's liberation was presented as a valuable contribution to the possibilities of healthier personality for women. Age roles were seen to be challenges to grow, and also invitations to act "old," even to die at the age deemed appropriate by society. However, one may internalize certain values, such as dignity, not as a role but as a way of being.

Healthy Personality   *The ability to disengage from social roles and to interact with others as persons, in a personal relationship, is an essential complement to living one's life in roles.*

1. For a discussion of role theory from the psychologist's point of view see M. E. SHAW and P. R. CONSTANZO, *Theories in Social Psychology* (New York: McGraw-Hill, 1970).

2. A good discussion of caste, class, and status is given in R. BROWN, *Social Psychology* (New York: Free Press, 1965), Chapter 3. Role theory from the point of view of an eminent sociologist is seen in E. GOFFMAN, *Interaction Ritual: Essays on Face-to-Face Behavior* (Garden City, N.Y.: Doubleday, 1967).

3. M. S. WEINBERG, and C. J. WILLIAMS, *Male Homosexuals: Their Problems and Their Adaptations* (New York: Oxford U.P., 1974).

4. See T. SCHEFF, *Being Mentally Ill: A Sociological Theory* (Chicago: Aldine, 1966); E. GOFFMAN, *Asylums* (Garden City, N.Y.: Doubleday, 1961).

5. See CAROLE TAYLOR, *In Horizontal Orbit: Hospitals and the Cult of Efficiency* (New York: Holt, 1970) for an anthropologist's account, sometimes hilarious, about roles and status in a major university hospital. Also, D. L. ROSENHAN'S, "On Being Sane in Insane Places," *Science*, 1973, Vol. 179, pp. 250–258.

6. A good discussion of roles is given in T. SARBIN, "Role Theory," in G. LINDZEY (Ed.), *Handbook of Social Psychology*, I (Reading, Mass.: Addison-Wesley, 1954).

7. H. HARLOW, "The Affection System in Monkeys," *American Psychologist*, 1962, Vol. 17, pp. 1–9.

8. The chapters on nursing in S. M. JOURARD, The *Transparent Self*, 2nd ed. (New York: Van Nostrand Reinhold, 1971) came out of this experience.

9. R. D. LAING and A. ESTERSON, *Sanity, Madness and the Family* (London: Tavistock, 1964); see also A. ESTERSON, *The Leaves of Spring: Schizophrenia, Family and Sacrifice* (London: Tavistock, 1970). See also the very moving account of Mary Barnes' struggle to transcend her family's definition of her, in MARY BARNES: *Two Accounts of a Journey Through Madness* (New York: Harcourt, 1971).

10. D. COOPER, *Death of the Family* (New York: Random, 1971).

11. Perhaps the most widespread availability of preparation for family development is found in the Parent Effectiveness Program developed by Dr. Tom Gordon and discussed in one of his many excellent guidebooks, *P.E.T. in Action*

*Social Roles
and Healthy
Personality*

(New York: Wyden, 1976). Written with Judith G. Sands.

12. See T. PARSONS, "Age and Sex in the Social Structure of the United States," in his *Essays in Sociological Theory* (New York: Free Press, 1954); MARGARET MEAD, *Male and Female* (New York: Morrow, 1949); BETTY FRIEDAN, *The Feminine Mystique* (New York: Norton, 1963).

13. D. R. FOLLINGSTAD, R. R. KILMAN, and E. A. ROBINSON, "Prediction of Self-actualization in Male Participants in a Group Conducted by Female Leaders," *Journal of Clinical Psychology*, 1976, Vol. 32, pp. 706–712; J. A. DOYLE, "Self-actualization and Attitudes Toward Women," *Psychological Reports*, 1975, Vol. 37, pp. 899–902; L. A. HJELLE and R. BUTTERFIELD, "Self-actualization and Women's Attitudes Toward Their Real Roles in Contemporary Society," *Journal of Psychology*, 1974, Vol. 87, pp. 225–230.

14. D. CHRISTIANSEN, "Dignity in Aging: Notes on Geriatric Ethics," *Journal of Humanistic Psychology*, 1978, Vol. 18, pp. 41–54.

15. JOURARD, op. cit., Chapters 4, 9, 10.

Healthy Personality

11

SELF-DISCLOSURE, PERSONAL RELATIONS, AND HEALTHY PERSONALITY

INTRODUCTION

Next to the death penalty, the gravest punishment that can be inflicted upon persons is to deprive them of intimate human company. Not to have someone to talk to, to share life with, is to be dehumanized. Enforced solitude can lead persons to madness unless they have strong egos and can discipline themselves to retain their identity and values. People need one another simply to be human.

In some families the relationships among the members are those of strangers among strangers. Everyone plays his or her part. The father is paternal, the mother does motherly things, and the children do their filial duties; not one knows the experience of the other. Their relationships with each other are impersonal. In my research in self-disclosure, I found many instances where the members of a family were completely ignorant of one another's hopes and fears, likes and dislikes, problems and joys. They simply did not discuss "personal" things among themselves.

The experience of feeling at a standstill in one's relationships with friends, where the relationship does not seem to be "going anywhere," is likewise common. "Where" can a relationship with another person "go" anyway?

It is in the intimacy of personal relationships that an individual's upbringing receives its most rigorous test. The ability to stay in growing relationships with a few others, in such a way as to continuously raise the level of each other's existence, is what healthy personality is about.

In this chapter, we provide a set of criteria in the light of which a person can evaluate his or her friendships and relationships with family members, to discern the extent to which these are life-giving to the self and the other, and the degree to which they diminish health and block personal growth. These same criteria provide goals for assessing whether or not one's relationships are "moving," and the direction of such movement.

Characteristics of Healthy Personal Relationships

The following characteristics describe relationships between two persons that engender growth and well-being in both parties:

1. The two people communicate authentically with one another and stay in touch with each other's perspectives.

2. Their demands and claims upon one another are reasonable.

3. They are actively concerned with one another's growth and happiness.

4. Each treasures the freedom of the other to be himself or herself and does not try to control the other.

No relationship begins this way, neither within the family, nor outside it. People make contact with each other as persons in many ways—through sheer physical nearness, as at home; through shared hobbies and interests; and through accidental meeting. According to one investigator, the first four minutes of any acquaintance are decisive for the fate of that relationship—whether it will move in the direction of greater intimacy or will remain distant and superficial.[1]

Healthy Personality

268

Once people have met, however, a period of mutual exploration begins. The desire to know the other as that person *is*, rather than seems to be, motivates the mutual "interviewing" that goes on between persons. Getting to know one another is like unveiling a mystery that may further bind the two people in friendship, or it may serve to terminate the acquaintance.

Authentic Communication

There is only one way for people to come to know one another, and that is through mutual self-disclosure. This is what differentiates personal relationships of love and friendship from formal role relations—the participants seek to make their subjective worlds known to one another, in an ongoing dialogue.[2]

The experience of freedom to tell another person of one's hopes and fears, joys and sorrows, plans for the future, and memories of the past is the essence of relief from loneliness. But such freedom appears to be rare. More common is the fear of disclosure, limiting self-revelation to topics that are "safe" and superficial.

I devised a simple exercise to provide people with a feel for the pleasure and anxieties of mutual self-revelation. My students and I have used the technique in our experimental research, and I have also employed it in conducting encounter groups. The game calls for two people—a pair of roommates, friends, or people going together—to take turns telling each other all they feel comfortable in telling about the following topics. (These are sample topics; the two people can choose other topics of interest to them.)

1. My hobbies and interests.
2. My likes and dislikes in food and drink.
3. What I like and dislike about my parents and siblings.
4. What I like and dislike about my appearance.
5. My chief personal problems and concerns.
6. My experience with the opposite sex.
7. My personal religious views or philosophy of life.
8. My past problems with health and present concerns about health.
9. How I feel about you (the present partner).

I have found that people sometimes feel awkward at the artificiality of beginning a conversation in such a structured way, but once the partners begin actually to disclose themselves, they find the experience rewarding.

SOME FACTORS IN SELF-DISCLOSURE

Under what conditions will persons disclose themselves fully and authentically to others? One factor is the perception of the other person as trustworthy. This places the onus upon the other individual to be trustworthy.

Another factor seems to be a considerable measure of security and self-esteem. Individuals who are relatively unafraid of others and who regard themselves as acceptable will be readier to let themselves be known than will insecure, dependent individuals.

Curiously enough, some individuals feel freest to disclose themselves to strangers, such as a casual companion on a plane, a hairdresser, or bartender. This freedom to disclose the self to strangers probably stems from the conviction that it does not matter what the other person thinks, because one is unlikely to encounter that person in one's everyday life.

One of the most powerful factors in self-disclosure is the willingness of the other person to disclose the self. My research has shown that people tend to disclose themselves to one another at a mutually regulated pace and depth. If one person volunteers a great deal of intimate disclosure, the other person is likely to reciprocate. If the other person is a "low discloser," one is less likely to confide in that person, because there is no reward for disclosures of comparable intimacy.

Other later studies have corroborated this relationship between two persons—we tend to disclose to people who disclose to us. Sometimes one person or the other takes the initiative in disclosure, but the other person generally reciprocates.[3]

BARRIERS TO SELF-DISCLOSURE

Social Norms. Although honest communication is valued in our society, there is another value that is often more strongly affirmed than honesty. "If you can't say something nice about another person, don't say any-

Healthy Personality

thing." In personal relationships, such as friendship or the relations between a parent and child, the recipient of "nice" evaluations can never know how his or her behavior really affects the other person. Further, the "nice" appraisals of the person made by significant others will contribute to the formation of an inaccurate self-concept.

Another socially derived precept holds that people should not be demanding or complaining. A wife who would lose self-esteem if she made demands on her husband may refrain from so doing. Because he has no sign that he is thwarting or depriving her of legitimate satisfactions, he will continue blithely to behave in his accustomed ways. The upshot will be that the wife will preserve her self-esteem, true enough, but the cost may be a life of suffering and repressed resentment. The same holds for complaints. Complaints are to an interpersonal relationship what pain is to the body—a sign that something is wrong, a sign that something must be done in order to restore the valued state of affairs. Vigorous complaints will at least create an impasse, which is the first step in the direction of adjustments. In my therapeutic and counseling work, I have advised quietly martyred spouses to learn the art of complaining. It may happen that a person complains on the basis of irrational and unrealistic needs and demands. In such cases it is to the other's advantage to rebut the complaints with as much vigor as they have been presented. This reaction insures that all sides of the issue are brought into the open, where they can be more effectively resolved.

Dependency. A helpless person may avoid full disclosure of self to the one upon whom he or she is dependent, because of fear that the other will withdraw support. The dependent employee doesn't tell the boss how she feels about her out of dread she will be discharged from a job she needs. The dependent wife doesn't tell her husband all her feelings, needs, thoughts, and opinions, because she fears he will leave her. The dependent friend doesn't tell his buddy what he thinks and feels, because he fears he will be abandoned. Any factor that promotes dependency and interferes with the attainment of independent security is a factor that interferes with full communication.

Self-disclosure, Personal Relations, and Healthy Personality

It should not be assumed that the sheer amount of self-disclosure between participants in a relationship is an index of the health of the relationship or of the persons. There are such factors as timing, interest of the other person, appropriateness, and effect of disclosures on either participant that must be considered in any such judgment. In one research study, it was found that of the two least liked and most maladjusted members of a work setting, one was found to be the most secretive and undisclosing, and the other was the highest discloser in the group. If a relationship exists between self-disclosure and factors of health, it is likely curvilinear, not linear; that is, too much disclosure and too little disclosure may be associated with unhealthy personality, whereas some intermediate amount, under appropriate conditions and settings, is indicative of healthier personality. However, as a general principle, it may be proposed that persons who feel obliged to lie to others about their inner being are making themselves sick. Honesty may yet prove to be the best policy—in this case, the best health insurance policy. And we may find that those who become sick most frequently, physically and mentally, have long been downright liars to others and to themselves.[4]

Realistic Demands on the Other Person

In a healthy personal relationship, the demands that each partner imposes on the other as conditions for the continuation of the relationship are realistic, mutually agreed upon, and consistent with the values and happiness of the other. What does this prescription imply? What is a realistic demand?

As we have seen, people enter into personal relations to enrich their existences. Each partner needs the other to act in certain ways in order to attain those ends. In most friendships, the participants are willing to accede to the requests, demands, and needs of the other. But it can happen that one of the partners has unusual needs—needs deriving from an atypical life history. That person needs the other to act in atypical or perhaps impossible ways in order to produce satisfactions. Where one partner has *Healthy* unusual needs, or where each has an inaccurate concept *Personality* of what the other is capable of doing, the demands may be unrealistic and impossible of fulfillment.

There is a distinction between a demand that is difficult to conform with and one that is impossible for the other to fulfill. In the case of difficult demands or challenges, efforts to fulfill these may well contribute to growth. In fact, challenges made by one person to the other may serve to motivate new efforts and creative achievements that would not have materialized without the challenge. In the case of impossible demands, they may be physically impossible to fulfill, or they may cost so much that other values would have to be sacrificed, thus making it not worthwhile.

A sweetheart may demand of her lover that he abandon his work in order to spend all his time with her. Or a parent may demand a straight-A average from a child of below-average intelligence. In these instances, the demands cannot be met. Growth would not consist in one person conforming with the other's demands; rather, growth would be promoted if the individual refused to conform and strove instead to show that the demands were unrealistic. If these attempts were successful, and the demanding one accordingly adjusted the demands, to bring them into reasonable limits, then we would assert that the one who modified the demands had grown.

As two persons interact over a period of time, revealing their thoughts, feelings, and needs to one another, they will of course come to know one another better. But beyond mutual knowledge, honest disclosure of demands and wishes inevitably will produce an impasse in the relationship. It is in the resolution of these impasses that growth can be fostered.

IMPASSES AND THEIR RESOLUTION

An impasse between two persons exists when one has a need or expectation that, if fulfilled by the other, would promote satisfaction. The other person, however, either will not or cannot comply with this wish. Impasses may be open or covert. Only open impasses can be resolved in growth-promoting ways. Covert or hidden impasses are likely to result in a gradual deterioration of the relationship.[5]

Self-disclosure, Personal Relations, and Healthy Personality

The most obvious sign that an impasse has arisen in a relationship is open conflict. However, many impasses occur before they are recognized as such: they manifest themselves as boredom, irritation, restlessness, dissatisfaction with the other, nagging, recurrent criticism, or anger. These symptoms indicate that one of the partners is being thwarted in the relationship but is unable or unwilling to specify in what precise ways the other person is failing to satisfy. A woman found herself getting increasingly bored with her fiancé and overcritical of his appearance, eating habits, hobbies, and other minor matters. When he changed his grooming and eating habits, and abandoned his hobbies for the time, she still remained bored and irritated. She had not yet put her finger on the precise way in which he was thwarting her needs. It was only when he spontaneously lavished affection upon her that the impasse was resolved. She did not realize that this was what she had wanted.

The simplest case of an interpersonal impasse consists in one person disclosing his wish or demand that the other person do something, or stop doing something; the other person refuses openly. The simplest case of impasse resolution consists in either (1) the person withdrawing the demand, (2) the other person complying with the demand, or (3) some compromise between (1) and (2). The resolution of an impasse fosters growth if it results in changes in either partner such that

1. Each displays the behavior that is appropriate to his or her age.

2. The person's self-structure changes correspondingly, so that the self-concept remains accurate, the self-ideal remains congruent with social mores and with actual behavior, and the various public selves remain accurate and mutually compatible.

3. The growing person becomes increasingly capable, through learning, of a broader repertoire of skills.

4. The person's action and self-disclosure become increasingly authentic.

Everyone is involved within the family and outside it in a number of personal relationships. Some of these relationships may be neutral with respect to growth, others may produce regression, others may prevent growth, and *Healthy* still others may promote growth.
Personality

Perhaps one of the most predictable impasses in one's life involves the teenager and the parent. One of the most successful teachers of parents was the popular Haim G. Ginnott,[6] who in a series of books provided much good-humored and good-sense help to parents. From *Between Parent and Teenager*, some of his suggestions include:

Accept the teenager's restlessness and discontent.
Don't try to be too understanding.
Differentiate between acceptance and approval.
Don't invite dependence.
Don't hurry to correct facts.
Don't violate his privacy.
Avoid clichés and preaching. [p. 21]

Personal Relationships and Growth

RELATIONSHIPS THAT ARE NEUTRAL WITH RESPECT TO GROWTH

Any relationship with another person that does not produce change in that person's personality is neutral with respect to growth. In this category of "growth-neutral" relationships we would include all brief encounters with other people for specific purposes: the brief contact with a garage mechanic fixing your car; a person sitting beside you on a train, with whom you converse about assorted subjects, perhaps sharing a drink, but that is all; it could also be a relationship with a brother, sister, or roommate. We should not assume, however, that brevity is the sole characteristic that defines a "growth-neutral" relationship. Some relationships with others last for years, but neither partner changes his or her reaction patterns or values one whit. Other relationships may last five minutes, but the partners may have been radically changed. Thus, a stranger may say something to you that produces a marked change in your self-concept, a marked change in your values, or a marked change in your behavior.

RELATIONSHIPS THAT INDUCE REGRESSION

Self-disclosure, Personal Relations, and Healthy Personality

Students of personality development have developed crude norms that describe the range of reaction patterns "normal" for each of several age levels. Thus, we can divide a total life history into infancy, early childhood, late childhood, adolescence, early adulthood, middle adulthood, late adulthood, old age, and senility. Different behavior patterns are expected in each society from persons falling into each age bracket. Sociologists speak of this kind of categorizing as age-grading. Whereas growth means progressive change in behavior consistent with age norms, regression means growth in reverse.

Experimental psychologists have formulated the general proposition that frustration or, more generally, stress are factors that promote regression. A stressor is any factor that interferes with the ongoing course of activity. Thus, physical danger, illness, frustration, interference are all stressing agents and as such can induce regression, or growth in reverse. Adult persons will usually display childish behavior when they are ill, thwarted, or in danger.

There are some relationships that produce stresses resulting in permanent regression in one of the partners. Thus, one of the participants in a friendship or marriage may act in such a way that it literally "childifies" the other person, who otherwise can act in ways appropriate to his or her age. The wife may impose such impossible demands on her husband that in attempting to implement them he is forced by stress to act in childish ways. Bettelheim described the regressive behavior of concentration camp inmates, behavior that derived from the physical stresses of prison camp life as well as from the arbitrary behavior of the guards.[7] Many of the prisoners were reduced to childlike levels of behavior. Dependency relationships promote regression in the dependent person.

We must distinguish between situational regression and more generalized, or stabilized, regression. A person may display regressive behavior only in one kind of relationship whereas in all others he can act his age. A husband may behave in a childish manner with his wife (not much different from the way he behaved as a child toward his mother), but toward other women he may act in mature fashion. Or an employee may act like a grudgingly obedient child toward her boss and other authority figures, but toward her peers she may act her age.

Healthy Personality A truly regression-producing relationship is one that produces permanent regression in the participant—regression that carries over to other relationships, so that other people are impressed by the juvenile or childish behavior of the individual. Such relationships reverse a slogan adopted by many schools: "Send us the boy, and we'll return a man." Instead, some people, by virtue of their demands and their power over anyone with whom they get involved, seem to say, "Send me a man, and I'll return a boy."

In this discussion we have overlooked the very important fact that in a healthy relationship, the participants can allow each other to regress; they do not necessarily demand perpetual adultness from each other. This is an entirely different state of affairs from what we have been discussing. There is a difference between a relationship that enforces regression and one that permits both regressive behavior and growthful behavior to occur. There is even reason to believe that genuine personal growth is not possible unless the individual is able to abandon present modes of behaving, regressing for some time to a more infantile level of behaving and experiencing, and then progressing to an even more adult level.

RELATIONSHIPS THAT PREVENT GROWH

There are some relationships that continue on the unspoken condition that neither partner will grow. Thus, a man and woman marry. Each holds a certain concept of the other that each has deliberately constructed in the mind. At the time of the marriage his concept of her personality was inaccurate and incomplete. She did not know him as he "really" was. However, he believed she had all the traits of an ideal wife. If either behaved contrary to expectations, then the other would be disappointed, would feel let down and deceived: "You are not the person I married or the kind of person I want to stay married to." In order to preserve their marriage (for whatever satisfactions it does provide), each partner would strive to remain unchanged; each partner might believe that a change in personality would result in the dissolution of the marriage—a consequence that is dreaded. Such a marriage prevents growth.

A bachelor, living with his parents long after his peers have been married, does not grow. His present behavior repertoire may be acceptable to his parents; they are willing to support him, cook his meals, and do his laundry; they make no demands on him he cannot readily fulfill. For him growth is contingent upon moving away, exposing himself to new challenges and to new people who make new demands upon him.

Some parents actively prevent growth in their children, either through ignorance, because they do not place a value on their children attaining maturity, or because their own self-esteem is dependent upon playing the parental role. So long as their child is getting satisfactions out of the child role, she will not break away and expose herself to growth-promoting influences.

RELATIONSHIPS THAT MAKE ONE SICK

When one is thrust into prolonged, intimate contact with other persons of a certain kind, the chances of illness—physical or personality illness—are increased. For example, if an individual is obliged to remain in close contact with someone on whom he is dependent for any reason, and this other person is obnoxious, depressing, overdemanding, or irritating, it can literally give rise to a "pain in the neck," headache, digestive upsets, and other byproducts of suppressed emotion. Of course, poor relationships between husband and wife are perhaps the most potent destroyers of physical health—this has been substantiated by recent studies showing high correlations between marital dissatisfaction and visits to physicians.[8] The experience of psychotherapists has amply shown that when parents make excessive or contradictory demands on their children, when they will not let their children be themselves, the children are likely to develop neurotic or psychotic disorders. Two Dutch researchers, Groen and Bastiaans, find considerable evidence for the role of interpersonal stress and anxiety and suggest that the adolescent particularly is forced to be in close relationships with many people (including parents, peers, teachers) over whom he or she has no control because of economic dependency. Should any of these relationships be truly lethal, the adolescent is subject to enormous, escape-proof frustration.[9]

Healthy Personality

Many physicians who have become alert to interpersonal sources of stress have been able to prove that for given patients, their symptoms of asthma, hemorrhoids, skin eruptions, hypertension, diarrhea, and so on, arose and lasted as long as the patient was inescapably involved with another person, and disappeared as soon as the relationship was ended.

Probably there exist some few people with a special talent for spreading misery, who always depress or sicken, disorganize, and undermine the self-confidence of all they come in contact with. It is meaningful to regard such individuals as today's witches. The comic character Joe Btflsk, in Al Capp's strip "Li'l Abner," is a fictional representative of the modern witch. In the comic strip, Joe always walks with a rain cloud over his head, and whenever he appears, expert workers hit their thumbs with their hammers, hens do not lay, and the most robust people feel miserable. There is need for further study of those persons like Joe Btflsk who affect others in a deleterious fashion.

HOW DOES SELF-DISCLOSURE PROMOTE GROWTH?

Growth in personality occurs as a consequence of meeting conflicts and impasses head on and reconciling them. Interpersonal conflicts and impasses constitute problems that require solution so that a satisfying relationship may be maintained. Whenever persons encounter a problem in their everyday living, they are obliged to vary their behavior until they discover some mode of responding that is successful in achieving a solution. With no conflicts, with no impasses, there would be no instigation to change—one would, in short, not learn. If persons had no need to keep afloat and move in water, they would never learn to swim. If they had no occasion to keep records or to communicate by letters, they would not learn to write. If nobody made demands upon them, they would never learn ways of behaving that would please the other person.

Self-disclosure, Personal Relations, and Healthy Personality

In interpersonal relationships, it is often when there is open conflict between the participants that an occasion is provided for growth. Interpersonal relationships, besides being a rich source of satisfactions for the participants, also provide a rich source of problems. Studies have shown that as the level of disclosure in a group becomes higher, the group members become closer to one another.[10]

Mutual Respect for Freedom and Individuality

FREEDOM

Ours is a democratic society in which personal liberty is treasured. This emphasis upon the autonomy of the single person contrasts with concepts of the ideal person that are held in other societies. Thus, it could be said that in Nazi Germany, the ideal person was the "obedient person," obedient to the leaders of the state. Nazi parents raised their children toward this goal of obedience; Nazi wives admired husbands who showed unflinching obedience to superiors and condemned those who were so "weak" and "selfish" as to put private interests above those of duty.

In a healthy personal relationship, each partner will value the autonomy of the other, and, further, will value the goal of growth toward self-actualization of the other. When these values are clearly stated, it becomes apparent that many other values can readily conflict with them. In a marriage, for example, a husband may refuse his wife's wishes to resume her education, because he is afraid of her freedom; he wants her to be dependent and compliant. A parent may force unwilling compliance from the child in order to maintain his own self-esteem. In each case, we observe a lack of respect for the individual needs of the other person. This is a subtle point but one that warrants elucidation because of its importance.

Perhaps no professional in human behavior has been as persistent in emphasizing the role of personal freedom as a major boost to the healthy personality as has Carl R. Rogers.[11] In his earlier book, *Becoming Partners*, Rogers has pointed out that the new "person-centered" approach to all forms of marriage, as well as in personal relationships in general, calls for both partners giving each other *Healthy* greater personal freedom. In *Carl Rogers on Personal* *Personality* *Power*, he suggests:

280

So it becomes only realistic to recognize that each partner will need to grant the other more living space for outside interests, outside relationships, time alone—all of the elements that enrich life. This in no way contradicts the continuing search for a wider and deeper mutual life. . . . Experiencing that greater freedom leads them to a more rewarding life together [p. 52].

Rogers is advocating more freedom in all directions. The person-centered position of Rogers is intriguing in a society where we search for greater and greater freedom. But the demands of reality indicate that for most people some limitations are always involved. The freedom to travel anyplace in the world still requires that one stop for traffic lights. Maturity of the persons involved can make considerable freedom possible, and it is the freedom that is particularly effective in helping people grow. The limitation in that freedom may well come from the insistence on the part of most partners that the single, centralized relationship, usually thought of as marriage, not be threatened by other sexual partners. Rogers seems to be permitting such explorations or "satellite" relationships. Most would perhaps draw the limiting line at that point of sexual involvement.

In a healthy relationship, each partner wants the other partner to do what he or she wants to do. Certainly friends or spouses choose one another because of similarities in values, i.e., similarities in what each wants to do. In our society, because of the high value placed on free will, few spouses would want the other to remain married unwillingly. What we are here saying is that a sign of a healthy relationship is present when each participant shows an active concern for the preservation of the integrity and autonomy of the other, even when this involves at some time the dissolution of the relationship. If a divorce, break-up of a friendship, departure from the parent's home, or resignation from a job is an important means of promoting growth and increasing autonomy, then in a healthy relationship, the other person will want this to occur.

Very often a concern and respect for the other person's right to integrity and autonomy involves some pain.

Self-disclosure, Personal Relations, and Healthy Personality

For that matter, to be concerned with one's own freedom may often involve a good deal of social pressure—especially in those instances where one's wishes differ from those of the majority of people. The "nerve of failure," as Riesman and others have called it, is rare. By this is meant the courage to continue to assert one's difference from the mass of other people, despite economic and social pressure to conform.

INDIVIDUALITY

To respect and to value another's individuality means that one sees that person's unique qualities as priceless and irreplaceable. Individuality includes not only those characteristics that are considered socially valuable, but also traits that might be called faults. Yet in a healthy interpersonal relationship, the participants seek to learn one another's distinctly idiosyncratic qualities and to affirm them.

Martin Buber [12] stated this appreciative view of the other person's idiosyncrasies in elegant terms:

> The basis of man's life with man is twofold, and it is one—the wish of every man to be confirmed as what he is, even as what he can become, by men; and the innate capacity in man to confirm his fellow-men in this way. . . . Genuine conversation . . . means acceptance of otherness. [Everything] depends, so far as human life is concerned, on whether each thinks of the other as the one he is (and) unreservedly accepts and confirms him in his being this man and in his being made in this patricular way [p. 102].
>
> Man wishes to be confirmed in his being by man, and wishes to have a presence in the being of the other [p. 104].

The concept of confirmation, as employed by Buber in these passages, has a precise meaning, one that amplifies our assertion that respect for individuality of the other characterizes healthy interpersonal relationships. To "confirm another man in his being" means that one *Healthy* acknowledges he is what he is. One may not necessarily *Personality* like all that he is, but at least one acknowledges and respects the fact that he is that very person, with those very characteristics, and not someone else. This is the direct means of respecting another's individuality. I feel confirmed by the other person when I recognize myself as the person he addresses. I can tell by his words and actions directed to me if his concept of me is valid, that is, matches my experience of myself.

Rogers referred to it as "unconditional positive regard," and he sees it as a necessary condition for helping others fulfill their individuality. Perls expressed this ideal in his Gestalt "prayer": "You do your thing, and I do mine. . . ." [13]

Concern for the Welfare and Growth of the Other

In a healthy personal relationship each partner is actively concerned for the welfare of the other. What is meant by concern? Out of what conditions does it emerge? What do we mean by active concern?

Concern for the other person means that his or her well being *matters*. The first person wants the other to be well, happy, and growing.

When we say active concern, we mean that the happiness of the other is not passively longed for; rather, we mean that the concerned person *acts*, engages in action, the aim of which is to provide the conditions for happiness and growth of the other person.

We become concerned about the other person because our life would be diminished without her sharing it. She will enrich our life most if she is herself satisfied. Thus, we acquire a vested interest in her welfare, happiness, and growth. Concern for the happiness of the other person is insurance for one's own satisfactions. A workhorse cannot work for us when he is ill treated. We use the horse's energy as a means for the attainment of our own goals. Thus, we have a vested interest in tending the horse's needs very carefully.

Self-disclosure, Personal Relations, and Healthy Personality

It may offend the reader thus to be compared to a horse, yet the analogy is not farfetched. The other person, like the horse (though in different ways), embodies qualities and powers that we need to enrich our lives.

His affection is important to us for security and self-esteem. His very company serves as entertainment and relief from loneliness. In order for him to continue to satisfy us, it is important that he be happy. Therefore, each dissatisfaction of his promises a withdrawal of satisfactions from us. In order to avoid this eventuality, we learn to anticipate his wants and fulfill them. We help him when he asks for help. We help him to grow, because a mature partner is more satisfying than one who is immature.

Parents are concerned for the happiness and growth of their children for a number of reasons. Happy children are signs of success in child rearing, and this is an important condition for the parents' self-esteem. This also provides satisfactions for the parents—even security, for it is possible that the parents may need the future economic support of their children in old age.

A wife is concerned for the happiness and growth of her husband, because a happy and mature husband is a much richer source of satisfactions for her than a miserable, thwarted, and childish husband.

It should not be construed that all concern for others is an outgrowth of the calculated view that "if I take care of that person, then she will take care of me." A healthy personality is capable of *disinterested* concern for others; it gives a feeling of fulfillment, or of abundance, to be able actively to care for another person. Thus, grandparents may delight in the growth of their grandchildren, whom they indulge and nurture, yet they get no reward other than the experience of pleasure from watching the children's antics.

A further determiner of concern that must not be overlooked is the fact of identification with the other person. In a healthy interpersonal relationship—say, one between spouses—one partner identifies very closely with the feelings and needs of the other. Where this has occurred, the satisfactions of the other person are felt as deeply as satisfactions for the self.

It appears, then, that concern for the other person is a kind of devious concern for one's own happiness and growth. This may appear offensive and selfish. Yet, with Fromm, we shall ask this question, "Why should we not

Healthy Personality

284

be concerned about our own happiness and growth?" There is growing evidence that one can love another only if one loves oneself; that love and concern for the self and the other person are not mutually exclusive. Rather, they are correlated, and derive from something else, a common factor which, for want of a better name, we shall call the "power to love." [14] In other words, only if one can be concerned for the self can one be concerned for the other.

One of the major principles shared by all civilized religions is known most familiarly in the selection from Leviticus 19:18: "And thou shalt love thy neighbor as thyself." This statement as is, or in its form as the "silver rule": "Do not unto thy neighbor that which is distasteful to thyself," is found as a Confucian analect, a Jainist precept, and as a Christian and Judaic admonition. It also appears as a psychological law or principle, which suggests that in order to do well by one's neighbors one must love one's self. The concept of the beautiful and noble person suggests the highest level of actualization to be the compassionate self—one who cares for others but also, following this universal principle, who yields primacy to the concept of the passionate self—actual love of self.

People who appear to be totally unconcerned for themselves, and who instead make all manner of "sacrifices" in order to help another person (they are called "unselfish"), usually demand a terrible price in return and usually get this price—absolute conformity with their wishes. We are all familiar with the "unselfish" parent who sacrifices a great deal to help a child get through school. Would it not be ungracious if the child then, against the parent's "reasonable wishes," married someone of his or her choice but not his parent's?

THE WISH TO CHANGE THE OTHER

Self-disclosure, Personal Relations, and Healthy Personality

Psychologists know that human nature is not fixed, that behavior and personality structure are quite subject to change within broad biological limits. Psychologists even have acquired some rudimentary knowledge of the conditions under which behavior and personality will change, and they stand in a position where they can influence the rate and direction of changes in behavior and personality structure. Teachers, psychotherapists, social workers, military training personnel, all seek to influence the process of change in other people, with or without their knowledge and consent. One would have to raise questions about the depth of love that one partner had for another if that one constantly nagged the other to change. "Love is not love which alters when it alteration finds," admonishes Shakespeare in the Sonnets (CXVI).

A person may get into difficulty in relationships because of an inaccurate estimate of the changeability of the other person. The person may overestimate or underestimate the changeability, or fail to identify the conditions under which personal change is most likely to occur.

The Effects of Underestimating Changeability. A person may believe that the other's behavior is unyielding and immutable. In consequence, he may develop fixed modes of relating to the other that perpetuate the undesirable behavior of the other person by evoking it. For example, a man may believe that human nature is basically evil, that people are "just no damn good"; no matter what is done for them, they will remain untrustworthy, dishonest, selfish, animal-like, lustful, and everything else that is bad. If a person with this belief has children, his child-rearing behavior will necessarily be influenced. It makes a difference to a parent whether he is dealing with a child who he believes will turn into a savage beast unless curbed or whether he is dealing with a malleable piece of "clay" who will become, roughly, what he is expected to become. In the former instance, child rearing will consist primarily of a tense battle between the parent and the forces of evil that are assumed to be inherent in the child; one false step, one weak moment of unwatchfulness, and catastrophe will result.

Probably many marriages have been terminated, or endured with resignation and martyrdom, because one spouse has incorrectly diagnosed the changeability of the partner. The husband may assume his wife cannot be changed, and the wife has tried unsuccessfully to change her man. The couple then "digs in" for a life of dissatisfaction, or they institute divorce proceedings. Many a spouse, following a bitter divorce, has been dumbfounded to observe that, like magic, the discarded partner became everything that was desired during the marriage. The husband about whom the wife forever complained, "He is such a stodgy, unimaginative, unromantic man," becomes attentive to his appearance, more considerate of women, more romantic after she divorces him. This is certainly evidence that he was capable of change, but more than this, it is evidence he did not *want* to change for her, and that she did not know how to behave so he would want to change for her.

The Effects of Overestimating Potential for Change. Although behavior is mutable, there are powerful forces that militate against change. These factors include the need to feel safe, the need to maintain self-esteem, the need to maintain a sense of identity, and other people's expectations. Each time a person alters some accustomed mode of response, she may feel anxious about disapproving responses of others; she may lose self-esteem if her present value system opposes the new behavior; she may fear that other people will no longer recognize her. These factors thus operate to restrict behavior to a fixed range. But someone may choose a friend, or a spouse, with a view to transforming this person, like Pygmalion, into something new and different. The person "as is" is not acceptable. A sort of silent wager is laid down that the chooser will in time be able to change the other person. Thus, a woman may displace her zeal as a sculptress from clay to people. She chooses a bum or a criminal as husband, not because he is attractive the way he is, but because she believes she can change him into a new man. In theory, it is possible to arrange conditions so that someone will change his or her reaction patterns, but few laypersons are so skilled that they can manipulate conditions in precisely the ways that will promote behaivoral change. For that matter, trained psychotherapists, criminologists, and other professional personality changers have a difficult time doing their job, because knowledge about personality change is as yet incomplete and incompletely tested. Therefore, the layperson is advised not to choose friends and lovers with the aim of changing them. If the other is not acceptable the way he or she is, do not accept that person. The major consequence of over-estimating changeability of the other person is disappointment and failure in effecting the changes.

How to Change the Other Person. The most effective and the most healthy way to produce change in the other person is to invite him or her to change. People choose their action, and they can choose to change it. If a person's behavior is unsatisfactory to themselves, they can usually modify it. If their behavior is unsatisfactory to another person, they can alter the behavior so it will satisfy the other person, if they wish. Naturally, it may not always be easy, but it is possible.

If the relationship is one that provides satisfactions for both participants, then each will want to please the other.

But there is a difference between a cold, calculated attempt to *bribe* another person into conformity with one's wishes, and a spontaneous wish that the other person, who is loved, will change. In the former instance, the one being bribed will eventually discover he is being manipulated. In the latter, the relationship is more likely to be one of mutual requests to change and mutual compliance with the other's wishes.

It should not be overlooked that we can change another person by force, by threats, or by "brainwashing" procedures. Although change induced by threat, manipulation, or sanction may be effective in the short run, it will usually be achieved at the cost of resentment and hostility toward the person dictating the terms. The overbearing parent or teacher seldom takes into consideration the other person's needs and values. As these are violated and thwarted, hostility is provoked. Whenever the subject becomes less dependent upon the other, she will rebel, and either terminate the relationship or inflict violence upon the would-be manipulator of her behavior.[15]

Manipulation of Others' Experience and Behavior. Some people dream of being able to manipulate other people into doing what they want them to do. The average student is fascinated with accounts of the effects of propaganda in shaping the attitudes of the populace, of the shrewdness of advertisers at molding the buying habits of people, at the skill of the college Romeo who can boast of his conquest with the opposite sex by virtue of a "smooth line." The extreme case of manipulation of others is provided by hypnosis, in which the subject will comply with the wishes of the hypnotist.

In a startling book, *Man the Manipulator*, Everett L. Shostrom [16] has taken direct aim at the manipulative behavior of persons:

> A manipulator may be defined as a person who exploits, uses and/or controls himself and others as things in certain self-defeating ways. . . . The opposite of the manipulator is the actualizor . . . who may be defined as a person who appreciates himself and his fellowman as persons or subjects with unique potential— an expresser of his actual self. The paradox is that each of us is partly a manipulator and partly an actualizor, but we can continually become more actualizing [p. 15].

When manipulation becomes the usual mode of interacting with others, it is a serious sign of impaired personality health. It implies, among other things, a profound distrust of the other person, even a contempt for him. Furthermore, the habitual manipulator of others must repress his spontaneous feelings, thereby promoting further self-alienation.

The contriving, manipulative insincere individual, often without conscious awareness, places popularity and "success" at the peak of his value hierarchy. He sells his soul (his real self) to achieve it. He strives to determine what kind of behavior the other person likes and then pretends to be the kind of person who habitually behaves that way.

The major factor responsible for habitually contrived interpersonal behavior is the belief, conscious or implicit, that to be one's real self is dangerous; that exposure of real feelings and motives will result in rejection or ridicule. Such a belief stems from experiences of punishment and rejection at the hands of parents and other significant persons. In order to avoid punishment in the future, the child represses the real self in interpersonal situations and learns to become a contriver, an "other-directed" char-

Self-disclosure, Personal Relations, and Healthy Personality

acter. Of course, more serious outcomes are possible too: neurosis, psychopathic personality, and psychosis.

Scientific students of the learning process, following the lead of Pavlov, Watson, and Skinner, have been able to demonstrate that people's behavior can be manipulated without their awareness.[17] A psychologist was able to get subjects in an experiment to increase the frequency with which they uttered plural nouns simply by murmuring "Mm-hmm" whenever the subject spontaneously uttered the desired class of words. Many other experimenters have demonstrated that the content of another's conversation can subtly be controlled by properly timed "reinforcing" stimuli, such as saying, "That's good." There seems little doubt that, with a little training, anyone could improve the efficiency with which he or she could thus influence the behavior of others without their awareness that they had been so manipulated. All it calls for is study of the other person, to discern what things will function as reinforcers to his or her behavior, and then supplying these things whenever the desired behavior occurs. However, most people resent being manipulated, and they become properly angry when they discover that they have been treated like puppets or animals.[18]

A nineteen-year-old male student once consulted with me, seeking help in improving his relations with people. He stated that he had studied Dale Carnegie's book *How to Win Friends and Influence People* and found the advice given there extremely helpful to him in "conning" others, especially girls. He was successful as a campus lover and had six of the most attractive coeds in love with him at the time of seeking help. The help he sought was any suggestions that psychology might offer to him in his campaign to win over the affections of the campus queen, who rejected him, telling him he was a "phony." This rejection upset him. He wondered if there were some new gimmicks he might learn in order to seem authentic. Parenthetically, he mentioned that, once he won a girl's affections, he rapidly became bored by her, stating, "Once you've won a girl, it's like a book you've just read; you don't want to have anything more to do with her." I refused to help him learn new manipulative meth-

Healthy Personality

ods. In a number of interviews, I helped him gain insight into his motives and background, and he became more authentic and less the unscrupulous user of other people.

Friendship and Love Between the Sexes

In the preceding discussion I did not specify whether I was talking about friendship between partners of the same or opposite sex, between members of the same family, or between spouses. Different norms and expectations guide each of these relationships, and there are differing degrees of commitment and of self-disclosure in each type of dyad. However, most of what has been said applies in some degree to any personal relationship. My concern was to show some dimensions along which any personal relationship can grow. In the next chapter I explore love relationships, mostly between the sexes, but not exclusively so. Love occurs between friends, and, of course, among family members other than a husband and wife. But the ability to love is a criterion of healthy personality, and I have devoted a chapter to its exploration.

Some Existential Suggestions

As Buber sees it (and I concur), personal relations call both for "distance" and "relation." This means being able to disengage from dialogue with the other, and to enter into relationships of authentic revealing with the other. It is useful, then, to see the extent to which you can sustain dialogue with each of the "significant others" in your life. You probably will find that with each person, there is a point of mutual knowing to which you have arrived, and where you may be content to rest. If any of your relationships have become unrewarding, it might be worthwhile to renew disclosure and see if the bases of discontent can be brought into the open. One of the major change problems that student couples have centers about the more rapid growth in one in contrast to the other. This is particularly true where perhaps only one of the pair is in a graduate school program, while the other is tied down to family responsibilities. High rates of breakup in such marriages strongly suggest that cou-

Self-disclosure, Personal Relations, and Healthy Personality

ples should find ways to, first, understand each other's work and lives outside of the home; and second, take active measures to provide growth opportunities for both members of the marriage. These might include the spouse's taking courses, seeking cultural enrichment, and active participation in the work of the graduate student spouse.

A review of the demands one makes upon others will sometimes be shocking. You may find you have been depending upon others in almost infantile ways, to entertain you, to guide you, to govern *their* lives in the light of *your* hopes and anxieties. The other person "is not in the world to live up to your expectations." See the extent to which you can enlarge your sphere of independent security by learning new skills.

The most difficult thing to discover in oneself is one's efforts to manipulate and control other persons rather than to stay in dialogue with them, inviting them truly to be free agents. Study your relations with parents, friends, and siblings to see if you can identify the "games" you play with them, subtly to induce them to conform to your wishes.

Can you recognize the possible damage to another person whom you might be manipulating for your own wishes? Freeing one's self and freeing another person of your manipulation can result in growth toward psychological health for both of you.

SUMMARY

Personal relationships call for mutual knowing through authentic self-disclosure. Self-disclosure is inhibited by social norms and by dependency upon others, which makes persons fear they will be rejected if they are truly known. The most powerful factor in one person's self-disclosure is the other person's willingness to disclose information of comparable intimacy.

In healthy personal relationships, the participants make realistic and feasible demands upon one another. Relationships become frozen into impasses when one partner makes demands that are not being met by the other. Impasses are vital for fostering both personal growth and

Healthy
Personality

the growth of the relationship, but they must be brought out in the open and resolved in ways that enhance the maturity and self-reliance of the participants. Some relationships actually inhibit or reverse personal growth, and some foster sickness.

Self-disclosure between persons fosters growth because it reveals the impasses that inevitably arise in an honest personal relationship.

Mutual respect and confirmation of one another's individuality are essential in personal relationships. The participants are concerned about one another's wellbeing and growth, and they strive to act in ways that foster these goals. They do not try to change one another through devious manipulations, but openly express any desires for change in the other.

NOTES AND REFERENCES

1. L. ZUNIN, *Contact: The First Four Minutes* (Los Angeles: Nash, 1972).

2. For the classic exposition on dialogue, see M. BUBER, *I and Thou* (New York: Scribner, 1970); and *Between Man and Man* (Boston: Beacon, 1955), pp. 1–39.

3. R. GELMAN and H. McGINLEY, "Interpersonal Liking and Self-disclosure," *Journal of Consulting and Clinical Psychology*, 1979, Vol. 46, pp. 1549–1551; J. D. DAVIS, "Self-disclosure in an Acquaintance Exercise: Responsibility for Level of Intimacy," *Journal of Personality and Social Psychology*, 1976, Vol. 33, pp. 787–792.

4. See S. M. JOURARD, *Self-disclosure: An Experimental Analysis of the Transparent Self* (New York: Wiley-Interscience, 1971) for a review of our scientific studies; the significance of self-disclosure in everyday life is explored in JOURARD, *The Transparent Self*, 2nd ed. (New York: Van Nostrand Reinhold, 1971). For an excellent review of the literature in self-disclosure, see the paper by JACQUELYN RESNICK and MARTIN AMERIKANER, "Self-Disclosure," in R. WOODY (Ed.), *Encyclopedia of Clinical Assessment* (New York: Jossey, 1979).

5. For further discussion of expectations, impasses, and their resolution, see C. WHITAKER and T. MALONE, *The Roots of Psychotherapy* (New York: Blakiston, 1953); C. WHITAKER, J. WARKENTIN, and NAN JOHNSON, "The Psychotherapeutic Impasse," *American Journal of*

Self-disclosure, Personal Relations, and Healthy Personality

Orthopsychiatry, 1950, Vol. 20, pp. 641–647; F. PERLS, *Gestalt Therapy Verbatim* (Lafayette, Calif.: Real People Press, 1969), pp. 28–40.

6. Perhaps the most readable, charming, and witty collection of advice on child-rearing is contained in the series of books by Haim G. Ginnott, a child psychotherapist who also became a television personality. His most popular works are *Between Parent and Child* (New York: Macmillan, 1965); *Between Parent and Teenager* (New York: Macmillan, 1969); and *Teacher and Child* (New York: Macmillan, 1972).

7. B. BETTELHEIM, *The Informed Heart* (New York: Free Press, 1961).

8. R. L. WEISS and B. M. AVED, "Marital Satisfaction and Depression as Predictors of Physical Health Status," *Journal of Consulting and Clinical Psychology*, 1978, Vol. 46, pp. 1379–1384.

9. R. D. LAING and A. ESTERSON, *Sanity, Madness and the Family* (London: Tavistock, 1964) gives a strong argument for this point. See also J. P. SPIEGEL and N. W. BELL, "The Family of the Psychiatric Patient," in S. ARIETI (Ed.), *American Handbook of Psychiatry*, I (New York: Basic, 1959). An excellent overview of the dynamics of stress and anxiety is found in the volumes edited by C. D. SPIELBERGER and I. G. SARASON, *Stress and Anxiety* (New York: Hemisphere, 1975). In that publication you will also find the paper by J. J. GROEN and J. BASTIAANS, "Psychosocial Stress, Interhuman Communication and Psychosomatic Disease," p. 27–49.

10. B. J. KIRSHNER, R. R. DIES, and R. A. BROWN, "Effects of Experimental Manipulation of Self-disclosure on Group Cohesiveness," *Journal of Consulting and Clinical Psychology*, 1978, Vol. 46, pp. 1171–1177.

11. Carl R. Rogers, pioneer "inventor" of client-centered psychotherapy, is one of the leading figures in humanistic psychology. Some of his current books that discuss the "person-centered" approach in a number of areas of life and that stress personal freedom include: *Becoming Partners: Marriage and Its Alternatives* (New York: Delacorte, 1972); *Freedom to Learn* (Columbus, Oh.: Merrill, 1969); and *Carl Rogers on Personal Power* (New York: Dell, 1977).

12. M. BUBER, *The Knowledge of Man* (New York: Harper, 1965).

Healthy Personality

13. C. R. ROGERS, "The Necessary and Sufficient Conditions of Therapeutic Personality Change," *Journal of*

294

Consulting Psychology, 1957, Vol. 21, pp. 95–103; PERLS, op. cit.

14. This discussion is based on E. FROMM, *Man for Himself* (New York: Holt, 1947), pp. 96–141.

15. Contrasting theories and methods for promoting change of personality and behavior are given in C. B. TRUAX and R. P. CARKHUFF, *Toward Effective Counseling and Psychotherapy: Training and Practice* (Chicago: Aldine, 1967), Chapter 2; and L. KRASNER and L. P. ULLMAN (Eds.), *Case Studies in Behavior Modification* (New York: Holt, 1965); and their more recent volume, *Behavior Influence and Personality: The Social Matrix of Human Action* (New York: Holt, 1973). An effort to reconcile "humanistic" and "behavioristic" approaches to behavior change is given by F. J. SHAW, *Reconciliation: A Theory of Man Transcending* (New York: Van Nostrand Reinhold, 1966); and A. LAZARUS, *Behavior Therapy and Beyond* (New York: McGraw-Hill, 1971).

16. E. L. SHOSTROM. *Man, the Manipulator: The Inner Journey from Manipulation to Actualization* (Nashville: Abingdon, 1967).

17. See Jourard's critique of "behavioristic" methods of influence in *The Transparent Self*, op. cit., Chapter 16, "Dialogue Versus Manipulation in Counseling and Psychotherapy."

18. When she discovered that she had been thus "manipulated," the heroine in Koestler's novel shot her lover. See A. KOESTLER, *The Age of Longing* (New York: Macmillan, 1951).

Self-disclosure,
Personal
Relations,
and Healthy
Personality

CHAPTER

12

LOVE AND HEALTHY PERSONALITY

INTRODUCTION

Can one look realistically, even scientifically, at love? We had better do so, for there is scarcely any other subject, force, or phenomenon that is given so heavy a responsibility. Love, among other functions, is supposed to make the world go around, to turn day into night; it also extends as far as your soul can reach. It must be pretty important, not merely to the poets, but to people of all ages, to children to assure the health of their personalities, and to the aged to give meaning to each sunrise.

Freud once remarked that lieben *and* arbeiten, *loving and working, were the crucial signs of maturity and healthy personality. Yet love is among the least understood of all human activities.*[1]

What is perhaps more important is its tremendous significance to all generations and in all cultures, and the fact that, like the thing that cannot buy it, it is often counterfeited, and possessing it is not always a happy experience.

Some, for example, have claimed that drug abuse can be cured with love,[2] as in the SEED program, while others report that the same loving program is a matter of brainwashing and is deeply destructive. Another study reports that most college students do express great pleasure in love, yet over 50 per cent also report depression, and some 25 per cent have talked of suicide in relation to love problems.

Fromm[3] has been almost singular among writers on the subject by defining love in terms of action as well as experience. In his work, love is not exclusively a passion or emotion; rather, it is partly action. A love relationship exists when a person behaves toward the object of love in ways that show the lover knows, cares for, respects, and feels responsibility for the other.

The Definition of Loving Behavior

I will modify Fromm's definition and speak of loving behavior. Loving behavior is distinguished from other kinds of action by its motives and by its consequences. We can speak, with Fromm, of the "power," or capacity, to love. It should be possible to determine whether loving behavior is effective in achieving its aims, and it should be possible to study the relationships between loving behavior and the healthy personality.

Loving behavior refers to all action that a person undertakes to promote happiness and growth in the being he or she loves. Another fuller definition of love is as follows: [4]

Love is (1) a feeling and behavior toward an entity, usually a person but also an idea or a thing (as in love of one's country). It is intense or of a high degree of passion. (2) Includes the intense desire and acts intended for that entity's wellbeing or highest level of existence. The existence of the beloved is valued equal to that of the lover's own. (3) It includes the intention and desire to be present and intimately with that entity in almost all conditions. (4) In its fullest realization, it is experienced as requited—the beloved carries out similar feelings and acts for the lover.

Probably love begins as a feeling or a commitment—both subjective reactions. But if these feelings or the commitment to another's wellbeing are real, they will inevitably become manifest in loving behavior.

Kinds and Classes of Love

One of the best ways to understand a concept that can be as vague as love is to try to organize its many forms and to discover its internal organization. Many systems have sprung up in recent years, and they each give a new perspective on this charming subject.

John Lee[5] has identified three primary styles of loving:

Eros: the search for the perfect lover.
Ludus: viewing love as pleasant pastime.
Storage: love that develops slowly and naturally.

Other terms sometimes used are

Agape: altruistic or religious love.
Platonic: sexless love.
de Clerambauit syndrome: a woman's delusion that an older, high-status male is in love with her.

The two major forms of love identified by Landsman[6] center about the dynamic relationship between love in childhood and in adulthood. They are referred to as:

Natural love: the one-way giving of love unconditionally from parent or adult to child.
Conditional love: the two-way, reciprocal, giving and taking of love between two psychologically mature adults. *Earned and learned love.*

This is a radical, nonromantic view of love in the adult world and is likely to be hard to take on the part of a person who sees in love a free ride—that he or she will be loved by the spouse regardless of the reciprocal giving demanded in the adult stage. This suggests that adult love must be continuously fed.

Healthy Personality

Natural or unconditional love is only characteristic of childhood and is essentially instinctive or "natural." A child will usually retain the love and affection of the parents even when the child has grossly misbehaved. Such unconditional love in early childhood is fundamental to the ability to give and take love that gradually becomes the pattern in adulthood. Even the child's attitude toward the parents as he or she grows up becomes governed by the reciprocating principle. The now-grown child sees the parents as peers and recognizes that he or she must give love to the parents as well as receive it.

If the unconditional, natural, early childhood, one-way love is not present, as in the case depicted in the book *Sybil*,[7] the capacity for the reciprocating form of love seems diminished or, in some instances, nonexistent. Sybil was deprived of mother love in childhood by a psychotic mother who often tortured her. She developed a complex multiple personality, with some thirteen selves, which were eventually fused into one person with the help of a dedicated psychiatrist.

Emotional Experience and Loving Behavior

When somebody loves another person (or an animal, or a country), he identifies with him. Because the lover is concerned with the happiness and growth of the other, he will feel the pleasures and pains, the dangers to and the happinesses of his loved one as if they were his own. It is as if he had extended the contact surface of his organs for feelings and experiencing. He reacts emotionally to the events that affect his loved one, just as he does to the events that affect him personally.

Just as the lover becomes angry when someone hurts or insults her, so she becomes angry when something hurts the being she loves. Just as she is happy at her own successes, so is she affected by the successes and gratifications of her loved one. Just as she is concerned about her own growth, so is she concerned for the growth of the other. Identification, empathy, and sympathy are all involved in loving. Empathy involves the correct interpretation of cues that reflect the feelings and wishes of the other person.[8] Identification, becoming

Love and Healthy Personality

like the other, in imagination, for longer or shorter intervals of time—makes sympathy (literally, feeling *with* the other) possible.

Experiences that affect the loved one provoke emotions in the lover. These in turn serve as important motives for loving behavior. Under the impetus of emotion provoked by whatever has affected the loved one, the lover strives to do those things that will promote happiness and reduce unhappiness in the loved one.

SEX IN LOVE

It should be pointed out that there can be sexuality without love, and there can be love without sexuality. We would not call sexual intercourse that was desired by one partner but not by the other an expression of loving behavior. And we could call it a love relationship between a man and his friend, male or female, when there was active concern for happiness and growth, but no sexuality. We will discuss sex more fully in the next chapter.

However, the sexual act, intercourse, is not referred to as "making love" without reason. Many people think the two are inevitably associated, love and sex. We do know that when they are associated, we obtain a remarkably high moment, or even a lifetime of beauty and intensity. The orgasm is often thought of as the epitome of positive experience when it is associated with the overall relationship of deep loving. Some of the current behaviorists have minimized this phenomenon. They choose to see sex and sex problems as essentially mechanical, controllable processes. An example would be the use of a technique involving the squeezing of the penis by the female to prevent premature ejaculation. Sex may be thought of separately from the emotional life of the person or it may be raised to a high level, emotionally and perhaps even spiritually, when it occurs within a context of caring and loving.

CHOICE IN LOVE

Healthy Personality

One has to wonder about the personal characteristics that first attract a possible lover and the characteristics that build a lasting, successful relationship. There can be no doubt that physical attractiveness ranks first. In studies of college students at a dance, it was clear that the physically attractive persons, male or female, were seen as more desirable for dates.[9] It is also true, however, that as time goes on, we settle for someone who may be less than ideal, and we generally settle for someone who is at about the same level of physical attractiveness as ourselves, who has similar interests and background and, of course, someone who likes us, thereby closing the reciprocal circle of attraction. The role of physical attractiveness in the relationship seems to hold throughout the entire life cycle.[10]

Is it bigger than both of us? For some, one of the excitements of love is that it can seem to overpower. It seems to be true that under circumstances of any kind of emotional arousal, positive or negative, we are more likely to fall in love or see the other person as physically attractive. One ingenious pair of researchers [11] had males interviewed by a female while both were on a scary suspension bridge and found the males more sexually aroused than when on the solid ground. Thus, as many a passionate lover has discovered, creating the right arousal situation, whether it is a moonlit night or a candlelight dinner, can make things go much faster. Primary, to a certain extent, among the factors involved in choice of a partner seems to be what is called propinquity, but which simply means being in the right place at the right time, living in the same neighborhood, and so on. People choose people whom they live near, sit near in class, or who happen to be at the same dance at the same time. Thus, mixers and computer dating agencies provide for an enhancement of the propinquity principle.

In principle, a person can choose anything or anyone to love, if the person wants to love at all. But it is well known that when choices are made from among a variety of possible alternatives, the motivations may be complex. As the psychoanalysts say, choices are "overdetermined."

A person may choose someone on the basis of certain estimable characteristics. Or the person may choose someone he or she thinks will give much love. Let us explore some of the more common bases for choice in love.

Love and Healthy Personality

Helplessness and Need. One may be moved to love another because the other seems to be helpless and in need of loving behavior. Thus, most people find it easy to love small children or helpless animals, without necessarily expecting anything in return.

Conformity with the Lover's Ideals. A potential lover may have ideals of appearance, personality, and behavior with which the other must conform before love will be offered. The concepts of the "ideal wife" and "ideal husband" may be decisive factors in determining whom a young man or woman will select to fall in love with. The young adult observes someone who accords with his or her ideals and then pursues this person as the one he or she will love. There is considerable cultural stereotyping in the characteristics that define the beautiful and/or ideal person whom a person seeks, but there may be much individual variability as well. Langhorne and Secord, in one study, showed that unmarried college males sought a pleasing personality, tenderness and consideration, moral uprightness, and a complex trait that included health, emotional maturity, stability, and intelligence. Freud described a class of men who were most attracted to women who were the "property" of another man, or whose fidelity and sexual propriety were questionable. I know of men who can only love women much older or younger than themselves. A sociologist gathered evidence to show that people select mates on the basis of complementary needs, for example, dominant men choose passive women. Some men may choose women who will not make them feel inferior, for example, someone less intelligent or from a lower socioeconomic status, and some unconsciously choose mates who resemble one parent or the other. The range of possible variability in choosing someone to love is remarkable.

RATIONAL CHOICE OF SOMEONE TO LOVE

Ability of the Loved One to Reciprocate Love. A person may not experience the desire to love another person until and unless the other person shows clear signs of a desire to love first. In other words, the person can be moved to love if and only if she has been first

Healthy Personality

assured that she is loved. It is almost as if the would-be lover is afraid to risk rejection of her love, or is not willing to love, unless there is some guarantee that the love will be returned.[12]

The following discussion applies mainly to marriage, where mutuality of love is almost a *sine qua non* of a successful and happy marriage. In our culture, it is the custom that would-be spouses must first "fall in love" with each other before they consider marriage. The process of falling in love is itself a nonrational phenomenon, probably based on deprivation of sex and on loneliness. When a person in our culture is "in love," he or she displays most of the characteristics associated with deprivation: preoccupation with the need object, "overestimation" of the value of the object, a desire to possess and "consume" the object in order to appease the hunger, and so on. In fact, what is called romantic love sometimes resembles narcotic addiction. The lover will do anything to experience the loved one's company and embraces. If there is separation, the lover will do anything to be reunited. If the lover is rejected, he or she shows the withdrawal symptoms of a heroin addict.

So apparent is this phenomenon that a number of investigators have suggested the parallel between love and addiction, including Simon and Peele.[13]

Romantic love becomes active loving when the lovers actually behave in ways that will produce mutual happiness and that will promote growth in each other. The hunger to "be loved" may serve as a factor that brings people together. But whether or not love can emerge from romantic love depends on the actual loving capacity of each partner, and the actual suitability of each person's traits for promoting happiness and growth in the other.

The person who would choose wisely for marriage should soberly ask himself the question, at some time prior to marriage, "Can I make this person happy, and can I help her to grow?" Obviously the more reality-based the answers are to these questions, the more likely it is that a rational choice will be made.

Whether or not a given choice of a spouse has been suitable can be determined only by observation of the subsequent relationship through time; time will tell. It is possible, however, to make a choice of a spouse in ways that will increase the *probability* of the relationship moving in a healthy direction. The guiding philosophy of choice would be to state, as clearly as possible, (1) the needs and values of the choosing person and (2) the traits of the person being chosen in as detailed a fashion as is practicable. If choices are predicated on such a broad base, the chances are greater that they will be fortunate choices. Naturally, though, there are many purely technical problems involved in specifying the needs and values of the chooser. Because these are psychological problems, or problems within the professional realm of the psychologist, one can sometimes obtain professional help in making a judicious choice of a partner in such important interpersonal relationships. Thus, to an increasing degree, engaged couples consult professional marriage counselors to assist them in clearing up misconceptions about each other and about marriage. This is not a very romantic practice, but it can be helpful.

One's family and friends frequently serve as an investigating committee to examine and pass judgment on a lover's choice of a spouse. "Lovers are blind," it is assumed with some validity; and so the well-intentioned family and friends try to examine all the fiancé's traits that have been ignored as unimportant by the love-blinded youth. She may have fallen in love because of some one need-related trait and may ignore all the rest of his characteristics. The uninvolved others look the man over from many other standpoints, looking at such things as his health, his income, his religion, his attitudes and values, his tastes, and so on. If these judges know the overall needs and value hierarchy of the young lover, they may be able to see he has attributes that make him unsuited to her. She may not pay attention to their advice.

FACTORS THAT PROMOTE UNWISE CHOICES IN LOVE

Healthy Personality

Let us consider some of the factors that will impair the capacity of a person to make a suitable choice of someone to love.

Chronic Needs. An individual with strong, unsatisfied needs will be likely to perceive other persons in autistic fashion. He will seek satisfaction of his immediate needs and ignore other traits in a person that are important to his growth and overall happiness. In consequence, he might choose a person who can gratify these needs. He doesn't realize he has other needs and values that will become important when the present needs have been satisfied.

Thus, the inadequate man who needs to be taken care of and to have decisions made for him may fall in love with a dominant woman. Eventually, he may outgrow his need to be dominated and require other modes of behavior from her. If she cannot change her ways of behaving toward him, an impasse may arise that will result in termination of the relationship.

Lack of Self-knowledge. The person who is alienated from her real self will not know what she needs to make her happy or to help her grow. Because her choice is not based upon consideration of these important factors, it will be based on other criteria that are irrelevant to growth and happiness. Thus, she might choose a possible husband just on the basis of appearance alone, because other people regard the man as desirable. She doesn't know if she really desires the man; rather, she wants him because she believes she ought to. This would be the case with the other-directed character described by Riesman. Or she may choose a man as a possible mate because her parents, or her conscience, demand she make that choice. Again she is ignoring her own needs and wants. It is not rare for a person to fall in love, court, and marry someone, and then, much later, come face to face with her real self and wonder, "How did I ever get joined to this person?"

Lack of Knowledge of the Loved One. I pointed out earlier that there is only one way to know another person: that is, to observe, to come to tentative conclusions, and then continuously to modify these conclusions as more observations are made. This calls for time to make many observations of the other person's behavior in a wide range of situations.

Love and Healthy Personality

When this procedure has not been adopted by the

would-be lover, then it follows that his concept of stable traits of the other will be autistic, or inaccurate. That is, it will be based on need-selective observation, attribution, disowning or assimilative projection, hearsay, or other mechanisms that guarantee inaccurate concepts of the other (see Chapter 4).

Optimally, of course, in anything so intimate as marriage, the couple should explore each other, perhaps for a long time, so that each will come to know the other's stable traits before they become legally committed to one another. This is unromantic, however, and seldom done; the longer-range consequence is either divorce or a long life of boredom or martyrdom. But even more, each person may strive to *hide* many of his characteristics from the other because he needs the other person. He is afraid he will be rejected should the other person discover these traits. And so a courtship, instead of being a period of mutual self-disclosure and study, becomes a period of mutual deception and the construction of false public selves. Many a person has experienced tragic disillusionment with his spouse once the ceremony has been completed and the marriage begun. Even more tragic, however, is a longer-run consequence—that of striving to conform with a false public self that has been constructed during the courtship. The "perfect lovers" in "The Chocolate Soldier" found their relationship too idealistic, too perfect. It was a strain, and so the nobleman married the maid, with whom he could be himself, and the girl of high degree married the bourgeois chocolate soldier-innkeeper for the same reason.

The Need to Love and to Be Loved

We are born helpless, and so we need to be loved by our parents if we are to survive. Good physical care is not enough to insure healthy personality growth. Unless the child has received loving care, including emotional displays of affection and attention to her idiosyncratic needs, she is likely to grow in deviant ways. Spitz showed that children raised from birth in a foundling home, with adequate physical care but no personalized attention from a mother figure, were retarded in physical

Healthy Personality

306

growth, were less resistant to disease, and were retarded in their overall "development quotients," compared to infants raised by their own mothers. Goldfarb showed that institution-raised children, by the time they reached adolescence, were severely handicapped in their ability to relate to others on an emotional and loving basis. Ribble saw lack of adequate mothering as a causal factor in the development of infantile marasmus, a rare disease in which the infant literally wastes away. And Spitz showed that depression in infants was the byproduct of separation from the mother. It is a definitely established fact that loving is needed to foster a child's physical growth and the growth of healthy personality.[14]

Harry Harlow, the gifted psychologist, was able to demonstrate that even infant monkeys who were denied access to a mother during their earliest days and were instead reared with a "mother" constructed out of terry-cloth or wire reached maturity with impaired ability to mate.[15]

It is doubtful if anyone ever completely loses the need to be loved. The strength of conscious longings for love, however, is probably related to the amount of love a person has experienced. If from early infancy, a child has had no love, he may grow into a psychopath who is incapable of active loving and who experiences no conscious longings for love. If the child has had a "taste" of love, just enough to learn that it feels good, but not enough to satisfy, then he may develop what Levy called "primary affect hunger" and pursue love for the rest of his life, at any cost.[16]

The ability to love actively is an outgrowth of having one's love needs gratified earlier in life. There is logical basis for such a statement, as well as empirical grounding. A person whose needs are thwarted is a "hungry" person, seeking to be filled. When one is empty, one can hardly give. Active love seems to rest on the economics of plenty rather than of scarcity. The healthy lover is as one who is "filled" and who gives freely to his loved ones not only because of their need, but because of his abundance.[17]

No one, however, is so "full" that she can love endlessly without receiving love in return. In relationships of mutual love, where the partners have chosen wisely, each can give freely what the other needs, and each receives in return, freely given, what is needed for happiness and growth. Thus, it is doubtful if a parent could actively love young children without receiving love from the spouse, or eventually from the children, or from some source. It is doubtful if a psychotherapist could meet the needs of her patients if she was not receiving love from her spouse or friends.

But once a person has approached mature years, society expects him or her to have the capacity and the desire to become an active lover. If the person has been sufficiently loved in the past, the likelihood will be increased that he or she will be able to establish a mutual loving relationship with another person, rather than a relationship of continued passivity and dependency, or of "receiving" love only.

It would be magnificent if somehow the world were ordered such that all children were guaranteed a childhood full of natural, unconditional love. Reality dictates that this is hardly to be. What can be done for those of us who, through the transmitted deficiencies of our parents, might have less than ideal childhoods? Some have suggested a complete reparenting experience where the person, now an adult, goes through a second childhood with surrogate, loving parents.[18] However, more practical would be a gentle search for loving friends and colleagues; in some cases, counseling with a caring but not dependency-building therapist would be helpful. Perhaps above all, the person must be careful in choosing a mate who can recognize his or her deep-seated needs for affection and also, should that be the case, be aware of the limitations of the childhood-deprived spouse in providing affection. Both should embark upon a sensitive, loving journey aimed at increasing the capacity for loving and the achievement of a comfortable balance in love-giving and love-receiving.

FACTORS THAT ENLARGE A PERSON'S
CAPACITY FOR ACTIVE LOVE

Healthy
Personality

Gratification of Basic Needs. As a general rule, a person who has experienced rich need gratification will be in a position to become an active lover. He is not obliged to devote all his energies to personal need satisfaction. He can afford to use some of his time, skills, and energies for other people's happiness and growth.

Affirmation of the Value of Love. If a person has acquired a strong sense of the worth and value of love in and for itself, she will undoubtedly seek opportunities to love. Her self-esteem will be based, at least in part, on her ability to love actively. In other words, unless, she is involved in an active loving relationship, she may feel less than whole and fully "actualized"—less than a whole person.

High Frustration Tolerance. Loving another person often involves deprivation of one's own needs. The more fully the lover's ability to tolerate periods of privation is developed, the better able will he be to love.

Self-love. Fromm has pointed out, in an important essay, that love of self and love of some other person are not mutually exclusive as was long believed. He states emphatically that one can love another only if one loves oneself. The rationale behind this precept may be stated in these terms: To love oneself means that one is concerned with one's own growth and happiness and will behave in ways that implement these values. Self-loving, in a real sense, gives one actual practice in loving; to the extent that others are similar to the self, then these ways of acting that constitute self-love will make another person happy if they are directed to that person. Self-love makes one attentive to one's own needs and probably increases one's sensitivity to the needs of others; if one has experienced needs and gratifications, one can visualize more vividly what the partner's needs and gratifications feel like.

It should also be pointed out that healthy self-love is an outgrowth of having been loved by parents and other significant persons, and we have shown that the experience of having been loved enlarges one's capacity for active love.

When a person ignores or hates himself, he is less able to love others. The self-hater cannot love others, because he usually claims total obedience from those for whom he has "sacrificed" so much. The mother described by

Love and Healthy Personality

309

Philip Roth in *Portnoy's Complaint* was such a martyr, who "loved" her son more than she did herself; she sacrificed her happiness on his (unasked) behalf. All she wanted in return was complete conformity with her wishes and demands, which is incompatible with genuine love. Mrs. Portnoy was a tyrant, whose love for her son nearly destroyed him.

Psychoanalysts regard excessive unselfishness as a neurotic trait, and personality hygienists such as Maslow and Fromm place a positive value on "healthy" selfishness. This is no more than a recognition on the basis of clinical experience that the person who is concerned for his own growth and happiness will have acted in such a way to promote it; in consequence, he is a better person and better able to give.[19]

Competence. The more skills a lover has, the more diversified will be the needs she can gratify through her loving behavior. This presumes, of course, that the individual has few inner barriers, such as an unhealthy self-structure, to the full use of her entire behavior repertoire. If she has, then she will experience threat whenever she is about to behave in a loving manner, and so she will suppress the loving behavior.

Healthy Self-structure. If the lover has a self-concept, a self-ideal, and public selves that permit him to function freely and fully, then his capacity for loving will be promoted. In other words, the lover will have access to all his behavior potential. He will not be obliged to exclude some ways of behaving in his love relationships because of the need to defend an unrealistic self-concept or to conform with a false public self or an excessively strict conscience.

Thus, if the loved one wants tenderness, affection, or domination, the healthy lover will be able to sense these needs and behave in a gratifying way without a sense of forcing, faking, or threatening himself.

In principle, the more diversified the personality structure of an individual and the healthier his self-structure, the broader the range of persons he can effectively love. Practically, however, the healthy lover probably prefers to seek someone who has an equally diversified personality and healthy self-structure, because his needs may require just such a person to love him. Anyone

Healthy Personality

with a less complex personality would be less able to meet his needs.

Reality Contact. It takes knowledge of the loved one to be able to love effectively; the person with autistic other-concepts will be unable to act in ways that meet the loved one's needs.

Reasonable Ideals. A person may construct such impossible ideals and expectations as conditions for expressing her own love that no human could ever hope to qualify. She may then engage in an endless and fruitless quest for the "worthy" and "perfect" recipient of her love. Of course, she will never find this paragon, or else she will experience perpetual disillusionment. If it happens that a person has married on grounds other than love, she may place such stringent conditions on her love that it is never given. The spouse doesn't "deserve" her love and must meet her impossible demands for perfection before it will be given. Sometimes a person who has only limited capacity to bestow affection will show remarkable skill in finding out what her mate *cannot* do; once she discovers these inadequacies, she uses them as the reason for not loving the other.

Reasonable demands and ideals apropos of the other are likely to be held by a person who holds reasonable demands and expectations of herself.

Emancipation from Parents. A person who is not alienated from his real self will be better able to govern his loving behavior in accordance with the needs and wishes of his loved one, and with his own real feelings and wishes. But if the person behaves only to please his parents, his capacity to love may be reduced. The reason for this lies in the fact that much of the behavior that might be necessary to promote happiness in the spouse may be tabooed or condemned by the parents, and the individual does not dare to displease his parents. The psychoanalysts have shown that sexual difficulty in marriage, such as impotence and frigidity, stems from failure to emancipate the self from parental control, and failure to withdraw unconscious sexual interest in the parents. It is as if the spouse cannot devote love and sex to the partner because, unconsciously, love and sex "belong" to the opposite-sexed parent.

Love and Healthy Personality

Some persons cannot accept the deepest expressions of the real self of another person who loves them. They find such expression cloying, threatening, or embarrassing. When someone loves them, they become suspicious of the lover—the lover may be just pretending to love in order to disarm her and make her vulnerable. Or the lover may be trying to get the individual to do something. The person who cannot accept love may believe that the need for love means one is weak, and such an admission may diminish her self-esteem.

We may generalize and suggest that the factors that might prevent a person from accepting authentic love from others include (1) fear of being hurt and (2) repression of the need to be loved.

Fear of Being Hurt. Because of past experiences with people, the individual may project or attribute motives to others that they do not possess. He may assume they do not, or cannot, love him. If he believes this, then he will probably misinterpret loving behavior from others; he will believe their behavior toward him is motivated by sentiments other than concern for his welfare.

Repression of the Need to Be Loved. In the past the individual's longings for love may have been thwarted, or she may have been hurt in her quest for love. She may then repress her wish for love; she may, indeed, develop reaction formations against her love needs and make loud protestations of her independence from others: "I don't need anybody for anything." Such a person may strive to *prevent* others from loving her, with considerable success in such efforts.

The healthy personality is able to accept freely given love just as she is able to give love freely. She does not demand love from her lover as a duty for her partner to fulfill. Rather, she assumes that if she is loved, the lover is giving out of free will, with no strings attached, and so she can accept it without guilt or fear.

Variety of Loves. Our definition of love uses the phrase love of an "entity" rather than of a person. One *Healthy* must excuse the seemingly impersonal term. It is meant *Personality* to point out that one can love self and other persons, but also can passionately love ideas and objects, such as:

One's country.

A neighborhood.

A special place, such as a lake, a woods, or a mountain.

Children.

A deity or the deity.

An activity such as sailing or one's work.

A poem, painting or sculpture, or melody or symphony.

Animals and pets.

The list is endless and the capacity for the individual human to express and experience love, while it may not be endless, is beyond the love of self and even of others. Such loves contribute to the person's joy of living and expand his capacity to love self and others. Especially, of course, love of one's work would have great consequences in contentment with life.

LOVE AND DEPENDENCY

Self-sufficiency—independent security—is important for healthy personality, but this is relative. In the first place, it is impossible for a person to be completely self-sufficient; indeed, attempts directed toward complete independence may be regarded as pathological, because they are likely to be predicated on a profound distrust of all people.

In the second place, it is undesirable for a person not to need people for some things. People *want* to feel needed by those to whom they feel close. There are occasions where dependency upon another person is an expression of active loving, for it implies trust and accords dignity to the one who is needed.

A healthy love relationship involves two persons who are relatively self-sufficient in most ways but who are mutually dependent for important gratifications. The love relationship involves mutual giving and mutual taking, mutual needing and mutual willingness to provide what is needed.

HOW MANY PEOPLE CAN AN INDIVIDUAL LOVE?

Love and Healthy Personality

Love is action, and there are limits upon how many things a person can do. If one devotes more time and attention to one sphere of activity, then other spheres of activity will suffer relative neglect. A farmer has numerous fields, livestock, and buildings to maintain, and a family to look after. If he spends all of his time and skill at cultivating his corn fields, then his wheat fields and vegetable plots will become overrun with weeds; his farm buildings will begin to deteriorate from neglect, and his livestock may fall victim to diseases. He has to apportion his time so that everything is attended to according to its requirements.

An adult has many things to attend to, not the least in importance being the needs of the people whom he loves. Thus, the husband must earn a living and satisfy his own urges toward productivity and status, but he also wants to promote growth and happiness in his wife and children. How much of himself should he give to his work and how much to his wife and children? His friends? His parents? Is there room in his life for other loves in addition to his wife and children?

There is no simple answer to these questions. The needs of the lover and the needs of the other persons have to be taken into consideration. In addition, there will be broad individual differences from love relationship to love relationship, with respect to the "amount of self" that must be invested.

In some marriages, for example, the husband is quite happy with only occasional contacts with the wife, who may be immersed in a career or traveling at her occupation. In others, the husband may receive the loving attention of his spouse for all of her time away from his work, and yet it is not enough to make him happy. One of the advantages of the loving relationship is the increased ability to handle crises through mutual support. Ziller,[20] for example, has shown that couples who successfully come through these crises become strengthened in self-esteem. This, in turn, would seemingly enable them to love each other more fully and also to be able to extend their loving relationships to others in a controlled fashion.

Because there is a limit on how many things a person can do, there is thus a limit on the number of people a person can love.

Healthy Personality

Many a wife has complained that her husband loves

314

his work or his hobbies more than he loves her. If he devotes more of his undivided attention to these than he does to her needs, then to that extent she is correct.

The healthy personality is able, like the good farmer, to apportion his time and his care so that he is able to harmonize his own needs with the growth and happiness of his loved ones. This is not a simple task, but one that requires continuous reassessment, readjustment, and vigilance. A healthy personality actively loves as many people as he can, without doing violence to his own growth and happiness and the growth and happiness of his loved ones.

ATTRACTING LOVE FROM OTHERS

A person may assume she is unlovable and that she is powerless to induce someone to love her. This belief may stem from a childhood that was devoid of parental love and an adolescence devoid of friendship.

How does one induce others to love her? Ignoring for the time being such factors as attractive appearance, we can assert that love begets love. Active concern for the needs of another individual will, in general, tend to motivate the other person to become actively concerned for the growth and happiness of the giver. Unfortunately, a vicious circle often appears. The unhappy person who believes no one can love her is usually in such a chronic condition of need deprivation that she cannot give freely to others. Hence, although she may be pitied by others, she is unlikely to be loved. How can one break this vicious circle? How can one arrange it so that the person who "hath not" love will be given love? The Biblical precept "to him that hath shall be given" seems to hold true for love.

In our society the love-deprived individual may be able to love only through effective therapy. The professional psychotherapist is, in a sense, a source of love for the deprived individual. The therapist behaves toward her patient in ways that will promote her growth and happiness—and this is love, albeit without romance. Through successful therapy, an individual may acquire the capacity to love others and thus make it possible to induce others to love her.

Love and Healthy Personality

315

Love and Self-disclosure

When two people love one another, they open themselves to one another's gaze; they become transparent to each other. Such openness makes it possible for each to know the other's needs and to know what the other is up to. There is no room for duplicity or inauthenticity in loving relationships.

Love *is* self-disclosure. When one person loves another, he reveals his love by his actions as well as his words. A loving act is a nonverbal way of saying, "I love you." Love cannot be faked for long, because when it is authentic, it enlivens the loved one as well as expresses the vitality of the lover. If a person pretends to love, but instead is indifferent or even hostile, then in time the "loved" person will notice that he does not feel loved in the company of the other. Instead, he may feel trapped, smothered, or even drained of energy.

Because love and self-disclosure are related, each person in a loving relationship knows the other, and knows that the other knows him. However, because love implies respect, lovers respect one another's right to privacy when it is requested. I do not have to be chronically open and transparent to the people who love me, nor do I wish for them to be that open, always, with me. Sometimes the most loving thing a person can do for another is to withhold self-disclosure, so that the loved one will not have additional burdens to cope with.

Love, Marriage, and Divorce

When and whom should a person marry? When should a divorce occur? In this age, one marriage in three terminates in divorce, and persons who remain married often feel trapped or unhappy in the relationship.

The reasons for undertaking marriage in the first place are varied. Young couples enter marriage for companionship, for an opportunity to raise a family, for sexual gratifications, to change their status in the eyes of the community, or, in a more general sense, to find greater happiness in the married state than in the single state. *Healthy Personality* Although many achieve these desirable outcomes, others do not.

In Chapter 11 I provided some criteria for assessing whether a relationship such as marriage is healthy. When a marriage relationship deviates strikingly from these criteria, the participants experience the marriage as flat, dead, devoid of meaning or satisfactions; more emphatically, they may experience the marriage as positively agonizing, stifling to the self and partner. When there are children in the family, an additional problem is presented, because the children will require some care that will help them attain maturity and a healthy personality.[21]

If the partners are unable to work through interpersonal impasses themselves in a growth-productive manner, then ideally each should consult a psychotherapist or marriage counselor. With expert assistance, each partner can often be helped to grow, so that an autonomous, responsible, and mutually agreed-upon reconciliation or divorce can be arrived at. When the partners will not avail themselves of such help, or seek it out, then the probability is high that whatever decision they make will be incompatible with their own wellbeing and that of the children. It is an open question whether children are better off, from a personality-hygiene point of view, living with two unhealthy parents enmeshed in an unhealthy marital relationship. A strong case could be constructed to show that children raised by one parent who is divorced from the other, where the divorce was a healthy one, have a greater chance of attaining personality health than the children raised in a miserable marriage.

When Is a Divorce Healthy? A divorce is healthy when it becomes apparent that the changes necessary to improve the marriage are just not practicable. There are limits to how much a person can change her personality to meet the other's needs; often the changes required to keep a marriage going would be personality changes in a direction away from health. Thus, one partner may need the other to be a paragon of moral perfection in order to be happy. No amount of feasible change could make the partner attain those ideals. Further, no amount of therapy is successful in altering the needs of the spouse who demands perfection. They may be too deeply rooted. Perhaps, in such an impasse, the best that can happen is

Love and Healthy Personality

divorce, in the fervent hope that each will be better able to grow when separated from the other (something that happens quite often) or that if they don't grow, and still want to marry, they will find a spouse with a personality that complements their own.

I know several marriages that went stale, and where insurmountable impasses existed between the partners. Each needed the other to be different, but neither partner could comply, or wanted to comply, with the other's demands and needs. When a divorce finally occurred, each partner became, almost like magic, the embodiment of the desires of the former spouse (perhaps out of unconscious or conscious hostility). It seemed, then, that their prior relationship blocked growth, rather than promoted it. The traits that drew the couple together into marriage in the beginning later became obstacles to growth.

In one marriage, the man had fallen in love with his wife because of her cute, childish innocence, dependency, lisping manner of speech, and so on. He evidently needed to enact a fatherlike role for assorted reasons, and she needed to be fathered. As time passed, he began to feel the need of an adult peer, and he made this need known to his wife. She reacted always with tears and the assertion, "You don't love me any more." She could not, or would not change. He divorced her and remarried. She suffered considerably through the divorce, sought therapeutic help, and eventually achieved an understanding of the reasons for her infantile characteristics; she was assisted in growing to a healthier level. She remarried, and the new marriage appeared to be healthier.

Living Together. The U.S. Census Bureau reported recently that the number of persons living together, unwed, had doubled since 1970. More than a million couples have apparently made this choice, and such an alternative to formal marriage cannot be ignored as a viable choice for two loving persons. However, it is still too early to have substantial data on the success of such a structure and upon the particular kinds of persons most suited to it. At risk of appearing negative to the structure, let us point out what appears from our clinical experience: (1) breakups in the living-together pattern, when they occur, are no less traumatic than are breakups in formal marriages. The license to marry does not protect you from heartache and neither does the lack of license do so; (2) as preparation for marriage, the arrangement is scarcely a good test. The major stresses of marriage occur not in the first few years, but in the child-rearing years and with stress upon old roles of new demands—such as feeding the baby at 2 A.M. What seems to be an obvious conclusion emerges: such an arrangement should not be attempted with any less commitment than is found in a formal marriage, nor with any less forethought.

The Power to Love and Healthy Personality

In the last analysis, love is a gift, freely and spontaneously given by the lover to his loved one. The being who is loved may be the self, a spouse, a child, a friend, and so on. The gift that is proffered to the loved one is the real self of the lover. He gives himself—he focuses his powers so that the loved one may be happier and may better actualize her potentialities. The criterion of the success of loving behavior is evidence of happiness and growth in the loved one.

The individual who is alienated from his real self cannot love. He cannot even love himself, because he does not know what he needs. The individual with a personality illness—neurosis, psychosis, or character disorder—is a person who cannot love. Many patients who have undergone psychotherapy report they have acquired, for the first time in their lives, the power to love themselves and others. Probably what the psychoanalysts refer to as "genitality" or as "orgastic potency" refers to more than sexual adequacy; it may be interpreted as the power to love in the broader sense in which we have interpreted the word *love*. The neurotic who does not "command" his sexual functions, who is "alienated" from control of his own sexuality, is a person in whom sexuality is symbolic of all that is summed up by the term *real self*. Just as he cannot give sexuality to his loved one, so he cannot give his real self.

Love and Healthy Personality

Love is art and science, romance and fact. As an art, loving can improve with age, practice, and knowledge. It would be both pleasurable and meaningful if you were to search out new ways of showing caring and loving to someone special. What is it that your friend finds most delightful, and can you help create that or provide it? You can also deepen your existential capacity to give and receive love by experiencing love in a number of differing media—in addition to love of self and love of others, which are basic, you can learn to love an activity or an art masterpiece, good music, and so on. Knowledge about the activity or the art increases your capacity to develop a true love for it.

If you are planning soon to enter into one of the many loving relationships, such as marriage, you should explore the deepening of the relationship in marriage enrichment groups and of course, with each other alone. A meaningful degree of self-disclosure is of great consequence in such a preparation.

Can you improve your love for your friends—those relationships that are not necessarily as intense as the marriage relationship but that are increasingly important as you go through life. Good friends are to be prized and and loved, and such friendships need regular nurturance through acts of love—visits, phone calls, being with friends in times of stress or tragedy as well as on joyous occasions.

Are you a one-way lover—capable only of giving love, reluctant to accept it, or the reverse? If so, you should consider developing that other neglected side of your art of loving. Mutuality in the relationship provides the greatest source of satisfaction.

SUMMARY

Love is a commitment to another's wellbeing. Loving behavior is motivated by knowledge and concern for the wellbeing of the loved one. This concern is an outcome of identification, empathy, and sympathy with the loved one's condition. Sexuality is a factor in heterosexual love, but there can be love without sex, and sex without love.

People choose someone to love on the basis of the

Healthy
Personality

other's helplessness, in conformity with the lover's needs and ideals, and in return for being loved. Strong needs, lack of self-knowledge, and lack of knowledge of the loved one are factors in unwise choices of someone to love.

Love may be defined in terms of a feeling and of behavior. Being close to the loved one, caring for the other's wellbeing as for the self and mutuality are all involved, along with strong feeling or passion. There are many ways of looking at love. One suggests that adult love is not unconditional, but is earned and is two-way giving and taking between two adults, while natural, or unconditional love is the special love given children by parents, which is one-way, from parent to child. Unconditional love in childhood is necessary to prepare the person for adult, two-way, earned love. Yet many successful lovers have re-invented themselves after compensating for such deprivation. Physical attractiveness plays a large role in mate selection. There is also evidence that any kind of emotional arousal helps to trigger off a love response.

One may enrich the capacity to love by learning to relate with passion and love to many entities, things such as a painting, music, or a mountain—as well as self and others.

Healthy personality is fostered by both giving and receiving love. The capacity for loving is fostered by basic need gratification, affirmation of the value of love, frustration tolerance, competence, a healthy self-structure, reality contact, self-love, reasonable ideals, emancipation from parents, and through loving a wide variety of entities such as one's work, and the world of nature or of art.

People reject love out of fear of being hurt and repression of the need to be loved. It is compatible with healthy personality to love as many people as one can without jeopardizing other values. Love from others is attracted by offering love first. A healthy self-structure liberates a person to act in loving ways. Impasses arise in marriage. Struggle with these may enrich the relationship; if the impasse cannot be resolved alone, or with help from a

Love and Healthy Personality   *marriage counselor, divorce may be essential.*

Being able to receive and give love wholeheartedly and skillfully is a crucial sign of healthy personality.

1. See, however, ROLLO MAY's magisterial treatise *Love and Will* (New York: Norton, 1970). Perhaps one of the most complete and scientific approaches to love is seen in ZICK RUBIN's book, *Liking and Loving: an Invitation to Social Psychology* (New York: Holt, 1973). Another useful recent book is edited by MARY E. CURTIN, entitled *Symposium On Love* (New York: Behavioral Publications, 1973).

2. J. MILLER, "The Seed: Reforming Drug Abusers with Love," *Science*, 1973, Vol. 182, pp. 40–42.

3. E. FROMM, *Man for Himself* (New York: Holt, 1947), pp. 96–101; *The Art of Loving* (New York: Harper, 1956). For an account of love as experience, see S. M. JOURARD, *The Transparent Self* (New York: Van Nostrand Reinhold, 1971), Chapter 6, "The Experience and Disclosure of Love." See also H. OTTO (Ed.), *Love Today* (New York: Association, 1972).

4. T. LANDSMAN, "Love: The Serpent's Tooth and the White Knight," unpublished paper presented at Conference on New Frontiers in Counseling, University of Florida, 1977.

5. J. A. LEE, "The Styles of Loving," *Psychology Today*, 1974, Vol. 8, pp. 43–50.

6. LANDSMAN, "Love: The Serpent's Tooth . . . ," op. cit.

7. F. R. SCHREIBER, *Sybil* (New York: Warner, 1974).

8. D. A. STEWART, *Preface to Empathy* (New York: Philosophical Library, 1956); R. KATZ, *Empathy* (New York: Free Press, 1963); R. D. LAING, H. PHILLIPSON, and A. R. LEE, *Interpersonal Perception: A Theory and a Method of Research* (New York: Harper, 1972); M. BUBER, *The Knowledge of Man* (New York: Harper, 1965), pp. 78–85.

9. E. WALSTER, V. ARONSON, D. ABRAHAMS, and L. ROTTMAN, "Importance of Physical Attractiveness in Dating Behavior," *Journal of Personality and Social Psychology*, 1966, Vol. 4, pp. 508–516. See also J. P. CURRAN and S. LIPPOLD, "The Effects of Physical Attraction and Attitude Similarity on Attraction in Dating Dyads," *Journal of Personality*, 1975, Vol. 43, pp. 528–539.

10. G. MARAYUMA and N. MILLER, "Physical Attractiveness and Classroom Acceptance," *Social Science Research Institute Research Report 75–2*, University of Southern California, Los Angeles, 1975.

11. D. G. DUTTON and A. P. ARON, "Some Evidence for Heightened Sexual Attraction Under Conditions of

Healthy Personality

High Anxiety," *Journal of Personality and Social Psychology*, 1974, Vol. 30, pp. 510–517.

12. S. FREUD, "On Narcissism: An Introduction," in S. FREUD, *Collected Papers*, IV (London: Hogarth, 1953); M. C. LANGHORNE and P. F. SECORD, "Variations in Marital Needs with Age, Sex, Marital Status, and Regional Location," *Journal of Social Psychology*, 1955, Vol. 41, pp. 19–37; S. FREUD, "Contributions to the Psychology of Love: A Special Type of Choice of Object Made by Men," in FREUD, op. cit., Chapter 11; R. F. WINCH, *Mate-Selection* (New York: Harper, 1958).

13. S. PEELE and A. BRODSKY, *Love and Addiction* (New York: Taplinger, 1975). See also J. SIMON, "Addiction or Road to Self-Realization?," *American Journal of Psychoanalysis*, 1975, Vol. 35, pp. 359–364.

14. R. A. SPITZ, "Hospitalism: An Inquiry into the Genesis of Psychiatric Conditions in Early Childhood," *Psychoanalytic Study of the Child*, I (New York: International Universities, 1945); W. GOLDFARB, "Emotional and Intellectual Consequences of Psychological Deprivation in Infancy: A Revaluation," in P. HOCH and J. ZUBIN (Eds.), *Psychopathology of Childhood* (New York: Grune, 1955), pp. 105–119; MARGARET RIBBLE, *The Rights of Infants* (New York: Columbia U.P., 1943).

15. H. HARLOW, "The Heterosexual Affection System in Monkeys," *American Psychologist*, 1962, Vol. 17, pp. 1–9.

16. D. M. LEVY, "Primary Affect-Hunger," *American Journal of Orthopsychiatry*, 1937, Vol. 94, pp. 643–652.

17. A. H. MASLOW, "Love in Self-actualizing People," in A. H. MASLOW, *Motivation and Personality* (New York: Harper, 1954).

18. J. L. SCHIFF and B. DAY, *All My Children* (New York: Pyramid, 1972).

19. E. FROMM, *Man for Himself*, op. cit., pp. 119–140; P. ROTH, *Portnoy's Complaint* (New York: Random, 1969).

20. R. ZILLER and J. ROSEN, "Monitoring the Meaning of Love," *Journal of Individual Psychology*, 1975, Vol. 31, pp. 51–64.

21. There are numerous books dealing with love, marriage, and divorce which offer different perspectives on this most difficult of institutions. See, for example, I. CHARNY, *Marital Love and Hate* (New York: Macmillan, 1972), which I regard as most instructive; NENA O'NEILL and GEORGE O'NEILL, *Open Marriage: A New Life Style for Couples* (New York: M. EVANS, 1972); H. OTTO (Ed.), *The Family in Search of a Future* (New York: Appleton, 1970).

13

SEX AND HEALTHY PERSONALITY

INTRODUCTION

Even though most people feel that the sexual revolution has peaked and is in the midst of a quieter phase, there is still much chaos, confusion, and embarrassment in it for young and old. It would seem that it was a long revolution, extending from the time of Freud until the present, perhaps almost 90 years, and that the long struggle was won by sex. However, perhaps it was more of an evolution, a gradual awareness of the importance of sex in human affairs—and a parallel effort to avoid exaggerating its role in relationships between the two genders. In these recent years, sex was brought out of the closet and into the movies. There are some who would prefer to return sex, if not to the closet, at least to the closed-door bedroom. We are probably not yet at the end of the evolution, and it would be wise for young people to also be prepared for drastic changes in sex customs and mores in their early and middle adulthood. The nature of that change is difficult to predict. Various arms of the popular media, in the 1960s, announced that God was dead; it was also pronounced that sex was dead. Both seem to be quite as alive as before, and the worst that may be said about the future of sex is that it might well be of lesser importance for its having been brought into the bright light.

Sex is a source of boundless delight, and a means to express the profundity of love between man and woman, yet sex is a problem to many people in our society. The problem stems, in part, from the obvious fact that children are conceived through the sexual relationship. Every society restricts sexual behavior to insure that when children are born, they will be born to parents who are willing to assume responsibility for their upbringing. Our society, perhaps, has been overzealous in seeking to instill a sense of caution and responsibility regarding sex; as a result, many people grow to adult years regarding sex as dangerous and immoral. Healthy personality is difficult to achieve unless the individual is able to reconcile sexual needs with such other values as the integrity of others, some measure of conformity with prevailing morality, and a sense of self-esteem. Persons unable to integrate sexuality with other values will suffer; they will create great pain for self and for those close to them.

Sexual Evolution

Along with love, its sometime companion, sex, requires a perspective of reasonable distance, particularly for young adults. Although we don't intend to keep the reader entirely at a distance from this attractive subject, a description of its historical context first may also help readers formulate their own pattern of dealing with, not the strongest, but one of the most powerful of human drives.

The sexual revolution, evolution, or war, as you may choose to see it, is usually assumed to have begun with Sigmund Freud at the turn of the century. Other major milestones include the publication by Kinsey et al. of *Sexual Behavior in the Human Male* [1] in 1948. Involving some 5,000 subjects, the study was perhaps the first that attempted to get so much information about so intimate

Sex and Healthy Personality

325

a subject. Though originally intended by its authors to be a purely scientific publication, it quickly became a popular bestseller. It was a startling book. Some of its surprising data, for example, indicated masturbation experience for some 92 per cent of all males and 62 per cent of all females. Extramarital experiences were reported by 50 per cent of all males and 27 per cent of the female population. The bellwether figure of the progress of the sexual evolution, however, was the frequency of premarital intercourse reported among females. In 1953 Kinsey et al. reported 33 per cent of women under twenty-five having had such experience (and 80 per cent of males).

The third revolutionary force was loosed by Masters and Johnson,[2] who published detailed laboratory studies of the orgasm and other sexual responses. In a sense, Kinsey and others took the macrocosmic viewpoint, Masters and Johnson attacked the still shy subject from a microscopic stance. Secrecy, prudishness, and even the double standard could hardly recover from this attack from both directions. Openness about sex became the password of the liberated society. Some of Masters and Johnson's findings with regard to male and female orgasm may be summed as follows:

PHASES	MALE RESPONSE	FEMALE RESPONSE
excitement	penile erection	vaginal lining moistens
plateau	testes enlarge	clitoris retracts
orgasmic	rhythmic contractions of penis	contractions of muscles in vagina
resolution	return to unstimulated conditions	return to unstimulated conditions

Masters and Johnson have reshaped the thinking concerning the differences in response; sexual pleasure to them seems fundamentally alike for both sexes.

A fourth phase in the evolution takes a surprising turn. Contemporary magazines, from the frivolous *Playboy* to staid women's publications such as *Redbook*, do their own surveys and bring under study a population size ordinarily unheard of in any kind of human research.

Healthy Personality

Redbook, for example, received more than 100,000 responses to a survey of sexual satisfaction among women. Although some of the studies are of doubtful validity from a scientific point of view, *Redbook*'s study, for example, was carried out by two respected sociologists, Robert and Amy Levin.[3] They found that the frequency of sexual intercourse among women under twenty-five had almost tripled from the 33 per cent reported by Kinsey in 1953 to 90 per cent in 1975.

Although smaller studies of sexual behavior cannot be described as commonplace today, they are appearing with frequency and aiding not only in determination of average sexual behavior but also in illumination of high-level or healthy sexual behavior. In a review of some twelve studies of sexual behavior in adolescence by J. R. Hopkins[4] of the incidence of coitus in late adolescence (which he describes as the college years), the frequencies reported for females in the 1970s varies from 19 per cent to 85 per cent; males reported frequencies varying from 36 per cent to 82 per cent. These enormous variations suggest that our scientific researchers have yet to structure their samples adequately.

Nevertheless, the present sexual era is marked by acceptance and discussion of sex in unprecedented fashion by newspapers, magazines, and especially motion pictures. There are many loosely structured surveys and a host of improvable studies by scientists. It is also noteworthy that many social scientists feel the acceptance of abortion, vasectomy, the development of inexpensive contraceptives such as the birth control pill, the intrauterine devices, supplementing the condom and the diaphragm, have contributed to the changes in attitudes and behavior. Strangely enough, the frequency of teenage pregnancy and of venereal diseases has steadily risen during the 1960s and 1970s. The irrational aspect of much of sexual behavior, as well as difficulty in self-control involved, clearly require that sex education involve more than facts. The emotional aspects, its power and its potential for extreme delight and extreme pain, must not be hidden. The ideal norm up to a decade ago was for young people to be asexual until they married, at which time they were to learn how to make sexual love

Sex and Healthy Personality

with their spouse. Of course, this ideal was violated by most people, as Kinsey's classic study showed. Masturbation, premarital intercourse, extramarital sex relations, and homosexuality were all viewed as sins, sicknesses, or crimes. Now growing numbers of people who were raised with those moral convictions have the opportunity to act differently, without having to face social shaming.[5]

The liberalization of attitudes toward sex does not eliminate problems, however. In my psychotherapeutic work, I have found that people, however "emancipated" from the morality of their parents, or practiced in the varieties of sexual conduct, still experience jealousy, possessiveness, impotence, frigidity, and false expectations about what sex will and will not do for them. In America, our sexual mores are in continuing transition, and so people are obliged to grope for a solution to the conflict between their sexual needs and their wishes to be free of guilt and shame.

Before examining sex in relation to healthy personality, I will review the psychoanalysts' contribution to our understanding of this important topic. Freud was the first of the modern psychologists to attempt to trace the changing patterns of sexuality all the way from infancy to adulthood.

Psychoanalytic View of Sexual Development

Freud [6] devoted considerable attention to the sexual side of his patients' lives, correctly recognizing that in his time, people were especially prudish about sexual matters. Such excessive prudery played some part in the development of neurotic disorders. He postulated that early in infancy sensual gratification centered around the child's mouth, in sucking behavior especially. He termed this period the *oral* stage of "psychosexual development," and it was considered to last into the second year of life. During the second year and up until about the third or fourth year, Freud claimed, the most important bodily focus of sensory pleasure shifted from the mouth to the excretory organs, especially the organs of defecation. He termed this phase the *anal* stage. Readers of his writings at the time were disgusted at this acknowledgment that pleasure might be associated with bowel evacuation. Many contemporary readers may share this disgust. That Freud had some empirical warrant for his assertions can be readily attested by candid observation of small children or upon frank self-examination.

By about the fourth or fifth years of a child's life, the zone of the body directly concerned with pleasure appeared to shift to the genital organs. Freud termed this phase the *phallic* stage, applying the term to girls as well as to boys. The main source of pleasure for children in this stage, he claimed, was direct manipulation of the genital organs, as in masturbation. During this stage, too, the child of either sex typically becomes involved in the so-called Oedipus complex. Freud used the term *Oedipus complex* to describe a common infantile fantasy. The little boy wishes, in his imagination to possess his mother and to exclude the father from her attentions and affection. The little girl wants to own or marry her daddy and be done with mother. Yet each child has positive feelings toward the rejected parent, and to make matters more complicated, each child fears retaliation from the rejected parent—retaliation for secret wishes that the rival parent would die. It may be seen that the period of the Oedipus complex is fraught with acute conflicts. Freud claimed that the conflicts were commonly resolved in the following manner: The child would give up the wish for exclusive possession of the parent of the opposite sex. Further, the child would strive to become like the parent of the same sex. This solution, if successful, would permit growth to resume. The child was then said to enter the *latency* period.

The latency period was said to last from about the age of five to twelve or thirteen, when puberty brings it to a close. Sex play during this time is not united with romantic or Oedipal fantasies; instead it is pursued out of curiosity, or for the excitement and pleasure it yields. As the child enters adolescence, however, he or she has begun the process of rapid physiological maturation, with its attendant strong sexual urges. The adolescent may participate in solitary or in shared sexual play, but by this time, the real or imagined partners become increasingly suitable as possible marriage partners. That is, they are of

Sex and Healthy Personality

appropriate age and sex, as contrasted with the fantasied partners of the Oedipal period. Unless earlier conflicts have prevented growth, the adolescent gradually enters what Freud called the *genital* stage of psychosexual development. By the time the person reaches adult years, he or she is ready to integrate the quest for sexual pleasure with other values, such as love and respect for the parent. The person is increasingly ready for marriage.

Persons who have successfully passed through the "pregenital" stages become "genital characters." Again, this term may seem somewhat outrageous to the thoughtful student, but it is a term that derives its meaning from the complex theory of development that has been sketched out above.

For the psychoanalysts, the *genital character* is the healthy personality.[7] Adults who have successfully become genital characters have been described as follows: They are able to love and work effectively. They are not hampered by unresolved conflicts with their parents, conflicts arising from earlier childhood. They are not obligated, by guilt or anxiety, to repress their imaginations or their feelings. They can reconcile their sexual feelings toward a partner with feelings of tenderness and esteem. Hence, they can be affectionate, spontaneous, creative, playful, able to work productively, and able to love other people.

Some Factors in Sexual Behavior

Freud showed that experiences in childhood can have a decisive effect upon the sexual life of the adult. Frightening experiences relating to sex and prudish attitudes learned from parents can make it difficult to achieve a healthy pattern of sexual behavior. Let us now discuss sex in its relation to healthy personality.

MOTIVES FOR SEXUAL BEHAVIOR

Healthy Motives. The main purpose for which sexual behavior is commonly undertaken is pleasure. This holds true for children and adults alike.

Healthy Personality

However, the distinctive character of the sexual relationship is that it provides *mutual* pleasure. One of the many challenges in the sexual experience is for each partner to anticipate, of course, his or her own ecstatic pleasure, but at the same time to make the physical and psychological relationship equally of meaning and joy to the other partner. Thus, this sometimes magical, human capacity holds the ideal potential: the giving and taking of pleasure and of deep interpersonal meaning—love, if you will. The sexual climax, or orgasm, is probably among the most intense pleasures that humans can experience, and so it is no wonder that it is sought even into advanced years, as long as persons are in reasonably good health. Contrary to common expectation, not only do very young children have a rudimentary sex life, but people in their eighties and nineties are known to maintain their sexual activity at a level compatible with their physical health.[8]

Pleasure, however, is not the sole motive for which healthy personalities will engage in sex. Sex is heavily freighted with symbolic meaning, and in our society it is generally regarded as a symbol of love. In fact, it is probably only within the context of an authentic loving relationship, where both partners feel free to express themselves fully, that sexual experience is the source of the richest pleasure.

Married couples will engage in the sexual relationship not only for love and for pleasure but also to conceive children. We live in an age when the means of preventing conception have been developed to a high degree so that, in principle, married couples can have more freedom to choose the time of conception as well as the size of their families. It should be recognized, however, that interference with conception is forbidden among some religious groups, such as the Catholics.

Thus, the attainment of pleasure, expression of love, and conception of children are all motives for sexual behavior that fall within the healthy range. Now let us explore some motives that are less healthy.

SOME UNHEALTHY MOTIVES FOR SEXUAL BEHAVIOR

We shall select for discussion the following: (1) sexual behavior as reassurance, (2) sexual behavior as an opiate, (3) sexual behavior as an exchange commodity, and (4) sexual behavior as conquest or as punishment.

Sex as Reassurance. It is not uncommon for males in our society to have grave doubts concerning their adequacy, sexual potency, or general competence as men. Sexual behavior is a primitive proof of one's masculinity, and so a man might seek numerous sexual experiences to demonstrate his prowess to himself. So long as he continues his "conquests" he can maintain his self-esteem; if any factor, such as illness or enforced abstinence, prevents him from maintaining a certain level of sexual activity, he is likely to undergo feelings of depression, inferiority, or anxiety.

A woman might have grave doubts concerning her attractiveness to males and her "womanliness." Where this is the case, she might become sexually promiscuous to reassure herself that she is indeed desirable.

The use of sex as reassurance is deemed unhealthy in these cases because it does not get to the root of inadequacy that motivates the need for reassurance.

Sex as an Opiate. Sexual gratification is a fundamental pleasure. For many persons, everyday life may be quite "gray" and devoid of satisfactions. Their work may be boring and their relationships with people superficial and unsatisfying. Under such conditions, a person might engage in very frequent sexual relations or masturbation as compensation for the emptiness of his or her life. Again, such a use of sexual behavior is unhealthy because it does not get to the root of the difficulty. Instead, the sexual pleasures may so "tranquilize" persons that they lose some of the impetus for efforts that could change their circumstances. If there is no other recourse, however, sex is at least a pleasant way to pass the time.

Sex as Exchange Commodity. Persons might engage in sexual behavior as a means of getting things they believe cannot be gotten in any other way. The most obvious example of sex as an exchange commodity is provided by the practice of prostitution. The prostitute sells sex for money.

Healthy Personality

Less obvious examples, but apparently quite common, occur in some marriages. A wife "starved" for affection may engage in sexual relationships with her husband when she does not really want to; she feels it is only through such submission that she can gain her husband's affection.

In one case (mentioned later in this chapter) a frigid wife would abstain from sexual intercourse with her husband whenever she wanted to force him to comply with her wishes for a major household purchase or a trip. She would "submit" only after her husband came around to her point of view. She was employing sex as a reinforcer, to "shape" his behavior according to principles of operant conditioning.

The use of sex as an exchange commodity runs counter to our social mores. More important, it implies that the "vendor" is treating himself or herself as a commodity. This is degrading and dehumanizing to the "buyer" and the "seller."

Sex as Conquest or Punishment. Perhaps among the most reprehensible aspects of the use of sex is its use to demonstrate supremacy or power over another. As such, it may be employed by both males and females, by the latter in situations where the female may demand more sexual activity than a particular male can provide, in order to demonstrate conquest. The male form of conquest often takes the ugly form of rape, which many insist should not be classified as a sexual experience at all. Intermixed with rape is often the rapist's perception of the victim as representative of someone who humiliated him or deprived him. He sees the rape as humiliation for the victim and punishment for past injustices that in no way would have involved his present victim.

HEALTHY CONDITIONS FOR SEXUAL AROUSAL

A man in our culture is likely to become sexually interested when he looks at an attractive, shapely woman clad, partially clothed, or nude. For the man to respond with interest probably signifies that he is "getting the message"; that is, he is in good health and in contact with reality.

Sex and Healthy Personality Women, typically, can be aroused by expressions of love, tenderness, and caresses. They may give off signals meaning they would welcome advances from a man, but whether they will respond to these advances depends upon many other conditions being met. These conditions include reassurances of the love and esteem in which they are held by the other, safety, and the degree to which ethical precepts are being observed.

In a socially sanctioned relationship like marriage, many of the barriers that ordinarily might block full sexual arousal will be absent. If the couple truly love one another, they will learn the idiosyncratic conditions for full mutual arousal, and they will find little difficulty in providing these for one another, for example, tenderness, expressions of endearment, caressing, and the like. Now let us consider some of the unhealthy conditions for arousal.

UNHEALTHY CONDITIONS FOR SEXUAL AROUSAL

A failure to respond sexually to the usual forms of sexual stimulation is called *frigidity* in a woman and *impotence* in a man. The most common cause of these conditions is emotion that is incompatible with sex, such as guilt, anxiety, or disgust. Thus, a woman may have irrational fears associated with sex. The signals that would arouse a healthy person serve only to induce anxiety and disgust in this woman. Likewise, a male may have various fears pertaining to sex that preclude his becoming aroused, even under conditions where there is no rational basis for these fears. Such fears usually stem from early training and from traumatic experiences with sex. For such persons to become capable of sexual responsiveness, it is necessary that the incompatible emotional responses to sexual stimuli be removed.

Some persons will respond sexually to stimuli not generally regarded as sexual symbols in our society. The homosexual, for example, is a person who fears, is repelled by, or is indifferent to persons of the opposite sex; he or she can only be aroused by members of the same sex. The fetishist is aroused by the objects of his or her fetish, such as a pair of stockings, and not by a receptive partner of the opposite sex. The sources of these deviations are to be found in an intensive study of the life history of the persons who suffer from them. There is no evidence that deviant sexuality is innate or caused by endocrine disturbances.

Healthy Personality

Sacred and Profane Love

Many persons, because of strict sexual training, are unable to fuse the tender and sexual aspects of love. They cannot respect and care for the same person toward whom they experience sexual feelings. Thus, a man may marry a woman because she has admirable traits, but he finds he cannot become sexually aroused by her. He may be quite potent with other women whom he does not respect. Similarly, a woman may admire and respect her husband but not be able to respond sexually to him; with a lover (who is quite unsuitable as a marriage partner), she may find herself sexually responsive.

This state of affairs is common. Freud thought it was a derivation of an unresolved Oedipus complex. That is, a man might choose as a spouse some woman who resembles his mother. Sexual feelings are tabooed toward the mother; it is as if the man transferred many of the same feelings and attitudes from his mother to his wife. The woman might likewise transfer many of her attitudes and feelings from her father to her husband.

Healthy Sexual Behavior

Sexual behavior is compatible with healthy personality when it produces satisfactions without transgressing the limits of good taste and integrity of the participants. If the aim is to achieve a climax for the self and the partner, the healthy personality will display the capacity to achieve these ends. If the aim is to express love and esteem for the partner, the healthy personality will behave in ways that convey these sentiments. Among healthy personalities, sex is a source of satisfaction and enjoyment with considerable freedom in the choice of modes of sexual behavior.[9]

Among some persons, the conscience may impose certain restrictions on the variety of sexual behavior. Thus, certain modes of sexual stimulation, caressing, and sexual intercourse may be deemed desirable by one partner and distasteful by another. Such incompatibilites in values and ideals may produce dissatisfaction with the sexual relationship between the spouses. Sexual behavior cannot be discussed without attention to the person's self-

Sex and Healthy Personality

structure. Healthy sexual behavior presumes a healthy self-structure in the individual and, of course, a loving relationship between the partners.

Some partners find their sexual relations becoming boring, but fear that if they change their mode of intercourse they will be doing something perverse. This is absurd. Variety in styles of intercourse is good, because it keeps interest high, although it cannot in any way compensate for a lack of genuine love.

Freedom and spontaneity in sexual lovemaking is most possible when the couple have established a loving relationship within which they have learned to know, respect, and trust one another.[10]

Other Patterns of Sexual Behavior

Let us discuss some patterns of sexual behavior that deviate from conventional ideals. These patterns are neither healthy nor unhealthy in themselves. Whether they influence the health of personality for better or worse can only be ascertained after careful study.

MASTURBATION

The practice of masturbation is well-nigh universal among members of our society, yet it runs counter to official social mores. This implies that many persons undergo acute moral conflicts at some time during their lives because they masturbate.

Many parents instill erroneous beliefs into their children concerning the supposed effects of masturbation. The children may be told that this practice will weaken them, will destroy their minds, make them insane, or render them impotent later in life. There is no evidence to support these beliefs. Some parents even make dire personal threats to their children in connection with "self-abuse." [11]

Children with strict training in regard to masturbation will have severe guilt feelings because they cannot withstand the impulse to masturbate. These guilt feelings often produce feelings of inferiority and worthlessness. Some *Healthy* children become so threatened by the supposed conse-
Personality quences of masturbation that they completely repress sex-

uality. Such a means of handling sexual feelings can lead to serious personality illnesses.

The sternness with which masturbation is condemned has gradually diminished. More and more parents regard masturbation as a natural part of growing up, they may attempt to discourage their children from masturbation, but they no longer punish it with severity. Some parents overlook it completely.

PREMARITAL INTERCOURSE

A strict taboo used to be directed toward premarital sexual behavior. The reasons behind the taboo were partly moral and partly practical, for example, the possibility of pregnancy, venereal disease, and so on. Almost everyone in our culture has been raised to regard premarital sexual relations as morally wrong. Now the taboo is bypassed by a growing number of young people.

Many of the practical reasons for avoiding premarital relationships are less pressing than they were at an earlier stage in history. Methods of avoiding conception have improved and are more available to married and unmarried persons. These methods do not guarantee 100 per cent effectiveness, but they reduce the possibility of conception. Methods for preventing and curing veneral diseases are easily available, and so this reason for premarital continence is less urgent than it once was.

These observations mean that spokespersons for premarital chastity have primarily religious grounds to support their arguments; practical reasons for avoiding premarital intercourse have been solved by technology and better sex education.

Yet, as indicated earlier, the frequency of teenage pregnancy and of venereal disease has increased steadily. This gives additional force to the awareness that the sex drive can be "bigger than both of us" unless the couple, individually and together, is careful to make decisions and to work out the necessary controls ahead of time. Responsible sex experience requires use of one's rational capacities, recognizing the necessity to make some decisions away from the intense pressures of the moonlight night and soft music. This will apparently be true and always be necessary, regardless of how technologically

Sex and Healthy Personality

337

effective are the contraceptive aids. Mechanical or engineered devices are no better than the brain on the body that is about to use them.

HOMOSEXUALITY

Throughout this chapter I have been speaking only of heterosexual love. There are, however, some whose love and sexuality are expressed to a person of the same sex. It used to be believed that homosexuality was a mental disease. With greater enlightenment has come the realization that, if someone has been "bent" in a homosexual direction by his or her upbringing, this does not mean that person is criminal or sick. Many states regard homosexuality as a criminal offense; this is an unenlightened policy.

It is true that some "gay" persons (as homosexuals sometimes describe themselves) are unhealthy personalities, but there is no evidence that they are more neurotic or psychotically incapacitated, as a group, than any other group in the general population. Of course, if homosexual people live in a "straight" society with conventional sexual morality, they run the risk of ostracism, or of being fired from their jobs. I agree with the aims of the Gay Liberation Society, and hold the view that, among consenting adults, any way of expressing sexuality is a private matter.

I have served as a psychotherapist to numerous people who were homosexual, and in some of these cases, their avoidance of the opposite sex was grounded in irrational fears. Through the therapeutic interviews, it was possible for them to overcome their fear of the opposite sex and to establish heterosexual relationships. Other patients learned how to live nondestructively with their homosexuality, when it become apparent that the homosexual way was deeply established. Some patients learned to "swing both ways."

Various Responses to Sexual Arousal

Healthy Personality

Let us examine some of the ways in which a person can respond to sexual feelings once they have arisen. First, let us discuss the healthy pattern and then comment upon some of the less healthy responses.

The healthy personality will have formed a set of ethical and perhaps aesthetic conditions under which she will feel free to express her sexual feelings. She will be aware of sexual feelings whenever they arise, even under conditions that for her are inappropriate. She does not feel threatened by her own feelings, and hence does not need to deny their existence through repression. When the preceding conditions have not been met, however, she will suppress (not repress) her sexual feelings and refrain from sexual behavior. The reason for such suppression, fundamentally, is that sexual intercourse is not satisfying when the conditions are not right. We may call this pattern *selective suppression and release*.

SOME UNHEALTHY PATTERNS

Immediate Release of Sexual Tensions. A person may find it impossible to delay sexual gratification, so intense or urgent are his tensions and desires. Consequently, he may seek release in any way immediately available to him. The quest for immediate release reflects an inability on the part of the person to control his impulses. This inability to impose control is likely to result in sexual behavior that jeopardizes many values. If the person seeks sexual release with a partner, he may choose that partner only on the basis of immediate availability, ignoring other important criteria for the choice of a sex partner. Thus, the person chosen may be unsuitable because of age differences, ill health, intelligence level, or social class. Probably many unwanted pregnancies, instances of venereal disease, hasty marriages, rapes, and other undesirable occurrences derive from the inability to tolerate delay in the attainment of sexual gratification.

Repression. Repression of sexual feelings is likely to occur in persons who have rigid sexual morality and who fear sexuality in general. Repression of sex manifests itself in (1) an absence of conscious sexual wishes or desires or (2) a denial of any sexual intent. All of us repress sexuality at various times because we have been trained to observe certain taboos, for example, the incest taboo. Most of us would become upset if we become sexually aroused by members of our immediate family. Yet psy-

Sex and Healthy Personality

339

choanalysts have shown that such feelings may well occur early in our lives.

Repression of sexual desire in the right times and places is compatible with personality health, provided the repression is not too general. Social living would be impossible if persons were chronically aroused sexually. Imagine being sexually aroused all day, every day, every year. It would interfere with other pursuits, to say the least. But if sexuality has been totally repressed, many unhealthy consequences ensue. The represser carries a virtual "well" of unconscious sexual desire, manifested in unpredictable and uncontrollable ways, in accidents, gestures, and unwitting sexualization of interpersonal relationships. Chronic unconscious sexuality disturbs the person's capacity to work effectively and it disturbs her relationships with people by making her unduly defensive or autistic. The psychoanalysts assert that repressed sexuality contributes to the development of neurosis and to other patterns of unhealthy personality.

The worst danger associated with a total repression of sexuality is the fact that from time to time the repression may be overcome in explosive fashion. This may occur when the sexual tensions become too strong or when the energy required to maintain the repression is decreased, for example, in fatigue or intoxication. On such occasions, the represser may engage in impulsive sexual behavior, or she may become overwhelmed with guilt and anxiety without really understanding why.

Chronic Suppression. A person can be fully aware of his sexual tensions but suppress sexual behavior for a number of reasons: fear of disease, fear of pregnancy, guilt, ideals, and so on. Chronic suppression sets the stage for unremitting sexual tension.

Chronic sexual tension will produce many undesirable effects. The most obvious is unhappiness and a sense of frustration. In addition, the suppresser will be plagued with chronic sexual fantasies so that he cannot concentrate on his work. His relationships with people will be impaired for a number of reasons; for example, he may not be able to appraise the feelings of others with accuracy, or he may be irritable and short-tempered.

Healthy Personality

Suppression of sexual behavior is unhealthy when the

consequences to which it leads are unhealthy, and when the reasons for the suppression are unrealistic and unwarranted. The ability to suppress, however, is a desirable ability, as we shall see in the next section.

Some Factors in Healthy Sexuality

Healthy sexuality in an adult is no accident, nor is it a natural phenomenon. Some of the factors that foster a health-engendering sex life include (1) sensible sexual instruction, (2) early nontraumatic sexual experiences, (3) availability of suitable sex partners, (4) a wide repertoire of other satisfactions, (5) the capacity to establish love relationships, and (6) knowledge about the use of contraception.

Sensible Sex Instruction. Humans have to learn how to behave sexually, and they have to learn when it is socially appropriate to become sexually aroused. Some of this learning results from deliberate parental instruction of children. Much of this instruction in our society is negative; it consists in admonishments about what is taboo. Children are told not to masturbate, not to display their bodies; in fact, from an early age many children are actively trained to be ashamed and afraid of things pertaining to sex. Because many parents are embarrassed or tense about sexual matters, their children may be afraid to ask questions about their sex organs or about reproduction. The children may then acquire false beliefs concerning these matters.

Healthy sexuality is most likely to be promoted if the sexual instruction that the children receive is matter-of-fact, accurate, and in response to the children's spontaneous curiosity.

Nature of Early Experiences with Sex. Healthy adult sexuality is most likely to be achieved against a background relatively free of fears and guilts pertaining to sex. Many children have undergone severe punishments for childhood masturbation or sexual experimentation. These punishments have made sexual situations a stimulus for emotions incompatible with sex. The severely punished child may, if other contributing factors are present, develop impotence, frigidity, various perversions, and

Sex and Healthy Personality

other unhealthy patterns. Healthy sexuality will be promoted if the parents handle the children's deviations from their own sexual ethics with kindness, understanding, and explanations the child can understand.

Thus, if a child is observed masturbating or if there is evidence of his masturbation in discharge on the bedsheets, parents have a choice of ignoring the matter; discussing and explaining the matter with the child so that he is freed of guilt feelings; gently, without condemnation, requesting that he try not to masturbate; or, finally, suggesting that it be done only in private, as are many things that people do. It should be explained in simple language relative to the child's level of understanding. The choice of which of these approaches is to be used is a legitimate responsibility of parental judgment. It is a parent's perogative—except that truth must be the basis of the choice and that guilt must be ruled out. Our recommendation is that it be explained and thereafter ignored.

Availability of Suitable Partners. It is not uncommon for homosexuality to occur among students in all-male or all-female schools; among prisoners in jails, camps, and penitentiaries; and among sailors. In rural areas, where the population is scanty and the opportunities for marriage are limited, sexual contacts with animals may occur.

The incidence of such deviant patterns could be reduced if appropriate partners were available to persons living under these conditions. The policy of denying prisoners any access to spouses or lovers is particularly brutalizing.

A Generally Satisfying Life. The probability of attaining and maintaining healthy sexuality is increased if a person is gaining satisfactions in other realms of life. Adequate sexual relationships will promote a person's ability to function satisfactorily in her work, her leisure, and her nonsexual relationships with people. The reverse also appears to be true: If a person is able to derive satisfaction from her work, her leisure, and her relationships with people, she is likely to be better able to achieve healthy sexuality. A person filled with unresolved tensions arising from other areas of her life may try to compensate by means of sexual activity. She may demand more of sex than it can deliver. And further, the burden of nonsexual tensions that she is carrying may prevent

Healthy Personality

her from performing adequately in a sexual situation. A tense, thwarted person can't be a relaxed, effective sexual lover.

Love for the Partner. Many barriers to healthy sexuality will not arise in a healthy love relationship. If a person has the capacity to love another person, he will doubtless have the capacity to develop a satisfying sex life within that relationship. Loving involves knowing the loved one, caring for him or her, behaving in ways that will promote the other's growth and happiness, and making the self known to the other. If a couple has been able to establish such a relationship, then neither will be afraid or ashamed to make needs and desires known to the other. Each wants to please the other and to promote the happiness of the other. At the outset of a marriage, a loving couple may not achieve full harmony and mutual satisfaction in sexual relationships, but in time they should be able to accommodate each others' changing needs and wishes. The richest sexual satisfactions occur in the context of a love relationship, where the communication barriers between the partners are reduced to a minimum.

Knowledge and Use of Contraceptive Methods. Responsible, brain- and body-controlled sexual experience requires knowledge of the available devices to prevent pregnancy: the diaphragm, the condom, vaginal jellies, the pill, sterilization, the IUD, and vasectomy. A deterrent to the use of these devices is perhaps the hidden fear on the part of both members of the couple that the interruption in the stimulation and arousal in preparation for intercourse will cause the other partner to change his or her mind. This is hardly likely under conditions of arousal; on the contrary, one may expect that the mutuality and enjoyment of the experience will be heightened through the knowledge that fear of pregnancy is dispelled. High-level, healthy sexual activity requires informed responsibility to one another.

Therapy for Unhealthy Sexual Patterns

The individual with an unsatisfactory sex life suffers. The sexual represser is afflicted with prolonged sexual privation. The person with deviant sexual behavior may suffer from fear of punishment, and possibly losses of self-esteem. The impotent husband and the frigid wife suffer from disturbances in the overall relationships with the spouse.

Such persons may seek psychotherapy. Although assistance cannot always be guaranteed, often guidance, instruction, or more intensive therapy may be effective in removing some of the obstacles to healthy sexuality.

A woman undertook therapy because of marked difficulties in her relationship with one of her children. During the course of therapy, it was discovered she was not sexually responsive to her husband. She merely endured the sexual aspects of marriage. Indeed, she used her sexual compliance as a way to control her husband. It was soon discovered that her lack of responsiveness derived largely from attitudes acquired from her mother. Her mother had instructed the patient to view sex as dirty. The patient, when she became aware of the origins of her attitudes, came to see them as silly. Her lack of responsiveness vanished, and with it vanished also the lack of zest in the marriage, a lot of tension, and finally, the difficulties in her relationship with her child.

Although counseling is often sufficient to help a person overcome difficulties with sex, other approaches have been employed by psychologists and psychiatrists. Masters and Johnson,[12] the pioneer researchers of orgasm in women, developed sophisticated methods for supervising the sexual behavior of married couples who have not been successful in bringing each other to a sexual climax. Classical aversion conditioning techniques have been employed to help men overcome impulses to engage in fetishistic or homosexual activities. For example, a man who found himself unable to resist the impulse to fondle young boys might have electrodes attached to some part of his body; each time he is shown a picture of a young boy, or thinks of a young boy, a mild shock is administered to him. The rationale is that he will then experience anxiety, rather than sexual arousal, each time he is confronted by the "forbidden" sex stimulus.

In my opinion, such a direct attack upon the symptoms of unhealthy sexuality should occur only within the context of a counseling relationship where the person's over-

Healthy
Personality

344

all life style is explored; the aim would be to seek ways of changing other aspects of life that have contributed to the development of the sexual difficulties.

Some Existential Suggestions

A very distinct specialization in sex therapy has grown in recent years and offers considerable benefit in an age of increased sexual activity. A person with problems in this area, premature ejaculation, uncertainty about sex role, inability to enjoy sex, and so on, should seek out a fully qualified sex therapist. Perhaps because of the intimate nature of the matter, one should be extra careful in his or her choice of therapists. The name of a qualified person can be found through referral by a qualified general counselor, psychologist, psychiatrist, or social worker.

Cultural customs and religious beliefs cannot be separated from activity in sex. What is condoned for another cultural community or religious faith may not be suitable to you. Therefore, you need to consider the constraints and the commitments that are part of your faith in making these choices. It is also understandable that some persons choose to break with their old cultural ties. You may find some cultural constraints too restrictive, and may elect to change despite cultural taboos. In such circumstances you should be certain your changes come out of conviction and not out of convenience.

The new orientation to sex behavior encourages openness, truthfulness, and avoidance of secrecy. Yet you may wish to maintain some of the mystique of sex without being repressive and without dishonesty. Openness in sex activity requires not flaunting your affections but cherishing them in privacy, and avoiding behavior that is conducive to guilt, such as exploitation, seduction, or heightening frustration through teasing.

There is still no better aphrodisiac, however, than authentic, committed, responsible love for the partner.

Sex and Healthy Personality

SUMMARY

Sexual mores have changed in the past decade in a revolutionary way. Premarital sexual relationships are more

345

common, and there is more widespread interest in ways to make sexual love more fulfilling.

The sexual evolution began with Freud's frank and open insights concerning sex and personal adjustment, continued with the classic surveys of Kinsey, Pomeroy, and others. The laboratory research of Masters and Johnson made sexuality a legitimate scientific study and took society to the point where discussion of sex in the media and movies became commonplace.

The psychoanalytic theory of sexual development, with its division of sexuality into the oral, anal, phallic, and genital stages was presented.

Some unhealthy motives for engaging in sexuality include using sex as a quest for reassurance, as an opiate, and as an exchange commodity.

Inability to become aroused sexually is termed frigidity in the female, impotence in the male. Such unresponsiveness may signify unhealthy personality.

Among loving partners, great freedom in the expression of sexuality is an expression of healthy personality and enlightened attitudes. Some patterns of sexual expression, once regarded as evil or dangerous, are now viewed less critically, for example, masturbation, premarital intercourse, and homosexuality. The ability to control one's sexuality is important for healthy personality; repression and uncontrolled expression of sexuality are destructive. Some factors in healthy sexuality are proper early instruction, nontraumatic early sexual experiences, availability of suitable sex partners, a generally satisfying life, and the capacity to love. Psychotherapy is available for persons with sexual difficulties.

NOTES AND REFERENCES

1. A. C. KINSEY, W. B. POMEROY, and C. E. MARTIN, *Sexual Behavior in the Human Male* (Philadelphia: Saunders, 1948); see also A. C. KINSEY, W. B. POMEROY, C. E. MARTIN, and P. H. GEBHARD, *Sexual Behavior in the Human Female* (Philadelphia: Saunders, 1953).

2. W. H. MASTERS and V. E. JOHNSON, *Human Sexual Response* (Boston: Little, Brown, 1966); W. H. MASTERS and V. E. JOHNSON, *The Pleasure Bond* (Boston: Little, Brown, 1974).

Healthy Personality

3. R. J. Levin and A. Levin, "Sexual Pleasure: The Surprising Preferences of 100,000 Women," *Redbook*, 1975, Vol. 145, pp. 51–58; R. Levin, "Premarital and Extramarital Sex," *Redbook*, 1975, Vol. 145, pp. 38–44, 190–192.

4. J. R. Hopkins, "Sexual Behavior in Adolescence," *Journal of Social Issues*, 1977, Vol. 33, pp. 67–85.

5. See A. Ellis, *Sex Without Guilt* (New York: Lyle Stuart, 1958). Other general discussions of love and sex that you will find useful include Z. Rubin, *Liking and Loving: An Invitation to Social Psychology* (New York: Holt, 1973); L. A. Peplau and C. L. Hammen (Eds.), "Sexual Behavior: Social Psychological Issues," *Journal of Social Issues*, 1977, Vol. 33, pp. 1–96.

6. S. Freud, *Three Essays on the Theory of Sexuality* (New York: Basic, 1962).

7. See W. Reich, *Character Analysis* (New York: Orgone Institute, 1948), for discussion of the genital character.

8. G. Newman and C. R. Nichols, "Sexual Activities and Attitudes in Older Persons," *Journal of the American Medical Association*, 1960, Vol. 173, pp. 33–35.

9. S. M. Jourard, *The Transparent Self* (New York: Van Nostrand Reinhold, 1971), Chapter 5, "Sex and Self-disclosure in Marriage."

10. There are many "how-to" books available on sexual love. One that I find aesthetically pleasing and that is presented in a spirit of joy is A. Comfort (Ed.), *The Joy of Sex: A Gourmet Guide to Love Making* (New York: Crown, 1972).

11. See the list of parental reactions to children's masturbation—some brutally sadistic—complied in M. Huschka, "The Incidence and Character of Masturbation Threats in a Group of Problem Children," *Psychoanalytic Quarterly*, 1938, Vol. 7, pp. 338–355.

12. W. H. Masters and Virginia E. Johnson, *Human Sexual Inadequacy* (Boston: Little, Brown, 1970).

14

WORK, PLAY, AND HEALTHY PERSONALITY

INTRODUCTION

Now and then, writers lay the blame for the emphasis upon work and working in America on "the Protestant-Judaic ethic," which has built many of the moral rules of American society. Such blame suggests that only those brought up in this ethic feel the need to work. On the contrary, work is valued in all societies for a rather uncomplicated reason; it is necessary to produce the basic needs of people: food, shelter, even safety. But beyond basic needs, work also has the potential for the satisfaction of the higher needs: aesthetic needs, cognitive needs, and the need for self-realization. From a sociological perspective, work is the activity that persons undertake to keep the social system going. The total labor necessary to sustain life in common is divided among the participants in the society, and each person thus fulfills his or her occupational role, just as they fulfill their various social roles.

In some societies work is separated, with one kind of

work for the very young, usually quite menial; other work for the young adult; and a limited kind of work for the aged. Especially is work "segregated" for the disadvantaged, for example, for blacks and for women. As a matter of fact, almost all societies seems to have limited the career opportunities for women to child-rearing-related jobs, such as teaching; food preparation jobs, such as waitressing; or jobs as "assistants" to men. To add insult to injury, even those jobs that are shared by men and women often pay less when the holder is female.

The job and the identity of the person are often the same. If maintenance and enhancement of the self is the basic need, then the job one holds is the basic self for most people. Thus the dignity of one's job is often one of the major criteria involved in choosing a life career.

One of the great threats for a large group of young people, and a challenge for others, is the increasing cybernation of the work-world, i.e., the increasing automation and control of large, complex processes in industry by computers rather than by people. The unemployment that results is a great stress common to industrialized society. In agricultural and hunting and fishing cultures, work is needed at all times from all members; no one is without essential and meaningful work to do. But the specter of being "laid off" from the job because of overproduction, strikes, or automation haunts workers in our society.

Most people are obliged to work more than one third of their waking adult lives; it is obvious that work has a decisive influence on one's sense of identity [1] and on one's physical and psychological health. There is a relationship between various trades and professions and assorted kinds of disease. Ulcers of the stomach and intestine are more common among upward-mobile executives in corporations than among secretaries employed in the same firms. British conductors on buses, who regularly climb stairs and move about in the two-story buses, usually live longer than do the drivers, who are sedentary. Moreover, if a person is obliged to work at menial or monotonous tasks, the sheer boredom of daily existence can undermine morale and contribute to physical and psychological breakdown.

Work, Play, and Healthy Personality

On the other hand, being at a job that provides excitement, dignity, and even fun can facilitate longevity. Arthur Fiedler, famed conductor of the Boston Pops orchestra, when honored on his eighty-second birthday, said, "He who rests, rots," and his enjoyment of his work was apparent in his youthful exuberance and sense of humor, let alone in the enormous range of music he conducted.

No matter how absorbing one's work, humans need meaningful leisure as a balance to work. Whether it is the law of variety or the fact that leisure is carefree, play seems to be an important part of life. Some studies [2] suggest that a childlike sense of humor or playfulness is a characteristic of the high-level-functioning personality. Leisure is necessary for the healthy personality, and significant social and labor movements recognize this by creating greater opportunities for leisure. Thus, it becomes important to make plans for one's free time and to utilize the opportunities for personal growth in leisure. Healthy personality calls for hobbies and interests, for activities that provide enjoyment and sustain joie de vivre, *the joy of life. It may seem unreal to the tired worker, but unless people are educated early in life to use leisure time in rewarding ways, they may find such time oppressive.[3]*

Choice of Vocation

The *Dictionary of Occupational Titles* [4] lists 20,000 occupations at which people can earn a livelihood in the American society.

When the number of options open to a person was slight, the problem people faced was vocational *adjustment*—how to make life bearable in the vocational slot to which one was fated. As in all realms where freedom is encountered, for some the freedom is terrifying and paralyzing, but for others, it is exhilarating. Many college freshmen and high school seniors face a career choice in a state of total confusion and with a feeling of desperate urgency that a choice must be made now, and it must be the right one, or disaster will be forthcoming.

*Healthy
Personality*

The profession of vocational counseling was developed

to help young persons choose a vocation that would utilize their talents and aptitudes and fulfill their economic aspirations.

SOME BASES FOR VOCATIONAL CHOICE

Parental Choice. Some young men and women are guided into a vocation that their mother or father now occupies, or that either parent *wishes* he or she had entered. In such cases, the child is seen as an extension of the parent, or a family representative whose task it is to fulfill dreams and goals of someone other than himself. There is nothing intrinsically healthy or unhealthy in such a basis for a choice; everything depends upon the personal characteristics of the child. I have known many students who were contented and productive in a career path that simply seemed ready and waiting for them as soon as they finished high school. One person enters the family business because it was always expected of him, and another starts training to become a lawyer or physician with as little conflict.

Difficulty arises in such cases when there is conflict with the parents over goals in life, or where the student is struggling to achieve some measure of emancipation from parental control. Parents often equate obedience with their wishes with love for them—a fallacy that produces agonies of guilt for students who find themselves unhappily enrolled, say, as a student of dentistry when they would prefer to study art. Any expression of discontent is encountered with a barrage of criticism: "You must be out of your mind to want to study art. You can't make a living at it. You know you'll be happy as a dentist. You never did know your own mind. Besides, do you know how much money we've invested in your training so far . . . etc., etc." A student has to have courage to follow her choice under such onslaughts of disconfirmation.

There are students who find training for *any* vocation meaningless, and the experience of being in junior or senior college absurd. Such a student may drop out of college for a time and travel, take an unskilled job, or enter a skilled trade for training. Although parents might become alarmed to find their children thus dropping out,

Work, Play, and Healthy Personality

I have on occasion encouraged students to withdraw from college when it seemed meaningless for them to be there. The period of being out has enabled such persons to find their own aims in life and to pursue them with more mature resolve than they experienced when they merely went automatically into a career under family prompting, without a responsible commitment.

Professional Vocational Counseling. Perhaps the most rational way to make decisions concerning a career involves the use of qualified, well-trained vocational counselors. These counselors usually form the backbone of the staff of college and high school counseling and placement centers. In addition, often community college counseling programs offer these same services to the entire community, regardless of whether the client is a student at the college or not. Sometimes these are also called *assessment centers.*

The counselor, rather than making a choice for you, will help you study yourself and will help you consider a wide variety of issues that might affect your career choice. The counselor probably will offer you the possibility of taking a number of tests, which would indicate your qualifications for various careers. Most of all, the counselor will leave the decision to you; however, he or she will not let you sink into a morass of your own uncertainty. The discussion of your potential decision and the use of valid testing should enable you to make a much wiser decision than one that might come to you by default—that is, a choice made simply because you could think of nothing else. Among the factors to be taken into consideration in either vocational counseling or in any decision made in the quiet of your own thinking are the following:

1. *Aptitude.* This refers to specific physical or psychological *capacities,* rather than what you actually accomplished. For example, being a dentist requires some special finger dexterity, such as is necessary to handle a small, specialized tool in a small space.

U.S. Employment Service publications often refer to 11 different aptitudes: intelligence, verbal, numerical, spatial, form perception, clerical perception, motor coordination, finger dexterity, manual dexterity, eye-hand-foot coordination, and color discrimination.

More often intelligence itself is considered as a special category, particularly because some professions, such as medicine and engineering, require measured estimates of intelligence for admission to training. On the other hand, and particularly in these days of some oversupply in the professions, some persons may be overqualified intellectually for some routine jobs, such as assembly work. The prediction is that the person would not be happy in work that does not utilize his or her intellect and therefore would be a poor prospect.

2. *Achievement*. As contrasted with aptitudes, which deal with potential, some careers may require specific achievement or attainment of particular levels of skill or knowledge. Graduation from college or knowledge of advanced mathematics would be examples.

3. *Personality*. In particular, many of the helping professions, such as social work, nursing, and clinical or counseling psychology, require some indications of the person's general psychological health. In some instances, as in the case of trainees for management positions, some assertiveness and other special personality qualifications might be considered. Past history of psychological problems should not in itself be grounds for the student rejecting those kinds of professions or for those professions rejecting him or her. In many instances, someone who has had such problems and had been able to overcome them brings to the profession a special strength, which of course cannot be taught academically.

4. *Interests*. This area has been perhaps the most researched in vocational guidance and career choice profession. A typical test given by a counselor to help a student determine his or her interests would be one that, for example, matches the student's interests with those of successful persons in the field.

5. *Job and situational factors*. Not the least factors to be considered in making a career choice are the salary level, possibilities for increased responsibility and skill, the prediction of crowding of openings in the future, and the working conditions, for example, office work versus outdoor field work.

Work, Play, and Healthy Personality   The counseling offered by a counseling psychologist or a vocational counselor should include the areas just stated, as seen pertinent by the client. In addition, you should expect to have an opportunity to think freely, range widely in your deliberations, and feel free to bring in especially awkward or uncomfortable issues, such as parental pressures, your own concerns about yourself, and so on. A good counselor will help the client to feel free to discuss all aspects of the matter, and above all, will leave both the responsibility and the final decisions as the prerogative of the client.

There is a tendency to ascribe magical properties to the testing, both by the counselor and by the client. An effective counselor will be careful to state the limitations of the tests and to rely more upon the opinions and motivation of the client than upon the tests themselves.

Some of the tests that you might encounter include:

1. The General Aptitude Test Battery [5] developed by the U.S. Employment Service for a variety of aptitudes.

2. The Wechsler Bellevue Intelligence Test. An individually administered intelligence test that yields scores that may help you know your strengths and weaknesses in differing areas of intelligence.

3. The General Educational Development Exams. An achievement test useful particularly for those who have not had a formal high school education.

4. The Minnesota Multiphasic Personality Inventory. A highly developed group test, administered to groups of clients at one time, which is often used as a general measure of personal psychological health.

5. The Strong–Campbell Vocational Interest Battery, the Kuder Occupational Interest Survey, and the Ohio Vocational Interest Survey. New forms of these standard interest tests are now available that minimize sex bias and take advantage of new developments in the job market.[6]

The healthy personality is heavily dependent upon job satisfaction, and thus one should leave no stone unturned in utilizing what science has to offer to help make what could be one of the two most crucial decisions in a lifetime (the other being a choice of a spouse!).

Also like some marriage patterns, there is the probability that one job choice is not necessarily a lifetime commitment. Second careers are now commonplace and may occur for any number of reasons, particularly at age 40; the possibility exists at all age levels. They may occur

Healthy
Personality

for a number of reasons: [7] physical disability (a musician injures her fingers); psychological change (Ralph Bugg, an Atlanta night editor, wearies of his job and becomes a freelance writer); [8] personal factors (early retirement from the army); technological change (a large industry goes out of business in a small town and hundreds of assembly-line workers now must seek jobs in a limited job market).

Independent Security in Vocational Choice. As I noted earlier (Chapter 2), Blatz [9] saw independent security as the goal of child-rearing and personal growth. According to this view, *insecurity* is inevitable and desirable in the course of life. It is the state of being that a person undergoes when some need is unmet, or some challenge or problem confronts a person, requiring decision and action. A person can evade the problem or need and employ various defense mechanisms in order to avoid the necessity to do anything different. This solution to insecurity is deemed unhealthy. The person can turn to someone to solve the problem for her or to act in her behalf. This solution is called the way of *dependent* security; it is deemed immature if the person assigns responsibility to the other for failure to solve the problem. It is regarded as *mature* dependent security if the person takes the responsibility for the other's intervention in her life. Thus, mature dependent security is displayed if a student asks her parent to advise her on some problem but accepts as her own responsibility the consequences of following the parental advice. The greatest contribution to personal growth is provided by the way of *independent security*—the person encounters insecurity in the conduct of her life, accepts it, and addresses it with the resolve to master it by learning a skill and by gathering information in order to make an autonomous decision.

A person achieves independent security in the vocational sphere of her life if she has made a choice—*any* choice, for *any* good reason—and has then pursued it with commitment, accepting the difficulties as well as the satisfactions as part of her lot.

Work, Play, and Healthy Personality

When I finished high school, I had no idea what I wished to do for a career. I knew I wanted further education, but I didn't know in what area. I did not think I would like to be a businessman, a lawyer, a dentist, a doctor, or a worker, skilled or unskilled, in a factory. My parents left me alone with my dilemma; my father told me he would back me in any career plan I chose, but that I would have to make the decision. One option he offered was to enter the retail clothing business, which was our family livelihood, but he put no pressure on me to do so. I chose to enter college in an unspecialized liberal arts program. As it happened, my psychology teacher, Dr. Mary Northway, was a fine lecturer; I read a great deal of psychology under her influence. We had to choose a "major" in our sophomore year, and for want of any other inspiration, I chose psychology. I had no idea about careers in psychology. I had no information about the ways of life open to people with undergraduate or graduate degrees in this discipline; I made the choice because we had to make some decision. Once in, however, I began to find interest and challenge. I retained a lively interest in many other areas, such as sociology, anthropology, literature, and languages, but I have stuck to the profession of psychology and have found challenge, boredom, excitement, financial reward—in short, satisfaction with the career that I chose with about as much foresight as one displays if he sees a body of water, closes his eyes, holds his breath, and jumps in to see if he can swim in it. Once in, however, one has to swim.

The point of this personal anecdote is that choice of a vocation can be made upon *any* constructive basis; once the choice is made, it contributes to healthy personality if the person remains the responsible agent of his existence and lives with the consequences of his decision until these become untoward, when he will again have to make a decision.

Being in a Profession

There are many ways to be at, and in, one's work. A person can view her vocation as something miserable she has to do, and endure, in order to earn enough money to "really live." However, there are times of economic hardship when people are forced to take employment that is boring, even humiliating, in order to eat and to

Healthy Personality

provide for their dependents. Thus, many people work at physical labor, as waiters and waitresses, or at unskilled trades, to put themselves through school or to support children. There is nothing incompatible with healthy personality in having to work for one's livelihood. Unrewarding work, however, can drain a person of vitality and morale, rendering the rest of her life unlivable. The interests of healthy personality and self-actualization are served by changing vocations when one's present work has lost zest and meaning. This is not always easy, and it frequently is costly, but if the change offers hope of more challenging and rewarding work, then the period of transitional seeking and training, with its expense, is worth it. Unrewarding work is one of the sources of the stress and dispiritedness that undermine physical health. Changes in vocation, after long periods of stress and boredom, can be rejuvenating.

Meanings of Work. One can work to earn a livelihood, to avoid boredom in life, or to fulfill the meaning of one's life. There are many meanings that a person's work can have for him. A common basis of meaning, especially within some of the professions, is to test oneself in comparison with others—the *achievement motive*, as McClelland called it.[10] The striving for excellence, for conquest, for being the best, is a powerful motive in American society, and, of course, in other societies around the world. The pursuit of high excellence, or recognition, is one of the basic human needs. High achievement is the basis for enhancing one's status in the eyes of contemporaries, and it is at the heart of self-esteem. While work is not the only source of such enhanced status and self-esteem, for many it is the most important. Each profession and trade offers its challenges and rewards for high achievement, and these rewards reinforce the persistence and the creativity of the workers. A person is fortunate, and has chosen his vocation wisely, if he finds challenge and reward in the daily activities that define his work.

A person may work "religiously"; that is, she sees her work as a "calling," whether from God or from the world, that she feels needs her, and only her, to do some essential tasks. Thus, a person may enter the

Work, Play, and Healthy Personality

357

ministry in response to the experience of a "call," or she may enter politics, or the profession of teaching, because she feels that she can make a unique contribution that is needed. People often enter and remain in helping professions, such as medicine, psychology, social work, and teaching, because they feel uniquely called upon to help solve problems in the world or to relieve ubiquitous suffering. I feel some of this motivation in my work.

Meaningful work is essential for healthy personality. It is common for people to deteriorate, sicken, and die within a few years of retirement from some lifetime career of work. It is also unfortunately common for people in their vigorous years to develop illnesses related to stress and dissatisfaction in their work. Heart attacks, peptic and gastric ulcers, heightened susceptibility to infectious ills are all common occurrences among people whose daily activity generates more stress and meaninglessness than satisfaction.

Change of Vocation

In my opinion, Marx was correct when he stated that a person's "relation to the means of production" imposed a powerful influence upon all aspects of his or her—beliefs and attitudes, future, family life, health, even life expectancy. Work uses one's time and energy, and these are all that anyone truly "has." In return, work yields money or a product. If it also yields boredom and sickness, then a change is essential for healthy personality. But as in changes in personal relationships and in one's own personality, powerful barriers often oppose such change.

BARRIERS TO CHANGE

Fear. A person who is unhappy in her vocation may remain in it, nonetheless, because she simply fears change. Although her present situation is miserable, she remains in it because at least it is familiar misery; she dreads the unknown challenges she would face if she were to drop out to seek a career that *might* (no guarantees) be more life-giving.

Healthy Personality

Present Sense of Identity. A person may base his sense

of personal identity upon his present vocational activity, so that to withdraw from that work, or place of work, is tantamount to a dreaded loss of identity. Although such a narrow basis to identity and self-esteem is incompatible with healthy personality, that may be a person's present status. Under such circumstances he may remain at unrewarding work because he cannot envision himself at any other. His imagination and confidence in his powers of rejuvenation are repressed.

Others' Expectations. The expectations of others, that a person will remain as they have known her, can keep that person in unrewarding social roles and in stressing work, long past the time it was good for her. Frequently a person's family may, with the best of intentions, keep a person "at" her present work, even if it is sapping her morale and vitality, because the *other* family members dread change. I have counseled several people at times when they were in despair over the meaninglessness of their work, and they have told me that whenever they would discuss changing jobs or careers, their spouses or friends met the suggestion with barrages of disconfirmation. "You'd be a fool to give up this job. You are well-liked, you earn a good living, you can handle the responsibilities . . . etc." Such persuasion often sufficed to keep a person in sickening (for her) work. It takes courage and encouragement to make such changes, in face of fear, limited senses of personal identity, and others' disconfirmation.

CHANGE IN VOCATION AND HEALTHY PERSONALITY

Many men and women are making drastic career changes in mid-life and finding such change invigorating. It takes self-assurance and some confirmation from significant others to make such major changes, but I have witnessed many of them, and I've been impressed with the liberating effects of the decision. For example, one person sold a small business that he had struggled to develop for fifteen years. He had found that the life of a storekeeper had become absurd for him. He bought a trailer, traveled with his family until he found another city in which he thought they would like to live, and

Work, Play, and Healthy Personality

returned to college as a forty-year-old student. His wife worked to help support him, and his children likewise worked at after-school jobs. In another case, a woman in her early fifties, who found the life of a middle-class housewife enervating, went across the country to resume graduate work for a doctorate in counseling psychology. She lost 30 pounds as a student and looked much more alive. Her husband and children, across the continent, discovered they could run the household without her and found new interests in common.

As a psychotherapist, I have often seen connections between stresses in work and the suffering that led my patient to seek help. This has been especially true among the people in mid-life. Often they have entertained fantasies of "chucking it all," and running off to the seaside, or to a hippie commune with a teenaged mistress. Some have checked out of their dispiriting family and occupational roles. Others have explored the possibility of resigning from their present work to start on a new vocation, even if it called for a return to school or university. Change is good for you, when it is responsible change. Impulsive change can be disastrous; but even if it is, at least a person has moved from stultifying places, and he can then pick himself out of the disaster to explore more life-giving possibilities for vocational change.

SPECIAL PROBLEMS IN WORK AND CAREER CHOICE

Four groups deserve special understanding from the point of view of the sense of identity and self-worth: women, minority groups, the physically handicapped, and the older person.

Women. For centuries and reaching well into modern times, women have been relegated to jobs relating either to the home or to the rearing of children. When they have been permitted to enter the extradomicile world of work, they found themselves still in positions that "assisted" men: nurses, secretaries, salesclerks, and so on. The technological fields, such as automobile repair, and those involving physical danger, such as heavy machinery operation or telephone lines work, were off limits for the female. However, an advancing society has opened al-

Healthy Personality

most all such opportunities in this quarter of the century, thus creating a new vista for self-realization possibilities in work for willing women. No doubt there will be many isolated pockets of resistance to this work revolution; meanwhile, by law and changing custom, women have far more complex choices now ahead of them.

Pioneers in the work equality of women were the Israeli kibbutzim, which had as part of their ideological base the principle of equality of women. Communal child care freed women in the collective settlement to work in the fields or in production. Yet, recent studies have shown a choice on the part of women to return to the more feminine kinds of work: raising the family, preparation of food, and so on. Tiger and Shepher [11] report of their study:

> If our data are accurate and our explanation valid, we can conclude that insofar as women are dissatisfied in the kibbutz, it is not principally because of polarized sexual division of labor and politics and an oppressive familism, as it so clearly is elsewhere. Rather, it is because familism does not yet provide women with as much "feminine" activity and family life as they desire [p. 259].

This does not mean that women generally wish to return to home and family. However, if they do so, they will do so out of choice rather than out of oppressive demands of a constricting society. The physiological bond between mother and child is often cited as predetermining some sexual division of labor. It may well be that the course of the job revolution for women will bring some back to the traditional home role, but the prediction on the basis of the recent past is that the greater numbers will move into the world of work, and that some significant, smaller numbers also will return to the child-rearing jobs, such as teaching and "homemaking."

The Disadvantaged. Despite a number of federal programs aimed at providing additional employment for young blacks, it is apparent that the teenaged black will continue to have a rough time finding and advancing in a career. Quoting reports from the U.S. Bureau of Labor

Work, Play, and Healthy Personality

Statistics, Herber [12] notes that more than a fourth of teen-age blacks are unable to find employment, compared to perhaps 15 per cent of young whites. Ginzberg,[13] quoted in the same report, says that young white females have increased their employability. "For black youngsters, however, the employment-population ratio has . . . been tending steeply downward for the past two decades" (p. 44).

This suggests that our society will have to create more successful employment programs than those of the past, such as CETA. Other studies do show the black increasing in attendance at American universities. The gloomy picture of black teenage employment does not mean career opportunities are not available to the motivated black student. It does mean that the student must recognize that he or she will have to be inventive in creating a career. It also suggests that our society must be more creative in its efforts to provide such groups having histories of discrimination and prejudice against them with realistic opportunities to be constructive and to participate in the self-worth-engendering experience of work, career, and dignity.

The Handicapped. Through federal legislation, handicapped children and adults in recent years have earned broader opportunities for training and personal development and increased likelihood of employment in the general labor market. The various pieces of legislation have provided for funds to offer special programs for handicapped children in public schools, including psychological services, support for equipping public buildings with ramps and railings to facilitate more comfortable mobility, and scholarship and support monies for education and training. The U.S. Rehabilitation Services Administration has reported that 345,000 persons were rehabilitated (restored to income-earning jobs) in 1974, compared to 88,000 in 1960.[14]

There is a special consideration with regard to the healthy personality for the handicapped. One of the major criteria used by researchers in identifying the healthy or beautiful and noble person is the person's ability to integrate negative experiences into the self or, in a sense, to change the meaning of a disaster into that of an ad-

Healthy Personality

362

vantage. Many handicapped persons have been able to manifest this change and have emerged as stronger, healthier personalities—but only with the help of understanding friends. Ziller,[15] for example, has shown that most people encountering a person in a wheelchair turn their faces aside. More handicapped persons would find their way to fullest rehabilitation if we showed understanding rather than avoidance.

Older People. These members of society, especially those faced with enforced retirement, face a dilemma not encountered in other, nonindustrialized societies. There is nothing for them to do, and they often die of boredom. In our society, retirement communities of old people's homes have flourished, yet some older people regard them as ghettos and storage depots for obsolete flesh. Many retired people have prepared themselves for meaningful lives of leisure after retirement, for example, by travel; return to school and community college; and pursuit of hobbies such as woodwork, art, music, and sailing. (Francis Chichester [16] sailed alone around the world in his sixties, with only one lung functioning.) Until education insures that more people will reach retirement age with inspiriting activity to engage in, there will be need for counselors of the aged, to help them find rewarding work with avocational pursuits.

THE IMPORTANCE OF SABBATICAL LEAVE

Some universities offer their faculty the opportunity to spend one year in seven away from usual teaching and scholarly duties. The purpose of such sabbatical leave is to provide the teacher with an opportunity for self-renewal, so that he will not stagnate in his work. Everyone is susceptible to becoming "efficient," stereotyped, boring, and bored in his way of being a professional person. Sabbatical leave, when needed, is invaluable. A person's situation imposes a hypnotic spell upon him, so that he may not be able to envision other, more creative ways to work at his calling. A prolonged absence from home base, with opportunity for leisure and study, "dehypnotizes" the person, such that on his return, he can work in more enlivening ways. A person might leave a profession because he found it unrewarding, yet he could have re-

Work, Play, and Healthy Personality

mained in it in productive ways, if he had had sabbatical leave when it was needed. As our nation becomes sufficiently affluent, I believe that it would be a contribution to the quality of existence to make it *mandatory* for people in all vocations to take sabbatical leave each year, or every few years, in order to renew themselves. I suspect that the cost of such leave would be made up by savings in medical costs incurred by bored, miserable, uncreative working men and women.[17]

Play and Healthy Personality

If work is activity that produces a product, play is activity or inactivity that yields the reward of fun. Work can be playful, and yet be work; play is undertaken out of exuberance, out of interest, out of the opportunities that life provides when work to sustain itself has been completed. Everyone needs meaningful avocational pursuits to make the quality of life worth living.

INSTANT PLEASURE: THE QUEST OF BORED AND UNIMAGINATIVE PEOPLE

People who are engaged in meaningful work, who have rewarding personal relationships and a vital leisure life, seldom become addicts to overeating or excessive alcohol consumption, or users to excess of such intoxicants as marijuana, LSD, or of various sedative and antidepressant drugs. These indulgences for instant consciousness change are the refuge of the bored, the uninvolved, and the unimaginative. Although intoxicants and overeating have always been part of every culture, their chronicity is usually destructive of health and life itself.

The trouble with and the attraction of food and drugs is that they afford the experience of instant, unmistakable pleasure. When a person's life is dull or stressing, she will seek to enrich it in any way that she can—seeking to produce a "high." There are periods of productivity, stress, and monotony in everyone's existence, but healthy personality is fostered by countering them with the bases for natural highs, that is, with challenging work and play, *Healthy* enjoyment of beauty, and authentic loving and friendly *Personality* relationships with others. As a psychotherapist, I have

364

observed that indulgence in drugs and overeating has carried a person through some difficult times harmlessly enough, but such indulgence becomes destructive when it becomes a life style. Many people get drunk or stoned on marijuana when life has dealt them a hard blow, and then they regain strength and perspective, and return soberly to their tasks, none the worse for the blow or the intoxication. However, there are many other therapists who feel that even casual use of the mind-changing chemicals is detrimental psychologically and physically. In particular, other therapists have reported motivational reductions in frequent users of marijuana; combined with the apparent irresistableness, if not addiction of some of the drugs, the weight seems to be clearly on the side of complete avoidance of chemical agents aimed at change in consciousness, according to these therapists.

Most young people have apparently learned that the hard drugs have at best questionable effects and after-effects. However, many of them staunchly defend marijuana, and arguments to the contrary clearly alienate the two generations represented by students and their parents. A recent view by Archer and Lopata [18] makes available summaries of all known studies on the effects of marijuana. The authors carefully avoid taking sides and suggest rather that emphasis be placed on "an approach that encourages potential users to make an informed choice" (p. 248). Further, they suggest that "there is evidence that marijuana users are often more antisocial, independent, and less achievement oriented than their non-user counterparts" (p. 248).

The rapid spread of drug use during the Vietnam war days and its often disastrous effects upon family unity suggest that positive-experience, "earned" highs, coming from preparation for and successful completion of a project, may be the harder way to joy but may provide a greater payoff in actual positive change in the self-concept.

More leisure time available makes "earned" highs even more important. As the length of the work week diminishes (futurists state that in a few decades, no one will work longer than ten or twenty hours weekly, to keep the economy going), the need for "nonproductive"

Work, Play, and Healthy Personality

365

avocational activity will become more apparent.[19] At the present time, it has been noted that among many factory workers, much leisure time is spent watching television and drinking beer; when the work-week has been shortened, the response has been to watch more television and drink more beer.

Undemanding, entertaining literature, movies, television, and radio programing serve the same function as drugs and overeating; they offer the experience of pleasure without personal effort. They prevent personal growth and the enlargement of awareness of one's possibilities. Thus, blatant pornography, violent, blood-spattering films,[20] and commercial advertising against a background of popular rock music all insure that the audience will not engage in serious thinking about the human condition, including its own.

Healthy personality is not fostered by any of the sources of instant pleasure, although they may make life endurable for a time. Healthy personality *is* fostered by seeking to cultivate meaningful and absorbing ways to spend time apart from work. Independent security in the avocational sphere of existence is displayed by the person who encounters boredom and the opportunity presented by leisure with efforts to learn new skills; new dimensions of appreciation of beauty, both created and natural; new, challenging games and sports to play; and perhaps, most importantly new friends and new passions.

Some Avocational Pursuits

Play is truly a uniquely human characteristic, although there is reason to suspect that animals also engage in play for the sheer hell of it. Not all animal life is spent in the struggle for survival. Anyone who has seen dogs wrestle to get possession of a stick, or otters slide down a bank,[21] or cats chase a ball of string can hardly doubt that they get bored and are looking for fun. But humans can obtain more respite from brute necessity than animals, and, paradoxically enough, they need to find fun or they will sicken. In our society, with the heavy emphasis that has been placed on upward mobility and professional achievement, many people have spent so much time at their ca-

Healthy Personality

366

reers that they have not *taken time* to learn how leisure can be spent. In the following pages, I will offer an overview of some kinds of avocational pursuits.

Sports. The value of sports is that they provide a way to obtain physical exercise in an absorbing way. Most city people lack the opportunity for regular use of their bodies in strenuous ways, and unless they take exercise, they become flabby. It is enriching to master a variety of games as one grows up, so that one can play throughout the life span. Thus, winter and water sports, like skiing, skating, swimming, diving, and sailing can provide solitary and shared play from infancy into old age. An advantage of the more physicaly active sports is that they afford intellectuals with an opportunity to "still their chattering minds" with involving activity. (I have always found it difficult to stop thinking about aspects of my work, so absorbing has it been. A challenging game of handball never fails to turn off obsessive thinking.)

There are so many sports available to anyone, including those that call for expensive quipment, that no one need be without several sports to turn to in various seasons, or when one becomes bored.

Hobbies and Arts. The world of hobbies is inexhaustible. Collecting things, ranging from stones to match covers, has always been rewarding for people. The cultivation of an art—painting, drawing, sculpture, gardening, mastering a musical instrument—develops dimensions of the human possibilities for creating beauty that *should* be developed if we are to broaden our awareness of the possibilities in the world. Jung pointed out how humans overdevelop some of their possibilities as they grow up, earn a living, and raise a family. Hobbies and involvement in some of the arts insures that other, dormant possibilities will be awakened, to enrich the person's experience of her life and her contribution to the lives of her friends. No one is more boring as a companion than a person without interests outside her work.

Sedentary Games. There is an entire world of games to be played alone and with others. Chess and checkers, bridge and rummy, Monopoly, Careers, and Scrabble— all challenge one's wits and afford an opportunity to do something with others besides engage in conversation

367

that may not be challenging, or drink. One outcome of commercial television is that it diverted many youngsters from learning games that could be enjoyed with others.

Nature. Nature can balance a person's way of life. In Chapter 4, I noted that contact with nature is a basic human need. It provides rich recreational and life-giving experience to persons in their leisure time. Backpacking, camping, skiing, bird watching, fishing, and hunting (though animal lovers and conservationists rightly protest) are all ways to be in nature in ways that lift one out of the mechanizing influence and rhythms of customary work.

Being with People. Just being with friends or family to laugh, reminisce, plan, listen to music, walk is one of the most rewarding avocations. The challenge, of course, is to find friends and to establish the kind of mutually confirming personal relationships that makes being with others a source of joy rather than stress (see Chapter 11). Ted Landsman [22] spoke of the "magnification effect" that is produced when one listens to music or watches a sunset with a loved person. Without a loving and confirming relationship, the presence of another person can make one so defensive and "uptight" that the beauties of nature and art cannot be savored. One has to be *open* to appreciate beauty, and a defensive attitude protects one from danger and anesthetizes one to the experience of beauty.

Meditation. Leisure affords an excellent opportunity for meditation. Meditation is a way of leaving or transcending one's everyday situation, in order to get perspective upon one's life, and to see new possibilities in stagnant situations. In recent years, Eastern techniques of meditation have been taught in colleges and at growth centers and institutes around the country. Meditation of any kind—transcendental meditation, Raja yoga, Hatha yoga, and so on—is a valid approach to personal growth and a meaningful way to spend leisure time. [23]

Personal Growth. The growth centers (see Chapter 16) have become a community resource for meaningful use of leisure time. As people come to spend less time earning their living, they experience boredom more readily and become increasingly aware that they have other possibilities than the ones they have cultivated. Growth

Healthy Personality

"guides" or counselors may advise a person to take part in encounter groups or other programs that have been developed to evoke new potentialities in persons. Some centers for personal growth offer weekend or longer, programs, during which people explore themselves and each other, seeking to awaken and confirm new ways to relate to others and to involve themselves in work and play.[24]

Adventure and Excitement. There are many who find meaning in adventurous hobbies, such as ocean racing, mountain climbing, automobile racing, motorcycle racing, sky diving, underwater exploration, and the like. Everyone needs some measure of excitement in their life or it palls with boredom. The element of risk to life and to health must be taken into account when a person chooses a more adventurous avocation. Energetic people, however, find that they must take part in such absorbing activities or they cannot take their mind off regular pursuits.

Helping Others. A rich arena for avocational activity is the realm of helping others, either individually or through some kind of community participation. Volunteer activity at boys' and girls' clubs, at crisis centers, old people's homes, hospitals, all afford the person an opportunity to extend himself or herself, to know the lot of others, and to devote some time and resources to their betterment. There are some who see such involvement in helping to improve others' lives, and the quality of the community, as their civic and religious duty.

Being an Amateur "Professional." For every profession there are amateurs who work at it for the fun of it. There are amateur astronomers, pilots, mechanics, sculptors, biologists, zoologists, physicists, and psychologists. An amateur is someone who does what he or she is doing for the love of it, not for gainful employment. Some great discoveries and contributions to knowledge have been made by amateurs who never made their livelihood at the activity they love. Darwin, for example, was not a professional biologist, in the sense of being salaried by a university or commercial research laboratory, and his contribution to knowledge can hardly be seen as trivial.

Learning and Study. As leisure increases, the impor-

Work, Play, and Healthy Personality

tance of schools and community colleges increases. Some observers have estimated that before the twenty-first century is reached, continuing education will be the most important activity for the world's population—assuming problems of poverty, war, and destruction of the environment have been solved. Perhaps a ceaseless life of learning is the means whereby everyone can renew themselves, find new ways to appreciate the world, and enrich their quality as companions to others. So long as a person has life, he or she can always learn a new language, a new art, a new body of knowledge.

Healthy Personality and Leisure

A rich avocational life yields many benefits of value for healthy personality. Most obvious, it lends balance to life especially when one's vocation calls for specialized use of the self. My work calls for me to be sedentary, and in the experiental mode of thinking (see Chapter 3) I find that competitive games (handball, tennis, water sports) are effective at lending balance to my life, affording an opportunity for release of tension engendered at work.

Another benefit lies in the fact, noted above, that the demands, challenges, and companionship found in one's leisure pursuits foster personal growth in enriching ways. One's regular occupational and household duties call for the development of some human possibilities, but these are in the realm of practical functioning. The beauty of one's hobbies is that they call for the development of aesthetic, athletic, emotional, and intellectual powers that otherwise would remain dormant. So important has the non-job life become that one investigator suggests that there has been an overemphasis on career planning and that there are many other worthy tasks other than the pursuit of money, status, or ease. Arnold [25] points out the need for dedication in one's career or leisure to issues such as self-realization, world peace, population control, and the elimination of poverty, pollution, prejudice.

Some Existential Suggestions

Healthy Personality If you are not fascinated with or passionate about the vocation you are in (or training for), it is valuable to go on a retreat, to seek some perspective, and perhaps some new aspects or opportunities in your work. I find that if I can get completely away from my work for periods of time, I re-enter it renewed. As you plan your career, visit settings and people who are associated with the kind of work you think would hold your interest for a significant length of time. Successful people in all areas are pleased to be approached by a sincere student. Private agencies are offering vocational counseling packages at rates up to $500 per person for a two-day study. You can obtain the same services free at college counseling centers. Take advantage of these vocational counseling services while they are available to you. A good way to familiarize yourself with some jobs is to do volunteer work in agencies related to your choice. Whom do you know who is passionately in love with his or her job? Talk to and get to know such people, regardless of whether or not their work matches yours. It is a deeply meaningful experience to even observe someone who is excited about his or her work.

What are some of your most intense yearnings? Can you identify some of the things you would most like to do in your lifetime—and can you take preliminary steps to accomplish them, regardless of how ambitious they are?

It is enriching, as well, to find leisure activity that is diametrically opposed to one's work in as many ways as possible. When I was a student, I sought part-time jobs at heavy physical labor, I worked on a carnival, in stores, and at a children's camp. The experience these jobs afforded me was enriching, and it counterbalanced the heavy emphasis upon the intellect I found in college. Sedentary people might well balance their existences with hobbies of a more physical sort.

Solitary leisure pursuits are invaluable. One cannot always have company, and so reading, playing a musical instrument, painting, or engaging in some craft are all enriching avocations.

Work, Play,
and Healthy
Personality

SUMMARY

Work and leisure both play important roles in healthy personality. Choice of a vocation especially is important, because it is the means of making a livelihood, and one spends nearly a third of one's life at work. Professional career counseling offers you an opportunity to study your aptitudes and to evaluate your intelligence, personality, achievements, and especially your interests, and to make rational decisions about your future. People choose their work on the basis of parental influence, psychological tests, and sometimes on impulse. Whatever the basis for the initial choice, persons serve the interest of healthy personality if they face the consequences of their choice realistically. If there is little satisfaction in their work they will change it. However, many factors make vocational change difficult, for example, one's sense of identity and other people's expectations.

Women are now faced with the necessity to make many more choices than in the past, and they find that new fields formerly monopolized by men are becoming available. Black teenagers, however, have not yet been sufficiently helped to move into today's labor force and have high unemployment rates. Handicapped persons are finally getting aid in using their abilities in the economic sphere. Retirement can mean death to the older citizen or it can mean the beginning of a new career.

Absorbing avocational pursuits contribute to the enjoyment of life and provide balance to one's working activities. The quest for instant pleasure through drugs, alcohol, or television usually signifies a deficient avocational life. Challenging sports and hobbies, games, relaxation with nature, meditation, pursuit of growth, adventure, company of friends, learning, and study all serve valuable avocational purposes.

NOTES AND REFERENCES

1. Meaningful work is essential for a firm sense of identity. Erikson calls work the "sense of industry." See E. H. ERIKSON, *Identity, Youth and Crisis* (New York: Norton, 1968), pp. 122–128.

2. W. PUTTICK, "A Factor Analysis Study of Positive Modes of Experiencing and Behaving in a Teacher College Population," unpublished doctoral dissertation, University of Florida, 1964.

Healthy Personality

3. Blatz recognized this problem before the age of automation and increased leisure. He insisted that training for "avocation" was as important as vocational training. See W. E. BLATZ, *Understanding the Young Child* (New York: Morrow, 1944).

4. U.S. Department of Labor, *Dictionary of Occupational Titles*, 4th ed. (Washington, D.C.: Government Printing Office, 1976).

5. S. E. BEMIS, R. L. BONNER, T. F. FEARNEY, and and K. G. VON LOBSDORF, "The New Occupational Aptitude Pattern for the GATB," *Vocational Guidance Quarterly*, 1973, Vol. 22, pp. 189–194.

6. For the student who would like to consider career counseling as a career and for the student who would like to know more about the experience of consulting a vocational counselor, two recent books would be useful: L. E. ISAACSON, *Career Information in Counseling and Teaching*, 3rd ed. (Boston: Allyn, 1977); and R. HOPPOCK, *Occupational Information*, 4th ed. (New York: McGraw-Hill, 1976).

7. ISAACSON, *Career Information in Counseling and Teaching*, op. cit., pp. 504–505.

8. A courageous tale of change is seen in a well-written book by a nonguidance-trained writer, who himself wearied of the strain on his family life and on his own body of the tensions as a night editor of the *Atlanta Constitution*. Despite the responsibilities of a large family, he struck out as a free-lance writer. The book is RALPH BUGG, *Job Power* (New York: Pyramid, 1976).

9. BLATZ, op. cit.

10. D. McCLELLAND, *The Achieving Society* (New York: Free Press, 1967). The Greeks called it *areté*, which means, roughly, "courage in battle," or more generally, "prowess"; it was the goal of classical education in ancient Greece. See W. JAEGER, *Paideia: The Ideals of Greek Culture*, Vol. I: *Archaic Greece: The Mind of Athens* (New York: Oxford U. P., 1965).

11. The fascinating social experiment, the Israeli kibbutz, and its relationship to women's satisfaction is unfolded in a scientific study by L. TIGER and J. SHEPHER, *Women in the Kibbutz* (New York: Harcourt, 1975).

12. Grim portents of a yet unsolved social problem are indicated in the report by J. HERBER, "Young, Black and Unemployed," *The New York Times*, March 11, 1979, Vol. 1, p. 44.

13. E. GINZBERG, "The Job Problem," *Scientific American*, November 1977, Vol. 237, pp. 43–51.

14. Rehabilitation Services Administration, *State Vocational Rehabilitation Agency Program Data* (Washington, D.C.: Office of Human Development, 1974).

15. R. ZILLER, "Psychology in Photography," *The Photographer*, Fall 1975, No Vol., p. 7.

16. F. CHICHESTER, *Gypsy Moth Circles the World* (New York: Coward, 1967).

17. See W. HARMON, "Humanistic Capitalism: Another Alternative," *Journal of Humanistic Psychology*, 1974, Vol. 14, pp. 5–32.

18. J. A. ARCHER, JR. and A. LOPATA, "Marijuana Revisited," *Personnel and Guidance Journal*, 1979, Vol. 57, pp. 244–251. This is a most dispassionate, terse summary of research studies and reports and should be useful for a young person considering use or abstinence from such chemical agents.

19. For a perspective on life in the future, see J. C. BROWN, *The Troika Incident* (Garden City, N.Y.: Doubleday, 1970). Brown has explored work, play, family life, and other aspects of human existence as it can be in less than 100 years. His utopian vision seems more feasible and more fit for human beings than Skinner's in *Walden Two*.

20. For a discussion of passive violence watching as a new neurosis, see T. LANDSMAN, "The Humanizer," *American Journal of Orthopsychiatry*, 1974, Vol. 44, pp. 345–352.

21. The late Gavin Maxwell knew the fun and mischief of otters. See G. MAXWELL, *Ring of Bright Water* (New York: Dutton, 1961).

22. T. LANDSMAN, "Positive Experience and the Beautiful Person," presidential address, Southeastern Psychological Association, 1968.

23. C. NARANJO and R. E. ORNSTEIN, *On the Psychology of Meditation* (New York: Viking, 1971).

24. See W. SCHUTZ, *Here Comes Everybody: Bodymind and Encounter Culture* (New York: Harper, 1971) for an exposition of what growth centers can offer. See also JANE HOWARD, *Please Touch* (New York: McGraw-Hill, 1970).

25. D. L. ARNOLD, "Life Purpose and Career Planning," *Character Potential*, 1972, Vol. 6, pp. 12–15.

15

RELIGION AND HEALTHY PERSONALITY

INTRODUCTION

*Religion, spirituality, ethics, morality are all both within
and without the province of even humanistic psychology.
In some aspects, such as guilt, leadership, "followership,"
they influence the personality and potentiality for enhancing the meaningfulness of life; they all intersect with
concerns about the healthy personality. However, it
must be also recognized that religion is a discipline in
and of itself and, in a sense, contains mysteries, demands,
and interpretations that require the explanations of professionals in the field. Thus, in this chapter, we will try
to discuss the healthy personality's participation in spirituality and religion from the psychological viewpoint
and in this existence or world. Discussions concerning
the nature of heaven or hell and of the nature of God
must be the prerogative of priests, ministers, sheiks, mul-
lahs, and rabbis.*

*Earlier we pointed out the significance of commit-
ment of the healthy personality to something beyond*

self—to justice, helping others, political change, a community drive, and so on. One of the greatest of these commitments can be to a deity, a god, or an ethical-religious system. Such a commitment has the possibility of propelling an individual and those about him or her into heights of real ecstasy, great passionate feelings, magnificent works of kindness and beauty. Yet spiritual commitments can also mislead young people into efforts that simply enrich a small group of people, or worse, lead to intensities of hatred, great grief for helpless families in the face of commanding, charismatic leaders, and, as in the case in 1978 in Guyana, to mass suicide. Clearly where one places one's spiritual commitment is crucial to the healthy person.

For millennia, religion provided humans with reasons for continuing to live when living became difficult, and courage to master the hostile forces of untamed nature. These functions of religion are evident among primitive people, and they are also evident in modern, industrialized free societies. Efforts have been made to force people to change their religion under threat of great political or physical pain, as during the Inquisition. Some societies, notably communist Russia, attempted to stamp out religion entirely, but have now switched to relying on the newer generations to be successively less religious.

Religions attempt to provide guides and values with which humans might create a high-level-functioning society. For example, choice is thought of by existentialists as a precondition for humanized existence. In Deuteronomy 30:19 Moses transmits God's message of choice, to gether with the advice concerning which choice would make for a better society: " . . . I have set before thee life and death, the blessing and the curse; therefore, choose life." Then Ten Commandments, the extended accounts of laws, ordinances, and prohibitions contained in Deuteronomy, have been likened to divinely presented instructions to humans in agriculture, ecology, intergroup relationship, family counseling, dietetics, and morale building. The Sermon on the Mount is an explicit lesson on how to live with one's companions. All of these are

Healthy Personality   *efforts toward the perfectability of humans [1] and reveal a hidden hope that such perfection is possible.*

In primitive religions the myths tell of how the world began and how the gods showed the way to hunt, fish, till the soil, live with one another, and make tools and weapons. At sacred times of each year, primitive peoples retell the account of their beginnings and celebrate their good fortune at having been blessed with ancestors who chose to start the world and show them how to live in it. The ways of living in primitive societies are sacred; there is no aspect of life that does not require the blessings of the gods for its success and that is not regulated by strict taboos. Indeed, in such societies, to fail to observe the taboos is to threaten the existence of the group, and so violation is punished by expulsion or death.[2] There is no need for Eskimos to execute someone who does not hunt in the way revealed by their gods. If he does not hunt seals in the way of his people, he will not kill any, and he will die. Eskimos would kill only those who violated taboos about ways to live harmoniously with one another, because these would create group dissension.

Religion in modern life takes many forms,[3] from ancient rituals, such as the Catholic Mass and the Passover Seder, to contemporary meditation, simple "witnessing," and quiet private prayer in one's own home, room, on a mountaintop, or in the middle of a wood. Small cults that practice rare rituals outlawed by state and local laws, such as snake handling, polygamy, or drug-induced hallucinations, are still extant in the free society that is basically reluctant to regulate religious practices.

Modern human beings have desacralized most of their lives, and they have few sacred aspects of their existence. Yet religion underlies much of what we do, including the beliefs of agnostics and atheists, for whom no formal religious symbols are experienced as sacred. Some worship science, some sacralize the state, and some sacralize money. The human is incurably religious. What varies among humans is what they are religious about.

What Is Religion?

Beyond all else, religion is an *experience*, the experience of being in a divine presence, of being called, of elevation of spirit, of ethical obligations too. William James' [4] classic *The Varieties of Religious Experience* gives many accounts of persons who felt their ego dissolve and experienced union with all life, indeed all the universe. The lives of the Christian saints and Hebrew prophets also offer first-person accounts of what it feels like to be spoken to by God, or to believe oneself to be Jahveh's spokesperson.

Religion is also the experience of the sacred and holy. The symbols and representatives of God inspire an attitude of awe and reverence among the faithful adherents to any formal religion. The experience of the sacred involves fear of the power of God, and sometimes an attitude of loving surrender, entrusting one's life to the good will of the deity. [5]

The great religions also function as *ethical systems* for their followers, providing them with instructions in living that are deemed to be of divine origin. The assumption is that if people will live with one another in the ways described in their scriptures or in the oral traditions, then life will be long, fruitful, and peaceful.

Religion provides humans with the definition of *ultimate concern* and value. [6] "God's will" is held to be the highest purpose of living in the Judeo-Christian and Muslim faiths. Some aspects of God's will are explicitly stated in the scriptures of those religions, whereas others are left unclear, calling for guidance from priests, rabbis, and holy persons. Whatever a person takes to be the highest value in life can be regarded as her God, the focus and purpose of her time and life. Thus, a person may devote her life to the accumulation of wealth or the acquisition of political power. She may live for eating, for indulging in sex, or for keeping the love of her parents at all costs. Whatever a person spends her time and effort for, even to the point of endangering her health and her life, can be seen as her equivalent to God, the ultimate concern of concerns. The Old Testament regards such uses and aims of one's life as the gravest sin of all, the sin of *idolatry*. [7]

Many students raised in some various religious traditions abandon them when they attain the capacity for independent thought and criticism. After taking courses

Healthy Personality

378

in psychology, sociology, and comparative religion, they find that what their parents or the clergy presented as absolute truth was not "necessarily so." Indeed, some students find that the Bible has been used to justify outright tyranny, as in the case of white exploitation of black peoples and the anti-Semitic attitudes of bigoted Christians. After reading and discussion, many students come to see the faith of their childhood and of their parents as superstition and as an obstacle to life itself. Others take up modernized versions of their childhood, familial faith and continue to share this experience with their parents and their extended family. Some even choose more fundamental practices of their parental religion (such as Hasidism) as a reaction to a lack of spirituality in their parental families. Yet religion of some form is part of the human condition. One does not have the choice between being religious or not. One only chooses what one will be religious about, and the ways in which one will be religious.

Religion is thus a *way of being*. To act religiously means that one will not let anything interfere with the action in question. The primitive person would never consider living an any way other than the way of his people, which he believes was taught by the founding gods. Even to think about some other way of relating to parents than the prescribed way would inspire dread. The experience of dread is the anticipation of some unspeakable punishment and death for violating a taboo. Many supposedly nonreligious students do things religiously, such as take exercise, study their textbooks, or pursue popularity, motivated by vague feelings of dread.

Everyone begins his life indoctrinated with the religion of his family and community. The family religion is part of the "facticity" that each person has to do something with, as he must do something with all other aspects of his situation. He can acquiesce and follow in his religious tradition, ignore it, change it, rebel against it—but as in all other existential situations, he is free to take a stand. His personal religious orientation, like his *Religion* conscience, becomes his responsibility. We can speak, *and Healthy* then, of personal religious orientation as an achievement *Personality* and a challenge. Further, we can evaluate whether a person's religious orientation is conducive to growth and to satisfaction in living, or whether it is an impediment to healthy personality. Some students may prefer to use the term *philosophy of life* rather than religion, because the latter term may signify a belief in a supreme being, and they prefer to be atheistic or agnostic. For our purposes, it does not matter, because we are using the term *religion* in a way that reconciles any contradiction between belief in a God as such and a philosophy of living that a person follows religiously, as his view of the good life.

A religious orientation is healthy if it enhances life and fosters growth of one's powers as a human being, including the power to love, to be productive and creative. Thus, no matter whether a person be Christian, Jew, Muslim, Hindu, or Buddhist, the criterion of whether her religion is healthy is provided not by the piety and scrupulousness of her ritual observances, but by its effect upon life. Is she a vital, loving, strong, growing person who does not diminish others? Or is her piety accompanied by prudery, inability to love others, and lack of joy in living? I have often served as a psychotherapist to the clergy and members of their families. I found that much of the suffering was a direct outcome of their need to *appear* pious before themselves and others. The action essential to make their lives more livable was initially experienced by them as sinful. Actually, their religion, the object of their ultimate concern, was not God so much as a "respectable" appearance, in the name of which they were sacrificing the joy and vitality of their lives. Some members of the clergy felt they could only begin to live religious lives, that is, lives that served their God (life itself, not a church, or a church organization) if they left the organized church. And so they did.

Idolatry: Unhealthy Personal Religions

In the times portrayed in the Old Testament, idolatry was taken to be the ultimate sin.[8] Idolatry meant worshiping and living for the products of human hands, or natural objects—in any case, gods that are less than the "one and true God" (Jehovah, or Jahveh). In an effort

Healthy Personality

to demystify some aspects of the Judaic and Christian faiths, I have tried, as an hypothesis, to replace the word *God* with the word *Life*, or Life itself. Thus, where the Old Testament might say, "God spoke to Moses," I would restate is as "Life 'spoke' to Moses." This is another way of saying that Moses, in a moment of keen insight and ultimate concern, "saw" the connection between some way of living and the flowering or destruction of life itself. "Idolatry" would mean equating some part of life with *all* of life. Thus, no animal, stone, place, or person could merit "worship"—living in ways to enhance the "God"—without peril to the worshiper. If idolatry was a "sin," then a sin must mean action that destroys life, if not at once, then ultimately. Indeed, the word *sin* means "off the mark," as in archery when the bowman is aiming and shooting inaccurately. A more contemporary interpretation of sin would be "off the beam"—as an airplane straying off the radar track.

True devotion to God would mean "living in a life-giving way." Sentences like "God loves a repentant sinner" would mean that, if a person had been living in a sickening, even lethal way, then to repent would mean to "turn," to stop living in a destructive way. Such cessation of devitalizing ways of life would instantly start a healing process—which may account in part for "miracle" cures and faithhealing. If the sinner then lived in a more vitalizing way, he would enjoy abundant health and a more richly livable existence. In this way, I can see a connection between the religious teachings of the Jewish and Christian bibles and the secular principles of healthy personality.

The secular problem, of course, is akin to the formal religious problem of how to discern what God, or Life itself, demands of a person if "God's will is to be done," or if life itself is to be enhanced. Authoritarian answers, learned by rote from some scriptural source, or from some member of the clergy, may not be viable guides to action, nor do they foster growth in the persons dependent upon such authority for guidance. There is some doubt also as to whether church attendance alone is characteristic of the self-actualizing person. One study, using Shostrom's POI test, found higher scores for the nonat-

Religion and Healthy Personality

tenders on inner-directedness, existentiality, feeling re-activity, and capacity for intimate contact.[9] Clearly, to live in the way demanded by life itself calls for continuous independent study and learning, for growth of the abilities to perceive, think, reason, and see connections between one's condition and ways of living. Thus, a person whose life is blocked or vexed by disease, failure, stagnation, or other decrements of vitality must enlarge his perspective to see vitalizing ways out of the dilemma. Authentic prayer to God works for some. When they say they prayed, and God "showed them the way out," what happened was that the act of "surrender" involved in dialogue with the deity enabled a person to suspend his present perspective and experience a larger view (see Chapter 3).

It would be elegant if the experience of vitality functioned as a steady beam in the background of a person's awareness, so that she could swiftly notice when her experience and action were sapping her life. She could then change something in her situation before she sickened. Reich believed that persons had the capacity to "tune in" to their vital energy to avoid devitalizing relationships and roles. The re-embodying techniques mentioned in Chapter 7 can serve this function by enhancing sensitivity to the body.

Idolatry of grades or of popularity has produced suffering among many students. They pursue these goals at the expense of their health and of close, loving relationships with others. I have served as therapist to students who failed to develop a single close friendship during several years at college, so obsessed were they with the necessity to maintain a straight-A average.

A love affair becomes idolatrous, ceasing to engender and enhance life for the lovers and others when its pursuit results in the neglect of true interests on the part of one or the other of the lovers. A true interest is any activity, relationship, or object that is essential to life, and the neglect of which diminishes life. Thus, a student might enter an affair which at first lends zest to the existence of the lovers. When continuation results in neglect of work, when jealousy and possessiveness endanger health, then to continue the affair is to neglect true

Healthy Personality

interests. The affair has become idolatrous, destructive to life.

Suicide and Bases for Existence

Suicide is illegal in our society, and it is regarded as contrary to the teachings of the Judeo-Christian religions. There are times when to give up one's life or to take it can be seen as the most meaningful and loving action a person can undertake, as an expression of the affirmation of life. Thus, in times of war a person may give up his life to save many others. It is not that such a hero detests his life; rather he sees that he can fulfill the meaning of his life best in that situation by giving it up so that others may live. Some suicides can also be seen as expressions of the affirmation of life, as when an elderly person chooses to die rather than face years of invalidism, pain, and loneliness.

A person may come to equate her present identity with the only basis that she has for the possibility of living at all. It is as if she is saying to herself, "The only way in which I know that I can exist, and that I deserve to exist, is if I have the love of my parents, or if I get the highest grades, or if I am loved by that man." The problem with such flimsy bases for identity as warrants for existence is that when the parental love is taken away, the affair breaks up, or a course is failed, the person becomes convinced that she can no longer live at all. She may then attempt suicide. When someone has been seen by the community as an honest person and she is proven to have stolen sums of money that have been entrusted to her, she may commit suicide rather than acknowledge to the world that she has been living under false pretenses.

The wish to be dead thus can function as a test of the life-giving power of one's personal religion or philosophy. If it is a healthy religion, a person will be able to find new possibilities in life even when she has lost that which had previously given life its zest.

Religion, Guilt, and Humanistic Conscience

The voice of the conscience is *guilt;* for some it speaks in a whisper and for others it is a commanding shout.

The concept and its forms earns almost two full pages of definitions in the classic Oxford English Dictionary.[10] There are those who would dedicate a good portion of their lives to its claims upon them. May [11] has suggested that neurotic guilt, that related to unnecessary, unearned, imagined guilt be separated from real guilt. And neurotic guilt is, of course, what most psychotherapists must deal with. However, the healthy personality in many instances must deal with real guilt and at times it proves as elusive and ephemeral as its maladjusted mate. Perhaps one may distinguish at least three points of view toward real guilt and conscience:

1. That guilt may be clearly defined as the consequences of disobeying any lawful authority (parents, police, government), and this often includes self-selected moral authorities. It is an absolute position, simple in its statement but complex in its utilization because the potentialities for being overwhelmingly governed by guilt are considerable. Those who choose this position are severely vulnerable to the guilt-givers, who delight in transmitting and magnifying guilt in others.

2. A second position centers about the concept of a humanistic conscience. Steady contact with one's sense of vitality and enlivenment, functions as the basis of humanistic conscience.[12] It will be recalled that humanistic conscience functions as a "call" to desist from some way of living that was "sinful" ("disobedient" to the laws of life), or off the beam, and a moral command to "come round right." If authoritarian sources of conscience have truly been replaced by a humanistic conscience, a person can then entrust his experience of guilt to guide him in ways of living that insure healthy personality. Authoritarian conscience refers to moral precepts that have been taken uncritically from parents and clergy; conforming with these precepts engenders diminished life. Thus, to a person still afflicted beyond childhood with an authoritarian conscience, sin would be defined as violation of taboos, and virtue as obedience (to authority, not to life), without reasonable consideration of whether the taboos have any relevance or contribution to the quality of life. The person who has achieved a *Healthy* health-engendering humanistic conscience has a different *Personality* sense of sin and guilt. Guilt is engendered when he di-

minishes life in himself and others, not when he violates some rule imposed upon him by his parents, through the medium of an authoritarian conscience. The latter represents another kind of "idol," obedience to which diminishes life.

The words to a hymn attributed to the Shakers (a now nearly defunct Christian sect that flourished in the late nineteenth century in the United States) express the concept of sin and of humanistic conscience in a beautiful way. The irony is that the Shakers died out because they did not believe in sexual intercourse; the articles of their religious faith were authoritarian and nonlife-giving, despite the hymn:

Simple Gifts

'Tis a gift to be simple, 'tis a gift to be free
'Tis a gift to come down, where we ought to be
And when we find ourselves in the place just right
We will be in the valley of love and delight.
When true simplicity is gained
To bow and to bend we will not be ashamed
To turn, turn, will be our delight
'Til by turning, turning, we come round right. [my italics]

3. A third position, also humanistic, suggests that guilt is the moral equivalent of pain and that it signals to the person when some behavior of hers has hurt someone else, is "wrong" in terms of her own moral code, and needs to be righted. As such, it needs to be listened to by the healthy personality in the same way we suggest you listen to your body, to signals indicating the health or sickness in the physical realm. "Wiping out" of the guilt does not ordinarily come from psychotherapy, but rather from sincere efforts on the part of the guilt-conscious person to correct the wrong, seek forgiveness, or make peace with one's self when neither of these is possible. Within this position is included the possibility not only of forming one's own ethical and moral code, as is implied in the second position, but also permits the introjection, "taking into one's self," of moral principles from other sources, such as parents, friends, or more likely, ethical positions derived over ages and often en-

Religion and Healthy Personality

coded in biblical or near-biblical sources, such as religious authorities, Talmudic decisions, and so on. This point of view continues to differ from the humanistic conscience position, in that the person does not take full responsibility herself for knowing the reasons behind some ethical principles, but acknowledges the possibility that some principles, only those truly time-tested for ages, rather than years, may hold some considerable truth for today.

Religion, Attitude Toward Death, and Healthy Personality

Only humans, among all living creatures, can know they will die. A person may experience death as an abstract concept that has no connection with his life and no influence upon the way that he lives. He may live his life routinely, giving no thought to the way in which he spends his days. Existential philosophers designate such automatic, unreflective lives as inauthentic. According to these philosophers, *authentic* existence begins when one's own death becomes a reality, when a person encounters death in some inescapable way such that after the realization, he knows his years are finite. It often takes serious illness or a nearly fatal accident to give vivid meaning to death. Such experiences confront a person with the challenge to *choose*, to decide how he will spend his life, where he will live it, with whom he will live, and how he will make his living. Death forces a person to question the meaning of life in general, and of his own life in particular. Many people make radical changes in their lives following the encounter with death, such as marrying or divorcing, changing jobs, spending more time with children or in nature, than they had hitherto.

Death is so inexplicable and so terrifying for many that they repress all awareness of it; they refuse to think about the death of parents or friends, and they may believe vigorously in a life after death, so that death will "lose its sting." Although hopes for an afterlife in some version of Heaven may give comfort to people whose actual lives are dismal, such hopes make people resign themselves to miserable conditions that could conceivably be ameliorated.

Healthy Personality

One of my students, Sharon Graham, did an experiment to explore the relationship between attitude toward death and styles of interpersonal relationship. She found that college students who believed in some form of afterlife did not enter relationships in ways as intense and mutually self-revealing as did students who accepted the reality and finality of their personal deaths. It was as if, because they had acknowledged that they would die, they could not waste time in trivial or superficial personal relationships.[13]

One's personal religion, if it functions to foster and maintain healthy personality, can be expected to help a person live authentically with the fact of her death. A healthy religious philosophy should encourage her to live decisively, intensely, and in growth-promoting ways. There is life-giving value in a religion that provides comfort and meaning to life when suffering and death must be experienced; however, it is an unhealthy religion, indeed, that functions only as a tranquilizer and does not encourage a person to live fully and with growing awareness in the time she has.

The reality of death is even denied in hospitals, where physicians and nurses frequently conceal the imminence of death from patients with terminal conditions. Thus, the patient is denied the opportunity to encounter death while she is still conscious and able to give structure and meaning to the life behind her. Elizabeth Kübler-Ross,[14] a Chicago psychiatrist, pioneered a seminar on dying, in an effort to help clergy, doctors, and nurses to handle their own fears of death, so that they, in turn, could help dying patients face death in noninfantile fashion.

The healthy personality faces two challenges with the concept of death: understanding and accepting (1) his or her own death and (2) the deaths of others, particularly of friends and family members. Thanatologists, specialists in death and dying, chide our culture for being unwilling to countenance or encounter death. With regard to the latter, Feder[15] wryly observes, "I don't have an idea how we help a person to die, but I am sure we can do much to help a person to live until the time of death" (p. 437).

Much has been made recently about death with dignity. Such dignity is essentially as chosen and wished by the patient. One patient may wish to be surrounded by family, another only to be with a particular person who may not be the closest relative legally, and another may choose to be entirely alone. St. Christopher's hospice is an institution near London dedicated to the care of the dying and the long-term sick. Dr. Cicely Saunders, its medical director, describes simply the dignified death of an independent man.[16]

> Mr. A., a brick layer of 61, came to the ward after Mr. P. left us. He was not very keen to let anyone into his flat, where he lived alone, protecting his independence even from his daughter. Throughout the weeks of his stay in St. Christopher's we had to help him maintain his fight for independence. Short of breath as he was, he would stump up and down the stairs to the garden or the Pilgrim Room, pausing to look very critically at the progress of the Play Group Wing building on the way. He made many friends and established himself as escort and guide to a blind patient in his bay. His relationships with the other patients were often colourful but always kind. Bed was definitely not on his schedule and he sat out beside it till his last day surrounded by the *Daily Mirror,* well spread out, ashtrays with endless cigarette ends and ash everywhere. On his last day, he was still in charge, dictating what he would let us give him and very much himself. In the evening, he checked that Sister had his sons' phone numbers correctly. When the night nurses came on he said, "I may give you trouble tonight." He died quietly in his sleep early next morning.

Religion, Culture Change, and Healthy Personality

Healthy Personality

Every person learns from his predecessors how to relate to others in "the right way," the way that is sacred; he learns, not just how to till the soil, hunt, fish, wear clothes, raise children, but how to do these things *in the way of his family, or his people.* These ways are deemed

388

sacred, not to be questioned, much less altered, because in being sacred they are held to be ways commanded by God or the gods, and hence essential to life itself. This is the authoritarian religion of which Erich Fromm wrote. So long as a group lives in a stable physical environment, with unchanging technology and resources, the traditional, religiously lived ways may be compatible with survival of the group and a rich, meaningful life for individuals. But when society changes, crises arise for the society as a whole and for individual members. The traditional way of life that gave meaning and direction to individual existence may become an obstacle to survival in the changed circumstances facing the group. Traditional ways and values interfere with new learning essential for adaptation to the changed times for some young people. But the new ways may be deemed sinful from the perspective of the traditional religion. Thus, immigrants to America often found themselves scandalized at their children's "immorality" as they became acculturated. For others, traditional religious values provide stability and security in the midst of social change.

In developing countries facing industrialization and overpopulation as in India or Indonesia, the young people are addressed by the challenge and temptations of a way of life made possible by modern technology, but the clutch of tradition and traditional religion produces powerful conflict. In contemporary America, children born after World War II have lived in a world of increased affluence and technological magic, so that television and world travel by cheap jet transportation are a normal part of their existence. The possibilities for living in ways that differ from their parents' have increased radically. And so young people, especially of the age of high school and college students, face conflicts between tradition, in the form of parental expectations, and the realities of their present situation. Traditional religions in the West have not been helpful in the solution of the problem of how to live.

Religion and Healthy Personality

Healthy personality calls for a sense of values and meaning in life that give existence a purpose. Rapid cultural change challenges institutionalized authoritarian religions. Many young people in America have begun to explore native American Indian religions, such as the Peyote cults, and Eastern religions, such as Hinduism, yoga, and Buddhism, for guidance in their lives. Others are exploring mystical branches of traditional faiths, such as Hasidism within Judaism, Sufism—a mystical branch of Islamic faith—astrology, the I Ching, tarot. Others become "reborn Christians" and dedicate themselves fervently to following in the ways of Jesus Christ. All these current explorations of guides to existence can be seen as expressions of a sense of uncertainty about how to live in the midst of changing times.

For some whose parents were themselves removed from spirituality or their own traditional religions, a return in greater depth to the religions of their ancestors provided contentment and satisfaction for the spiritual hunger and for the yearning for an identification over the ages with an eternal deity.

MYSTICISM AND HEALTHY PERSONALITY

People turn to mysticism when traditional ways of life are no longer possible because of catastrophe, conquest by another people, or the effects of technology. Mystical religions and practices can function as sources of creativity and inventive ways to live. They also can encourage a kind of anti-intellectual attitude, a distrust of reason that ultimately proves disastrous. There is mystery in life, and rational thinking is not always a reliable way to solve riddles of existence. Mystical practices may indeed enable a person to tap sources of creativity buried within her, so that problems of existence can be solved as if by inspiration. If mystical practices eventuate in more creative ways to live, then they are compatible with healthy personality. If they serve as evasions of responsibility for the search for viable ways, so that a person depends upon her horoscope or some equally impersonal guide to choice, then she is replacing one rigid religion with another. Her health and personal growth are not likely to be fostered through such dependency. There is no alternative to a personal search for meaning and direction when traditional guides to existence have been outdated by changing times. Although the search is seldom easy, no one can do it for another person, any more than someone else can do one's own dying.

Healthy Personality

Religion and Cultism

In some instances, the yearning for spirituality has been so insistent and the pain of the present so pervasive that young people are drawn to the colorful, hypnotic leadership of cults. Many of these groups are oriental in origin, but some, such as the People's Temple in California and Guyana, are entirely domestic. Poverty-stricken blacks who have always found comfort, if not material support, from religion, were particularly drawn to the People's Temple promises of a new economy in a new Christianity. The madness of the cult's leader, Jim Jones, was seen as religious fervor, and over 900 members followed him in frightful mass suicide. In other cults such extremism is avoided, but other, similarly blind loyalties are demanded, plus money, gifts, mindless mouthing of slogans, constant repetitions of simple statements of blind faith, and perhaps most distasteful, constant badgering of possible recruits into the cult with threats of eternal damnation and promises of equally eternal bliss.

As indicated in earlier chapters, any person drawn to such cults must first ascertain his or her own intellectual and emotional freedom—is the choice to join or not a free one, uninfluenced by either promises or threats? Can your mind stay free? Can you leave easily and immediately? Are both the doctrines and the behavior of group members free of racist hatred and self-glorification of one group above another? Further, the dangers of commitment are such that any young person caught up in a fervor to join should at least give himself or herself a cooling-off period of several months before becoming a member. Like many good things in life, overindulgence in religious fervor can be irremediably destructive. The enormous amount of fakery in cultist religion, its irrationality and demand for mindless loyalty, has brought renewed interest in traditional religions that have withstood the test of time and that have learned how to cope with frauds from within. A healthy person may well be one with a deep spirituality, and is someone who has chosen a method of expression of that spirituality with exquisite care. A healthy spirituality may be discovered in many religions, Buddhism, Christianity, Hinduism, Islam, and Judaism, among others.

Religion and Healthy Personality

Sick people do not always respond to conventional medical treatment and some turn in desperate hope to religious systems of healing, or to healers who work from the standpoint of a different theory of illness and its treatment. The Catholic shrine at Lourdes, in France, attracts millions who make the pilgrimage there in search of a medical miracle. Many regain their health, or at least arrest the lethal development of the symptoms that brought them to their quest. Members of the clergy are consulted by the gravely ill, to pray with and for them, that they may overcome their diseases and gain new hope and life. From time to time, new healers with extraordinary powers appear and gain a following.

Evangelizing clergy often carry out healing ceremonies, characterized by prayer and the laying on of hands. Laypeople abound who discover that they can heal by a touch, or a massage, and that they see an "aura" of diverse color emanating from the body, which changes magnitude and hue with changes in health.

I have never seen an aura, which does not mean it does not exist. I retain an open mind about the more (to me) astonishing aspects of healing through faith, but I hold to a theory of illness that helps me to make sense out of confirmed instances of healing through prayer, ritual, and the healer's charisma.

According to this view, people sicken because they do not "live right," as one faith healer puts it. When ill, they are frightened, and frequently without hope. The initiation of an attitude of hope is itself healing, or it initiates the healing reflexes. Anyone that arouses hope and faith will arrest a progressive disease and permit healing to begin. If the sick person will then change her life from the style that engendered her disease to one that is more life-giving, then she will not only regain her health, but she will keep it. One faith healer insists that patients must change their lives if they are to stay healthy.

This rationale appears to underlie the Christian Science system of healing. The emphasis upon understanding how one has become sickened, the mobilization of hope, *Healthy* and the changing of style of life from one that sickened *Personality* to one that heals appears to be a common denominator in

392

the nonmedical healing approaches. Probably in those cases where such treatment is both effective and harmless, it accounts for healing brought on by conventional medical intervention too.

I believe that as more research is done, medical approaches to healing will be altered in the direction of the religious ways, so that pharmaceutical and surgical methods will increasingly be replaced by rest, meditation, and alteration of life style to one that engenders and maintains health.[17]

Religion and a Good Society

A person's religious orientation, if it is to foster healthy personality, must be re-examined at various stages in life. Children begin life with an authoritarian religious orientation. If they are growing persons, they will eventually come to doubt and challenge the arbitrariness of the taboos and commandments that comprise this faith. As individuals learn about life, it is to be expected that they will modify their religious views in the light of reason. Many people simply replace one orthodoxy with another, when their faith in the first has been shaken. Thus, an authoritarian Baptist may become converted to Judaism or Catholicism and be more strict in ritual observance than persons reared in those faiths. Some students abandon their family religious tradition and pursue astrology, psychology, transcendental meditation, or yoga with the same fanaticism and lack of critical perspective they showed toward the family faith. If one's religious orientation is health- and growth-engendering, then it will prove itself by its consequences. The test of one's religion is in the quality of existence that it evokes, in the meaning it gives to life, and in the life-enhancing effect it has in the midst of life itself. Religion, in its truest sense, is a relentless *search* for life. Organized religion—the churches—frequently provide *answers*, and interfere with, even prevent, the search.

Religion and Healthy Personality

History is a record of oppressive social and political systems in which masses of people were exploited in cruel, dehumanizing ways. History likewise provides accounts of the way in which organized religion did noth-

393

ing to encourage exploited people to act courageously and intelligently to improve their lot. The history of the majority of today's faiths yields at least some evidence to show that their official leadership often colluded with the political leadership to maintain the political and economic status quo. The orthodox church of czarist Russia did little to reduce the aristocrats' exploitation of workers and peasants, and in World War II persons of the same faith slaughtered each other, presumably in the conviction that God was on their side.

Healthy personality calls for enlightened perspectives upon the society within which one lives, and it calls for active engagement in providing social conditions suitable for humans to live and to develop their potentialities. If personal religion does not encourage one to grow in understanding of society, and to protest unjust policies, then it is no more than a tranquilizer; it is then the "opium of the masses," as Marx saw it, or culturally shared compulsion neurosis, which Freud maintained it was.

One of the functions of organized religion should be to produce heaven on earth. In less ornate language, this means striving to find ways to govern and to organize society in ways that are just. Justice, in this sense, means that everyone has the opportunity to realize their possibilities as human beings, no matter what their class, religious or ethnic origins, or sex. In a sense, religion is a quest for, and offers a vision of, a utopia.

UTOPIAS, CHURCHES, AND HEALTHY PERSONALITY

There have been many efforts to describe utopian societies, for example, Samuel Butler's *Erewhon*, Plato's *Republic*, Aldous Huxley's nightmare utopia *Brave New World*, and George Orwell's chilling vision of life in *1984*. Even Hitler's view of society, as described in *Mein Kampf*, was a kind of utopia for Germans, but not, of course, for the victims of the Nazi regime he organized. Canaan, the promised land, was to be utopia for the ancient Hebrews. B. F. Skinner described a utopian society in *Walden Two* organized along lines suggested by his theories of human conditioning. James Brown has described how the world might be in 2070 A.D. in his novel *The Troika Incident*. The student is encouraged to read as much of the utopian literature as he or she can find, because everyone is a utopian thinker, implicitly or explicitly; everyone affirms some view of the good life in a good society, and one should be informed about the way some good thinkers have portrayed these.

The trouble with utopias is that one person's heaven is another person's hell. A way to organize society, distributing resources and wealth in order to enrich the life of one group, produces tyranny, mystification, and exploitation for another. A male-dominated society may be utopian for men in our culture, but it hardly pleases those women who have become aware of limitations imposed on them because of their sex. South Africa produced a near-utopian society for white native-born Afrikaaners, but the more than 15 million blacks hardly see the policy of apartheid as utopian for them.

The challenge for organized religion and churches is to examine whether their preaching has contributed to economic and political regimes that are just and utopian for *all* sectors of the population. Throughout history, churches have taken sides with the ruling elite, in opposition to larger sectors of the population, which have felt themselves unjustly exploited. There is no record of protest from church officials at the annihilation of Aztec, Inca, Mayan, or North American Indian cultures and religions. The Christian utopian view was not utopian for the "natives." A religious denomination and its church is compatible with healthy personality if it champions and works for the establishment of a just society in which none feels exploited, because none is, and where the means to foster healthy personality and the fullest personal growth are available to all.

Those who attend churches and synagogues can work toward the "de-dogmatizing" of official church positions on contemporary affairs. There was hardly a ripple of comment when a news item issued by a Protestant church economic council appeared showing that the organized Protestant churches in the United States had investments of over $300 million in prime war industries—at a time when the United States was involved in the Vietnam war.

The so-called Protestant ethic, which affirms the virtue

Religion and Healthy Personality

of hard work, postponement of pleasure, and accumulation of capital, is itself under challenge by growing numbers of people. The character structure that made the development of the capitalist economy possible is incompatible with living in the affluent society that that "driven" character type produced. The antisensuality of the Protestant ethic is the special target of several authors who were reared in that world view, for example, Thomas Hanna (*Bodies in Revolt*), Sam Keen (*To a Dancing God*), Norman O. Brown (*Love's Body*), and Michael D. Lowman (*The Phoenix*). The religiosity with which human energy and natural resources were dedicated to the expansion of capital destroys the quality of life for many, and so Protestantism itself is under serious re-examination, in order to undo the apparent collusion between political and economic systems and church doctrine.[18]

So long as there is poverty, exploitation of people, and destruction of the environmental conditions for life, there is ample challenge to everyone's religion to seek to make the world and its myriad societies a place where healthy personality is possible for everyone.

In contrast, during the agonies of efforts to obtain first-class citizenship for blacks in the United States, a small number of clergy of all faiths, black and white, in the South and in the North, risked, and in many cases, lost their pulpits, through their preachings in favor of integration. Many dedicated Christians risked their lives, and in many instances lost their lives, in efforts to hide Jews from the Nazis during World War II. One of the most deeply moving descriptions of great risk undertaken through such religious motivation is described by Corrie ten Boom [19] in the book *The Hiding Place*. The ten Boom family, deeply Christian in its commitment, was, with the lone exception of Miss ten Boom, completely wiped out by the Nazis for protecting Dutch Jews.

Some Existential Suggestions

Healthy Personality Institutionalized religion can become more institutionalized than life-giving to the persons it is supposed to serve. It is enlightening for people to learn about religions

396

other than the ones in which they were reared. If they have prejudices and misinformation about other faiths, they will be serving the interests of healthy personality by correcting their misconceptions and outgrowing their prejudices.

It is especially good to learn about Eastern religions, as their influence spreads from the East to this hemisphere. It is rewarding to reread the Old and New Testaments as a grown person, struggling to identify with the perspectives of Moses, Jesus, and the various prophets, as an exercise in historical and sociological imagination.

At the same time, it is equally important for the young person to obtain an in-depth understanding of his or her own religion before making commitments to others. Take time to thoroughly familiarize yourself with the tenets, beliefs, and also changes that have occurred over time.

Visits to other religious group services are almost universally welcomed by churches, synagogues, and mosques when undertaken with serious motives.

Take time, periodically, to "consult" your own internal spirituality, to repair it with meditation, prayer, or rational thought, and consider ways to enliven this often-neglected aspect of the self.

SUMMARY

Religion provides humans with reasons for living, with a system of ethics, with the experience of the sacred, with a focus for ultimate concern. A religious orientation contributes to healthy personality if it enhances life and fosters growth of one's capacities to love and grow.

Idolatry, in contemporary life, means living for something less than life itself, for example, for success, wealth, or one's family. One's religion is idolatrous if it does not provide daily existence with life-giving challenge and meaning. One needs to safeguard one's own existential freedom from cults. A healthy religion enables a person to live decisively and to face death with courage. It preserves human values during times of culture change. There is healing power in profound religious faith. A healthy religion does not collude with the ruling elite of

Religion
and Healthy
Personality

a nation, but instead helps people struggle to achieve a just society.

NOTES AND REFERENCES

1. A distinguished philosopher explores a theme critical to humanistic psychology and a synonym for healthy personality in a manner of speaking in J. PASSMORE, *The Perfectability of Man* (New York: Scribner's, 1970).

2. See M. ELIADE, *The Sacred and the Profane: The Nature of Religion* (New York: Harper, 1961). This book was an eye-opener for me and taught me much about religion as experience of the sacred.

3. One of the most readable, yet accurate, descriptions of a number of religious approaches is presented in E. K. THOMPSON (Ed.), *The World's Great Religions* (New York: Time Incorporated, 1957). This is part of the Time-Life series of publications.

4. W. JAMES, *The Varieties of Religious Experience* (New York: Macmillan, 1961). (Originally published in 1902.)

5. ELIADE, op. cit.; R. ORRO, *The Experience of the Holy* (New York: Oxford U. P., 1958).

6. P. TILLICH, *Systematic Theology*, 3 volumes (Chicago: U. of Chicago, 1963).

7. E. FROMM, *You Shall Be as Gods: A Radical Interpretation of the Old Testament and Its Tradition* (New York: Holt, 1966), pp. 44 ff. See also his *Psychoanalysis and Religion* (New Haven: Yale U. P., 1950).

8. My debt to Fromm, in this discussion, is obvious. See FROMM, op. cit. I have also been influenced by Martin Buber's writings. See M. BUBER, *Eclipse of God: Studies in the Relation Between Religion and Philosophy* (New York: Harper, 1957); *Two Types of Faith: A Study of the Interpenetration of Judaism and Christianity* (New York: Harper, 1961).

9. The POI, or "Personal Orientation Inventory," is one of the few standardized tests available to measure self-actualization. The study referred to is R. LEE and F. P. PIERCY, "Church Attendance and Self-Actualization," *Journal of College Student Personnel*, 1974, Vol. 15, pp. 400–403.

10. *Oxford English Dictionary* (New York: Oxford U. P., 1971), pp. 496–497.

11. R. MAY, *The Meaning of Anxiety*. (New York: Ronald, 1950).

12. FROMM, *Psychoanalysis and Religion*, op. cit.; *Man for Himself* (New York: Holt, 1947).

13. SHARON GRAHAM, quoted in S. M. JOURARD, *Self-disclosure: An Experimental Analysis of the Transparent Self* (New York: Wiley-Interscience, 1971), Chapter 21.

14. E. KÜBLER-ROSS, *On Death and Dying* (New York: Macmillan, 1970); A. STRAUSS and B. G. GLASER, *Awareness of Dying* (Chicago: Aldine, 1965).

15. S. L. FEDER, "Attitudes of Patients with Advanced Malignancy," in E. S. SCHNEIDMAN (Ed.), *Death: Current Perspectives* (Palo Alto, Calif.: Mayfield, 1976), pp. 430–438.

16. C. SAUNDERS, "St. Christopher's Hospice," in E. S. SCHNEIDMAN (Ed.), *Death: Current Perspectives*, op. cit., pp. 516–523.

17. Christian Science, of course, is the best-known non-medical system of healing in the United States, where it was founded by Mary Baker Eddy. A review of current shamanistic healing practices around the world is given in A. KIEV (Ed.), *Magic, Faith, and Healing: Studies in Primitive Psychiatry Today* (New York: Free Press, 1964). I think the "psychic surgeons," like Tony Agpao, are authentic healers, but their "surgery" is sleight of hand. I don't know about de Freitas' ability to stick a knife into someone's body, apparently doing surgery without sanitary precautions. See the personal account by ANNE DOOLEY, "Psychic Surgery in Brazil," *Psychic*, 1973, Vol. 4, pp. 22–38.

18. S. BUTLER, *Erewhon* (London, 1872; numerous reprints); F. M. CORNFORD (Trans.), *The Republic of Plato* (London: Oxford U. P., 1941); A. HUXLEY, *Brave New World* (New York: Harper, 1932); G. ORWELL, *1984* (New York: Harcourt, 1949); A. HITLER, *Mein Kampf* (Boston: Houghton, 1943); B. F. SKINNER, *Walden Two* (New York: Macmillan, 1948); J. C. BROWN, *The Troika Incident* (Garden City, N.Y.: Doubleday, 1970); T. HANNA, *Bodies in Revolt* (New York: Holt, 1970); S. KEEN, *To a Dancing God* (New York: Harper, 1970); N. O. BROWN, *Love's Body* (New York: Random, 1966); M. D. LOWMAN, *The Phoenix: An Existential and Conceptual Account of Personal Growth* (Boulder, Colo.: Shields, 1974).

19. C. TEN BOOM, with J. and E. SHERRILL, *The Hiding Place* (Old Tappan, N.J.: Revell, 1971).

16

PSYCHOTHERAPY AND HEALTHY PERSONALITY

INTRODUCTION

When a person's life is bogged down in painful impasses so that he cannot work, play, or enjoy satisfying relationships with others, it is time for him to seek help. The professional psychotherapist or personal counselor can help him understand how he has behaved his way into a devitalizing trap, and how to grope his way out. There are millions of "therapeutic people" in society. These "social therapists" are increasingly being sought to serve as volunteers at crisis centers and mental health clinics. Gerald Goodman [1] trained college students to serve as nonprofessional therapists for delinquent children, and laypersons answer telephones at suicide prevention centers. People who have conquered some affliction such as blindness, loss of limbs, drug addiction, or alcoholism will often devote part of their time to helping others transcend their difficulties. The professional psychotherapist seeks to understand the theory of personal disintegration and growth, in order to help people through the most complex difficulties in living.

A professional psychotherapist may be a psychiatrist, a clinical psychologist, a counseling psychologist, a social worker, or a member of the clergy who has undertaken training as a personal counselor.

A distinction is often drawn between personal counseling and psychotherapy. Despite efforts to relegate counseling to the professions of psychology and education and psychotherapy to medicine or psychiatry, such distinctions are not generally honored. Counseling is perhaps the generic term that applies to all forms of helping with problems of the self and its relationship to other people. Psychotherapy is more often used as that aspect of the counseling relationship that deals particularly with complex emotional problems, such as anxiety. However, the distinction is not always relevant and we prefer to use the terms interchangeably.

Some Theories of Psychological Suffering

Mental Disease. For some centuries psychological suffering and deviant behavior were held to be evidence of mental disease. The medical specialty of psychiatry was developed to understand, prevent, and cure these diseases. In the history of psychiatry, the "treatments" proposed for the so-called mental diseases were often more destructive of life than the suffering itself. For example, for several decades people diagnosed as "schizophrenic" were treated by electrical shocks applied to the brain and by a form of surgery called prefrontal lobotomy.

Largely through the influence of R. D. Laing in England and T. Szasz in the United States, the view that deviant behavior and difficulties in living are evidence of a "mental disease" is being reconsidered. As Szasz states,[2]

The concept of insanity, or mental illness . . . enables the "sane" members of society to deal as they see fit with those of their fellows whom they can categorize as "insane." But having divested the madman of his right to judge what is in his own best interests, the people—especially psychiatrists and judges, their medical and legal experts on madness—have divested themselves of the corrective restraints of dialogue. In vain does the alleged madman insist that he is not sick; his inability to "recognize" that he is, is regarded as a hallmark of his illness. In vain does he reject treatment and hospitalization as forms of torture and imprisonment; his refusal to submit to psychiatric authority is regarded as a further sign of his illness. In this medical rejection of the Other as a madman, we recognize, in up-to-date semantic and technical garb, but underneath it remarkably unchanged, his former religious rejection as a heretic [p. xvi].

Growth Impasses and Fostering Growth. In more recent years, psychological suffering has come to be regarded by many psychotherapists as evidence of an *impasse in personal growth.* Such therapists conceive of humans as organisms with a fundamental tendency to grow toward health and fuller functioning, who may need help in identifying the factors that block their growth. This "growth model" has gained increased acceptance as the medical or disease model is being abandoned.[3]

Inhibition of Learning; Fostering New Learning. "Behavior therapists" see psychological suffering as a by-product of inhibitions and distortions of the learning process.[4] According to this view, "maladjusted" persons persist with interpersonal and emotional habits that no longer meet their needs. Humans have incredible learning capacity, and when environments change, they have it in their power to learn new modes of conduct. Neurotic and psychotic persons are viewed as people who have not "extinguished" inefficient habits in order to learn more adaptive modes of behavior. Psychotherapy is viewed as a learning process, with the therapist functioning as a "behavior modification" specialist.

Inauthenticity. Therapists with an existentialist orientation view psychological suffering as the outcome of inauthenticity. The sufferer is seen as alienated from her real self, from her fellow human beings, and from her natural environment. The task for the therapist is to reactivate "authentic being" in her patients. This means helping patients to recognize, to be, and to disclose their real selves and to dispense with contrivance and phoniness in dealing with others.[5]

Healthy Personality

Duality and Promotion of Nonduality. Still another view of psychological suffering has been introduced into the thinking of American and some European therapists from the Eastern philosophies of Taoism and Buddhism, and the integration of these ideologies, as in Zen Buddhism.[6] This is the view that humans suffer in consequence of a "dualistic" view of the world. According to this frame of reference, humans have gotten into difficulty with themselves, their fellow humans, and the natural world by identifying their entire being with just a part of it—the ego that controls behavior. In so doing, they have made a fallacy comparable to identifying or equating an entire heating system with the thermostat that regulates it. The thermostat simply is *not* the entire heating system; it is only part of the whole. When persons see themselves as an ego or a self that is in control of their body, their behavior, or their personality, then they experience themselves as separate from, or different from, their bodies, their nature, and their fellow humans. This separation is most graphically illustrated by the phenomenon of self-consciousness—a close synonym for the more difficult term *dual mode of being*. When we are self-aware during transactions with people or when we perform some task, such as playing the piano, our behavior is effortful, exhausting, and likely to be ineffective. Self-consciousness presumes that we are suppressing our spontaneous response tendencies. We suppress spontaneity because we distrust our organisms. The therapist influenced by Zen Buddhism seeks to "trick" or to invite his patient to produce spontaneous, unpremeditated behavior, and to learn thereby that nothing dreadful will happen when he is thus unself-conscious. This mode of behaving is described as *nondual*. It corresponds with the experience of the swimmer who, when he is first learning the strokes, is very much aware of the placement of his arms and the rhythm with which he kicks his legs. At some point, however, the novice swimmer "lets go," "loses himself," and "lets swimming happen." If his training has been adequate, his stroke will be smooth, rhythmic, and effortless.

Summary. The preceding overview of causes and proposed cures of psychological suffering will give the student some idea of the ferment that continues to go on in

Psychotherapy and Healthy Personality

the psychological healing professions. All of the interpretations that were cited have some truth to them, but no single one of them explains all cases of suffering or all cases of successful treatment of suffering.

Who Is a Psychotherapist?

Psychotherapy is a profession that calls for extensive training. Although psychotherapy was long seen as a medical specialty (literally, treating diseases of the body and mind by psychological means), it is now legally practiced by members of other professions, notably, psychology, social work, the ministry, and teachers and educators. Despite differences in terminology, theory, and institutional affiliations, effective psychotherapists share many personal characteristics, and their training inculcates similar ways of being with their clientele.

What Effective Psychotherapists Do

Therapists Listen. The activity therapists engage in most is listening. They provide an understanding audience for a troubled person, often the first such audience the patient has ever had. The patient discloses herself to her therapist more than she has to any other person. Even with the reassurance of professional confidence, however, many patients are reluctant to trust the therapist; it is at the point where patients resist further disclosure that the tact and professional skill of the therapist are called upon.

The Therapist Respects the Patient. The relationship with the therapist is often the first time in the patient's life that he has been respected as a unique human being by anyone. The therapist reveals the respect by not manipulating the patient or putting conditions on his attention and interest.

Therapists Enlighten and Demystify. Frequently, a patient is suffering because she does not know what is going on in her family, her place of work, or, for that matter, in the world. She may believe that her parents *Healthy* love and confirm her when in fact they are doing all in *Personality* their power to interfere with her growth and her confidence in herself. She may not be aware that her spouse has been "playing games," pretending to be weak and helpless so that she would neglect her career in order to pay attention to him. If the therapist learns how these relationships affect her patient's experience and action, she strives to impart her understanding to her patient.

Therapists Are Attentive to Dreams and "Body Language." Therapists have learned that patients repress many possibilities of experiencing, and they seek to provide an atmosphere within which such repression is released. They encourage a patient to pay attention to his dreams, in order to discern hints about possibilities of growing, and perceptions too painful, initially, to be acknowledged, but that appear more or less disguised in dreams.

Therapists will also be attentive to their patient's bodies —not only facial expressions and "kinesics" (meaningful gestures), but also the very way the person looks.

Therapists Invite Patients to Greater Immediacy. It was Fritz Perls' great insight that patients, indeed most average people, spend much of their waking time *out of sensory touch with the here and now*. Rather, they worry compulsively about the future, or pick over their memories for recollections of failures and past pleasures. This reduces their sense of vitality, of being intensely alive. Perls' Gestalt therapy teaches patients to pay attention to what is going on in their bodies and their immediate surroundings, right now, to feel the excitement of living with the joy and pain of the present, rather than escaping into pale intellectuality or wistful remembrance of things past.

Therapists also are attentive, however, to a defensive flight into the present. If someone evades remembering the past, because of past pain, or refuses to think about a problematic future, the therapist may invite the patient to give each time dimension of his life its due consideration.

Therapists View People as Embodiments of Fantastic Possibilities. By the time a patient has come to seek professional help, his view of himself has come to be that of a person with little strength and little personal worth. Indeed, significant people in his life have encouraged him

Psychotherapy and Healthy Personality

405

to regard himself as useless, weak, of little moral worth, and so on. They may have told him, repeatedly, that he will never be any different, that he is fated to failure. Therapists know that descriptions of people are actually subtle invitations to become or remain as described. They know, as well, that a person can be in any way that anyone imagines, and in any way that has meaning to him. When a patient believes he cannot cope with his difficulties, that he has no reserves of strength, no hidden possibilities of growing in new dimensions, then he will act in such a way to confirm those views of himself. The patient views himself as weak; the therapist relentlessly attributes to him strength and untapped potential for growth. Why is the therapist so relentless in attributing the capacity to transcend difficulties to his patients? Because a psychotherapist, perhaps more than anyone, knows from personal experience and from the experience of others of human beings' great possibilities of growing and overcoming impasses in life; he will not be shaken in this belief, which he holds "religiously" because it is scientifically founded. The patient who does not experience his own possibilities of overcoming difficulty is simply out of touch with reality.

Therapists Inspire Faith and Hope in Patients. A therapist is a professional person, and she is consulted in her office. The very setting, as well as the decision to go to this setting, seem to inspire in the patient a certain confidence that help will be received, that there may be hope for a better life. These attitudes and expectancies are factors in recovery. One of the puzzles that continues to vex health researchers is the manner in which an attitude of hopelessness seems to foster illness, whereas the inspiration of hope and expectation of help seems to stimulate wellness. Patients frequently get well no matter what a therapist says or does. Researchers have likened psychotherapy to the "placebo effect," which has long been observed in the field of medicine. Physicians sometimes prescribe medicines that come in large, colorful capsules, or that taste vile, but are actually inert—sugar or colored, flavored water. Patients report that following the ingestion of these placebos, their symptoms are relieved. My hypothesis is that healing is a reflex process that goes on

Healthy Personality

by itself unless the person's attitude and beliefs interfere with it. If a sick person will simply relax and let healing go on, it will proceed at its natural pace. If she believes she will die or has no reason to go on living, these attitudes, mediated by certain brain functions, can impede the healing process. The placebo, seen by the patient as "powerful medicine," convinces her that she is in good hands. She then relaxes and permits healing to proceed by itself.

In psychotherapy, the hopeless patient is confronted by a professional person who inspires confidence, and who offers informed hope that the patient can transcend her difficulties and get on with more effective living. This hope, if communicated, changes the patient's way of experiencing her situation. She will then keep trying new approaches to her dilemmas until she discovers a mode of behavior that yields health instead of chronic misery.[7]

Therapists Function as Exemplars. There is a sense in which a therapist is a leader of his patients, guiding them to ways of acting that generate health and growth. As in all forms of leadership, the direction to be taken is most convincingly demonstrated by example. The effective military commander does not say "forward," he frequently says "follow me." The effective teacher is the one who is himself an exemplar of the joy afforded by dedication to study. One would hardly place much faith in a therapist who emphasized the importance of authenticity when he was himself phony, self-concealing, and manipulative. Indeed, recent research has shown that "modeling"—serving as an example—is the most powerful way one person can influence another, especially if the exemplar is seen as a person with desirable characteristics. In a later section, we shall see how many of the self-help therapeutic groups are effective because they are led by persons who provide living proof that an infirmity that incapacitates others can be conquered.[8]

Therapists Are Not Just Competent: They Are Good Human Beings. Anybody, whether a professional psychotherapist or not, who displays the preceding qualities in her life with others, is a good human being. I don't know anybody who is this way all the time, but I know that psychotherapists strive to be this way as steadily as

Psychotherapy and Healthy Personality

they can. Fundamentally, a person committed to these ways is a person with enlightened goodwill toward her fellows. A layperson can cultivate the same qualities and skills to be helpful to others, and to enrich the quality of her personal relationship (see Chapter 10).

PSYCHOTHERAPY AS A KIND OF INVITATION

It seems clear that professional and nonprofessional therapists are helpful because they persuade a suffering person to change his behavior in some way. I find terms such as *encouragement, invitation,* and *leading by example* more valid metaphors for describing the process of helping others than medical or behavioristic terms (*treatment, shaping, reinforcing*). Therapists are effective only when they succeed in presenting an invitation or challenge that seems worthwhile and feasible to the sufferer. Psychotherapists are most convincing and effective at helping persons overcome the difficulties that they have been able to transcend in their own lives. As exemplars, they can persuade a sufferer to try making changes, where someone else might not be effective at such persuasion. A sufferer needs to be convinced that there is some chance, some hope of overcoming the barriers to a better life. A hypnotist tries to convince a patient that he has the power to transcend by direct suggestion. A good psychotherapist persuades, sometimes directly ("You can do it, go ahead and try") and sometimes by attribution of strength to the patient, taking it for granted that he can conquer the circumstances that hitherto overpowered him.[9]

Finding the Right Psychotherapist

Should a high-level-functioning person with a healthy personality have to see a psychotherapist? While there is some evidence that high-level-functioning persons do deal with their problems by themselves,[10] it is apparent that all human beings could at times find themselves so entangled in their feelings and the feelings of those close to them that the most efficient way to deal with the problems would be to utilize the help of a trained, competent professional person. Choosing to enter psychotherapy is

Healthy Personality

thus an indication of strength for a healthy personality rather than an admission of weakness. It indicates she knows how to deal with her personal problems with efficiency.

How do you shop for a psychotherapist? Perhaps there are three matters to be taken into consideration and probably in the following order: (1) professional, formal qualifications; (2) personality of the therapist; and (3) the special point of view, methodology or technique he or she employs.

1. *Professional qualifications:* Most, but not all, states have their own requirements for licensure or certification. In addition, licensing is not required for most persons working in state agencies, such as a state university counseling center. Here are some things you might look for to evaluate the minimal professional qualifications of the psychotherapist whom you are considering.

a. Psychiatrist: M.D. degree plus Board certification in psychiatry, a two- or three-year residency in psychiatry. Avoid an M.D. without special training in psychiatry.

b. Counseling or clinical psychologist: Ph.D. degree in counseling or clinical psychology, state license or certificate to practice in most states. Avoid someone without a year-long internship.

c. Counselor: Two-year master's degree, educational specialist degree, or doctorate in counselor education, some internship. Licensure and certification now being discussed but probably not yet available in most states. Avoid someone whose training is not clearly stated as being in a counselor preparation program.

d. Psychiatric social worker: Two-year graduate training in psychiatric social work, master's degree, which includes a full year of field training. Avoid someone with bachelor's degree only or without field training.

2. *Personality:* It is entirely possible that you will find the first therapist you meet to be pleasant, understanding, and able to quickly establish a trusting relationship. Should you feel otherwise, after a reasonable length of time, you should not hesitate to discuss it with your therapist and make plans to seek another person more capable with your own personality. There should be no hesitation on your part to switch—nor should there be

any pressure on the part of the therapist to keep you.

3. *The school of psychotherapy:* It is here that you probably find the most confusion. Almost all therapies profess to treat all problems; yet some have been tested largely in one or two particular settings. It is also true that, because of the length of time necessary to gain adequate training, a particular therapist is competent in perhaps only two, or at most three, approaches to treatment. Thus, an enlightened client might wish to make careful judgments about what particular approach he or she would feel to be most helpful. It is beyond the scope of this book to present a complete list of psychotherapies and their descriptions. However, here are a few of the more prominent forms. With the exception of behavior therapy and of psychoanalysis, all would be considered to be heavily influenced by the humanistic movement.[11]

Client-Centered Psychotherapy. Also often called nondirective therapy. Places great emphasis upon the individual's own resources. The therapist attempts to create a set of freeing conditions, warmth, authenticity, and openness and facilitates the capacity of the person to correct himself. Reflection of feeling is used to help the client think through problems. Avoids pushing, confronting, or suggesting. Developed largely with student populations but also has forms for children in play therapy.

Gestalt Therapy. Therapist is more active in exposing problems and seeking solutions. Often involves confrontation, role-playing, and, in groups, use of techniques to facilitate expression, such as fantasy games. Therapist is a stronger, directing figure. Emphasis on the present, avoids dealing with past, "old tapes," and encourages client to live and think in the present. Developed for a wide range of clients, including students and middle-aged adults.

Psychoanalysis. The granddaddy of them all and still heavily in use. Involves interpretation of dreams, free-association (speaking of whatever comes to mind at the time), gentle interpretations by the therapist. Therapist is often seen as a benevolent parent. Elaborate theoretical underpinning as rationale for methodology. Emphasizes understanding of past and meaning of dreams. Developed largely among upper middle class but now applied to all age and income groups.

Behavior Therapy. Sees client's problems as unadaptive learned behavior and expects that client can learn new ways to behave. Utilizes full range of conditioning techniques, providing rewards for correct behavior and mild punishment (aversive technique) for incorrect behavior. A favorite technique is systematic desensitization, in which relaxation is used to counter anxiety-producing stimuli. Although many humanists object to some behavioristic approaches, when entered into voluntarily by the client, behavior therapy permits the client to select the behaviors to be extinguished and those to be substituted. Changes in behavior are closely monitored with charts.

Reality Therapy. Has many intimations of behavior therapy; involves contract between therapist and client. Regards bad mental health as irresponsibility. Oriented to present and to future, avoids the past. Aims at acknowledgment by patient that she is responsible for her own behavior. Teaches patient better ways to meet basic needs. Much of the research is with teenagers in institutions for the delinquent but is applicable to wide age range, students, middle-aged, and so on.

Rational–Emotive Therapy. Emphasizes the rational component in changing behavior. The therapist challenges the irrational beliefs of the person through the use of logic and persuasion, which theoretically causes the undesirable consequences, such as anxiety, to disappear. May use role-playing, exortation, modeling, and assigned homework. Has an impressive background of research. Adaptable to all ages and specifically for mild or serious emotional difficulties.

There may be some 300 different forms of psychotherapy in the literature, and no one psychotherapy can lay claim to being of indisputable, general utility. In other than the larger cities of the United States, you may not have your pick of methodologies; yet you should always be picky about the personality and professional qualifications of your choice.

Psychotherapy and Healthy Personality

There is a sense in which psychotherapists have moved into the domain formerly under the aegis of formal religion. Over the centuries, people relied on prophets, priests, witch doctors, and shamans for guidance in ways to live. When they encountered disease and failure, they would return to the priest for healing rituals and oracular pronouncements of the wishes of God (or the gods). A contemporary psychotherapist espouses a set of beliefs about life-enhancing ways to act. This set of beliefs is scientific in origin, but it is possible to reconcile the highest ethical precepts of Judaism, Christianity, Islam, Hinduism, and Buddhism with scientifically informed knowledge about the enlivening and devitalizing consequences of ways to live. At a later point in this chapter we shall explore more fully the similarity between contemporary psychotherapists and the teachings of biblical prophets.

Settings for Therapy and Promotion of Growth

THE CONSULTING ROOM OF THE PSYCHOTHERAPIST

The replacement of the medical model by a growth model makes it possible for therapeutic help to be provided for people in many settings besides the private consulting room of the private practitioner in a one-to-one relationship. Poorer and less educated people generally are treated in clinics, and the treatment is more often with drugs, electroshock, and hospitalization than lengthy psychotherapeutic sessions.

"CHECK-OUT" PLACES

Several psychiatrists, psychologists, and laypersons in London organized a group they called the Philadelphia Association. It was to be devoted to exploring different ways to treat the so-called mental diseases, especially schizophrenia. Ronald D. Laing and Aaron Esterson were among the founders of this association, the idea for which came out of some research into schizophrenia on which *Healthy* they had collaborated. It was their hypothesis that *Personality* "schizophrenic" behavior and experience was not evidence of a disease process, but a natural and desirable process of personal growth and self-healing. Their work with the families of people diagnosed as schizophrenic convinced them that the patient was not so much sick as reacting to attitudes of rejection and to the familiar mystification and disconfirmation to which they were subjected. Although the patients did indeed display "delusions," hallucinations, and altered perceptions of reality, Laing and Esterson showed that these symptoms were intelligible in light of the way the patient's family interacted. For example, if a patient complained her parents were always discussing her behind her back, the parents denied this to her face, and then talked about her as soon as she was out of earshot.

Laing and Esterson believed that conventional psychiatric treatment for schizophrenia was damaging rather than helpful to the sufferer; drugs, electroshock, and prefrontal lobotomy were viewed more as violence than as enlightened efforts at healing. As an alternative, the members of the Philadelphia Association acquired an old building in east London, called Kingsley Hall (Mahatma Gandhi had stayed in a small room at this place in the 1930s). The building was to serve as an experimental community, where people designated schizophrenic could come to stay, and rather than be treated, they would be encouraged to explore the personal meaning of their confusion and suffering. There would be psychiatrists living there, as well as students, artists, and nurses, but within Kingsley Hall there would be no distinctions among people based on profession or status. The theory was that the schizophrenic was in the process of struggling to find or create a viable identity for himself or herself when the old identity could no longer be lived. The stay at Kingsley Hall was to be viewed as a time to carry out a voyage of self-discovery, without being distracted by psychiatric intervention and treatment.

Out of the Kingsley Hall experiment, which ended after a couple of years, there emerged an informal organization of "check-out" and "blow-out" places, private homes or residences for communal living where people who were "losing their minds" could go, not to be treated—since the places were not hospitals—but to check out of their past life, go crazy if they needed to, and do this in the company of people who had been through similar experiences themselves.

Laing and his associates are professional psychotherapists who wished to "deprofessionalize" their profession—to show how people can learn to help one another without the necessity of medical or psychiatric intervention.

CRISIS CENTERS AND PSYCHOTHERAPY BY TELEPHONE

In the past ten years or so, "crisis centers" have been inaugurated in many cities around the United States, where persons with any kind of human difficulty can obtain immediate psychotherapeutic help and guidance from professional people about whom the troubled person might not have known. In some cities, these centers are listed in the telephone directories and the classified advertisements as "suicide prevention centers," whereas in others, they are called "hot-lines," or crisis centers. Typically, they are staffed by volunteer workers who have received some training in the arts of listening and responding helpfully to troubled individuals. Workers at suicide prevention centers seek, in addition to being helpful over the telephone, to locate the suicidal person, so that direct personal contact might be made with him.[12]

THE COMMUNITY MENTAL HEALTH CENTER AND "OUTREACH"

One of the major innovations in service to the community coming from increased federal funding is the community mental health center. These centers are organized with matching local funds to insure community control and involvement. Staffed by qualified professionals, they see their function as service to the entire community. They have made a sizable dent in the problem of providing services for the poor, the disadvantaged and the handicapped. For a minimal fee, and in some instances none at all, community clients can get high-quality professional care for psychological problems. In *Healthy Personality* addition, many of these agencies will operate "halfway" houses for people with drug, alcoholism, or other emo-

414

tional problems. In the halfway house, the client usually spends the night at the facility but works in the surrounding city, or in some instances, stays full time at the facility.

In addition, progressive mental health centers provide "outreach" services to people in rural areas requiring psychological help. Counselors, social workers, and other personnel from the centers drive out to the outlying towns and make home visits to those who otherwise would be institutionalized in order to get treatment or who would have to beg transportation from neighbors.

The community mental health center also serves as a convenient source of information and referral to all such agencies in the area.[13]

WOMEN'S SHELTERS

One of the major kinds of services in the expanding community is the treatment and housing facilities for "battered" or "abused" women. Wives and girlfriends who find themselves abandoned and hurt by spouses or boyfriends can now get help in readjusting and shelter from possible harm to themselves and to their children.

COLLEGE COUNSELING CENTERS

Perhaps the agency most available to young people is the college or university counseling center. Although some limit their services to their own students, most community college centers welcome young people considering enrolling as well as those already there. These centers inevitably employ highly qualified professional personnel, usually psychologists and counselors, and provide help with course selection, career choices, and a host of personal-emotional problems, such as parental relationships, feelings of inadequacy, boy–girl problems, drug problems, alcoholism, and social development. Many of these centers, along with student mental health centers, also provide enrichment experiences, encounter groups, marriage counseling, assertiveness training, consciousness raising, counseling for gay students, and other efforts within the growth concept in psychotherapeutic services. Ordinarily no fees are involved.

Nonprofessional Self-help Groups

Alcoholics Anonymous (*AA*). Alcoholics Anonymous is perhaps the best-known self-help group, and has been in existence longer than any other such association. Chapters of AA exist in nearly every city and town in the United States, as well as in Canada. The members are persons who have been addicted to alcohol, who had learned that they can avoid drinking by regular association with alcoholics who are struggling to remain "dry." A member tempted to take a drink may call upon another member who will sit with him, perhaps just to provide company or encouragement to overcome the urge to drink to the point of stupor. Spouses and children of alcoholics have organized a program called Al-anon to help cope with the alcoholic parent.

Integrity Groups. Integrity groups were begun under the leadership of Hobert Mowrer,[14] as ways for people to help one another stay honest. They are groups of eight or ten people who meet regularly at one another's homes and engage in absolutely honest talk with one another about the ways in which they have been conducting their lives outside the group meetings, and how they relate to one another within the meetings. Mowrer began experimenting with, and participating in, these groups when he discovered that conventional psychoanalytic therapy was ineffective in helping him overcome a tendency to profound depression. What ultimately proved of greatest avail to him in his struggle with depression was avoidance of inauthenticity in his dealings with others. Lying was, in a sense, an addiction comparable to alcohol or drug addiction; truth-telling, while frequently painful, was seen as the only path to a livable life for sufferers from intense guilt or depression.

Other Groups. Many other kinds of nonprofessionally led therapeutic groups and associations have come into being because the participants discovered such association to be less costly and usually more effective than conventional psychotherapy. For example, *Weight Watchers*, though a profit-making association, has proven that groups of overweight people can control their food intake and slim down through regular association with one another, sharing experiences of sadness and suffering associated with obesity and encouraging one another to adhere to their dietetic regimens. As with the other groups, the participants feel they understand one another's problems better than any outsider can, even if the outsider has medical or psychological training. Comparable groups have been started by tobacco smokers who wish to stop smoking and parents of mentally retarded children who wish to avoid the experience of guilt and shame frequently occurring in such parents. In fact, associations of people with common problems or impediments to a full life provide a hopeful and valid path to healthier personality without resort to costly professional help.

Some Common Therapeutic Factors in Self-help Groups

Self-help groups are effective because a participant encounters others struggling to transcend self-defeating ways of living. Those who have struggled longest, and most successfully, serve as leaders by example. Senior "strugglers" know the many ways to give up and the importance of relentless struggle. They share their experience with their fellows. The novice members can see living examples of the possibility of avoiding intoxication with alcohol or narcotics, of overcoming self-defeating habits, and of transcending handicaps of all kinds. In all the self-help groups, radical honesty with oneself and others is encouraged by the simple act of engaging in it. Participants are encouraged to come to know one another, to disclose themselves honestly, and to invite honest confrontation between themselves and others. Moreover, they are challenged to keep struggling with the difficulties rather than yield to them. This is the way some professional psychotherapists function, even sharing with their patients their own personal experience with neurotic or psychotic disturbances.[15]

Group Psychotherapy, Growth Groups, and Encounter Groups

Almost every theory of psychotherapy has both an individual form, involving only the therapist and one client, and a group form, involving a number of clients, usually from seven to fifteen, and one or more therapists. Techniques in group psychotherapy center about techniques related to the particular form of individual therapy, with some exceptions. They usually meet for an hour and a half each week or twice a week. However, an approach that has made a great impact worldwide is the growth group, and specifically the encounter group, attributed to Carl Rogers.[16] There are other terms that describe forms of encounter that are indistinguishable from the original. Some specific characteristics may be given in the title, such as the *marathon group*, which may begin on a Friday evening, continue on through the night until all have fallen asleep at their places, begin as people waken the next day, and go on through the night to midday Sunday. Sensitivity groups are another form of the encounter. All of these owe their origin to the T-Group, developed by followers of Kurt Lewin at the National Training Laboratories in Bethel, Maine.[17] The T-group is a *training* group with more specific aims and objectives—such as the development of better working relationships among staff members of an industrial office. The encounter group may be distinguished from the group therapy by its time structure alone—they usually follow the marathon plan, whereas group therapy is for a shorter period of time each week. Group therapy usually lasts for more weeks than would the encounter group.

However, the major appeal of the encounter group, which is considerable, is in facilitating interpersonal relationships, opening the person to new vistas of potentiality in his or her own life, self-renewal, exploration of barriers to growth, and the experience of healthy intimacy with others. The growth group in general should not be used for serious emotional problems or mental health-type symptoms, but should rather be oriented toward a development of self. An encounter group, if successful, is an emotional, happy, exciting experience—after it is over. There may be some deep emotions stirred up during the sessions, and helping these stirrings become growth-facilitating is where skilled leadership is demanded. This perhaps leads to a major problem in many such groups—lack of trained, qualified, experienced lead-

Healthy Personality

ers. Many group members are attracted to the charismatic, flamboyant leader—not unlike the allurement of a religious zealot. There are many studies of the encounter group; very few could stand a rigorous scientific evaluation. The better controlled studies, such as those by Lavoie,[18] show positive results and, in many instances, effects that last months after. The most elaborate study of them all was carried out by the team of Lieberman, Yalom, and Miles,[19] and, among other issues, pointed out that some harm can also be done by the groups. Which groups are likely to be most harmful? Of course, those led by the most colorful, enthusiastic, charismatic leaders. Nevertheless, the encounter group is an exciting new growth-facilitating structure and is perhaps one of the most important developments in psychotherapy since Freud.

One final word: neither group therapy, group counseling, nor the encounter group represent a cheaper, faster way to solve one's emotional problems. They add a different dimension to the group experience and cannot substitute for individual therapy.

Places for Personal Growth

For centuries India provided its educated people with places to which they could retreat for meditation and renewal of their lives. These *ashrams* were places sheltered from the bustle of everyday practical life, frequently in the countryside, but sometimes in the center of a large city like New Delhi. A *guru* (a teacher of spiritual truth) is the head of each establishment, and he or she provides the guidance to the people who come to live there or who seek an audience. The pace and style of life at an ashram is radically slowed down. The pupils, or seekers (it is difficult to find an appropriate Western term to describe them), are encouraged to spend much time in solitude for meditation and to carry out a program of Hatha yoga postures. Diet is simplified, meals are usually communal and vegetarian, and each person lives in a small private room or cell. People stay for a day, week, months, or years. Or they may continue their customary life, but go to the ashram as one might go to church or temple, for spiritual guidance.

The Western world has not had an exact equivalent of ashrams available for persons who have wanted to get away for self-renewal. In 1963 Michael Murphy, a Californian graduate of Stanford University, inaugurated a Western equivalent of the Sri Aurobindo ashram at Pondicherry, where he had spent eighteen months in retreat and meditation several years earlier. He utilized a piece of land with natural hot springs in Big Sur, California, as a place to invite scholars and therapists for weekends, where they could conduct formal seminars on the current status of their work. The first such seminar was conducted by A. H. Maslow in 1962. As the years went by, the center, now called Esalen Institute (the Esalens were a tribe of Indians who used to live in the region), came to be called a "growth center" where people could come for weekends or longer periods of time to participate in encounter groups, to experience various body-awakening disciplines (see Chapter 7), or to take part in Gestalt therapy workshops conducted by followers of Fritz Perls. Residential programs were inaugurated, where the students could spend up to a year participating in all the seminars and workshops concerned with the enlargement of their awareness and stimulation of growth, and perhaps become qualified to conduct workshops and seminars themselves.

Since Esalen Institute first came into being, the idea of a center devoted to personal growth has become widespread, and there are several hundred in existence around the Western world. Although growth centers are not identical with Indian ashrams, there is a similarity, in that there is the commitment to self-exploration, to reinvention of one's life, and to radical honesty in one's relationships with others. The people who operate Esalen Institute bake the bread, cook the meals, conduct encounter groups, and offer Rolfing sessions and massage. They live a kind of communal life and serve as exemplars of ways to be "in one's body," and ways to be with one another, which are believed to be most life-giving and conducive to personal growth.[20]

The Role of Prophet in Psychotherapy

Healthy Personality   Chapter 15 discussed formal religion from the standpoint of the consequences for healthy personality of living in accord with formal religious teachings. This chapter will conclude with some excerpts from two lectures that S. M. Jourard gave to professional psychotherapists, which develop this parallel between the social functions of the ancient prophets and contemporary psychotherapy.[21]

Over the years I have been examining and re-examining psychotherapies and psychotherapists from the standpoint of different models and metaphors. The one model most compelling for me over the past ten years is that of exemplar, or role model of authentic existence. Now the very term *authentic existence* means more than simply living in truth and choosing one's existence. It also implies increasing enlightenment, so that one can make choices compatible with life, growth, and self-actualization. Psychotherapists in increasing numbers have been taking their own lives and growth seriously, seeking to authenticate their professional contacts by being exemplars themselves of the quest for growth, truth, and self-fulfillment. And they are seeking, some of them, to share their visions and knowledge with masses of others; to function, in short, as prophets outside the consulting room.

The psychotherapist, according to this view, embodies part of the way of a prophet, that of being an exemplar of the way of life he wishes to invite others to follow for their own good, and, by implication, for the good of the community. And he is a prophet when he points out the truth about destructive behavior. Old Testament prophets were desirous that the polyglot aggregation of Hebrew tribes might overcome their limited and autistic perspectives and become a people, a community called Israel, united under one God, living in exemplary ways as a beacon and example to all mankind. An extraordinarily modest ambition.

According to Abraham Heschel,[22] a prophet is extraordinarily sensitive to evil; he feels it keenly, and refuses to excuse or ignore it. He shrieks of what he sees. He pays attention to what others regard as trivialities, too obvious to note, but which signify a person or a people hellbent on destruction of self and the very conditions that make life possible. A prophet is, without compromise, committed to the highest good of which man is capable, and he mourns, castigates, and incites in order that mediocre men might rise to those heights. Like the outsiders of whom Colin Wilson wrote, the prophet sees too much, hears the groans of pain to which others are deaf. Yet the prophets have a compassion for mankind and they seek to invite all men to take responsibility for the fate of man and life in this place and time. The prophets feel the blast from heaven; they inveigh against callousness, indifference, and yet take no pleasure in the lot to which they have been called. Prophets are seditious, cranky threats to the status quo.

This is the way Heschel answers the question, "What manner of man is the prophet?" I see adumbrations here, as I said, with Colin Wilson's outsiders—the raw nerve-endings of our time: Lawrence of Arabia, Nijinsky, and other characters who never could be swallowed up by the hypocrisies and false values of their times, but who, as Wilson points out, were destroyed because they lacked insight and didn't know what was going on.

What psychotherapist measures up to the stature of a prophet rather than a mere outsider? Which is a true and which is a false prophet? Wilhelm Reich,[23] I feel, was a prophet as well as a genius who had magnificent revelations to share; I cited his work in many places throughout this book. He died in prison in Lewisburg, after a fight with the government over some aspects of his work, which he lost. Many thought Reich had become psychotic. Perhaps he had. This does not minimize his prophetic functions. Brock Chisholm,[24] a Canadian psychiatrist, became a prophet after World War II, at risk of his reputation. He preached against the teaching of certain myths to children, such as the Santa Claus story, so they would be less vulnerable to incitements to war as adults. Israel Charny, a psychotherapist, has written of the viciousness that prevails in marriage, in families; Auschwitz can be foreseen in the German family structure. Ronald Laing and Aaron Esterson, both psychotherapists, are prophets in their writings, pointing out how the family serves as a place within which some members are sacrificed to the mental hospital rather than allow the cosmetic image of a happy family to be besmirched.[25] Thomas Szasz is serving a prophetic function in his writings on "The Myth of Mental Illness" and the "Manufacture of Madness." [26]

The psychotherapists whom we consider great, I have argued, are great not because of their theories, which are efforts to scientize existential courage and enlightenment, but because their lives were threatened by some aspect of facticity and they learned how to transcend it, and could teach others how to be free and upright in the face of doting, destructive parents, addiction to heroin, or lack of awareness of others' destructive games.

Sigmund Freud mastered some forces which could have prevented him from becoming the man who invented psychoanalysis. He suffered *Portnoy's Complaint*, as millions of people in the West have: a seductive, doting mother and a father who was both strong and weak, loved and feared. The result of struggling with such conflicting parental demands has been neurosis and diminished self-actualization for man. Freud's courage lay in facing his recollections and fantasies, his sexuality, his anger, and discovering that one's past need not preclude fuller functioning, whether genital, intellectual, or physical, in adult years. I believe he was most effective as a therapist with persons whose suffering grew out of anti-growth forces comparable to those which he tamed. The therapeutic technique he taught others has not been notorious for its effectiveness. Freud showed *in his very person* that it is possible to marry, make love, raise children, and defy all kinds of social pressures in one's time and place in spite of having been raised as a middle-class minority group member, with parents whose demands and expectations were not always compatible with free flowering of individuality. He might have helped his patients more swiftly if he were not so shy, so reluctant to share his experience with his patients.

Psychotherapy and Healthy Personality

Carl Rogers was reared in the American version of the Protestant ethic. Such upbringing produces a strict conscience, one which keeps people "at it" when there is a frontier to conquer, a fortune to be made, duty to be fulfilled. This is the way of the "inner-directed" character so well described by Riesman. This conscience makes for conditional self-regard; it obstructs empathy and makes it difficult for a person to be "congruent" in his dealings with others. I would propose that Rogers' greatness and greatest effectiveness lie not in his invention of the client-centered techniques, nor in opening psychotherapy to scientific research, nor in his theories, but rather *in his conquest of the upbringing that would limit his growth*. He is a model of a way to be, a way which, when adopted, makes for more mutually confirming and authentic relations with others and which averts sickness.[27]

The fact that seems obvious to me about life in the time of the Old Testament prophets is that no one knew how to live in a way that would sustain life for self and others; and no one knew how to live in a way that would foster growth of more than a brutish few of man's infinite possibilities. The statutes, commandments, ordinances that Moses received "from God" may be regarded as the inventions of a highly imaginative and intelligent and compassionate man. Perhaps God spoke through him. Moses fascinates me—how did he (or they) arrive at a statement of ways to live in that time? Perhaps being reared in a civilized culture (Egypt) without being of it was a factor. Moses' writings and teachings were the equivalent of the writings of Dr. Spock, Ralph Nader, Rachel Carson, Adelle Davis, Mohandas Ghandi, and other contemporaries who have tried to help people live in viable ways. Failure to live in a viable way is to court disease, stultification, and death. This is as true today as it was in Biblical times.

Today's psychotherapists treat people whose growth is stultified, who are not living right for themselves and possibly not right for others. The therapist is prophetic insofar as he has learned, and authenticated in his very being and presence, viable ways to live— *Healthy* what the ancients may have called "righteousness." If *Personality* they invite others to change their ways and threaten

424

them with dire consequences if they do not, they are being as much prophet as the times admit. The prophets tried to make men realize their freedom to choose and to choose to change from "sin" to righteousness. A psychotherapist who is not as sensitive to self-destructive behavior and who is not committed to learning and living and leading in viable ways is neither prophet nor therapist.

One of the defining characteristics of the Old Testament prophets was the idea that the one true God spoke through them. This, I believe, is the metaphor signifying that the prophet was able to achieve a perspective on his culture which enabled him to see what those more acculturated could not see. The psychotherapist in modern days must be capable of achieving such an outsider's perspective, of attaining what Buber calls distance, but he must also have the capacity to "enter into relation," in order to have his vision and message heard. In modern terminology, an effective psychotherapist, like an effective prophet, can detach himself from prior ways of being and then return into community with one another, or many others, and share his vision. But I hold the hypothesis that the prophetic psychotherapist and the psychotherapeutic prophets are effective to the extent to which they embody, in their very being, the ways to live that are most compatible with life together in this time and place. It is not possible, I argue, for a true prophet to preach one way and live another. This may require that the psychotherapist in his prophetic function (which is not incompatible with healing) may be, for the moment, a very irritating, infuriating person who discloses truth that hurts, that fosters guilt, anxiety, and intense suffering. But, like the prophets, he does not confront for the joy of inflicting pain, but out of profound concern. If the therapist, like the prophet, is angry, it is because there is something to be angry at. We can view Carl Rogers' wrath at certain dehumanizing aspects of graduate and undergraduate education and his promulgation of encountering as "a Way," as a case of a therapist "gone prophet." [28]

Psychotherapy and Healthy Personality

Frank Shaw,[29] my late friend whose ideas are not

widely enough appreciated, viewed talent in phenomenological–behavioristic terms: talent was a matter of a specialized fascination with something in the world that one could not resist tinkering with in order to make it "right." We might look afresh at prophets and psychotherapists in order to discern whether they might resemble one another in terms of talent, thus defined. It is clear that the therapist and the prophet are fascinated by "sin"—life-destroying behavior—and by suffering: they cannot neglect it in self or in others. It is as if they are receiving sets tuned in permanently on the wave length most interesting to them. But the fascination is not a passive one. No psychotherapist I know of, and no prophet who is recorded, could resist responding to the sufferer (the prophets felt God's suffering), in spite of the fact that many therapists claim that indifference to whether one is helping the other is, paradoxicaly, the best way to be helpful. Prophet and therapist alike will not rest until they are doing what they deem best to remedy the situation.

Some Existential Suggestions

Each of us can function as a psychotherapist, to some extent, with other people in our lives. Truly to listen to the other person, and to share one's own experience with difficulties compared to those he or she is undergoing, is a very psychotherapeutic thing to do. Advice to people with difficulties is seldom the most helpful thing to offer, unless it is requested. Even then, to offer advice to someone with difficulties in living may earn for the advice giver a new dependent.

Human sharing of ways of coping with, or even stoically enduring, difficulties, is a valuable gift for people to give one another. Of course, challenge and attributing strength to people who see themselves as weak and helpless will seldom do harm.

However, a wise friend knows when she needs to refer someone with complex problems for professional help. When making a referral, try to get information ahead of time for the troubled person and make the referral to the agency or to a therapist in a spirit of wanting to get the

Healthy Personality

426

best of help for your friend, rather than in wanting the burden of helping removed from your shoulders.

There are probably a number of opportunities for you to participate in encounter or sensitivity groups. The counseling center, community mental health agencies, or student union all usually conduct these groups at minimal charge or none. The encounter experience can be a deeply meaningful stimulus to growth. However, check up on your leader's qualifications and avoid the charismatic, flamboyant leader.

Don't be reluctant to search for help when you feel the need for it. Shop around for a qualified person with personal qualities you respect.

SUMMARY

Psychotherapists are trained to help people explore new ways of being when their customary ways have led them into impasses or sickness. They come from a variety of professional backgrounds—psychiatry, clinical and counseling psychology, social work, the ministry, and school counseling; and they espouse diverse theories that account for the causes of psychological suffering. The "medical model," which views deviant behavior as mental illness, is gradually being replaced by other perspectives. One of these regards psychological suffering as a byproduct of impasses in personal growth; the psychotherapist is seen as an expert at fostering further growth. Another view holds that suffering stems from inefficient habits; the psychotherapist then functions as an expert in learning. Yet another view holds that people suffer from the results of inauthentic being. The therapist who holds this view then functions as a guide and exemplar of authenticity. Some psychotherapists are influenced by Zen Buddhism, and they see psychological suffering as an outcome of a dualistic, self-conscious state of being. The therapist then functions as a kind of guru who unifies the sufferer's experience. When choosing a therapist, look for professional qualifications and healthy personality. Some representative psychotherapies include psychoanalysis, client-centered reality, rational-emotive, Gestalt, and behavioristic.

Psychotherapy and Healthy Personality

Psychotherapists provide a beneficial influence for their patients by being good human beings. They listen keenly to what their patients have to say, they respect their patients, and strive to make sense of their condition. They regard each person as the embodiment of fantasic possibilities, and they inspire them with hope and the courage to struggle further with the difficulties that have temporarily overcome them.

Although many psychotherapists continue to conduct their practice in a private consulting room, a movement has begun to provide "check-out places," where people can go to change themselves, without professional intervention. Many nonprofessional self-help groups provide psychotherapy for fellow sufferers; for example, Alcoholics Anonymous.

Encounter groups and growth centers have proliferated in recent years, as yet another resource for people who seek to pursue personal growth beyond their present levels of functioning.

NOTES AND REFERENCES

1. G. Goodman, *Companionship Therapy: Studies in Structured Intimacy* (San Francisco: Jossey-Bass, 1972). A good introduction to what psychotherapy is all about is E. Kramer, *Beginning Manual for Psychotherapists* (New York: Grune, 1970). Also K. A. Colby, *Primer for Psychotherapists* (New York: Ronald, 1950).

2. T. S. Szasz, *The Manufacture of Madness. A Comparative Study of the Inquisition and the Mental Health Movement* (New York: Harper, 1970); R. D. Laing, *The Politics of Experience* (New York: Pantheon, 1967).

3. See F. Perls, *Gestalt Therapy Verbatim* (Lafayette, Calif.: Real People Press, 1969); also his posthumous volume, *The Gestalt Approach and Eye Witness to Therapy* (Ben Lomond, Calif.: Science and Behavior Books, 1973); C. R. Rogers, *Client-Centered Therapy* (Boston: Houghton, 1951); C. A. Whitaker and T. P. Malone, *The Roots of Psychotherapy* (New York: Blakiston, 1953); J. Dollard and N. E. Miller, *Personality and Psychotherapy: An Analysis in Terms of Learning, Thinking and Culture* (New York: McGraw-Hill, 1950).

4. J. Wolpe, *The Practice of Behavior Therapy* (New

Healthy Personality

York: Pergamon, 1969); L. P. Ullman and L. Krasner, *Case Studies in Behavior Modification* (New York: Holt, 1965); also their book *Behavior Influence and Personality: The Social Matrix of Human Action* (New York: Holt, 1973), Chapters 10 and 11.

5. J. F. T. Bugental, *The Search for Authenticity: An Existential Analytic Approach to Psychotherapy* (New York: Holt, 1965); S. M. Jourard, *The Transparent Self* (New York: Van Nostrand Reinhold, 1971), Chapters 16, 17, 18; S. M. Jourard, *Disclosing Man to Himself* (New York: Van Nostrand Reinhold, 1968), Chapters 7, 8, 9.

6. A. W. Watts, *Psychotherapy East and West* (New York: Pantheon, 1961).

7. J. D. Frank, *Persuasion and Healing: A Comparative Study of Psychotherapy*, 2nd ed. (Baltimore: Johns Hopkins, 1973).

8. Jourard, *The Transparent Self*, op. cit., Chapter 18, "The Psychotherapist as Exemplar."

9. Frank, *Persuasion and Healing*, op. cit.

10. M. L. Horn, "The Integration of Negative Experience by High and Low Functioning Women," unpublished doctoral dissertation, University of Florida, 1975.

11. An excellent detailed introduction to these and other popular forms of therapy is included in R. J. Corsini (Ed.), *Current Psychotherapies*, 2nd ed. (Itasca, Ill.: Peacock, 1979), and in D. Wedding and R. J. Corsini (Eds.), *Great Cases in Psychotherapy* (Itasca, Ill.: Peacock, 1979). A serious student may want to go directly to some of the sources cited in both of these books. Approaches to psychotherapy in the chapter are the "inventions" of Carl R. Rogers, Fritz Perls, Sigmund Freud, Albert Ellis, William Glasser, and Joseph Wolpe, among others.

12. A helpful book on the crisis center and suicide prevention is R. K. McGee, *Crisis Intervention in the Community* (New York: University Park, 1974).

13. R. H. Williams, "Perspective on the Field of Mental Health: A View of the National Program" (Rockville, Md.: National Institute of Mental Health, 1972).

14. O. H. Mowrer, *The New Group Therapy* (New York: Van Nostrand Reinhold, 1964).

15. Jourard, *The Transparent Self*, op. cit., Chapter 19, "Self-disclosure and the Encounter Group Leader."

16. For an entirely readable, professional description of the encounter group, see C. R. Rogers, *Carl Rogers on Encounter Groups* (New York: Harper, 1970).

17. K. W. BACK, *Beyond Words: The Story of Sensitivity Training and the Encounter Movement* (New York: Russell Sage, 1952).

18. D. LAVOIE, "The Phenomenological Transformation of the Self-concept Towards Self-actualization Through a Sensitivity Training Laboratory," *Interpersonal Development*, 1972, Vol. 2, pp. 201–212.

19. M. A. LIEBERMAN, I. D. YALOM, and M. B. MILES, *Encounter Groups: First Facts* (New York: Basic, 1973).

20. W. SCHUTZ, *Here Comes Everybody: Bodymind and Encounter Culture* (New York: Harper, 1971), offers a perspective on growth centers. Growth centers are now to be found all over the world. A list can be obtained from the Association for Humanistic Psychology, 325 Ninth Street, San Francisco, Calif. 94103.

21. S. M. JOURARD, "Prophets as Pychotherapists, and Psychotherapists as Prophets," *Voices: The Art and Science of Pychotherapy*, 1971, Vol. 7, pp. 11–16; "The Transcending Psychotherapist," ibid., 1972, Vol. 8, pp. 66–69. See also S. KOPP, *Guru: Metaphors from a Psychotherapist* (Palo Alto, Calif.: Science and Behavior Books, 1971), for analogies between psychotherapists and other human endeavors.

22. A. HESCHEL, *The Prophets* (New York: Harper, 1969).

23. The magnificent as well as the sad aspects of Reich's life are given in accounts written by his son, and by a former wife. See ILSE O. REICH, *Wilhelm Reich, a Personal Biography* (New York: St. Martin's, 1969), and P. REICH, *A Book of Dreams* (New York: Harper, 1973).

24. B. CHISHOLM, "Can People Really Learn to Learn?" (New York: Harper, 1958).

25. R. D. LAING and E. ESTERSON, *Sanity, Madness and the Family* (London: Tavistock, 1964); E. ESTERSON, *The Leaves of Spring: A Study in the Dialectics of Madness* (London: Tavistock, 1970). See also I. CHARNY, *Marital Love and Hate* (New York: Macmillan, 1972).

26. T. S. SZASZ, *The Myth of Mental Illness: Foundations of a Theory of Personal Conduct* (New York: Harper, 1961); T. S. SZASZ, *The Manufacture of Madness: A Comparative Study of the Inquisition and the Mental Health Movement* (New York: Harper, 1970).

27. Rogers discusses the development of his work in C. R. ROGERS, "My Philosophy of Interpersonal Relationships and How It Grew," *Journal of Humanistic Psychology*, 1973, Vol. 13, pp. 3–16.

28. C. R. ROGERS, *Freedom to Learn* (Columbus, Oh.: Merrill, 1969).

29. F. J. SHAW, *Reconciliation, a Theory of Man Transcending*, S. JOURARD and D. OVERLADE (Eds.) (New York: Van Nostrand Reinhold, 1966).

*Psychotherapy
and Healthy
Personality*

17

THE HUMANISTIC
APPROACH TO
PSYCHOLOGY

INTRODUCTION

Sartre described a scene in which a voyeur peeps through the keyhole into a bedroom.[1] Suddenly he is discovered by another, and becomes, thereby, an object for the other, and for himself. His experience of his freedom oozes away, and he feels himself transmuted from a subject into a thing. Whenever a person is caught in the act, when someone hitherto concealed is seen, then the viewer turns the one looked at into stone. Psychologists have been inviting the subjects of their research to become as natural objects, like stones. The surprising thing is that the subjects have cooperated. I cannot fathom why, because I do not know of any good that has accrued to the subject as the consequence of being a subject, that is, an object. This is a strong statement; yet I do not believe that the quality of personal life has improved as a result of eighty years of scientific investigation of human consciousness and action. In fact, there is more basis for me to believe the knowledge of human beings we have acquired has been used to control and limit them rather than to enlarge their awareness, their dignity, or their freedom.

Psychology as a "Natural" Science

In research, as most psychologists have practiced it, subjects are recruited and asked to make themselves available to the psychologist for observation, interviewing, and testing. The psychologist records their speech, actions, and reactions with various kinds of equipment; analyzes the findings; and publicizes them. Typically, the psychologist defines psychology as a scientific discipline that seeks to understand the behavior of humans and other organisms. Proof of understanding is evident when the psychologist can *predict* the action or reactions under study, by pointing to predictive signs, or by bringing them under some kind of deliberate *control*. Great pains are taken to insure that the observer does not influence the behavior he or she is studying, so that the persons or animals under study will show themselves as they really are. Ideally the subjects of study would not know that they were being watched because the experience of being observed affects action.[2]

It is clear from this description that scientific psychology has been patterned, since its inception by Wundt, after the natural sciences. Although we now draw distinctions among natural, social, and behavioral sciences, in each of these, similar assumptions are held by the respective scientists, for example, that determinism prevails and that the laws that govern the phenomena under study can be discovered if the right questions are asked of the subject matter in the right way.

Science, so understood, embodies two ambitions that enchanted me as a youngster. One was the wish to read the mind of others. It was fascinating to try to discern what was going on behind my friend's or some stranger's opaque exterior. Did they like me? Were they going to harm me? If I could see into or through them I would have fair warning about their intentions, and I could govern myself accordingly. In fact, if I could read minds in this way, it would give me a certain power over others.

The Humanistic Approach to Psychology

433

Such power over others was the second childhood wish. I imagined what it would be like to be able to get other people, and animals, to do exactly what I wanted them to do. Snake charmers and hypnotists provided a model of the type of control I sought in entertaining these fantasies. To this day, I am intrigued by trainers who can get animals to perform intricate tricks.

Let us look at psychology, as a natural science, in the light of these childhood quests for omniscience and omnipotence. It seems fair to say that psychologists aim to read their subjects' minds, and to gain increments of power over their experience and action.

In the dawn of history, humans were probably victimized by nature; animals, plants, seas, and soil all acted with "minds" of their own, indifferent to humans' needs and wishes. When nature was seen animistically, early human beings could seek some measure of prediction and control by talking to the souls, spirits, and gods that moved natural happenings. They would try to propitiate or bribe those animated beings, in order to get them to tell their intentions; this would help a person get power over hostile nature, and over untrustworthy, unpredictable strangers. Presumably, those humans who could best foretell the future and influence the outcome of events were seen by their fellows as having either more powerful gods or a closer relationship with the gods. In any case, nature was seen as capricious and hostile; humans could improve their lot if they could read its mind (predict what was going to happen) and get it to act in ways that would serve their needs and interests. Natural science was developed to tame and demystify hostile nature.

The modern scientific psychologist faces her subjects and subject matter in a posture similar to that of the natural scientist. The other person's action is not always friendly to someone's interests. Someone can gain if a person's action can be predicted (i.e., if her mind can be read, if her face becomes a transparent mask through which her stream of consciousness can be read), and if she can be induced to act in ways that serve someone's interests. The subjects of research in scientific psychology are deliberately seen as Other, as one of Them, as *a part of nature different from the scientist and those other persons whom the scientist designates as Us.*

Yet we must remember that a psychologist is a human being, living in a time and place, in a society with a class structure, a power structure; and he has economic interests. Typically, he is salaried and the costs of his research are borne by private or public agencies. We have to assume that these agencies will not willingly countenance research that will undermine their power over people. A pharmaceutical firm is unlikely to spend millions of dollars in the study of placebos, so that drug use in medicine will be diminished. It does not seem far-fetched to me to regard the most rigorous, truth-seeking psychologist as a servant, witting or unwitting, of the agencies that pay him and his costs. The agencies that believe it worthwhile financing research into human behavior typically believe that their interests will be furthered if human beings' behavior becomes more predictable. They want people to be transparent to them (while they remain opaque to the others), and they want to learn how to make people's action more amenable to control. People who can be controlled can serve the controller's interests without knowing it—in which case we would say that they are mystified. If a psychologist studies people and makes their action predictable and their experience transparent to some elite—but not to the persons he has studied—then he is indeed a functionary, even though he may be a passionate seeker of truth. He may share the class interests of the elite, and he may serve those interests by viewing the subjects of his research as "Them," creatures not unlike natural phenomena—floods, earthquakes, animals—that must be understood in order that they can be tamed.

My hypothesis is that unless the behavior scientist explores the broader social, political, and economic implications of his work, he is a functionary indeed; worse, if he does not realize it, then he is being mystified by those who employ him.

The psychological testing movement, likewise, can be seen in this light, as a quest to read people's minds and to fathom their talents, strengths and weaknesses, to serve someone's ends, not necessarily the ends of the person being tested. Beginning with Binet's contribution, up to and including that of Rorschach, the ability of one person, the tester, to discover something about the testee is

The Humanistic Approach to Psychology

not necessarily good for the latter. I can remember the excitement I felt, as an undergraduate, when I first heard about tests of intelligence, and of personality, by means of which one person could literally make another transparent. But now the blacks and other so-called culturally deprived people are less than sanguine in their appreciation of what psychometrics are good for. In fact, quite properly, many blacks see the testing movement as one of several means by which their subordinate status in the education establishment, and hence the professional world, is maintained. And as we come to take a fresh look at psychiatry, for which profession the projective and many objective (like the MMPI) tests of personality were developed, we see that psychiatric classification is less an analogue of differential medical diagnosis, and more a subtle way to invalidate a human being.[3] Projective techniques can be seen as violations of the Fifth Amendment of the Constitution—sneaky means of finding out about a person. "Unobtrusive measures," which have come to be seen as an answer to uncooperative research subjects, or to experimenter bias, likewise are ways to get a person to reveal herself unwittingly, thereby giving information which may not help her.[4]

Am I saying any more than that knowledge of people, like knowledge of nature, gives power, and power corrupts? Perhaps not, but to say that is still to say something that we in psychology must take into account. Are we seeking the truth about humans that sets all people free? Or are the truths we discover only making some people more free and powerful, while others become more vulnerable to manipulation?

It seems clear to me that the image of human beings assumed by a psychologist will affect her research strategies, her theories, and her ways and areas of consulting. If she views people as natural objects, rather than as beings like herself, her science and its applications will be as I have described.

I will now look at the fields of psychotherapy and counseling, as well as at the behavior-modification movement.

Healthy Personality　　Once again, economics rears its head. Psychological practitioners who apply scientific knowledge of people artfully do not sell their services cheaply. If they are in private practice, they charge substantial fees to the individuals and agencies that engage their services. Otherwise, they are retained or salaried by government or private agencies, to utilize their know-how in order that the agency might fulfill its aims more fully. For example, psychologists are employed by advertising agencies and business concerns of many kinds in order that the public being "served" will more readily buy the company's products or in order that workers will produce more, and more cheaply. Sometimes the service sold by the psychologist is knowledge about how masses of people will respond to symbols; sometimes, he trains people in the art of seeming sincere, friendly, and authentic.

The arts of counseling and psychotherapy, seen from the perspective of a natural science of psychology, become arenas for the practice of techniques, ways to influence the experience and hence the action of the client or patient. Psychoanalysts, behavior-modification experts, and many kinds of counseling technicians are all encouraged to believe that if they master a repertoire of laboratory- or clinic-tested techniques, they will "get the patient to change." Of course, the techniques of behavior modification by environmental control, as in token economies, in mental hospitals, represent a subtle exercise of power. Hypnosis, shaping, and aversive conditioning all represent ways to alter someone's action. The person who employs these techniques can remain invisible behind a professional manner. If he practices his techniques well, he will earn a fine salary from a grateful agency, or high fees from those rich enough to afford his services. Those individuals who are rich enough to afford his services are seldom spokespersons for liberal change in the political and economic system within which they earn the money to pay for their "treatments." Moreover, as some of the more radical psychiatrists are beginning to assert, psychiatric intervention, of whatever sort, is a kind of social control aiming to invalidate, and perhaps avert, dissent.

The Humanistic Approach to Psychology

If the basic and applied behavior science we have developed thus far has primarily been a quest for knowledge that makes people predictable and controllable, then clearly what is called for is a complementary science, one that uses scientific discipline and knowledge to liberate a person from being the victim not only of the forces of nature, but *also of the concealed efforts of other people to influence him for weal or woe.*

People's action and experience are indeed affected by mass media, by leaders, by genes, by their past experience, by reinforcement contingencies, by their biology and physiology, and by the social and interpersonal setting within which they live their lives. Any way of discerning how these realms affect experience and action is of some use to the person, and to others. I think that we psychologists have not served that person. Perhaps this is what humanistic psychology, or psychology as a *human* science, can do.[5]

Psychology as a "Human" Science

In 1957 I began to study self-disclosure. This was before I ever heard of anything called humanistic psychology. I was trained in experimental as well as clinical psychology, and a program of research has always been part of my view of the practice of my profession. I chose self-disclosure as a subject for scientific study because I began to wonder what we knew about the conditions under which people would reveal personal information to others. Freud pointed out that psychoanalysis entailed overcoming a patient's reluctance to let her analyst know her, and psychotherapeutic practice called for being an encourager and listener to another's intimate disclosure. And so, using what I regarded (and still do) as appropriate techniques for research, I began collecting self-report data from thousands of people about their past disclosure to parents, friends, and other target persons. I wanted a scientific understanding of self-disclosure in order to predict and control this kind of behavior. Certainly that is what my scientific training in Toronto and Buffalo encouraged me to do and think. Ironically, I soon discovered that *one of the most powerful correlates, if not determiners, of one person's self-disclosure was self-disclosure from the other person in the dyad.* Several questionnaire studies pointed to this hypothesis, and we

Healthy Personality

438

confirmed it in numerous experimental interviews conducted under laboratory conditions. We found that we could maximize a person's disclosure of personal data by offering such disclosure first, as a kind of invitation, or as an example of what action was appropriate to the situation. My students and I, in conducting these experiments, did not *pretend* to disclose personal subject matter. We *really did*, and it was sometimes risky and embarrassing; but we functioned in the spirit of adventurous inquiry, and found the outcomes we have mentioned.[6]

I had begun to experiment with my ways of being a psychotherapist, beginning soon after I discovered that my training did not prepare me to be helpful to Southerners with difficulties in living. I had begun as far back as 1952 to break my professional anonymity, by sharing with a client any experience of mine with problems comparable to those she was exploring with me. I found that such authentic sharing, within bounds of relevance and common sense, encouraged my patients to explore and reveal their experience more fully and freely than was hitherto the case for me. It was as if I had bungled onto a new kind of technique, but one that entailed some risk, indeed, some inclusion of my patient into the world of Us, rather than seeing her as one of Them—the neurotics, the psychotics, and so on. This experience in conducting psychotherapy appeared to support my survey and laboratory findings in the study of self-disclosure. But my experience as a psychotherapist influenced my view of research more profoundly.

I was motivated to be helpful to the person who sought my professional help, and I found, increasingly, that one way to be helpful was to demystify the patient insofar as it was possible. The patient suffered from difficulties in living because he did not know what was going on. People lied to him, and he to them. Some patients were mystified by nature, others by social structures. It was difficult to know oneself, others, and the world. Our therapy sessions could be seen as an effort at authentic communication between two persons, so both of us would know what was going on. I found myself sharing *my* understanding of how people not only mystified

The Humanistic Approach to Psychology

439

one another, but invited others to be diminished creatures. I would show and role-play the way people attributed imaginary traits to one another, which they would then embody and act out—like Gênet becoming the thief he was defined to be early in life. Gradually, my understanding of what a psychologist's task might be underwent a change. I came to see that, if hitherto, research and practice grew out of a view of the human being as a natural phenomenon, to be studied by an elite in order that he might be better mind-read and controlled, it would be elegant to strive to do psychology *for* man. This, I came to see, must be what a humanistic psychology would be and be for.

Humanistic psychology could be defined, I saw, as an effort to disclose human beings and their situation to *themselves*, to make them more aware, by any and all means, of what forces were influencing their experience and hence their action. I could see that human subjects would not really disclose themselves, would not really let themselves be known to researchers or anyone else whom they had reason to distrust, and so we commenced a program of research within which the researcher was as much to be interviewed by the subject as vice versa. Though we made only a beginning at this, the results confirm that different perspectives on people will emerge when more research is done.

If various institutions aim to control people's action and experience in order to serve the institution's aims, then a task for a humanistic psychology could be to study the means by which the propaganda, rules, and environment produced conformity, so that a person could better choose to conform or not to conform. I discovered in the process of this inquiry that for one person to lie to another is an effort to control her experience and action, so that she will be mystified. This is exactly equivalent to the situation of humans facing a hostile nature that they do not understand. Not to understand is to be vulnerable to prediction and control—victimization, whether by mystifying nature, or by one's lying and self-concealing fellow human being. To be understood, and not to understand the one who understands you, is indeed to be *Healthy* vulnerable—to be a transcendence transcended, as Sartre *Personality* puts it.

George Miller, a past president of the American Psychological Association, urged his colleagues to "give psychology away." As natural-science psychologists learn about "determiners" of human experience and action, humanistic psychologists (who can be natural-science psychologists too) can make apparent to all the ways in which their freedom is being eroded by hostile nature or hostile people.

Psychological research, from this perspective, becomes an enterprise wherein the subject becomes privy to the aims of the researcher, where she is free to learn about the researcher as the researcher learns about her.

Counseling and psychotherapy, from the standpoint of humanistic psychology, become enterprises where patient and therapist share relevant experience, so that the former can become more enlightened, more liberated from influences that constrain his growth and self-actualization. Indeed, I find myself using the word *therapy* less and less, seeking some metaphor more aptly descriptive of what goes on in such helping transactions. Terms like *teacher, guide, guru, liberator* all suggest themselves, though all sound fairly pretentious. But in all these cases, one thinks not of a person manipulating another, reading his mind in order to gain power over him, but of a dialogue between I and You.

Some Existential Suggestions

Try this exercise of imagination: imagine that your closest friend or the person whom you love best has suddenly been transformed into a rat, or into a robot controlled by a computer program. How would you relate to him or her? Clearly, it would be a case of you having to control the rat, or choose a program for the robot. Certainly your relationship with that person would change from the way it was when you attributed freedom, dignity, and responsibility to the person. Now imagine that the person is a person once more. When he or she was a rat or robot, how would you go about studying this person, to understand how his or her behavior worked? How would you learn about the person when he or she was attributed personhood?

If you intend to pursue psychology as a research career, or as a profession for helping persons live more fully, which perspective on human beings will you select? The human being as an object, or the human being as a person, or both? There *may* be times when human welfare and knowledge of people are furthered by assuming the human being, as a topic of study, is a natural object totally subject to natural law. I am not certain that such times exist.

SUMMARY

When psychology is pursued as a "natural" science, human beings, the subject of study, are dehumanized. Frequently they are studied in order to help other people control and predict their behavior, and not necessarily for their wellbeing. An alternative way to study human beings is described—where investigators encourage the persons whom they are studying to interview them as thoroughly as they wish, in order to test their trustworthiness. I discuss my own research briefly, which shows that when a psychological researcher, diagnostician, and psychotherapist make themselves accessible to their subjects and patients, the latter behave differently from when the professional person preserves his or her impersonal anonymity.

NOTES AND REFERENCES

[This chapter also appears as an article: S. M. JOURARD, "Psychology: Control or Liberation," *Interpersonal Development*, Vol. 2, 1971–72, pp. 65–72.]

1. Research psychologists would do well to read Sartre's sensitive account of the experience of being looked at. See J.-P. SARTRE, *Being and Nothingness* (London: Methuen, 1956), p. 259.

2. Rosenthal produced much evidence to show that the experimenter is an important influence on the behavior and experience of subjects in psychological research. See R. ROSENTHAL, *Exprimenter Effects in Behavior Research* (New York: Appleton, 1966). Efforts to make allowance for the "experimenter-effect" are discussed in A. G. MILLER (Ed.), *The Social Psychology of Research* (New York: Free Press, 1972).

Healthy Personality

3. See T. SZASZ, *Ideology and Insanity: Essays on the Psychiatric Dehumanization of Man* (Garden City, N.Y.: Doubleday, 1970).

4. For a review of methods to study people without their awareness, see E. J. WEBB, D. T. CAMPBELL, R. D. SCHWARTZ, and L. SECHREST, *Unobtrusive Measures: Non-reactive Research in the Social Sciences* (Chicago: Rand McNally, 1967). See also A. WESTIN, *Privacy and Freedom* (New York: Atheneum, 1967).

5. An introduction to psychology as a human, rather than a natural, science, is A. GIORGI, *Psychology as a Human Science* (New York: Harper, 1971).

6. Jourard's research in self-disclosure is presented in S. M. JOURARD, *Self-disclosure: An Experimental Analysis of the Transparent Self* (New York: Wiley-Interscience, 1971). The implications of this research for theory, and for human life, are given in his other books: *The Transparent Self* (New York: Van Nostrand Reinhold, 1964; 2nd ed., 1971), and *Disclosing Man to Himself* (New York: Van Nostrand Reinhold, 1968).

MARRIAGE IS FOR LIFE

SIDNEY M. JOURARD

The title of my article has nothing to do with chronological time. When I chose a title "Marriage Is for Life"
I meant that marriage is to enhance life, and it is not so
much an answer as it is a search. I want to direct my remarks to that search, the search for life itself.

Ideal (and False) Images of Marriage

The image of the good marriage is perhaps one of its
most destructive features. The ideal marriage is a snare,
a trap, an image the worship of which destroys life. The
ideal marriage is like the ideal body or any other ideal,
useful only if it engenders the divine discontent which
leads to questing and authenticity. Whose image of a

NOTE: About a month before his death, Dr. Sidney Jourard delivered
the following plenary address before the annual meeting of the American Association of Marriage and Family Counselors and the National
Council on Family Relations in St. Louis, Missouri. Edited from the
tape of the meeting by Dr. Jourard's colleagues, it probably represents the last of his lively thinking to reach publication.—T. L.
Source: Vol. I, No. 3, *Journal of Marriage and Family Counseling.*
Copyrighted by and used with the permission of the American
Association for Marriage and Family Therapy.

way to live together will guide a relationship? This is a question relevant for a president and his electorate, a doctor and his patient, a parent and child, a researcher and his subject, or a husband and wife. Shall it be an exercise in the concealment and display of power or a commitment to dialogue? Failure of dialogue is the crisis of our time, whether it be between nation and nation, us and them, or you and I.

I had thought of putting together a book of my several writings on marriage, education, psychology, politics, and business and entitling it "Disaster Areas," for that indeed is what they are. The state of marriage and family life in this country can easily be called a disaster. I think it stems in part from unrealistic expectations and in larger part because of a culturally induced arrest of growth in adults. Perfectly good marriages are ended because something has gone wrong. Actually, I would say they are ended right at the point where they could begin.

There are two fallacies perpetuated which keep the disasters happening. One is the myth of the right partner. The other is the myth of the right way to act as to ensure peace, joy, and happiness. People believe, or are led to believe, that if they just find the right partner, the right answer to the riddle of their existence will be found. Once having found the right person and the way of relating that is satisfying at this time, the partners try to do everything to prevent change. That's tantamount to trying to stop the tide. Change, indeed, happens, but it happens underground, is concealed, and then it's introduced and experienced as a catastrophe. Instead of welcoming it, the partners find it devastating. Each may then seek to find someone who will not change, so that they never need face the need to change themselves.

Marriage as Dialogue

Marriage at its best, according to the image that is making more sense to me, is a relationship within which change is generated by the very way of relating— dialogue, so that growth as well as identity and a sense of rootedness are engendered. Change is not so much a

threat as it is the fruit of a good marriage, according to

this image. Marriage is for growth, for life. It's a place to call home, but like all homes one must leave it in its present form and then return, and then leave it, and then return, like Odysseus, leaving Ithaca and returning.

Kierkegaard refused to marry and thereby defied the nineteenth century. I have refused to divorce, and I defy the twentieth. When one marriage in three is dissolved, or maybe it's 2.6, to remain wedded to the same spouse is virtually to live an alternate life style. If so few marriages endure, then something is non-viable about the way of being married. I have tried in the 26 years of my marriage to be married in the ways designated by tradition, by the mass media, by my friends, by textbooks on marriage, by my wife's image of a good marriage, and none of these ways were for life. None were life-giving, but were rather images, or better, idols. To worship idols is idolatry, a sin. To worship means to live for, to sacrifice what is of ultimate value. To worship an image of marriage is like any other idolatry, the expenditure of one's own life, time, and vitality to enhance the image. That such marriage is disastrous is self-evident. When it endures it becomes a major cause of psychological distress and physical illness in our land.

Conventional medicine, psychiatry, and psychotherapy, and for that matter, marriage counseling and family counseling, frequently function very much like combat surgery. The illness and suffering which reach the healers stem from the stress and "dispiritation" engendered from inauthentic family relationships. Laing and Esterson documented the way a family image can be preserved at the cost of one member being scapegoated as a schizophrenic (Laing and Esterson, 1965). The wards for cancer, heart disease, gunshot and knife injuries, suicide attempts, and other stress ailments provide evidence that non-dialogic family life engenders unrelenting and destructive stress. To be married is not an unmixed blessing. If marriage is hell, and family life is a major cause of disease, which indeed it is, why stay in it, or get in it?

Is the family dead, as David Cooper observed (Cooper, 1971)? If it's dying, should we then kill it, put it out of its misery?

Appendix   What do people do who have tried marriage and then

447

gotten out of it? The overwhelming majority remarry, and try to live the second, third, or seventh marriage in a way that is more life-giving for the self and others then the first. Frequently, these marriages "fail," as did the first, and I put "fail" in quotes, because I don't think marriages fail; I think people fail marriages.

Wherever I go in this country I get uncomfortable. I think it's more so in California than elsewhere, and it's not with smog or even the inhabitants of Orange County, but with the people one encounters everywhere. I am a trained and rather experienced psychotherapist, tuned in to the non-verbal expressions of despair, loneliness, anguish, and need. So many of the adults I encounter casually or in depth are suffering a rupture of their last lawful or common-law marriage, and are desperately looking for a new one or despairingly avoiding all but superficial relationships in order to avoid risk. The silent shrieks of pain deafen me. To be married is for many boredom or hell. To be unmarried, legally or illegally, as many experience it is hell and despair. Is there an alternative?

Everything depends on the model or metaphor which defines the marriage one will live, seek, grow in, or die from. There are lethal images of marriage and family life, and there are life-giving models. I take it that enduring, growing relationships are essential for truly human life and for personal fulfillment and growth. I take it that happiness, pleasure, or growth if sought as ends in and of themselves will not happen. They are by-products of a fully-lived life. A life lived in continuing dialogue with some few others will encourage, even force growth.

I take it as true that there is no way to go through life without some pain, suffering, loneliness, and fear. We can help one another minimize the shadow side of life; none can avoid it completely. To seek to avoid pain at all costs is to make an idol out of pleasure or painlessness. To avoid solitude at all costs is to make an idol out of chronic companionship. To avoid anxiety and depression at all costs is to make an idol out of safety and elation. To have to achieve orgasm with somebody in *Appendix* particular is to make an idol of that person or of the

448

genital experience. To sacrifice everything for the breath-less experience of being in love is to make an idol of breathlessness.

Many people live in such idolatrous fashion. They marry for those ends and divorce when the other side of reality creeps or bursts into the magic circle, only to seek another playmate or protector in relation to whom the idol may once again be worshipped and the sacrifice of life continue afresh.

Marriage as dialogue through life is for me a viable image, one that engenders life and growth as the con-versation unfolds. Dialogue for me, as for Martin Buber (Buber, 1937), is the appropriate way for human beings to be or to strive to be with each other, not imposition, power plays, and manipulation. Family life is an ap-propriate place for dialogue to be learned and practiced. And through dialogue it's a place to grow in compe-tence, self-sufficiency, and self-esteem.

To me the great failure in marriage as in American education is that neither institution as lived and practiced fosters enlargement of self-respect, respect for others, or growing competence in the skills that make life livable. Deception, manipulation, bribery, and threats are as American as apple pie and mother. These skills are learned in relation with Mum, Dad, the teacher, or the teaching machine.

There is, as near as I now know, no assured way to practice marriage as dialogue except by living it. As soon as a relationship becomes habitual, dialogue has ended. Predictable, habitual ways for people to act with one another are simply non-verbal ways to say the same things to one another day after day, year after year. Habit is the great anesthetic, the annihilator of con-sciousness.

Non-dialogic ways of being married are either exer-cised in a chronic struggle for power and control or they are harbors to escape those aspects of life that would engender growth. Some people stay married so they will have someone to control. Some people stay married so they will have an ear to talk into. Some people stay married so they can suffer or make their partner suffer.

Appendix Most curiously, some get divorced when their partner

449

will no longer be controlled, will no longer listen, or will no longer consent to suffer. The other's changes may be, indeed, a sign of the other person's personal growth. The one who gets a divorce may find yet another partner with whom control can be practiced or who will listen to undisciplined chatter with apparent interest or who will accept pain.

All this is by way of saying that I think in America and in the countries that follow the example set by the American way of life, we expect more out of marriage than it could ever deliver and we expect the wrong things. God, in Her infinite wisdom, so designed us that we are of two kinds and we find one another irresistible at various stages in our lives, so much so that we decide to live together. So far, so good. It's joyous to find another person attractive who finds you attractive, then to make love, even to have children.

Then the honeymoon ends and the marriage begins. It is at this point that I think most divorce happens. We are hung up on honeymoons. My honeymoon was a disaster. I knew next to nothing about tenderness and solicitude, sex, women's sexuality, my bride's sexuality. I was incapable of dialogue. I wanted to be seen in a certain way. I needed my wife to be a certain way, and obliging girl that she was, she obliged. She seemed to be the kind of person she thought I thought she was, the kind of person she felt I would like. We carried out this double masquerade for about three years. It took me that long to cheat. By seven years I was an accomplished dissembler in the realm of my sex life, not my love life, where I was a truthteller in all realms except that.

With our first separation I had a modest collection of female scalps, so to speak, to my credit and my wife, to her credit, after the shock of disclosure wore off discovered the dubious joys of semi-guilty infidelity. Through some fluke, though, within a month of a decree of divorce, we decided to resume our by now somewhat scarred relationship, rather wiser and more honest with one another about who we were. This openness for those not practiced in it was pure hell. It was *Appendix*   painful, I assure you. It was painful for me to learn that

450

my wife had a mind, a perspective, and feelings of her own different from mine. She was not the girl I married; in fact, she never was. I married my fantasy, and so did she. She had some coping to do, discovering that I was not the saint I had once seemed. She learned I was, and still am to some extent, a scarcely bridled privateer, a pirate, and adventurer, barely domesticated to her or American conceptions of married males.

How do two or more eccentric and energetic people live together? With humor or not at all. I did not become selectively gelded upon marriage. The more I reflect upon it, the more I like myself, having had the courage to pursue those ways of keeping vital and alive as non-destructively as I did. I could have done worse. I could have sought a divorce or have been divorced by my wife. If the first three years were the honeymoon—actually only about one year was honeymoon—boredom and pretense at joy in our sameness is a better description of our next two years. My cheating was the beginning of a marriage with some authentic companionship, some lying and getting on with the career, and the experience of living with several very young children. This marriage or this way of being married lasted until seven years when I experienced the death of my father, the completion of my first book, and the dreaded disclosure of my rather complicated affairs with several other women. Here was a real opportunity to be taught a lesson or to learn a lesson. I didn't divorce, however, nor did my wife divorce me, because we retained some recollection of affection between us, we had some children to care for, and a vast amount of anger and mutual reacquaintance to go through. It is, I assure you again, a painful experience extended through time to make yourself known to the person with whom you live and to learn aspects of her experience, attitudes, hopes, fears, and so on which shatter your image of her.

But my marriage and family life were not all my life. I had friends, other interests, and I pursued these, as did she. My life did not begin when I met her nor end when we were out of contact with one another.

Appendix   My third marriage to her began with hope and resolve,

451

as we struggled to find some enjoyment in living and to care for our children. I suspect we were growing in experience, self-sufficiency, and self-esteem. I hesitate to use certain words, but I'll say them. The point I was going to make is that marriage and family life is a wonderful place to learn shit, fecal detritus, because if you don't know shit, you have not lived. But if that's all you know, you have not lived.

I don't know how many marriages I have had by now, but I am married at the present time to a different woman of the same name in ways that are suited to our present stage of growth as human beings. I am not breathlessly in love with my wife, nor is she with me. Now, she read this and there are some asterisks in her handwriting. It says, "Maybe not breathlessly, but I do love you now with more intensity and depth and true caring than I ever have in my life."

When we spend a great deal of time in one another's proximity, we can both know irritations, even rages of astonishing intensity. It is difficult for two strong and passionate and willful people to share space and time without humor and respect for the other, even though she is wrong, as from my point of view she is. It would be so much easier for me to divorce her and to live with, even marry, some younger woman who has firmer breasts, a smaller waist, who is as sexy as a civet, who worships me and wants to have an intense and meaningful relationship with me, who would attend to my every word, and think I was the Messiah or at least worthy of the Nobel Prize. Many of my colleagues have done that. I could never see—except when I was most exasperated with my wife and fed up with being a father—why these friends of mine, otherwise sensible, wished to play the same record over again. I find someone whose perspective is smaller than mine, or who wants me to be their father, or who is but an echo of my own perspective, rather boring. Flattering, but boring. And I don't want to father anybody because I've been a father. I find a grown person of the opposite sex incites me much less to rape or riot than a young girl more interesting by and large, at least to listen to.

Appendix   It takes a long time to give up manipulative and mystifying ways of relating to others in order to trust oneself in dialogue. My training and experience as a psychotherapist have influenced my conception and experience of marriage, or perhaps it's the other way around. My colleagues in the American Academy of Psychotherapists are indeed a rather eccentric lot with many backgrounds and theoretical orientations. All were trained in some way of acting with a patient which was believed to influence, heal, or otherwise impose magical power upon the sufferer. All learned through experience that whatever else they did, they helped people grow by entering into dialogue with them, by being fully present struggling through impasses, and growing through those struggles. Impasses were not to be avoided, they were to be sought out and celebrated, as painful as they were. They helped their patients grow by staying in relationship with them. The growth that is crucial in this conception of therapy is increased awareness to one's own worth as a person and a realization that one is vastly stronger than anyone had ever imagined. This sense of worth and of strength protects one from entering into and staying in a way of relating to another that is devitalizing and sickening.

A book on marriage which I have read—and I have read many including the O'Neills' (O'Neill and O'Neill, 1972)—which addresses this mystery of growth with some of the respect that it deserves is a small volume written by Israel Charny called *Marital Love and Hate* (Charny, 1972). Compared to his vision, many of the other books fail to acknowledge, I think, the depths of misery and destructiveness which are the other side of personal growth. Charny sees the family not strictly as haven or a place for fun and games, although it can be that, or as a place for sexual delights, but as a place where the most savage of all creatures, man, can learn to share time and space nonviolently and nondestructively. Armed by his vision, as well as by my own, I can see that many so-called successful marriages and happy families are that way because someone is repressing his perspective or is colluding with others in the destruction of his own perspective.

Appendix   According to this view, marriage is not for happiness,

453

I have concluded after 26½ years. It's a many-splendored thing, a place to learn how to live with human beings who differ from oneself in age, sex, values, and perspectives. It's a place to learn how to hate and to control hate. It's a place to learn laughter and love and dialogue. I'm not entirely persuaded that marriage and family counseling is a profession with any particular contribution to make to the quality of life. There is so far as I now know no way for people to live alone or with others that God endorsed as *the way* that She intended. (Laughter) Why is that funny? Certainly She intended that we cohabit to conceive and then to rear children, but the exact way we should live with one another was never specified. We have to grope and search, according to this view. As near as I can see, such groping for viable, non-destructive ways proceeds best within a context of dialogue.

Dialogue takes courage and commitment to honesty. When people find they can no longer live with their partner, it is not divorce or separation that is indicated. This is in some ways like suicide. The person who tries to kill himself is being unduly literal. By his act he is saying that he no longer wishes to live in the way he has been, and he is also saying that he can imagine no other way to live. He doesn't necessarily wish to stop living, just to stop living in that way. His failure is a failure of imagination as much as it is a failure of nerve.

Divorce too frequently means that one partner or the other refuses to continue living married in that way. The divorce then finds someone with whom some other dimension of himself can be expressed. This looks like change or growth. I have wondered whether hitherto unexpressed dimensions of self could not have emerged in relation to the spouse because with the new partner an impasse will arrive and there will be the necessity to struggle with it.

If there is growth in serial marriage—and there is— one wonders why there could not be growth in the first. I know of many marriages in which one partner or the other refused to acknowledge or value the change in the other. The unchanged one ordered the changed one to revert to the way he or she was earlier, on pain of divorce.

Appendix

454

The failure of marriage is the failure of our culture to provide models and reasonable expectations about human relationships. Because we lie so much about our relationships, especially to our children, and because the breadth and depth of authentic experience is not presented in movies, comics, books, or TV, nobody knows what is expectable or what is healthy or lifegiving or potentially lifegiving in marriage. People think that if they get angry or bore one another or fail to respond sexually that the marriage is finished, that they are out of love. Perhaps the overestimation of romantic love is one of the more pernicious patterns in our society.

When spouses deceive one another for the first time that is the time the potentially life and growth-promoting aspects of marriage can begin. When the couple finds themselves in rage, that is the time not for divorce but for celebration. Whimsically, I thought that the first betrayal of marriage should come on the honeymoon, so that it can be gotten over and the dialogue resumed.

Marriage is not an answer, but a search, a process, a search for life, just as dialogue is a search for truth. Yesterday's marriage or way of being married is today's trap. The way out of the trap is to resume the dialogue, not to end it, unless someone is pledged not to grow and change. One of my colleagues is being divorced after 22 or 23 years of marriage. He is a Southern fellow, his wife an extremely pious member of the Methodist Church, a "lousy lay" he assures everyone, and he explored another young woman. And the way he put it, "You know, when I went to bed with her she liked it." He carried on, "It was great and I discovered there was another way, but then my wife found out about it and she made me confess to our children and then made me give her up" and so on. And, sadly, he is divorcing her, or she is divorcing him, they are divorcing each other, because she wants to remain exactly as she was when she was 14 or 15. He's growing and searching. Yesterday's way of being married is today's trap. The way out of the trap is to resume the dialogue, not to end it.

If marriage counseling is not training and experience in dialogue, then it falls short in my opinion of its help-giving potential. How does one function as a marriage *Appendix* and family counselor? In the same way two porcupines

455

mate—with difficulty and great care. I know of no techniques for counseling individuals, or couples, or entire family units. There is something about the experience of having struggled to retain one's self-respect and joie de vivre in the face of marital disaster, one's own marital disasters, that helps one to listen with empathy and humor to others' difficulties. I think that inventiveness and a profound faith in every individual's capacity to overcome all disasters and to find his own strength is helpful. I am always astonished at how couples convince themselves that they cannot live more than five minutes if their partner changes in one way or if they are incommunicado from their partner for five minutes. That is astonishing when you think about it, two reasonably adequate human beings live together and then if one of them changes in one jot or tittle, the other person is either to commit murder, suicide, or divorce. Or if they split for a day, or a week, or a month to recenter themselves, the one who did not choose to be apart for a while will very frequently do everything in his or her power to punish the one who is seeking to recenter herself or himself.

In various earlier papers I have explored the importance of modeling, of being an exemplar of viable ways to live, or of the possibility of overcoming difficulties in living. Theory and technique are valuable in counseling, as they are in any other enterprise, but they can be the refuge of scoundrels and fools, like patriotism. If he or she is not a spokesman for and an exemplar of dialogue, integrity, and a relentless commitment to a search for viable ways to live and grow, then he or she will be found out. There is no way to impersonate integrity for very long. As in all realms where human beings deal with one another, there is no place in family counseling for dissembling and technical manipulation by the professional person. Marriage and family counseling to enhance or to terminate marriages proceeds best, perhaps only, through dialogue.

REFERENCES

M. Buber, *I and Thou* (Edinburgh: T & T Clark, 1937).
I. Charny, *Marital Love and Hate* (New York: Macmillan, 1972).

Appendix

456

D. Cooper, *Death of the Family* (New York: Random House, 1971).

R. D. Laing and A. Esterson, *Sanity, Madness, and the Family* (London: Tavistock Publications, 1965; New York: Basic Books, 1965).

N. O'Neill and G. O'Neill, *Open Marriage: A New Life Style for Couples* (New York: J. B. Lippincott, 1972).

Appendix

457

NAME INDEX

Name Index

Name Index

Name Index

SUBJECT INDEX

Abstinence, 61–62
Accidents, unconscious motivations for, 107
Aesthetics, 5, 10
Affection, 134–35, 170. *See also* Love
Age roles, 258–60
Aged, after retirement, 363
Aggression, 100. *See also* Hostility
Alcohol abuse, 364–65, 366
Alcoholics Anonymous (AA), 416
Analogies, 49, 50
Anger, 128–29
Anxiety, 18, 21, 104, 107–108, 127–28, 228
Aptitudes, vocational, 352–53
Arts, as avocation, 367
Authenticity, 63, 205–207, 260–61, 402, 421
Authoritarian character, 204
Authoritarian conscience, 196
Authoritarianism, 218, 384–85, 389
Autism, 51, 153–54, 214–15
Avocations, 366–70

Beautiful and noble person (BNP), 10–12
Beauty, standards of, 158, 159–63
Behavior, learning, 251–52, 290
perception related to, 77–79
wish to change, in others, 285–91
Behavior therapy, 411
Behaviorism, 25–26, 120
Being-cognition, 65, 84
Being motivation, 59, 110
Bioenergetic analysis, 32, 174–75
Biofeedback, 47, 178–79
Blacks, young, occupations for, 361–62
Body, 150–81
contact with one's, 99. *See also* Touching
handicaps and, 166–69
ideal, 158–64
image of, 52–53, 153–54
personality and, 156, 164–66
re-embodiment and, 169–75
security and, 156–58
self-esteem and, 158–59
somatic manifestations of enliven-ment and, 176–79
somatic specialization and de-specialization and, 175–76
unembodiment and, 150–56
Body-ideal, 158–64
Body image, 52–53, 153–54
Body language, 152, 405
Body posture, 106

Boredom, 5, 95, 98, 133–34, 227, 364–66
Brain, two sides of, 45–46
Brain damage, 62
Breasts, cultural emphasis on, 161–62

Catastrophic reaction, 62
Challenge, need for, 95
Changing. *See* Behavior; Growth
Check-out places, 412–14
Childrearing, 22, 254–55
Cognition, being-, 65, 84
Cognitive clarity, need for, 96–97
Cognitive dissonance, 97
Cognitive needs, 5
Commitment, 5, 111–12. *See also* Meaning
Communication. *See also* Dialogue
authentic, 269–70
avoiding, 223
effective, as indicator of healthy personality, 22
Community mental health center, 414–15
Compassionate self, 11
Competence, healthy personality based on, 65
need for, 93–94
Compulsive behavior, 220
Conative needs, 5
Concepts, in reality testing, 82–83
Conceptualizing, 48–50
Conditioning, operant, 25
Conflict, 102, 448. *See also* Stress
Conformity, 20, 250. *See also* Out-siders
Conscience, 193–99, 383–86
acquiring, 195–99
health and, 194–95
healthy, 197–99
humanistic, 383–86
ideal self and, 193–94
self-alienation and, 203–204
strict, 142
unhealthy, 195–97
Consciousness, 37–69
altered states of, 59–63, 96
characteristic states of, 54–58
definition of, 38
divided and unified, 42–54
enlarged, and healthy personality, 64, 65–66
healthy conscience and, 197–98
larger than one's own, 63–65
levels of, 27
higher, 232–34

463

Subject Index

Subject
Index

Subject Index

467

Subject Index